M Paul Holsinger

Essays in
Constitutional Law

Essays in
Constitutional Law

EDITED WITH AN INTRODUCTION BY

Robert G. McCloskey

HARVARD UNIVERSITY

19 | 57

ALFRED · A · KNOPF: NEW YORK

FIRST EDITION

The editor is indebted to the following individuals and periodicals for granting permission to reprint material in this volume.

Zechariah Chafee, and the Harvard Law Review Association, for "Free Speech and Its Relation to Self-Government," by Mr. Chafee. Copyright 1949 by Harvard Law Review Association.

Edward S. Corwin, and the Columbia Law Review, for "The Steel Seizure Case," by Mr. Corwin. Copyright 1953 by Trustees of the Columbia Law Review.

Edward S. Corwin, and the Virginia Law Review, for "The Passing of Dual Federalism," by Mr. Corwin. Copyright 1950 by Virginia Law Review Association.

John Raeburn Green, and the Michigan Law Review, for "The Bill of Rights, the Fourteenth Amendment and the Supreme Court," by Mr. Green. Copyright 1948 by Michigan Law Review Association.

Harvard Law Review Association for "The Origin and Scope of the American Doctrine of Constitutional Law," by James B. Thayer. Copyright 1893 by Harvard Law Review Association.

J. D. Hyman, and the Vanderbilt Law Review, for "Segregation and the Fourteenth Amendment," by Mr. Hyman. Copyright 1951 by Vanderbilt University Press.

Max Lerner, and the Yale Law Journal, for "The Supreme Court and American Capitalism," by Mr. Lerner. Copyright 1933 by Yale Law Journal Association.

John Courtney Murray, S.J., and Law and Contemporary Problems, for "Law or Prepossessions?" by Father Murray. Copyright 1949 by Duke University.

Nathaniel L. Nathanson, and the Harvard Law Review Association, for "The Communist Trial and the Clear-and-Present-Danger Test," by Mr. Nathanson. Copyright 1950 by Harvard Law Review Association.

Political Science Quarterly for "The Supreme Court—Usurper or Grantee?" by Charles A. Beard. Copyright 1912 by Political Science Quarterly.

Thomas Reed Powell, and the Journal of Philosophy, for "The Logic and Rhetoric of Constitutional Law," by Mr. Powell. Copyright 1918 by Journal of Philosophy, Psychology, and Scientific Method.

Robert L. Stern, and the Vanderbilt Law Review, for "The Problems of Yesteryear—Commerce and Due Process," by Mr. Stern. Copyright 1951 by Vanderbilt University Press.

Arthur E. Sutherland, and the Harvard Law Review Association, for "Restricting the Treaty Power," by Mr. Sutherland. Copyright 1952 by Harvard Law Review Association.

Prefatory Note

With the exception of J. B. Thayer's essay in Chapter II and the opinion of Judge Learned Hand in Chapter IX, the selections contained in this volume are reprinted in full, as originally published. Although there is of course a case for the book of readings that consists of truncated excerpts from many sources, there is also a case for providing the reader with examples of legal scholarship at its unadulterated best. Even the footnotes have been preserved intact in the hope that each essay will thus constitute, not only a stimulating introduction to the subject under discussion, but a guide to further inquiry.

Contents

Introduction   3

PART ONE: THE NATURE AND DEVELOPMENT OF
AMERICAN CONSTITUTIONALISM

I   Judicial Review and "the Intent of the Framers"   20

    "The Supreme Court—Usurper or Grantee?" BY
    CHARLES A. BEARD   24

II   The Scope of Judicial Review   59

    *"The Origin and Scope of the American Doctrine
    of Constitutional Law."* BY JAMES B. THAYER   63

III   The Judicial Process in Constitutional Law   81

    "The Logic and Rhetoric of Constitutional Law."
    BY THOMAS REED POWELL   85

IV   The Supreme Court and Industrial Society   102

    "The Supreme Court and American Capitalism."
    BY MAX LERNER   107

PART TWO: THE MODERN CONSTITUTION

V   The Modern Court and Economic Legislation   147

    *"The Problems of Yesteryear—Commerce and
    Due Process."* BY ROBERT L. STERN   150

VI A "Constitution of Powers" and Modern Federalism 181

"*The Passing of Dual Federalism.*" BY EDWARD S. CORWIN 185

VII International Agreements and Constitutional Amendments 211

"*Restricting the Treaty Power.*" BY ARTHUR E. SUTHERLAND, JR. 216

VIII The Power of the President 252

"*The Steel Seizure Case: A Judicial Brick Without Straw.*" BY EDWARD S. CORWIN 257

IX Freedom of Speech 275

Book Review BY ZECHARIAH CHAFEE, JR., of *Free Speech and Its Relation to Self-Government* By Alexander Meiklejohn 281

United States *v.* Dennis. Decision of the United States Court of Appeals 295

"*The Communist Trial and the Clear-and-Present-Danger Test.*" BY N. L. NATHANSON 300

X Separation of Church and State 310

"*Law or Prepossessions?*" BY JOHN COURTNEY MURRAY 316

XI The Constitution and Racial Equality 348

"*Segregation and the Fourteenth Amendment.*" BY J. D. HYMAN 357

XII Criminal Procedures and Judicial Control 381

"*The Bill of Rights, the Fourteenth Amendment and the Supreme Court.*" BY JOHN RAEBURN GREEN 385

PART ONE

The Nature and
Development
of
American
Constitutionalism

Introduction

I

WHEN MEN OF THE PRESENT LOOK BACK, THEY ARE LIKELY to regard the past as a simpler age than their own, and this error is particularly easy to make when we contemplate the Constitution and the Supreme Court in the 19th century. The world those institutions dwelt in appears to us settled and snug, almost childlike in its enthusiasms, its animosities, and its faiths. As for the institutions themselves, they seem to us a reflex of that world. The Constitution of the era looks, in retrospect, like a relatively unambiguous document, faithfully performing its traditional function of confining Government to the status of "friendly enemy." The judges of the federal bench are its high priests, securely established in the public mind as the watchdogs of eternal constitutional verities. We contrast the intricate problems that tease our understanding with the easy questions and answers that satisfied them, and our cup of superiority is heavily charged with envy.

Of course, this beautifully simple constitutional universe never really existed outside our fond imaginations. Our memory has blurred its complexity, and the categories we have devised for thinking about it have imposed a deceptive (but perhaps

necessary) order on its essential untidiness. Nothing about
America was ever so clear-cut or single-dimensional as this illusion suggests.

Yet allowing for all these reservations, it is nevertheless true
that the 19th century did achieve a comparatively well-accepted
consensus about the Constitution and the Supreme Court. Dis-
affection with the standard myths was not unknown, and skep-
tics could be found even in the contemporary legal fraternity if
one went looking for them. But John Marshall's exalted version
of the constitutional-judicial relationship had survived the squalls
of the Taney period, had emerged from the Civil War with
renewed vigor, and had won a breadth of acceptance that would
have gladdened the great Chief Justice immeasurably. Certain
assumptions about the nature of the Constitution may not have
gratified him so much, but they too seemed firmly established.
There was, for the moment at least, a kind of synthesis in
American constitutionalism.

For our purposes, that synthesis can be quickly characterized.
In the first place, it involved the idea that the Constitution is a
fixed and immutable inheritance from the Founding Fathers. In
the sweeping words of Mr. Justice Davis:

The Constitution of the United States is a law for rulers and people,
equally in war and in peace, and covers with the shield of its protection all classes of men, at all times, and under all circumstances. (Ex
Parte Milligan, 71 U.S. 281, 295 [1866].)

And in the words of Mr. Justice Sutherland, a latter-day ex-
ponent of this constitutional creed:

. . . the meaning of the Constitution does not change with the ebb
and flow of economic events. We frequently are told in more general
words that the Constitution must be construed in the light of the
present. If by that it is meant that the Constitution is made up of
living words that apply to every new condition which they include,
the statement is quite true. But to say, if that be intended, that the
words of the Constitution mean today what they did not mean when
written—that is, that they do not apply to a situation now to which
they would have applied then—is to rob that instrument of the
essential element which continues it in force as the people have
made it until they, and not their official agents, have made it other-

wise. (West Coast Hotel Co. *v.* Parrish, 300 U.S. 379, 402, 403 [1937].)

Closely allied to this view of the nature of the Constitution was an assumption about the nature of the judiciary's task of interpreting the fundamental law. We can hardly do better than to draw further on Mr. Justice Sutherland's Parthian salvos:

The judicial function is that of interpretation; it does not include the power of amendment under the guise of interpretation. To miss the point of difference between the two is to miss all that the phrase "supreme law of the land" stands for and to convert what was intended as inescapable and enduring mandates into mere moral reflections. (*Ibid.*, 404.)

It is true that between the time of Davis and Cooley and the time of Sutherland the Constitution *had* changed greatly in ways that were unauthorized by formal amendment; it is true that the judiciary, responding to the sentiments expressed by a very influential segment of "the public," had itself brought about those changes. (See Benjamin F. Twiss, *Lawyers and the Constitution* [1942].) Nevertheless, in the face of these facts, the *official* doctrine concerning the Constitution and the judicial process survived substantially as the trio had stated it.

A third feature of this 19th-century consensus on constitutional matters was the general understanding about what was the Supreme Court's business and what was not. Courts seldom hurry to keep their appointments with destiny, and, as Walton Hamilton once pointed out, the 19th century was fairly over by the time the Supreme Court had finished defining that century's judicial agenda. (See Conyers Read, ed., *The Constitution Reconsidered* [1938] p. 189). But the understanding about it had begun to assume recognizable form long before 1900, and with the benefit of hindsight we can easily spot its outlines. Plainly, it was the Court's broad business, as the judges saw it, to supervise the other branches of government in important fields as to the "justice or reason or wisdom" of their acts (Harlan, J., dissenting in Lochner *v.* New York, 25 S.Ct. 539, 551 [1905]). The rationale behind this self-imposed task was expressed with unmistakable clarity by Mr. Justice Field, on the occasion of his retirement from the Court in 1897. The Court, he explained, is

the only institution capable of maintaining order in democratic
America:

> It possesses the power of declaring the law, and in that is found the
> safeguard which keeps the whole mighty fabric of government from
> rushing to destruction. This negative power, the power of resistance,
> is the only safety of popular government. (168 U.S. 717.)

In other words, the essential business of the Supreme Court
is to say "no" to government. But for Field and most of his
brethren, this negativism was curiously circumscribed. More
specifically, it was the Court's assumed responsibility, as thousands of pages of scholarship attest, to protect the existing economic order against encroachment by legislatures with novel or
hostile ideas.

On the other hand, it was *not* the Court's business to make
room in the constitutional universe for government to experiment with the economic arrangements of the nation. It was not
the Court's business to protect substantive individual liberties
like freedom of speech and press, nor to superintend the states
in their administration of criminal law. It was not the Court's
concern to interfere with the *social* (as distinguished from economic) affairs of local communities by attempting to erase dis-
criminations between the races. (See Plessy *v.* Ferguson, 163
U.S. 537, 552 [1896]: "If one race be inferior to the other
socially, the constitution of the United States cannot put them
on the same plane.")

II

This then was the aspect that the judiciary and its Constitution
presented to the world not long ago. But even while the synthesis was assuming its contours, forces were assembling to destroy it. Perhaps the difficulty was, in part, that none but the
irretrievably naive had entirely accepted it in the first place, or
rather, that its acceptance had been achieved by one of those
extraordinary feats of doublethink that are so marked a feature
of political life. Surely the demise of this particular *ancien ré-
gime* was hastened by the birth of a general questioning spirit
in the America of the early 20th century, the spirit that sparked

the muckrakers, the "debunkers" of historical mythology, and the Progressive movement. Surely it was facilitated by the skepticism of the "legal realists" whose voices penetrated to the educated public more and more as the century wended its hectic course. Of course the final break-up was precipitated by the horrendous economic problems of the 1930's and the anti-judicial temper of the New Deal, though some of the judges themselves must be credited with an assist for their intransigence. Yet one feels that there is much more to be said about this whole process, and that our understanding of the natural history of ideas would be illuminated by a study of the decline and fall of the old constitutionalism.

Whatever such a study might reveal, however, there can be no doubt about the central fact that the 19th-century synthesis was tattered almost beyond recognition by the time the 1930's had come to an end. The extent of this metamorphosis, which Professor Edward S. Corwin called "Constitutional Revolution, Ltd.," should not be exaggerated. One of the enduring premises of American constitutional jurisprudence is the ideal of continuity, and thus it was necessary for the new constitutionalism to march under a banner that proclaimed it, not an excursion into an untried future but a reversion to the tested verities of the hallowed past. To quote Mr. Justice Douglas:

. . . the new Court did not make great innovations in constitutional law. Rather, it returned to first principles as early pronounced by Marshall and others. The last two decades of American constitutional development saw, in the main, the rejection of newly fashioned doctrines for more historic ones. (William O. Douglas, *We, the Judges* [1956], p. 431.)

Nor was this appeal to history by any means mere fustian. Marshall *had* written perhaps the most quoted sentence in our constitutional law: "We must never forget it is a *constitution* we are expounding." He had formulated a doctrine of national supremacy and a view of the commerce power that were broad enough to validate the most ambitious economic programs of the New Deal. True to the law of its being, American constitutionalism fought history with more history, and this strangely unrevolutionary method of this revolution should be duly noted. But it should also be noted that, whatever the method, the revolution did come off.

It would be pointless to retrace the often-told story of that revolution in any detail. The idea of a changeless constitution fell by the way as court and legislature developed the implications of the Marshall aphorism that has just been quoted. Their way was paved by frequent reiteration of a point that had long been familiar to close students of the Constitution when they chose to acknowledge it: that the Constitution had changed frequently and sometimes drastically in the course of its past history.

Similarly, the 19th-century ideas about the judicial process in constitutional law were shaken up badly. Justice Sutherland's vision of judges bound by the inexorable limits of precedent and "interpretation" was undercut by the blunt declaration of Mr. Justice Stone:

. . . while unconstitutional exercise of power by the executive and legislative branches of the government is subject to judicial restraint, the only check upon our own exercise of power is our own sense of self-restraint. (United States *v.* Butler, 297 U.S. 1, 78–9 [1936].)

A judge, it seems, does have some leeway; he is not simply a neutral instrument of the Constitution's will. Meantime, the Cooley-Sutherland idea of high-minded judicial indifference to public opinion was likewise brought into question, as it had to be by the logic of Justice Stone's assertion. If the Court does have leeway, that means it may often choose between one course of doctrine and another; and it is hard to imagine that judges, being now acknowledged as mortals, can in making that choice be impervious to a force that plays so important a part in the lives of all men today.

But perhaps most spectacular, because easiest to identify, is the shattering of the old concept of the Court's primary constitutional business. The almost breathtaking presumptuousness of the 19th century concept of judicial supervision is displaced by a new judicial modesty. Again Justice Stone puts it tersely: "Courts are not the only agency of government that must be assumed to have a capacity to govern." (*Ibid.*, 87.) The Constitution, he goes on, is not the exclusive responsibility of any one

of the three branches of government; and the majority decisions
of the Supreme Court become heavily dependent on another old
but heretofore often neglected idea: "even if the wisdom of
the policy be regarded as debatable and its effects uncertain, still
the Legislature is entitled to its judgment." (West Coast Hotel
v. Parrish, 300 U.S. 379, 399 [1937].)

In specific fields, the contrast with the old order is even
sharper. Suddenly—and the word is advisedly chosen—the
Court is no longer concerned with the protection of economic
man against governmental encroachment; it now restricts itself
in economic matters to umpiring the relationship between one
government and another, so that the question is no longer
whether government can rule the economy, but rather whether
more than one government can rule it at once. At roughly the
same time, though not quite so suddenly, the Court begins to
display an interest in matters formerly regarded as nearly irrelevant—the scope of freedom of speech and religion, state procedures in the arrest and trial of criminals, the prevention of racial
discrimination. If a judge of the early 1900's, say Justice Peckham, could return and cast his eye over the modern Court's
docket, he would feel a stranger indeed.

His sense of alienation would be attributable in part to un-
familiarity with the subject matter and doctrines of many of the
cases themselves. The judicial rationale that has been built
around freedom of expression had hardly begun to take shape
until 1919, years after he had left the bench. Some of the language in the criminal procedure cases would have a faintly familiar ring, but the applications of that language might seem
outlandish, and he would certainly be astonished at the amount
of time the modern court spends soberly considering petitions
from those who are in state penitentiaries or are trying to keep
out of them. Unless he had himself changed greatly, he would
certainly be unpleasantly surprised by the cavalier spirit in
which the modern court rejects claims that economic liberty has
been unconstitutionally infringed. And quite apart from the
novelty of the specific causes and the doctrines by which they
were decided, he would be ill at ease with the modern assumptions that the Constitution is an adaptable instrument of government, rather than a roadblock, and that judges are people, whose

judgment is sometimes no better than the judgment of someone else.

So far, we might be comparatively safe in feeling sorry for this anachronism who had so much to learn before he caught up with the times. But if he kept on with his survey of the modern constitutional scene, he might begin to notice another contrast with his own world; and the contemplation of it might cause him to feel a little patronizing in his turn. He might discover, in short, that although the 20th century had unsettled the constitutional order he knew, it had not achieved a settlement to replace it. His day may have been simpler, but it was a good deal more serene. Judges knew, or thought they knew, what their job was; scholars knew, or though they knew, what the Court was up to. And the result was a feeling of belonging, a sense of certitude, far different from the atmosphere in the unanchored present.

For the fact is that the evaluations that destroyed the 19th-century synthesis were almost without exception negative in their emphasis. True, they sometimes contained an affirmative inference, but in the first place the affirmation often had to be drawn out by a somewhat tortured process, and in the second place, one felt that it had seldom been thought through as carefully as had the criticism. Take Mr. Justice Holmes, who probably had more to do with scuttling the old assumptions than any other man. The judicial fondness for formulas as a surrogate for thought evoked some of his most telling critical rhetoric. He was convinced that "to rest on a formula is a slumber that, prolonged, means death," and he took special pleasure in troubling the slumber of his brethren by reminding them that the doctrine of "business clothed with a public interest" was "little more than a fiction intended to beautify what is disagreeable to the sufferers." (Tyson *v.* Banton, 273 U.S. 418, 446 [1927].) The faith in self-devised formulas was a vice of the old jurisprudence as well as one of its chief sources of comfort; and the particular formula Holmes ironically impaled in this case deserved its fate. But he then went on to say:

I think the proper course is to recognize that a state Legislature can do whatever it sees fit to do unless it is restrained by some express prohibition of the Constitution. . . . The truth seems to me to be that, subject to compensation when compensation is due, the Legislature may forbid or restrict any business when it has a sufficient force of opinion behind it. (*Ibid.,* 446.)

It is hard to be sure that he really meant it. Did he actually intend to suggest that the Court should forthwith cease to provide any standard of constitutional protection for economic rights? But whether he intended the implication of his words is not the point. The point is that the implication, whether intended or not, requires a justification that is not provided, here or elsewhere. The critique of the public-interest formula and of formulas in general is powerful and valid; this building block of the old constitutional order is thus successfully dislodged. But the cornerstone of a new order is not firmly laid in its place, if indeed it was meant to be laid at all. Are economic rights now to be constitutionally irrelevant? If so, why? If so, are there *any* rights that cannot be encroached when the drive to encroach "has a sufficient force of public opinion behind it?" If there are such rights, what is the basis for distinguishing between them and the rights of the property-holder? Until such questions are answered, or at least considered, we have simply exchanged a formulized world for a chaotic one, and it is not entirely clear that we have had a good bargain.

Or take, for another example, the work of Edward S. Corwin and Thomas Reed Powell, who between them have probably contributed more to the understanding of American constitutional law than any other non-judicial observers. Corwin's insights are so many that it is hard to choose among them, but perhaps the most influential was his perception, expressed in *The Twilight of the Supreme Court* and elsewhere, that the modern Court's background of precedent was now varied enough to warrant almost any course of judicial action the judges preferred in such crucial fields as the commerce clause, due process, and taxation. As for Powell, he worked with a scalpel, neatly disembowelling the Court's decisions and exposing their logic for the flimsy stuff it often was. It was plain enough that Corwin wanted the Court to acknowledge the flexibility of modern judicial review and to stop pretending that judicial hostility to the welfare state was an unavoidable premise of American constitutionalism. It was plain that Powell wanted the Court to be less irrational, less content with loose slogans and shibboleths. But sound though this advice may well have been, it was never at all plain what either of them thought the Supreme Court should be after it stopped being what it was.

III

My intent is not to disparage the memorable accomplishments of these men and others who helped upset the serenity of Mr. Justice Peckham's world. If judicial review as we know it in America can be justified at all, it must be justified as an attempt by men to think coherently about the ordering of human affairs, and the first requirement for coherency is that we rid ourselves of delusions. The 19th-century synthesis had to go, and such critics as Holmes, Corwin, and Powell performed a brilliant and necessary service when they hastened its departure. But in constitutional law as in nature, when a vacuum is created it must be filled; the 20th century needs and still lacks its own affirmative theory about the place of the Constitution and the Court in our social-political order.

It would be preposterous of course to expect such a theory to be universally acceptable, nor would it be healthy if if were. Since the day the Republic dawned, the judiciary's concept of itself and the Constitution has been a subject for ardent controversy. Agreement was always partial and tentative and was achieved out of conflict, as most effective agreements are. There will always be those who like the Court when it agrees with them and vilify it when it does not, or who think of the Constitution as the Ark of the Covenant when it defends their interests and an abomination when it allows their interests to be thwarted. Even among those who take a broader view, there will always be disagreement, and that is as it should be. No doctrine of American government should be above question, lest it lose the vitality opposition engenders.

What does seem fair to ask, however, is that the 20th century produce something affirmative for opposition to rub against.

And there seems little basis for arguing that it has done so. Twenty years ago a substantial segment of the liberal fraternity was convinced that constitutional limitations did more harm than good and that the Court should surrender its veto before the sovereign voter; today the same observers or their descendants want the Court to call a halt to popularly supported inroads on individual freedom. One looks in vain for a reasoned theory of the Court's place in American democracy, a theory on whose basis the new call for judicial action might be justified. The current enthusiasm for judicial review seems on the contrary to be mainly grounded on the *ad hoc* selection of causes for the Court to sponsor, quite apart from the issue of whether the subjects are appropriate for judicial control.

Perhaps indeed a full-blown modern doctrine of American constitutionalism could be developed in strictly *ad hoc*, pragmatic terms. Broadly, the argument might be that the Constitution is by definition a loose and contingent arrangement for getting things done with reasonable expediency and fairness, and that the judges serve it best when they feel their way along from decision to decision, following their cultivated instincts in each case and leaving the overall perspective to those who have nothing better to think about. The view is not entirely lacking in merit, and it serves a useful purpose if it reminds us that wrong-headed certitude is sometimes more disastrous than a policy of drift, or that a Court which today unthinkingly embraces an absolute may live to regret it tomorrow.

But it is hard to escape the feeling that a really thoroughgoing doctrine of constitutional pragmatism is an evasion of hard questions rather than a solution of them. The idea of a constitution involves the idea, in Mr. Justice Brandeis's phrase, that men can guide their affairs by the light of reason, and it seems too bad to fritter that noble assumption away altogether, simply because we know that reason is a hard taskmistress, or even because we suspect that our efforts will never quite satisfy her. Though we realize that the job is never-ending, we are bound to continue; though we realize that the answers will surely be imperfect, we are bound to ask the questions, or abandon the aspiration on which American constitutionalism was based.

IV

What are some of these questions? First we might put a question, or a set of them, about the nature and function of the Constitution in modern American life. We know that it is not a collection of inexorable and unalterable commands handed down by quasi-mythic forefathers for our eternal guidance in all the exigencies of political life. Very well, what is it then? Is it, for example, to be thought of as a practical guide for the conduct of government, or as an ideal? The difference may be important. In 1867, in Ex Parte Milligan, the Constitution was interpreted as flatly forbidding the military trial of civilians even in time of war, unless the area in question was actually invaded and the civil courts closed. Although still nominally a constitutional rule, this "Milligan doctrine" has never been honored in practice, the argument being that it imposed an impossibly strigent limit on the government's power to protect itself in wartime. Assuming *arguendum* that this is so, does it follow that the rule should have been less ambitious, so that it might have furnished guidance that lawmakers would follow? Or is it perhaps desirable for the Constitution to set a bench mark higher than we are likely to reach in practice, on the supposition that the challenge of the ideal will carry us higher than a more practical admonition might?

To take another, not unrelated, question: Is the chief purpose of a constitution to facilitate government or to inhibit it? Surely the American Constitution at least was designed in the hope that it would make the conduct of government more, rather than less, effective; and constitutional interpreters of the past have sometimes appeared to forget that historical truism. The restatement of the fact that the Constitution was meant to be a "tool of government" helped break down the stubborn negativism of the old constitutional law, and we are probably the better for it. But we have never really addressed ourselves to deciding just where this "positive" view of constitutionalism's function should leave off, if at all. Is there not some point at which a constitutional prohibition is justified, even though it may hamper the power to govern? Most of us would probably agree that there is such a point, but to what principles should we turn in order to decide where it lies? As is suggested later in this volume, the controversy over proposals to amend the treaty power would be greatly illuminated by a discussion of this question.

Still another closely connected question concerns the Constitution's supposed flexibility, its adaptability to shifting circumstances. We no longer accept wholeheartedly the dictum of Mr. Chief Justice Taney in Dred Scott (19 Howard 393, 426 [1857]) that the Constitution never changes in meaning or application, but neither have we faced squarely the question of how much it can change without losing its force as a symbol of continuity. One feels that Mr. Justice Sutherland was pressing the claims for a static constitutional universe too hard in New State Ice Co. *v.* Liebmann (285 U.S. 262 [1932]) when he refused to widen his conception of legitimate business regulation even in the face of profound economic emergency; and many felt that Mr. Justice Black was on the other hand too recklessly disregardful of settled views when he urged that a corporation should no longer be considered a person within the meaning of the Constitution (Connecticut General Life Ins. Co. *v.* Johnson, 303 U.S. 77, 85 [1938]). However, little thought has been given to the issue that underlies both these evaluations, *viz.,* how much continuity is too much? For a start, the reply might be that it depends in part on the kind of constitutional command that is being considered. Mr. Justice Frankfurter has wisely suggested that certain provisions, such as the "bill of attainder" clause have a clear-cut historical meaning that we are bound to adhere to strictly, while others, such as the "due process" clause were more ambiguous at the outset and thus allow room for wider play (United States *v.* Lovett, 328 U.S. 303, 321 [1946]). This is a promising beginning, but it seems reasonable to hope that analysis of the whole subject of continuity and change could be carried much farther.

Finally, we need to ask more searchingly than we have what kinds of values a constitution is designed to protect. Mr. Justice Holmes told us long ago that "a Constitution is not intended to embody a particular economic theory, whether of paternalism and the organic relation of the citizen to the state or of *laissez faire*" (Lochner *v.* New York, 25 S.Ct. 539, 547 [1905]), and this view, once so startling, has come to be accepted as the common coin of constitutional discussion. But what sort of values *is* the Constitution designed to embody? Holmes called *laissez faire* a "shibboleth," which is no doubt a good word to describe what we want to avoid. But we need to try to understand what are not shibboleths as well as what are, if we are to make our way beyond the stage of rejection to a new stage of affirmation.

Turning to the Court itself, the unsettled (and largely unconsidered) questions about its contemporary place in American life are legion. In connection with the nature of the judicial process in American constitutional law, for example, how far have we gone beyond the now rather primitive-seeming insight that judges are mortals, who make mistakes and nourish prejudices and are in general much like their fellow members of the human race? We now suspect what it was *lèse majesté* to suggest in earlier days—that judges are not entirely unaware of public opinion. But we have not attempted to understand in what sense public opinion may affect the judicial process, unless indeed we make the completely unwarrantable assumption that our constitutional judges simply check the latest Gallup polls or election returns and then hasten to their courtrooms to vote accordingly. It may be in fact that what seems responsiveness to public opinion is something subtly different; *concurrence* with public opinion, arising from the fact that judges are themselves members of the public. The distinction, if valid, is surely significant; it deserves to be considered further; and we should ask, incidentally, not only whether public opinion does play a part in determining the path of judicial doctrine, but whether it *should*.

The problem of *should* indeed raises a whole range of unsettled questions about the relationship of the Court to other branches of government and to democracy, and these questions bear in turn on the question of the proper scope of judicial review. Most of the older apologiae for judicial power rested on a frankly anti-majoritarian base. The Court must exist to insure justice against popular imbecility, and therefore the more judicial review the better. The modern reversion to judicial modesty suggests a rejection of that view; yet the Court still holds to the title of its traditional constitutional authority. It still says "no" to the popular will from time to time, but the nay-saying areas it selects are very different; the respect for legislative judgment, at least in certain fields, is much greater; confidence in its own expertise seems much less. Yet there is not, so far as I know, any systematic examination of the premises of this new position to be found anywhere, either in the opinions of the Court or elsewhere.

When the Court withdraws in the face of legislative authority, for example, is it doing so because it feels the legislature may possess superior knowledge and expertise about the matter in hand; or because, right or wrong, the popularly elected branch has the highest claim to deference in a democracy? To put the thing another way, is the judiciary to be thought of as the ally of majoritarianism or its critic and occasional censor? If the answer is, as it probably must be, a little of both, then further questions crowd on the heels of the answer. Insofar as deference to the legislature depends on its supposed superior expertise, it becomes relevant to ask in what fields the legislature really does stand on surer ground than the judiciary. Is it logical to respect the legislative judgment equally in such widely different areas as rate regulation and criminal procedure? One would hardly think so, and the distinction suggests that we need to re-think the issue of judicial competence, now that we have abandoned the notion of omnicompetence.

On the other hand, insofar as the judiciary is regarded as a democratic ally, we need to ask, in the light of modern insights, how it can serve that function best. With all respect to the others, Mr. Justice Frankfurter is the only member of the present Supreme Court who shows evidence in his judicial opinions of having thought about this subject in fundamental terms. Yet it is hard to see how a judge can decide a constitutional case or a student can criticize him for what he has decided, until each of them has established an operating premise that constitutes, for him at least, an answer to this question.

And the difficulty is that we are seriously handicapped in our quest for an answer so long as we remain committed to the negative spirit of the recent past. Even Justice Frankfurter seems to regard the judicial veto as a pure impediment to the popular will, and goes on to suggest that the Court should use it most sparingly in the hope that the people will learn to defend the Constitution themselves if the Court declines to defend it for them. Yet the Court's veto can and historically often has greatly stimulated popular awareness of constitutional problems, has set going the kind of discussion that is surely the best "training in democracy" that could well be contrived. One recent example of this educative impact of Supreme Court decisions is provided by the Segregation Cases of 1954. In spite of the deplorable extremism of some of the ensuing controversy, we can probably agree that such constitutional problems as federalism and racial discrimination have received a salutary popular airing and that general understanding of their intricacy and their importance has greatly proliferated.

All this may suggest that the Court can serve democracy affirmatively even when it says "no," partly by focussing popular attention on constitutional issues, but partly too by offering the majority at least tentative guidance at the same time. We need not swallow the philosophy of Jean Jacques Rousseau hook, line, and sinker, in order to recognize that he had a truth by the tail when he suggested that the "general will" may be different from the "will of all." For our purposes, his nettling distinction can be adapted to a commonplace but nevertheless important observation: that what people will when they have thought only of immediate interests may be quite different from what they will after they have been reminded that cherished long-term values are involved. History has so ordered things that the legislature in America tends primarily to reflect immediate interests. Indeed, it is hard to see how the legislature could avoid assuming this role, considering the pressures it is subjected to, and of course it is proper that the function of representing such pressures should be performed by some agency in a democratic system. But it is likewise important and in fact essential that long-term values—"constitutional" values—be given the kind of due consideration that the American legislature seems unable to provide. Until the legislature does so, at any rate, the judiciary seems to inherit the assignment by default; and if the assignment is judiciously performed, the Court can be regarded, not as an adversary, but as an auxilliary to democracy.

V

These then are a few—and only a few—of the questions that must be dealt with in order to arrive at a modern view of American constitutionalism, a view that goes beyond both the 19th-century synthesis and the critique that destroyed it. The essays in this volume have been chosen largely because they raise such questions, either directly or by implication, and the prefatory notes have been written with the same emphasis in mind. The essays embrace a broad range of subjects, and the essays in Section II touch on most of the major areas of modern constitutional law, but no attempt is made to cover the field. If the reader looks for gaps, he will find them, for I have preferred essays that were provocative and even perhaps tendentious over others that presented more systematic and neutral surveys of the material. The audience I have had in mind might be said to include both those who are in the process of learning some constitutional law or history and those who already know some. In the prefatory notes I have sometimes filled in background when I thought it might be especially needful to an understanding of the essay. Sometimes, as in connection with the racial discrimination issue, extremely important constitutional events have occurred since the essay was written, and I have felt it necessary to bring the story up-to-date. More often, I have used the prefatory notes to call the reader's attention to evidence that might bear on the viewpoint expressed in the essay itself, not in an attempt to refute the essayist, but in order to suggest that there is another side to be considered. But my chief interest throughout has been to raise the kind of question that has been briefly described in this introduction. For—let me say it once again—as we discuss such questions we move towards a modern restatement of American constitutional premises. And that restatement is, or ought to be, one of the most pressing items on the agenda of those who think and care about government in the United States.

CHAPTER ONE

Judicial Review
and
"The Intent of the Framers"

NONE OF THE ESSAYS COLLECTED IN THIS VOLUME IS CONCERNED
with an uncontroversial subject. Some of them treat with
issues that are or have been hotly contested on the battlegrounds
of contemporary politics; others were produced in the course of
those more private wars that scholars sometimes wage with one
another. Almost all are staunchly opinionated, and since in constitutional law as elsewhere there are often two sides to a question,
the task of editorial choice has seldom been an easy one.

The problem discussed in Charles A. Beard's essay affords an
excellent case in point. Whether the Supreme Court's power of
judicial review was intended by the framers of the Constitution
or whether its assumption by the Court was, on the contrary,
a "great usurpation"—this issue has evoked a large body of
scholarly conflict which has, from time to time, worked its way
into the arena of political combat. Opponents of Beard's posi-

tion have scored some impressive points, and it might there-fore appear that the choice of "Supreme Court—Usurper or Grantee" was either partisan or arbitrary. By way of rejoinder several things might be said. For one thing, it seemed important that a collection of this kind include at least one selection by the man who is unquestionably among the greatest and most in-fluential of American historians. By the same token, it seemed desirable that the reader be given an opportunity to sample the method of constitutional exegesis that Beard made famous in his seminal work *An Economic Interpretation of the Constitution* (1913), i.e., the method based on the idea that the intended meaning of the Constitution can be inferred from an individual analysis of the men who framed it. And finally, it must be said that, although Beard's argument in this essay has been qualified by scholarly critics, it has not been really overthrown. Like many of his historical insights, this one has survived the polem-ics that surrounded it with a significant measure of its validity still intact.

Nevertheless, the reader should be aware of some of the as-saults made on Beard's thesis and should be on guard against ac-cepting it without reservation. Edward S. Corwin, perhaps the most learned and discriminating of all modern constitutional scholars, has demonstrated pretty conclusively that the framers who can be lined up on the side of judicial review were fewer than Beard had supposed and that the statements they made about it were often extremely ambiguous. (See his review of Beard's book *The Supreme Court and the Constitution* [1913]; Corwin's *The Doctrine of Judicial Review* [1914]; and *Court Over Constitution* [1937], pp. 26–33.) A considerably more ex-treme but highly stimulating attack on the whole idea that judi-cial review was intended by the framers may be found in L. B. Boudin's *Government by Judiciary* (1932). Other citations both pro and con are listed in P. T. Fenn's *The Development of the Constitution* (1948), pp. 11–12.

The upshot, if one may venture to assess so controversial a question, was well expressed by B. F. Wright:

It is clear that the federal Constitution includes no clause expressly conferring this power upon the courts. There is, nevertheless, evi-

dence adequately demonstrating that a number of the framers assumed that the power of review would be exercised by federal, as
well as state courts, and over congressional as well as state legislation.
The number is not large and many of the statements relied upon
as evidence of a belief in judicial review are of an equivocal character.
But the very fact that such views were expressed, and only very
rarely questioned . . . is indicative of the existence of a belief that
no express constitutional sanction would be needed for the exercise
of that power. (*The Growth of American Constitutional Law* [1942],
pp. 15–16.)

A more sophisticated and thus more difficult question than
the one posed by Beard is what *kind* of judicial review the framers envisioned, insofar as they envisioned any kind at all. At first
blush it may seem that the form of judicial review we enjoy today is the inevitable form, but a little reflection will suggest that
numerous variations in the idea of a constitutional court are
quite possible. Suppose, for example, we ask what was the *scope*
of the judicial review which the framers had in mind, i.e., did
they think of the courts as being empowered to overrule Congress in all cases that raised any constitutional question or did
they see the power as applying only when direct constitutional
prohibitions were transgressed? The distinction is important,
since it might be regarded as making the difference between the
Supreme Court as a kind of Platonic supervisor of our governmental system and the Supreme Court as a *court* in the more
traditional sense of the word. Suppose, for another example, we
ask what conception the framers had of the *finality* of the
courts' judgments on matters of constitutionality, i.e., whether
they thought of Supreme Court decisions as binding all other
departments of government, or only the judiciary? On both
these questions, as Corwin has shown in *Court Over Constitution*, the founding fathers had only the dimmest of notions. It
follows that while the shades of the framers may be invoked to
warrant judicial review in *some* form, they are of little help
when we seek support for the precise kind of judicial review
that subsequent history has established in America.

Finally, Beard's essay and the controversy of which it was a
part raise, by inference, an intriguing question about the process
of constitutional interpretation: To what extent should modern

America feel bound by the intentions of the framers in 1787, rather than by the usages that have evolved since that time? To be specific, suppose it could be proved conclusively that the framers' intention was *not* to allow courts the power of judicial review. Would this proof be a legitimate basis for discontinuing a power that American courts have exercised for more than 150 years? Or, on the contrary, can "use and wont" legitimize a constitutional arrangement even though the men who wrote the Constitution itself might have intended to establish something quite different? This issue, with all its implications, underlies a recent monumental study by W. W. Crosskey, *Politics and the Constitution in the History of the United States* (1953). Mr. Crosskey has re-examined a vast body of evidence and concluded, to his own satisfaction, that accepted interpretations of such salient constitutional provisions as the commerce clause and the judiciary clause are in conflict with the intentions of the framers of the Constitution. He leaves no doubt that he would like to see these aberrant interpretations promptly abandoned. Mr. Justice Black of the Supreme Court made a similar suggestion in Connecticut General Life Ins. Co. *v.* Johnson, 303 U.S. 77, 85–90 (1938) where he argued that the Fourteenth Amendment (ratified in 1868) was not designed to protect corporations and that court decisions bringing corporations under its shelter should be overruled, even though they were hallowed by some fifty-four years of judicial acceptance.

It would be strange indeed to contend that what the framers though they were doing was irrelevant to the meaning of the Constitution they produced. But neither would it be good sense to scuttle established interpretations every time the weight of historical scholarship threw the scales into a new balance. The American Constitution is not merely the document of 1789; it also comprises the judgments attached to it by subsequent generations. The wisdom of John Marshall is no more to be taken lightly than that of James Madison. When the judge or the scholar is faced by a seeming conflict between historical intent and orthodox interpretation, no naive rule-of-thumb is available to make his task easy. He is forced to a delicate choice which might involve, for a beginning, such factors as the conclusiveness of the historical evidence, the weight of the precedents that

have been built up to support a counter-view, and the disturbance to settled institutions threatened by the proposed change.
And, like most questions in constitutional law, this one will ultimately be decided by a process of "judgment or intuition more
subtle than any articulate major premise." (Holmes, J., dissenting in Lochner *v.* New York, 198 U.S. 45, 75 [1905].)

The Supreme Court—Usurper or Grantee?[1]

by Charles A. Beard *

Political Science Quarterly,
Volume 27, Page 1 (1912)

Did the framers of the federal Constitution intend that the Supreme Court should pass upon the constitutionality of acts of
Congress? The emphatic negative recently given to this question by legal writers of respectable authority [2] has put the sanction of the guild on the popular notion that the nullification of
statutes by the federal judiciary is warranted neither by the letter nor by the spirit of the supreme law of the land and is, therefore, rank usurpation. Thus the color of legality, so highly
prized by revolutionaries as well as by apostles of law and order, is given to a movement designed to strip the courts of their
great political function. While the desirability of judicial control
over legislation may be considered by practical men entirely
apart from its historical origins, the attitude of those who
drafted the Constitution surely cannot be regarded as a matter
solely of antiquarian interest. Indeed, the eagerness with which

---

* (1874–1948), Professor and author.

[1] The author desires to acknowledge his indebtedness to Mr. Birl E. Shultz, a
graduate student in the School of Political Science of Columbia University, for preparing a bibliographical note on the writings of members of the Convention and for
special researches in the papers of Roger Sherman and of John Dickinson.

[2] Cf. Chief Justice Walter Clark, of North Carolina, Address before the Law
Department of the University of Pennsylvania, April 27, 1906; reprinted in *Congres-
sional Record,* July 31, 1911. Dean William Trickett, of the Dickinson Law School,
Judicial Dispensation from Congressional Statutes, American Law Review, vol. xli,
pp. 65 *et. seq.* L. B. Boudin, of the New York Bar, "Government by Judiciary,"
Political Science Quarterly, vol. xxvi (1911), pp. 238 *et seq.* Gilbert Roe, of the
New York Bar, "Our Judicial Oligarchy" (second article), *La Follette's Weekly
Magazine,* vol. iii, no. 25, pp. 7–9, June 24, 1911.

the "views of the Fathers" have been marshalled in support of the attack upon judicial control proves that they continue to exercise some moral weight, even if they are not binding upon the public conscience.

The arguments advanced to show that the framers of the Constitution did not intend to grant to the federal judiciary any control over federal legislation may be summarized as follows. Not only is the power in question not expressly granted, but it could not have seemed to the framers to be granted by implication. The power to refuse application to an unconstitutional law was not generally regarded as proper to the judiciary. In a few cases only had state courts attempted to exercise such a power, and these few attempts had been sharply rebuked by the people. Of the members of the Convention of 1787 not more than five or six are known to have regarded this power as a part of the general judicial power; and Spaight and three or four others are known to have held the contrary opinion. It cannot be assumed that the other forty-odd members of the Convention were divided on the question in the same proportion. If any conclusion is to be drawn from their silence, it is rather that they did not believe that any such unprecedented judicial power could be read into the Constitution. This conclusion is fortified by the fact that a proposition to confer upon the federal judges revisory power over federal legislation was four times made in the Convention and defeated.

A careful examination of the articles cited fails to reveal that the writers have made any detailed analysis of the sources from which we derive our knowledge of the proceedings of the Convention and of the views held by its members. They certainly do not produce sufficient evidence to support their sweeping generalizations. In the interest of historical accuracy, therefore, it is well to inquire whether the evidence available on the point is sufficient to convict the Supreme Court of usurping an authority which the framers of the Constitution did not conceive to be within the judicial province. If the opinions of the majority of the Convention cannot be definitely ascertained, any categorical answer to the question proposed must rest upon the "argument of silence," which, as Fustel de Coulanges warned the Germans long ago, is a dangerous argument.

Now at the outset of this inquiry one important fact should be noted.

No proposition to confer directly upon the judiciary the power of passing upon the constitutionality of acts of Congress was submitted to the Convention. On this point a statement made in Chief Justice Clark's address, cited above, is misleading. The proposition to which he refers, and which formed a part of the Randolph plan, was to associate a certain number of the judges with the executive in the exercise of revisionary power over laws passed by Congress. This was obviously a different proposition. Indeed, some members of the Convention who favored judicial control opposed the creation of such a council of revision.[3] The question of judicial control, accordingly, did not come squarely before the Convention, in such form that a vote could be taken.

How are we to know what was the intention of the framers of the Constitution in this matter? The only method is to make an exhaustive search in the documents of the Convention and in the writings, speeches, papers and recorded activities of its members. It is obviously impossible to assert that any such inquiry is complete, for new material, printed or in manuscript, may be produced at any moment. This paper therefore makes no claim to completeness or to finality. It is designed to throw light on the subject and to suggest ways in which more light may be obtained.

In view of the fact that no vote was taken on this issue, we are compelled to examine the notes of the debates on every part of the Constitution and to search the letters, papers and documents of the members of the Convention to find out how many of them put themselves on record, in one way or another.

I

There were in all fifty-five members of the Convention who were present at some of its meetings. Of these at least one-third took little or no part in the proceedings or were of little weight or were extensively absent. Among these may be included:

---

[3] Cf. *infra*, pp. 29, 31, 34.

Blount, Brearley, Broom, Clymer, Fitzsimons, Gilman, W. C. Houston, William Houstoun, Ingersoll, Lansing, Livingston, Mc-Clurg, Alexander Martin, Mifflin, Pierce and Yates. It is of course difficult to estimate the influence of the several members of the Convention, and between the extremes there are a few regarding whom there may reasonably be a difference of opinion. The preceding list is doubtless open to criticism, but it may be safely asserted that a large majority of the men included in it were without any considerable influence in the framing of the Constitution.

Of the remaining members there were (say) twenty-five whose character, ability, diligence and regularity of attendance, separately or in combination, made them the dominant element in the Convention. These men were:

Blair	*Hamilton*	Pinckney,
Butler	*Johnson*	Charles
Dayton	*King*	Pinckney, C. C.
Dickinson	*Madison*	*Randolph*
Ellsworth	*Martin, L.*	Rutledge
Franklin	*Mason*	Sherman
Gerry	*Morris, G.*	*Washington*
Gorham	*Morris, R.*	*Williamson*
	Paterson	*Wilson*

This list, like the one given above, is tentative; and it is fair to say that, among those whose judgment is entitled to respect, there is no little difference of opinion about the weight of some of the men here enumerated. It cannot be doubted, however, that the list includes the decided majority of the men who were most influential in giving the Constitution its form and its spirit. Among these men were the leaders, of whose words and activities we have the fullest records.

Of these men, the seventeen whose names are italicized declared, directly or indirectly, for judicial control. Without intending to imply that the less influential members were divided on the question in the same ratio as these twenty-five, or that due respect should not be paid to the principle of simple majority rule, it is illuminating to discover how many of this dominant group are found on record in favor of the proposition that the judiciary would in the natural course of things pass upon the constitutionality of acts of Congress. The evidence of each man's attitude is here submitted, the names being arranged, as above, in their alphabetical order.

John Blair, of Virginia, was a member of the Virginia court of appeals which decided the case of Commonwealth *v.* Caton,[4] in 1782, and he agreed with the rest of the judges "that the court had power to declare any resolution or act of the legislature, or of either branch of it, to be unconstitutional and void."[5] Ten years later he was one of the three judges of the federal circuit court for the district of Pennsylvania who claimed that they could not perform certain duties imposed upon them by a law of Congress, because the duties were not judicial in nature and because under the law their acts would be subject to legislative or executive control. These judges—Blair, Wilson[6] and Peters—joined in a respectful letter of protest to President Washington, April 18, 1792, in which they declared that they held it to be their duty to disregard the directions of Congress rather than to act contrary to a constitutional principle.[7] It may also be noted that, as a member of the federal Senate, Blair supported the Judiciary Act of 1789, which accorded to the Supreme Court the power to review and reverse or affirm the decisions of state courts denying the validity of federal statutes.[8]

John Dickinson, of Delaware, is usually placed among the members of the Convention who did not recognize the power of the courts to pass upon the constitutionality of statutes; for in the debate on August 15, just after Mercer[9] declared against judicial control, Dickinson said that "he was strongly impressed with the remark of Mr. Mercer as to the power of the Judges to set aside the law. He thought no such power ought to exist. He was at the same time at a loss what expedient to substitute."[10]

---

[4] Thayer's *Cases in Constitutional Law*, vol. i, p. 55.

[5] That the decision could have been reached without invoking this power, as Mr. Boudin argues, *loc. cit.*, p. 245, note I, does not affect the value of the decision as evidence of Blair's belief in the existence of the power.

[6] Wilson, as we shall see later, had taken a strong stand, both in the constituent Convention and in the ratifying Pennsylvania convention, in favor of judicial control of legislation. Cf. *infra*, pp. 37, 49.

[7] Hayburn's Case, 2 Dallas, 409.

[8] Cf. *infra*, p. 38.

[9] Cf. *infra*, p. 42.

[10] Farrand, vol. ii, p. 299.

Later, however, he accepted the principle of judicial control, either because he thought it sound or because he could find no satisfactory substitute. In one of his "Fabius" letters, written in advocacy of the Constitution in 1788, he says:

In the senate the sovereignties of the several states will be equally represented; in the house of representatives the people of the whole union will be equally represented; and in the president and the federal independent judges, so much concerned in the execution of the laws and in the determination of their constitutionality, the sovereignties of the several states and the people of the whole union may be considered as conjointly represented.[11]

Whatever his personal preference may have been, he evidently understood that the new instrument implicitly empowered the federal judiciary to determine the constitutionality of laws; and he presents this implication to the public as a commendable feature of the Constitution.

Oliver Ellsworth, of Connecticut, held that the federal judiciary, in the discharge of its normal functions, would declare acts of Congress contrary to the federal Constitution null and void. In the Connecticut convention, called to ratify the federal Constitution, he was careful to explain this clearly to the assembled delegates.[12] Later, he was chairman of the Senate Committee which prepared the Judiciary Act of 1789 and took a leading part in the drafting of that measure.[13]

Elbridge Gerry, of Massachusetts. When, on June 4, the proposition relative to a council of revision was taken into consideration by the Convention, Gerry expressed doubts

whether the Judiciary ought to form a part of it, as they will have a sufficient check against encroachments on their own department by their exposition of the laws, which involved a power of deciding on their constitutionality. In some States the judges had actually set aside laws as being against the Constitution. This was done, too, with general approbation. It was quite foreign from the nature of the office to make them judges of the policy of public measures.[14]

---

[11] Ford, *Pamphlets on the Constitution of the United States*, p. 184.
[12] Cf. *infra*, pp. 49, 50.
[13] Cf. *infra*, p. 38.
[14] Farrand, vol. i, p. 97.

During the debate in the first Congress on the question whether the president had the constitutional right to remove federal officers without the consent of the Senate, Gerry more than once urged that the judiciary was the proper body to decide the issue finally. On June 16, 1789, he said:

Are we afraid that the President and Senate are not sufficiently informed to know their respective duties? . . . If the fact is, as we seem to suspect, that they do not understand the Constitution, let it go before the proper tribunal; the judges are the constitutional umpires on such questions.[15]

Speaking on the same subject again, he said:

If the power of making declaratory acts really vests in Congress and the judges are bound by our decisions, we may alter that part of the Constitution which is secured from being amended by the fifth article; we may say that the ninth section of the Constitution, respecting the migration or importation of persons, does not extend to negroes; that the word persons means only white men and women. We then proceed to lay a duty of twenty or thirty dollars per head on the importation of negroes. The merchant does not construe the Constitution in the manner that we have done. He therefore institutes a suit and brings it before the supreme judicature of the United States for trial. The judges, who are bound by oath to support the Constitution, declare against this law; they would therefore give judgment in favor of the merchant.[16]

Alexander Hamilton, of New York. In *The Federalist*, written in defence of the Constitution, and designed to make that instrument acceptable to the electorate, Hamilton said:

The interpretation of the laws is the proper and peculiar province of the courts. A constitution is, in fact, and must be, regarded by the judges as a fundamental law. It must, therefore, belong to them to ascertain its meaning, as well as the meaning of any particular act proceeding from the legislative body. If there should happen to be an irreconcilable variance between the two, that which has the superior obligation and validity ought, of course, to be preferred, or in other words, the Constitution ought to be preferred to the statute, the intention of the people to the intention of their agents.[17]

---

[15] *Annals of Congress*, vol. i, p. 491. See also p. 596.
[16] Elliot's *Debates*, vol. iv, p. 393.
[17] *The Federalist*, no. 78.

Rufus King, of Massachusetts. In the discussion of the proposed council of revision which took place in the Convention on June 4, King took the same position as Gerry, observing "that the judges ought to be able to expound the law as it should come before them free from the bias of having participated in its formation." [18] According to Pierce's notes he said that he

was of opinion that the judicial ought not to join in the negative of a law because the judges will have the expounding of those laws when they come before them; and they will no doubt stop the operation of such as shall appear repugnant to the constitution.[19]

James Madison, of Virginia. That Madison believed in judicial control over legislation is unquestionable, but as to the exact nature and extent of that control he was in no little confusion. His fear of the legislature is expressed repeatedly in his writings, and he was foremost among the men who sought to establish a revisionary council of which the judges should form a part. In the Convention he said:

Experience in all the states had evinced a powerful tendency in the legislature to absorb all power into its vortex. This was the real source of danger to the American constitutions; and suggested the necessity of giving every defensive authority to the other departments that was consistent with republican principles.[20]

The association of the judges with the executive, he contended, "would be useful to the judiciary department by giving it an additional opportunity of defending itself against legislative encroachments." [21] He was evidently greatly disappointed by the refusal of the Convention to establish a revisionary council; for, in after years, he said that "such a control, restricted to constitutional points, besides giving greater stability and system to the rules of expounding the instrument would have precluded the question of a judiciary annulment of legislative acts." [22]

---

[18] Farrand, vol. i, p. 98.
[19] *Ibid.*, p. 109.
[20] *Ibid.*, vol. ii, p. 74.
[21] *Ibid.*
[22] *Writings* of James Madison, vol. viii, p. 406.

From the first, however, he accepted judicial control only with limitations; and complete judicial paramountcy over the other branches of the federal government he certainly deprecated. When it was proposed to extend the jurisdiction of the Supreme Court to cases arising under the Constitution as well as under the laws of the United States, he

doubted whether it was not going too far to extend the jurisdiction of the court generally to cases arising under the Constitution and whether it ought not to be limited to cases of a judiciary nature. The right of expounding the constitution in cases not of this nature ought not to be given to that department.[23]

The refusal of the Convention to establish a council of revision, in his opinion, left the judiciary paramount, which was in itself undesirable and not intended by the framers of the Constitution. In a comment on the proposed Virginia constitution of 1788, he wrote, in that year:

In the state constitutions and indeed in the federal one also, no provision is made for the case of a disagreement in expounding them [the laws], and as the courts are generally the last in making the decision, it results to them, by refusing or not refusing to execute a law, to stamp it with its final character. This makes the Judiciary Department paramount in fact to the Legislature, which was never intended and can never be proper.[24]

The right of the courts to pass upon constitutional questions in cases of a judicial nature he fully acknowledged; but this did not, in his mind, preclude the other departments from declaring their sentiments on points of constitutionality and from marking out the limits of their own powers. This view he expressed in the House of Representatives (first Congress) when the question of the president's removing power was under debate:

The great objection . . . is that the legislature itself has no right to expound the Constitution; that wherever its meaning is doubtful, you must leave it to take its course, until the judiciary is called upon to declare its meaning. I acknowledge, in the ordinary course of government, that the exposition of the laws and Constitution devolves upon

---

[23] Farrand, vol. ii, p. 430.
[24] *Writings*, vol. v, pp. 293, 294.

the judicial; but I beg to know upon what principle it can be contended that any one department draws from the Constitution greater powers than another, in marking out the limits of the powers of the several departments. The Constitution is the charter of the people in the government; it specifies certain great powers as absolutely granted, and marks out the departments to exercise them. If the constitutional boundary of either be brought into question I do not see that any one of these independent departments has more right than another to declare their sentiments on that point.

Perhaps this is an admitted case. There is not one government on the face of the earth, so far as I can recollect—there is not one in the United States—in which provision is made for a particular authority to determine the limits of the constitutional division of power between the branches of the government. In all systems, there are points which must be adjusted by the departments themselves, to which no one of them is competent. If it cannot be determined in this way, there is no resource left but the will of the community, to be collected in some mode to be provided by the Constitution, or one dictated by the necessity of the case. It is, therefore, a fair question, whether this great point may not as well be decided, at least by the whole legislature, as by part—by us, as well as by the executive or the judicial. As I think it will be equally constitutional, I cannot imagine it will be less safe, that the exposition should issue from the legislative authority, than any other; and the more so, because it involves in the decision the opinions of both of those departments whose powers are supposed to be affected by it. Besides, I do not see in what way this question could come before the judges to obtain a fair and solemn decision; but even if it were the case that it could, I should suppose, at least while the government is not lead by passion, disturbed by faction, or deceived by any discolored medium of sight, but while there is a desire in all to see and be guided by the benignant ray of truth, that the decision may be made with the most advantage by the legislature itself.[25]

Madison's views on the point may be summed up as follows: In cases of a political nature involving controversies between departments, each department enjoys a power of interpretation for itself (a doctrine which Marshall would not have denied); in controversies of a judicial nature arising under the Constitution, the Supreme Court is the tribunal of last resort; in cases

---

[25] Elliott's *Debates,* vol. iv, pp. 382, 383.

of federal statutes which are held to be invalid by nullifying states, the Supreme Court possesses the power to pass finally upon constitutionality.[26]

Luther Martin, of Maryland, although he opposed the proposition to form a revisionary council by associating judges with the executive, was nevertheless strongly convinced that unconstitutional laws would be set aside by the judiciary. During the debate on July 21, he said:

A knowledge of mankind, and of Legislative affairs cannot be presumed to belong in a higher degree to the Judges than to the Legislature. And as to the Constitutionality of laws, that point will come before the Judges in their proper official character. In this character they have a negative on the laws. Join them with the Executive in the Revision and they will have a double negative. It is necessary that the Supreme Judiciary should have the confidence of the people. This will soon be lost, if they are employed in the task of remonstrating against popular measures of the Legislature.[27]

George Mason, of Virginia, favored associating the judges with the executive in revising laws. He recognized that the judges would have the power to declare unconstitutional statutes void, but he regarded this control as insufficient. He said:

Notwithstanding the precautions taken in the constitution of the Legislature, it would so much resemble that of the individual states, that it must be expected frequently to pass unjust and pernicious laws. This restraining power was therefore essentially necessary. It would have the effect not only of hindering the final passage of such laws, but would discourage demagogues from attempting to get them passed. It had been said (by Mr. L. Martin) that if the Judges were joined in this check on the laws, they would have a double negative, since in their expository capacity of Judges they would have one negative. He would reply that in this capacity they could impede in one case only, the operation of laws. They could declare an unconstitutional law void. But with regard to every law, however unjust, oppressive or pernicious, which did not come plainly under this description, they would be under the necessity as Judges to give it a free course. He wished the further use to be made of the Judges,

---

[26] Cf. Madison's letter of August, 1830, to Everett; *Writings*, vol. ix, p. 383.
[27] Farrand, vol. ii, p. 76. For further evidence of Martin's attitude, cf. *infra*, pp. 48, 49.

of giving aid in preventing every improper law. Their aid will be the more valuable as they are in the habit and practice of considering laws in their true principles, and in all their consequences.[28]

Gouverneur Morris, of Pennsylvania, declared, in the debate on July 21, that some check on the legislature was necessary; and he "concurred in thinking the public liberty in greater danger from legislative usurpations than from any other source." [29] He was apprehensive lest the addition of the judiciary to the executive in the council of revision would not be enough to hold the legislature in check. Later, when Dickinson questioned the right of the judiciary to set aside laws, Morris said:

He could not agree that the judiciary, which was a part of the executive, should be bound to say that a direct violation of the Constitution was law. A control over the legislature might have its inconveniences. But view the danger on the other side. . . . Encroachments of the popular branch of the government ought to be guarded against.[30]

This view he later confirmed in the debate on the repeal of the Judiciary Act of 1801, when he said:

It has been said, and truly too, that governments are made to provide against the follies and vices of men. . . . Hence checks are required in the distribution of the power among those who are to exercise it for the benefit of the people. Did the people of America vest all power in the Legislature? No; they vested in the judges a check intended to be efficient—a check of the first necessity, to prevent an invasion of the Constitution by unconstitutional laws—a check which might prevent any faction from intimidating or annihilating the tribunals themselves.[31]

Edmund Randolph, of Virginia, does not seem to have expressed himself in the Convention on the subject of judicial control over congressional legislation. In the plan which he presented, however, provision was made for establishing a council of revision, composed of the executive and a convenient number of the judiciary, "with authority to examine every act of the National Legislature before it shall operate." He must, there-

---

[28] Farrand, vol. ii, p. 78.   [29] *Ibid.*, pp. 75 *et seq.*
[30] *Ibid.*, p. 299.
[31] Benton, *Abridgement of Debates in Congress*, vol. ii, p. 550.

fore, have been convinced of the desirability of some efficient control over the legislative department. Subsequently, as attorney-general, when it became his duty to represent the government in Hayburn's case [32] and he was moving for a mandamus to compel the circuit court for the district of Pennsylvania to execute a law under which the judges had declined to act on the ground of its unconstitutionality, Randolph accepted the view of the judges that they were not constitutionally bound to enforce a law which they deemed beyond the powers of Congress. The meager abstract of his argument before the Supreme Court in Dallas's *Reports* gives no hint of its precise character; but in a letter to Madison, dated August 12, 1792, Randolph said: "The sum of my argument was an admission of the power to refuse to execute, but the unfitness of the occasion." [33] That he approved the provision of the Judiciary Act of 1789, giving the Supreme Court appellate jurisdiction to review and reverse or affirm a decision of a state court denying the constitutionality of a federal statute, is apparent from his report to Congress on the judicial system in 1790. After enumerating the instances in which cases might be carried up to the Supreme Court from the state courts, he says: "That the avenue to the federal courts ought, in these instances, to be unobstructed, is manifest." The only question with which he was concerned was: "In what stage and by what form shall their interposition be prayed?" [34]

Hugh Williamson, of North Carolina, certainly believed in judicial control over federal legislation; for in the debate on the proposition to insert a clause forbidding Congress to pass ex post facto laws, he said: "Such a prohibitory clause is in the constitution of North Carolina, and though it has been violated, it has done good there and may do good here, because the judges can take hold of it." [35] It is obvious that the only way in which the judges can "take hold of" ex post facto laws is by declaring them void.

James Wilson, of Pennsylvania, expressed himself in favor

---

[32] 2 Dallas, 409.
[33] Moncure Conway, *Edmund Randolph*, p. 145.
[34] *American State Papers, Class X, Miscellaneous*, vol. i, p. 23.
[35] Farrand, vol. ii, p. 376.

of judicial control in the course of the debate on July 21, when the proposition to associate the national judiciary with the executive in the revisionary power was again being considered. He declared:

The Judiciary ought to have an opportunity of remonstrating against projected encroachments on the people as well as on themselves. It had been said that the Judges as expositors of the Laws would have an opportunity of defending their constitutional rights. There was weight in this observation; but this power of the Judges did not go far enough. Laws may be unjust, may be unwise, may be dangerous, may be destructive; and yet not be so unconstitutional as to justify the Judges in refusing to give them effect. Let them have a share in the Revisionary power, and they will have an opportunity of taking notice of these characters of a law, and of counteracting, by the weight of their opinions, the improper views of the Legislature.[36]

Speaking again, on August 23, in favor of giving the national legislature a negative over state legislation, he said that he

considered this as the key-stone wanted to complete the wide arch of Government we are raising. The power of self-defence had been urged as necessary for the State Governments. It was equally necessary for the General Government. The firmness of Judges is not of itself sufficient. Something further is requisite. It will be better to prevent the passage of an improper law than to declare it void when passed.[37]

The rejection of the plan to establish a revisionary council did not lead Wilson to infer that thereby the right of the court to pass upon the constitutionality of statutes was denied. On the contrary, in the debates in the Pennsylvania ratifying convention, he declared that the proposed Constitution empowered the judges to declare unconstitutional enactments of Congress null and void.[38]

Examination of the speeches, papers and documents of the influential members of the Convention enumerated above fails to disclose any further direct declarations in favor of the prin-

---

[36] *Ibid.*, p. 73.
[37] *Ibid.*, p. 391.
[38] Cf. *infra*, p. 49.

ciple of judicial review of legislation. However, there is reasonably satisfactory evidence that four other members of this group understood and indorsed the doctrine.

William Johnson, of Connecticut, *Robert Morris*, of Pennsylvania, *William Paterson*, of New Jersey, and *George Washington*. The evidence of their opinions is their approval of the Judiciary Act of 1789. Section 25 of that act provided:

A final judgment or decree in any suit, in the highest court of law or equity of a state in which a decision in the suit could be had, where is drawn in question the validity of a treaty or statute of, or an authority exercised under, the United States, and the decision is against their validity; . . . or where is drawn in question the construction of any clause of the Constitution, or of a treaty or statute of, or commission held under, the United States, and the decision is against the title, right, privilege or exemption specially set up or claimed by either party, under such clause of the said Constitution, treaty, statute or commission,—may be reëxamined and reversed or affirmed in the Supreme Court of the United States upon a writ of error.

In other words: the Supreme Court may review and affirm a decision of a state court holding unconstitutional a statute of the United States. It surely is not unreasonable to assume that the men who established this rule believed that the Supreme Court could declare acts of Congress unconstitutional independently of decisions in lower state courts. Indeed, it would seem absurd to assume that an act of Congress might be annulled by a state court with the approval of the Supreme Court, but not by the Supreme Court directly.

William Johnson, Robert Morris and William Paterson [39] were members of the first Senate and voted in favor of the Judiciary Act; [40] and Washington, as president, approved the measure.

In addition to these eminent members of the Convention who directly or indirectly supported the doctrine of judicial control over legislation there were several members of minor influence who seem to have understood and approved it. There is direct or indirect evidence in the following cases.

Abraham Baldwin, of Georgia, had no extensive faith in

---

[39] *Annals of Congress*, vol. i, p. 51.
[40] For further evidence in the case of Paterson cf. *infra*, p. 55.

the probity of a legislature based on a widely extended suffrage. In speaking on the composition of the Senate, on June 29, he said: "He thought the second branch ought to be the representation of property, and that in forming it, therefore, some reference ought to be had to the relative wealth of their constituents and to the principles on which the Senate of Massachusetts was constituted." [41] Baldwin does not seem to have spoken on the subject of the judicial control in the Convention; but two years later, on June 19, 1789, he participated in the discussion of the bill constituting the Department of Foreign Affairs. The point at issue was whether the president could remove alone or only with the consent of the Senate; and some members of the House of Representatives held that this was a judicial question. To this Baldwin replied:

Gentlemen say it properly belongs to the Judiciary to decide this question. Be it so. It is their province to decide upon our laws and if they find this clause to be unconstitutional, they will not hesitate to declare it so; and it seems to be a very difficult point to bring before them in any other way. Let gentlemen consider themselves in the tribunal of justice called upon to decide this question on a *mandamus*. What a situation! almost too great for human nature to bear, they would feel great relief in having had the question decided by the representatives of the people. Hence, I conclude, they also will receive our opinion kindly.[42]

Here is a direct statement that it is the duty of the judges to pass upon the constitutionality of statutes; and the statute in question was not one involving an encroachment upon the sphere of the judiciary but one touching the respective powers of the president and Senate. Baldwin here seems to think, however, that the court would, and ought to, receive with gratitude the expressed opinion of the House of Representatives. Such an opinion, he apparently thought, would aid the judges in reaching a decision but would not be binding upon them. In his later years, however, after the struggle between the Federalists and the Jeffersonians for the control of the national government had begun, Baldwin seems to have retracted his earlier

---

[41] Farrand, vol. i, p. 469.
[42] *Annals of Congress*, vol. i, p. 582.

view; for in a debate in the Senate concerning the powers of
the presidential electors, in January, 1800, he said:

Suppose either of the other branches of the government, the Executive or the Judiciary or even Congress, should be guilty of taking
steps which are unconstitutional, to whom is it submitted or who
has control over it, except by impeachment? The Constitution seems
to have equal confidence in all the branches on their own proper
ground, and for either to arrogate superiority, or a claim to greater
confidence, shows them in particular to be unworthy of it, as it is in
itself directly unconstitutional.[43]

It is small wonder that Baldwin thought the powers of the judiciary one of the questions that the Convention had left unsettled;[44] but his clear statement on June 19, 1789, may reasonably be taken to represent his understanding of the power conferred on the judiciary by the Constitution. At that time, at
least, he believed it a function of the judiciary to pass upon
the constitutionality of the statutes.

Richard Bassett of Delaware, was a member of the Senate
committee which introduced the Judiciary Act of 1789, and
he voted for the measure.[45] Bassett was also one of Adams's
Federalist judges, appointed under the act of February 13, 1801;
and when the Jeffersonians repealed the law he joined several
of his colleagues in a protest against the repeal, on the ground
that it was an impairment of the rights secured to them as
judicial officers under the Constitution. In a memorial to Congress the deposed judges declared that they were

compelled to represent it as their opinion that the rights secured to
them by the Constitution, as members of the judicial department,
have been impaired. . . . The right of the undersigned to their compensation . . . involving a personal interest, will cheerfully be submitted to judicial examination and decision, in such manner as the
wisdom and impartiality of Congress may prescribe.[46]

The memorialists proposed that their rights should be decided
by the judicial department; and such a decision would have involved an inquiry regarding the constitutionality of the repeal

---

[43] Farrand, vol. iii, p. 383.
[44] *Ibid.*, p. 370. Cf. *infra*, pp. 46, 47.
[45] *Annals of Congress*, vol. i, pp. 18, 51.
[46] *American State Papers, Class X, Miscellaneous*, vol. i, p. 340.

of the Judiciary Act of 1801.[47] That Bassett believed the repeal unconstitutional, as to his deprivation of judicial functions and salary, and held the judiciary to be the proper authority for deciding the point, is quite evident.

George Wythe, of Virginia, was a member of the Virginia court of appeals which decided the case of Commonwealth *v.* Caton [48] in 1782. Justice Wythe, in his opinion, referred to the practice of certain English chancellors, who had defended the rights of subjects against the rapacity of the crown, and exclaimed:

If the whole legislature, an event to be deprecated, should attempt to overleap the bounds prescribed to them by the people, I, in administering the public justice of the country, will meet the united powers at my seat in this tribunal; and, pointing to the constitution, will say to them, here is the limit of your authority and hither shall you go but no further.

The duty of a court to declare unconstitutional laws void could hardly be more energetically asserted. Of course this is not direct evidence that Wythe held that the federal Constitution embodied the principle, but it is clear that he favored the doctrine.

Willian Few, of Georgia, *George Read*, of Delaware, and *Caleb Strong*, of Massachusetts, who were members of the first Senate under the new government, voted for the Judiciary Act [49] and may therefore, for the reasons indicated above, be regarded as having accepted the principle of the judicial review of federal statutes.

Summing up the evidence: we may say that of the leading members of the Convention no less than thirteen believed that the judicial power included the right and duty of passing upon the constitutionality of acts of Congress. Satisfactory evidence is afforded by the vote on the Judiciary Act that four other leading members held to the same belief. Of the less prominent members, we find that three expressed themselves in favor of

---

[47] A proposition to make provision for submitting the case to judicial determination was defeated in the House on January 27, 1803. *Annals of Congress,* Second Session, 7th Congress, p. 439.

[48] Thayer's *Cases,* vol. i, p. 55. Cf. *supra,* p. 28.

[49] *Annals of Congress,* vol. i, p. 51. Cf. *supra,* p. 38.

judicial control and three others approved it by their vote on the Judiciary Act. We are accordingly justified in asserting that twenty-three members of the Convention favored or at least accepted some form of judicial control. That they all had equal understanding of the implications of the doctrine, that they clearly foresaw the possible development of the judicial power, cannot, of course, be claimed. But it seems to be unquestionable that they all understood that refusal to recognize unconstitutional enactments was a part of the judicial function.

II

We may now turn to the evidence that judicial control was not regarded by the framers of the Constitution as a normal judicial function under the new Constitution. The researches of those who contend that the doctrine propounded in Marbury *v.* Madison is sheer usurpation have placed only four members of the Convention on record against judicial control; and one of these, John Dickinson, of Delaware, must be stricken from the list.[50] The evidence in the case of the remaining three members is as follows:

Gunning Bedford, of Delaware, speaking in the Convention on June 4 on the subject of the executive veto, expressed himself as

opposed to every check on the legislative, even the council of revision first proposed. He thought it would be sufficient to mark out in the Constitution the boundaries to the legislative authority, which would give all the requisite security to the rights of the other departments. The representatives of the people were the best judges of what was for their interest and ought to be under no external controul whatever. The two branches would produce a sufficient controul within the legislature itself.[51]

John F. Mercer, of Maryland. On August 15 Madison moved that all acts, before they became laws, should be submitted to both the executive and supreme judiciary departments and, upon being vetoed by either or both of these departments, be repassed only by extraordinary majorities. Mercer

---

[50] Cf. *supra*, pp. 28, 29.
[51] Farrand, vol. i, p. 100.

heartily approved the motion. It is an axiom that the judiciary ought to be separate from the legislative; but equally so that it ought to be independent of that department. The true policy of the axiom is that legislative usurpation and oppression may be obviated. He disapproved of the doctrine that the judges as expositors of the Constitution should have authority to declare a law void. He thought laws ought to be well and cautiously made and then to be uncontroulable.[52]

Mercer evidently feared "legislative oppression," and when the motion to have acts submitted to the judiciary before they should become laws was rejected, he may have changed his mind on the subject of judicial control. However that may be, he stands on record as distinctly disapproving the doctrine.

Richard Spaight, of North Carolina, was undoubtedly opposed to judicial control over legislation, although he does not appear to have said anything on the subject in the constitutional Convention. In the spring of 1787 the superior court of North Carolina, in the case of Bayard *v.* Singleton, declared an act of the legislature of that state null and void on the ground that it was not warranted by the constitution of the commonwealth. The decision aroused much popular opposition and Spaight joined in the protest against the action of the court. In a letter dated Philadelphia, August 12, 1787, and directed to Mr. Iredell, Spaight wrote:

I do not pretend to vindicate the law which has been the subject of controversy; it is immaterial what law they have declared void; it is their usurpation of the authority to do it that I complain of, as I do most positively deny that they have any such power; nor can they find anything in the constitution, either directly or impliedly, that will support them, or give them any color of right to exercise that authority. Besides it would have been absurd, and contrary to the practice of all the world, had the constitution vested such power in them, as would have operated as an absolute negative on the proceedings of the legislature, which no judiciary ought ever to possess. . . .

He further declared that "many instances might be brought to show the absurdity and impropriety of such power being lodged in the judges." He was aware, he explained, of the desirability

---

[52] *Ibid.*, vol. ii, p. 298.

of a check on the legislature, but he thought an annual election the best that could be devised.[53]

Pierce Butler, of South Carolina, and *John Langdon*, of New Hampshire, were members of the first Senate of the new Union, and both voted against the Judiciary Act of 1789.[54] Their reasons for so voting are not apparent; and it may be questioned whether a vote cast against the act as a whole is evidence of opposition to the principle of judicial control of federal legislation recognized in the twenty-fifth section of the act. If, however, these two names be added, the list of opponents of judicial control contain five members of the Convention, and but one of the five, Butler, belonged to the influential group.

III

Mr. Boudin lays much stress on the silence of those who disliked judicial control of legislation. He says:

It is absurd to assume that the many avowed opponents of judicial control of legislation who sat in the convention would have agreed to the [judiciary] article without a murmur had they suspected that it contained even a part of the enormous power which our judiciary now exercises. Richard Spaight for one, whose fiery denunciation of this power I have quoted above, would have made the halls in which the Convention met ring to the echo with his emphatic protest, had he suspected any such implications.[55]

The "avowed opponents" do not seem to have been "many"; but whether they and the unavowed opponents were many or few, they must have been fully aware that most of the leading members regarded the nullification of unconstitutional laws as a normal judicial function. The view was more than once clearly voiced in the Convention, and any delegate who was not aware of "such implications" must have been very remiss in the discharge of his duties. On June 4 King definitely stated that the judges in the exposition of the laws would no doubt stop the operation of such as appeared repugnant to the Constitution.[56]

---

[53] Coxe, *An Essay on Judicial Power*, pp. 248 *et seq.* and 385.
[54] *Annals of Congress*, vol. i, p. 51.
[55] *Loc. cit.*, pp. 248, 249.
[56] Farrand, vol. i, p. 109.

On that day there were present representatives from Massachusetts, Connecticut, New York, Pennsylvania, Delaware, Maryland, Virginia, North Carolina, South Carolina and Georgia. In addition to members in the group of twenty-five enumerated above there were recorded as present on that occasion Bedford, McClurg, Pierce and Yates.[57] Several other members, including Spaight, were in Philadelphia at the time and were probably in attendance at that particular session, but as there was no preliminary roll call the list of those actually present must be made up from those who addressed the Convention or appeared in the roll on a divided vote. There was also a large attendance on July 21, when the doctrine of judicial control was again enunciated in even more emphatic tones. In view of these facts it cannot be assumed that the Convention was unaware that the judicial power might be held to embrace a very considerable control over legislation and that there was a high degree of probability (to say the least) that such control would be exercised in the ordinary course of events.

The accepted canons of historical criticism warrant the assumption that, when a legal proposition is before a lawmaking body and a considerable number of the supporters of that proposition definitely assert that it involves certain important and fundamental implications, and it is nevertheless approved by that body without any protests worthy of mention, these implications must be deemed part of that legal proposition when it becomes law; provided, of course, that they are consistent with the letter and spirit of the instrument. To go further than this—to say that the Convention must have passed definitely upon every inference that could logically be drawn from the language of the instrument that it adopted—would of course be an absurdity.

In balancing conflicting presumptions in order to reach a judgment in the case, it must be remembered that no little part of the work of drafting the Constitution was done by the Committee of Detail and the Committee of Style.

The former committee, appointed on July 24, consisted of Rutledge, Wilson, Ellsworth, Randolph and Gorham. Of these

---

[57] Farrand, pp. 96 *et seq.*

five men two, Ellsworth and Wilson, had expressly declared
themselves in favor of judicial control, and Wilson seems to have
been the "dominating mind of the committee." This committee
had before it the resolutions referred to it by the Convention
of July 23. It had also before it the Pinckney plan, or an
outline of it, and the New Jersey plan. The members of the
committee had been assiduous in their attendance upon the debates during the two months previous, and they prepared a draft
of a constitution which they presented to the Convention on
August 6. The article dealing with federal judicial power, as
reported by the committee,[58] contained most of the provisions
later embodied in the federal Constitution.

After lengthy debates on the draft submitted by the Committee of Detail, a committee of five was created to revise
and arrange the style of the articles agreed to by the Convention;
and Johnson, Hamilton, Gouverneur Morris, Madison and King
were selected as members of this committee. Of these five men
four, Hamilton, Morris, Madison and King, are on record as
expressly favoring judicial control over legislation. There is some
little dispute as to the share of glory to be assigned to single
members of the committee, but undoubtedly Gouverneur Morris
played a considerable part in giving the Constitution its final
form. Speaking of his work on the Constitution, Mr. Morris
later wrote:

Having rejected redundant and equivocal terms, I believed it as clear
as our language would permit; excepting, nevertheless, a part of what
relates to the judiciary. On that subject conflicting opinions had been
maintained with so much professional astuteness that it became necessary to select phrases which expressing my own notions would not
alarm others nor shock their self-love.[59]

That the Constitution was not designed to be perfectly
explicit on all points and to embody definitely the opinions of
a majority of the Convention is further evidenced by a speech
made by Abraham Baldwin, a member of the Convention from
Georgia, in the House of Representatives on March 14, 1796.

---

[58] Farrand, vol. ii, p. 186.
[59] Sparks, *Life of Morris,* vol. iii, p. 323.

In speaking of the clause of the Constitution which provides that treaties are to be the supreme law of the land, he said:

He would begin it by the assertion, that those few words in the Constitution on this subject were not those apt, precise, definite expressions, which irresistibly brought upon them the meaning which he had been above considering. He said it was not to disparage the instrument, to say that it had not definitely, and with precision, absolutely settled everything on which it had spoken. He had sufficient evidence to satisfy his own mind that it was not supposed by the makers of it at the time but that some subjects were left a little ambiguous and uncertain. It was a great thing to get so many difficult subjects definitely settled at once. If they could all be agreed in, it would compact the Government. The few that were left a little unsettled might, without any great risk, be settled by practice or by amendments in the progress of the Government. He believed this subject of the rival powers of legislation and treaty was one of them; the subject of the militia was another, and some question respecting the judiciary another. When he reflected on the immense difficulties and dangers of that trying occasion—the old Government prostrated, and a chance whether a new one could be agreed in—the recollection recalled to him nothing but the most joyful sensations that so many things had been so well settled, and that experience had shown there was very little difficulty or danger in settling the rest.[60]

IV

It is urged by the opponents of judicial control that, whatever may have been the purpose of the members of the Philadelphia Convention, the ratifying conventions in the states gave the final legal sanction to the Constitution, and a sound rule of interpretation would compel us to ascertain the opinion of these bodies on the point at issue. This contention cannot be gainsaid; but a full examination of the materials on the state conventions, as any one can see, would require years of research into the lives and opinions of several hundred members. The author of this paper does not pretend to have made this research, and this essay is limited principally to a consideration of the purpose of the framers, not the enactors, of the Constitution.

[60] Farrand, vol. iii, p. 369.

However, it is of interest to note what materials bearing on the purpose of the enactors with regard to this point are contained in Elliot's *Debates*.

If the members of the Virginia convention which ratified the federal Constitution were in the dark in this matter, or had any doubts as to the probable implications of the judicial article, they must have been enlightened by the clear and unmistakable language of John Marshall. In replying to objections which had been raised regarding the danger of an extension of federal jurisdiction at the cost of the states, he pointed out that the proposed federal government was one of enumerated and limited powers.

Has the government of the United States power to make laws on every subject? . . . Can they make laws affecting the mode of transferring property, or contracts, or claims between citizens of the same state? Can they go beyond the delegated powers? If they were to make a law not warranted by any of the powers enumerated it would be considered by the Judges as an infringement of the Constitution which they are to guard. They would not consider such a law as coming under their jurisdiction. They would declare it void.[61]

In the course of the discussion Mr. Grayson said: "If the Congress cannot make a law against the Constitution I apprehend they cannot make a law to abridge it. The judges are to defend it." [62] Mr. Pendleton declared: "The fair inference is that oppressive laws will not be warranted by the Constitution, nor attempted by our representatives, who are selected for their ability and integrity, and that honest, independent judges will never admit an oppressive construction." [63]

The Maryland convention was by no means uninformed regarding the possible functions of the judiciary under the proposed Constitution. In his famous letter directed to the legislature of the state, Luther Martin said:

Whether, therefore, any laws or regulations of the Congress or any act of its president or the officers are contrary to, or not warranted

---

[61] Elliot's *Debates*, vol. iii, p. 553.
[62] *Ibid.*, p. 567.
[63] *Ibid.*, p. 548.

by, the Constitution, rests only with the judges who are appointed by Congress to determine; by whose determination every state must be bound.[64]

If the members of the Pennsylvania ratifying convention had any doubts regarding the probable exercise of judicial control over legislation under the new Constitution, these must have been removed by one of Mr. Wilson's speeches in defence of the judiciary. Some members of the convention expressed the apprehension that, inasmuch as the federal courts were to have jurisdiction in all cases in law and equity arising under the Constitution and the laws of the United States, the power enjoyed by the judges might be indefinitely extended if Congress saw fit to make laws not warranted by the Constitution. On this point Mr. Wilson said:

I think the contrary inference true. If a law should be made inconsistent with those powers vested by this instrument in Congress, the judges, as a consequence of their independence, and the particular powers of government being defined, will declare such law to be null and void. For the power of the Constitution predominates. Anything therefore that shall be enacted by Congress contrary thereto will not have the force of law.[65]

In New York, the members of the Convention must have known the clear and cogent argument for judicial control made by Hamilton in *The Federalist*.

If the members of the Connecticut convention were unaware of the fact that under the provisions of the Constitution the judiciary would enjoy the power to pass upon the constitutionality of federal and state statutes, it was their own fault; for, in his speech of January 7, 1788, on the power of Congress to lay taxes, Oliver Ellsworth carefully explained the new system. He said:

This constitution defines the extent of the powers of the general government. If the general legislature should at any time overleap their limits, the judicial department is a constitutional check. If the

---

[64] *Ibid.*, vol. i, p. 380.
[65] McMaster and Stone, *Pennsylvania and the Federal Constitution*, p. 354.

United States go beyond their powers, if they make a law which the Constitution does not authorize, it is void; and the judicial power, the national judges, who, to secure their impartiality, are to be made independent, will declare it to be void.[66]

It would be entirely misleading to conclude from this fragmentary evidence, that the question of judicial control over acts of Congress was adequately considered in the state conventions. It was judicial control over state statues that aroused the most serious apprehensions of critics of the new frame of government. That they thought much—or cared much—about what might happen to acts of Congress is not apparent.[67] Still it cannot be said that they were kept in the dark in this respect, or that they could not easily have learned, if the matter had interested them, what the framers of the Constitution intended and expected. And it may pertinently be asked what our constitutional position would be today, if it were recognized that each branch of the federal government, in addition to the clearly expressed powers conferred upon it, possesses those additional powers only which were understood, by the ratifying conventions of the states, to have been impliedly conferred!

---

[66] Elliot's *Debates,* vol. ii, p. 196. Cf. Farrand, vol. iii, p. 240.

[67] It is interesting to note that when, ten years later, the Kentucky and Virginia Resolutions raised the question of judicial control, and the other states had occasion to express a direct opinion on this point, none of them seems to have approved the doctrine expressed in the Resolutions. *Cf.* Ames, *State Documents on Federal Relations,* p. 16. The Massachusetts legislature replied to Virginia, on February 9, 1799: "This legislature are persuaded that the decision of all cases in law and equity arising under the Constitution of the United States and the construction of all laws made in pursuance thereof are exclusively vested by the people in the judicial courts of the United States." *Ibid.* pp. 18 *et seq.* The Rhode Island assembly declared that "the words, to wit, 'The judicial power shall extend to all cases arising under the laws of the United States,' vest in the federal courts exclusively, and in the Supreme Court of the United States ultimately, the authority of deciding on the constitutionality of any act or law of the Congress of the United States." *Ibid.* p. 17. The New Hampshire legislature resolved: "That the state legislatures are not the proper tribunals to determine the constitutionality of the laws of the general government; that the duty of such decision is properly and exclusively confided to the judicial department." Elliot's *Debates,* vol. IV, p. 539 (ed. 1861). The Vermont legislature asserted: "It belongs not to state legislatures to decide on the constitutionality of laws made by the general government, this power being exclusively vested in the judiciary courts of the Union." *Ibid.* The House of Representatives of Pennsylvania replied to Kentucky that the people of the United States "have committed to the supreme judiciary of the nation the high authority of ultimately and conclusively deciding upon the constitutionality of all legislative acts." Ames, *op. cit.,* p. 20. The Senate of New York replied to Virginia and Kentucky that the decision of all cases in law and equity was confided to the federal judiciary and that the states were excluded from interference. *Ibid.,* p. 23.

V

Those who hold that it was not the intention of the framers of the Constitution to establish judicial control of legislation make much of the opposition aroused by the sporadic attempts of a few state courts to exercise such a control prior to 1787. Dean Trickett cites the cases and exclaims: "These then are the precedents!" Mr. Boudin cites them and also exclaims: "Such were the state 'precedents,' and such was the temper of the people at the time the Philadelphia Convention met to frame the Constitution of the United States." The only trouble with this line of argument is that it leaves out of account the sharp political division existing in the United States in 1787 and the following years.

The men who framed the federal Constitution were not among the paper-money advocates and stay-law makers whose operations in state legislatures and attacks upon the courts were chiefly responsible, Madison informs us, for the calling of the Convention. The framers of the Constitution were not among those who favored the assaults on vested rights which legislative majorities were making throughout the Union. On the contrary, they were, almost without exception, bitter opponents of such enterprises; and they regarded it as their chief duty, in drafting the new Constitution, to find a way of preventing the renewal of what they deemed "legislative tyranny." Examine the rolls of the state conventions that ratified the Constitution after it came from the Philadelphia Convention, and compare them with the rolls of the legislatures that had been assailing the rights of property. It was largely because the framers of the Constitution knew the temper and class bias of the state legislatures that they arranged that the new Constitution should be ratified by conventions. The framers and enactors of the federal Constitution represented the solid, conservative, commercial and financial interests of the country—not the interests which denounced and proscribed judges in Rhode Island, New Jersey and North Carolina, and stoned their houses in New York. The conservative interests, made desperate by the imbecilities of the Confederation and harried by state legislatures, roused themselves from their lethargy, drew together in a mighty effort to establish a government that would be strong enough to pay the national debt, regulate interstate and foreign commerce, provide for national defence, prevent fluctuations in the currency created by paper emissions and control the propensities of legislative majorities to attack private rights.

It is in the light of the political situation that existed in 1787 that we must inquire whether the principle of judicial control is out of harmony with the general purpose of the federal Constitution. It is an ancient and honorable rule of construction, laid down by Blackstone, that any instrument should be interpreted, "by considering the reason and spirit of it; or the cause which moved the legislator to enact it. . . . From this method of interpreting laws, by the reason of them, arises what we call equity." It may be, therefore, that the issue of judicial control is a case in equity. The direct intention of the framers and enactors not being clearly expressed on this point, we may have recourse to the "reason and spirit" of the Constitution.

Now the essence of the doctrine of judicial control is that the judiciary, rather than the legislative or executive department, is best fitted to pronounce the final word of interpretation on the Constitution in cases involving private rights. Assuredly it is best fitted to secure the purposes which the framers had in mind—the construction of a government strong enough to carry out certain great national functions and at the same time firm enough to secure the rights of persons and of property against popular majorities, no matter how great.[68]

No historical fact is more clearly established than the fact that the framers of the Constitution distrusted democracy and feared the rule of mere numbers. Almost every page of Madison's record bears witness to the fact that the Convention was anxiously seeking to solve the problem of establishing property rights on so firm a basis that they would be forever secure against the assaults of legislative majorities. If any reader needs a documented demonstration of this fact, he will do well to turn to the *Records of the Convention*, so admirably compiled by Professor Farrand. Let him go through the proceedings of the

---

[68] *The Federalist*, No. 10.

Convention and see how many of the members expressed concern at the dangers of democracy and were casting about for some method of restraining the popular branch of the government. The very system of checks and balances, which is undeniably the essential element of the Constitution, is built upon the doctrine that the popular branch of the government cannot be allowed full sway, and least of all in the enactment of laws touching the rights of property. The exclusion of the direct popular vote in the election of the president; the creation, again by indirect election, of a Senate which the framers hoped would represent the wealth and conservative interests of the country; and the establishment of an independent judiciary appointed by the president with the concurrence of the Senate—all these devices bear witness to the fact that the underlying purpose of the Constitution was not the establishment of popular government by means of parliamentary majorities.

Page after page of *The Federalist* is directed to that portion of the electorate which was disgusted with the "mutability of the public councils." Writing on the presidential veto Hamilton says:

The propensity of the legislative department to intrude upon the rights, and absorb the powers, of the other departments has already been suggested and repeated. . . . It may perhaps be said that the power of preventing bad laws included the power of preventing good ones; and may be used to the one purpose as well as the other. But this objection will have little weight with those who can properly estimate the mischiefs of that inconstancy and mutability in the laws which form the greatest blemish in the character and genius of our governments. They will consider every institution calculated to restrain the excess of lawmaking and to keep things in the same state in which they happen to be at any given period, as more likely to do good than harm; because it is favorable to greater stability in the system of legislation. The injury which may be possibly done by defeating a few good laws will be amply compensated by the advantage of preventing a number of bad ones.[69]

In the face of the evidence above adduced, in the face of the political doctrines enunciated time and again on divers occasions by the leaders in the Convention, it certainly is incum-

---

[69] *The Federalist*, No. 73.

bent upon those who say that judicial control was not within
the purpose of the men who framed and enacted the federal
Constitution to bring forward positive evidence, not arguments
resting upon silence. It is incumbent upon them to show that
the American federal system was not designed primarily to
commit the established rights of property to the guardianship
of a judiciary removed from direct contact with popular elec-
torates.[70] Whether this system is outworn, whether it has unduly
exalted property rights, is a legitimate matter for debate; but
those who hold the affirmative cannot rest their case on the intent of the eighteenth-century statesmen who framed the Constitution.

VI

The great justice who made the theory of judicial control operative had better opportunities than any student of history or law
today to discover the intention of the framers of the federal
Constitution. Marshall, to be sure, did not have before him
Elliot's *Debates*, but he was of the generation that made the
Constitution. He had been a soldier in the Revolutionary War.
He had been a member of the Virginia convention that ratified
the Constitution; and he must have remembered stating in that
convention the doctrine of judicial control,[71] apparently without
arousing any protest. He was on intimate, if not always friendly,
relations with the great men of his state who were instrumental in framing the Constitution. Washington once offered
him the attorney-generalship. He was an envoy to France with
two members of the Convention, Charles Cotesworth Pinckney and Elbridge Gerry. He was a member of Congress for
part of one term in Adams's administration; he was secretary of
state under Adams; and he was everywhere regarded as a tower

---

[70] See the article on this point by President Arthur T. Hadley of Yale University,
The Independent, April 16, 1908.

[71] Cf. *supra*, p. 48. In Marshall's argument in the case of Ware *v.* Hylton before the Supreme Court in 1796, Marshall said: "The legislative authority of any
country can only be restrained by its own municipal constitution. This is a principle that springs from the very nature of society; and the judicial authority can have
no right to question the validity of a law unless such a jurisdiction is expressly
given by the Constitution." 3 Dallas, 211. Here, however, Marshall was arguing as
counsel, not stating his own personal views.

of strength to the Federalists. It was, therefore, no closet philosopher, ignorant of the conditions under which the Constitution was established and unlearned in the reason and spirit of
that instrument, who first enunciated from the supreme bench
in unmistakable language the doctrine that judicial control over
legislation was implied in the provisions of the federal Constitution.[72]

Those who hold that the framers of the Constitution did
not intend to establish judicial control over federal legislation
sometimes assert that Marshall made the doctrine out of whole
cloth and had no precedents or authority to guide him. This
is misleading. It is true that it was Marshall who first formally
declared an act of Congress unconstitutional; but the fact should
not be overlooked that in the case of Hylton *v.* The United
States [73] the Supreme Court, with Ellsworth [74] as chief justice
and Paterson as associate (both members of the Convention),
exercised the right to pass upon the constitutionality of an act
of Congress imposing a duty on carriages. On behalf of the
appellant in this case it was argued that the law was unconstitutional and void in so far as it imposed a direct tax without
apportionment among the states. The court sustained the statute. If it was not understood that the court had the power to
hold acts of Congress void on constitutional grounds, why was
the case carried before it? If the court believed that it did not
have the power to declare the act void as well as the power to
sustain it, why did it assume jurisdiction at all or take the trouble
to consider and render an opinion on the constitutionality of
the tax?

The doctrine of judicial control was a familiar one in legal

---

[72] It has not escaped close observers, that the law which Marshall declared unconstitutional in Marbury *v.* Madison was a part of the Judiciary Act of 1789, which
had been drafted and carried through by men who had served in the Convention.
An analysis of the decision shows, however, that the section set aside was at most
badly drawn and was not in direct conflict with the Constitution. Had Marshall
been so inclined he might have construed the language of the act in such a manner
as to have escaped the necessity of declaring it unconstitutional. *The Nation,* vol.
LXXII, p. 104. The opportunity for asserting the doctrine, however, was too good
to be lost, and Marshall was astute enough to take advantage of it. In view of the
recent Jeffersonian triumph, he might very well have felt the need of having the
great precedent firmly set.
[73] 3 Dallas, 171 (1796).
[74] Ellsworth did not take part in the decision, for he had just been sworn into
office.

circles throughout the period between the formation of the
Constitution and the year 1803, when Marshall decided the
Marbury case. In Hayburn's case, already cited, the federal
judges had refused to execute a statute which they held to be
unconstitutional. This was in 1792. In 1794, in the case of Glass *v.*
The Sloop Betsey,[75] the Supreme Court heard the doctrine of
judicial control laid down by the counsel of the appellants:

The well-being of the whole depends upon keeping each department
within its limits. In the state governments several instances have
occurred where a legislative act has been rendered inoperative by
a judicial decision that it was unconstitutional; and even under the
federal government the judges, for the same reason, have refused to
execute an act of Congress. . . . To the judicial and not to the
executive department, the citizen or subject naturally looks for
determinations upon his property; and that agreeably to known rules
and settled forms, to which no other security is equal.

In the case of Calder *v.* Bull,[76] decided in 1798, the counsel
for the plaintiffs in error argued "that any law of the federal
government or of any of the state governments contrary to
the Constitution of the United States is void; and that this
court possesses the power to declare such law void." Justice
Chase however refused to pass upon the general principle, because it was not necessary to the decision of the case before
him. He said:

Without giving an opinion at this time whether this court has jurisdiction to decide that any law made by Congress is void, I am fully
satisfied that this court has no jurisdiction to determine that any law
of any state legislature contrary to the constitution of such state is
void.[77]

In the same case Justice Iredell said:

If any act of Congress or of the legislature of a state violates those
constitutional provisions, it is unquestionably void; though I admit,
that as the authority to declare it void is of a delicate and awful

---

[75] 3 Dallas, 13.
[76] 3 Dallas, 386.
[77] Of course, as everybody knows, Chase adhered stoutly to the doctrine of federal judicial control.

nature, the court will never resort to that authority but in a clear and urgent case.

In view of the principles entertained by the leading members of the Convention with whom Marshall was acquainted, in view of the doctrine so clearly laid down in number 78 of *The Federalist*, in view of the arguments made more than once by eminent counsel before the Supreme Court, in view of Hayburn's case and Hylton *v.* The United States, in view of the judicial opinions several times expressed, in view of the purpose and spirit of the federal Constitution, it is difficult to understand the temerity of those who speak of the power asserted by Marshall in Marbury *v.* Madison as "usurpation."

Note on the Views of Thomas Jefferson

The great authority of Jefferson is often used by the opponents of judicial control; and it is true that, after his party was in control of the legislative and executive branches of the government, he frequently attacked judicial "usurpation" with great vehemence. The Federalists were in possession of the Supreme Court for some time after his inauguration. Jefferson was not a member of the Convention that drafted the Constitution nor of the Virginia convention that ratified it. There is, however, absolutely no question that at the time the Constitution was formed he favored some kind of direct judicial control. In a letter to Madison, dated Paris, December 20, 1787, he said: "I like the organization of the government into Legislative, Judiciary and Executive. . . . And I like the negative given to the Executive with a third of either house, though I should have liked it better had the judiciary been associated for that purpose, or invested with a similar and separate power." [78] He had before him, of course, only a copy of the new instrument and the explanatory letters from his friends. In another letter from Paris, to F. Hopkinson, he approved the idea of a council of revision and added "What I disapproved from the first moment also was the want of a bill of rights to guard liberty against the legislative as well as executive branches of the government ["by"

---

[78] *Documentary History of the Constitution,* Part I, p. 412.

stricken out in the manuscript—it would be interesting to know whether he had in mind "the judiciary"], that is to say, to secure freedom in religion, freedom of the press, freedom from monopolies, *etc.*" [79] Jefferson favored a bill of rights because of "the legal check which it puts into the hands of the judiciary." [80]

---

[79] *Ibid.*, vol. v, p. 159.
[80] *Ibid.*, vol. v, p. 161.

CHAPTER TWO

~~~~~~

The Scope of Judicial Review

As we have seen, the framers of the Constitution did not undertake to spell out ready-made answers to all the great questions of governmental power that were sure to arise. If they had made such an effort, it is difficult to believe that the Constitution would have been flexible enough to survive the mutations of an expanding future and there is grave reason to doubt that it could even have been ratified. But whatever may be the truth about these matters, one thing is certain—that the silences and ambiguities of the Constitution imposed on posterity the weighty burden of thinking out and working out the problems the framers wisely neglected.

One of the most important and troublesome of these unresolved, inherited issues is the question of the scope of judicial review. The framers, as has been said, probably assumed that the courts would exercise some such authority, but neither the Constitution itself nor the speeches and writings of the Convention delegates tell us much about the contemplated range of judicial supervision. Judges, scholars, and citizens of the future have therefore been faced by the task of compounding their own answers, and this is a fairly neat illustration of the fact that the study of American constitutional law casts its followers, willy-nilly, in the roles of political theorists. For neither judge nor student can usefully ply his trade until he has evolved some premises of his own about the relationship between the judicial power and American constitutional democracy.

James Bradley Thayer's essay, here reprinted in part, provides us with one such formulation; and it merits the most respectful consideration, not only because the author was a wise and erudite man, but because, as Thayer shows, the rule he sets forth is solidly moored in constitutional history. And Thayer's argument—that the courts should overturn legislation only when it is unconstitutional beyond "rational question"—also hangs on several theoretical pegs, including the separation of powers doctrine, the postulate "that the people are wise, virtuous, and competent to manage their own affairs," and the conviction that the judicial process is inherently inadequate to save a nation from itself. In short, the essayist has sought to vitalize his legal precedents with a rationale drawn from the traditions of American political philosophy.

Thayer himself, writing in 1893, was perfectly aware that his rule had not always been followed by the Supreme Court, and subsequent constitutional history has seen it frequently honored in the breach. The author refers with apparent approval to Chicago, M. & St. P. Ry. Co. *v.* Minnesota, 134 U.S. 418 (1890), yet this case was an important link in a long chain of decisions involving the due process clause in which "the presumption of constitutionality" seemed often displaced by the judges' flat judgment of right or wrong. Mr. Justice Holmes repeatedly urged that his judicial brethren were denying statutes the benefit of the doubt and tried, in his dissents, to recall them to the tradition restated by Thayer. In Lochner *v.* New York, 198 U.S. 45, 75 (1904), he said:

I think that the word 'liberty,' in the 14th Amendment, is perverted when it is held to prevent the natural outcome of a dominant opinion, unless it can be said that a rational and fair man necessarily would admit that the statute proposed would infringe fundamental principles as they have been understood by the traditions of our people and our law.

Years later, he made it clear that he felt his injunctions had often gone unheeded:

I have not yet adequately expressed the more than anxiety that I feel at the ever increasing scope given to the Fourteenth Amendment in cutting down what I believe to be the constitutional rights of the States. As the decisions now stand, I see hardly any limit but the sky to the invalidating of those rights if they happen to strike a majority of this Court as for any reason undesirable. I cannot believe that the Amendment was intended to give us *carte blanche* to embody our economic or moral beliefs in its prohibitions. Baldwin *v.* Missouri, 281 U.S. 586, 595 (1930).

In 1937, the Court majority restored the presumption of constitutionality in issues involving economic regulation (West Coast Hotel *v.* Parrish, 300 U.S. 379), and it has adhered to the principle in such cases ever since. Not the least interesting aspect of the Parrish case, however, is that the four dissenters quite evidently believed they had never departed from the rule that rational doubts should be resolved in favor of challenged legislation. Mr. Justice Sutherland said, in effect, that he *had* been giving economic regulations the traditional benefit of doubt and that the statutes he voted to overturn were, in his opinion, unconstitutional beyond all rational question. Holmes, Stone, Brandeis, and others had argued that it was hard to hold a law indubitably unconstitutional when a large number of sane men were convinced it was valid, since this amounted to holding that these men were guilty of a completely irrational error in judgment. Sutherland, however, insisted that the question of rational doubt was a matter for private judgment, not determined by the conclusions that others may have reached. If a judge, after searching his soul, decides that the Constitution has plainly been infringed, he must act in accordance with that opinion even though the whole world may disagree with him.

Plainly then, the application of Thayer's rule is no simple and automatic process, and the limits it imposes on judicial supervision may sometimes be less stringent than the author imagined. Nevertheless, it is probably safe to say that the "beyond-rational-question" principle does imply a comparatively modest role for the judiciary, and this is of course all the more true if we apply the objective test of rationality of the Holmes-Stone-Brandeis contingent. The question remains whether the courts, in thus deferring to legislative power, would be serving the best purposes of constitutional democracy.

It is a question that cannot be answered here, if, indeed, a conclusive answer is possible. But it should be noted that Thayer's case is not altogether unchallengeable. He himself remarks, quoting Judge Cooley, that Americans commonly assume the courts will always provide a remedy against unconstitutional legislation. Is it altogether safe, in the face of that assumption, to confine judicial review to the very rare instance when the legislature is guilty of unconstitutional behavior beyond reasonable doubt? Of course, Thayer would argue that Americans should rid themselves of this delusion about the function of courts. He contends that courts are institutionally incapable of bearing so crushing a burden of responsibility, and he would presumably agree with Mr. Justice Frankfurter that the judicial veto deprives the people of that "training in liberty" which is our surest safeguard. (See Minersville School District *v.* Gobitis, 310 U.S. 586, 600 [1940]). But it is easier to condemn a delusion than it is to expunge it, and if Americans persist in passing the buck to the courts, while the courts persist in passing it back, the whole idea of constitutional government may fall by the way. No doubt it would be healthy for legislatures to be as concerned with constitutional principles as they are with expressing the popular will, but history, in its unreasonable way, has ordered things otherwise. American legislatures have tended to take "the will of the people" as their special concern, and the courts have traditionally been delegated a heavy share of the responsibility for maintaining constitutional safeguards. It is wise to recognize, as Thayer does, that the judiciary cannot save us from ourselves if we are determinedly bent on folly. But it is a long step farther to contend that the judiciary should so narrow its range that it would no longer play a vital role in marking the path of constitutional duty.

The Origin and Scope of the American Doctrine of Constitutional Law

by James B. Thayer *

Harvard Law Review,
Volume 7, Page 129 (1893).

[The early pages of Thayer's essay are concerned with a discussion of how the American doctrine, "which allows to the judiciary the power to declare legislative acts unconstitutional, and to treat them as null," came about.]

It is plain that where a power so momentous as this primary authority to interpret is given, the actual determinations of the body to whom it is intrusted are entitled to a corresponding respect; and this not on mere grounds of courtesy or conventional respect, but on very solid and significant grounds of policy and law. The judiciary may well reflect that if they had been regarded by the people as the chief protection against legislative violation of the Constitution, they would not have been allowed merely this incidental and postponed control. They would have been let in, as it was sometimes endeavored in the conventions to let them in, to a revision of the laws before they began to operate.[1] As the opportunity of the judges to

---

* (1831–1902), Professor of Law, Harvard University Law School, 1874–1902.

[1] The Constitution of Colombia, of 1886, art. 84 provides that the judges of the Supreme Court may take part in the legislative debates over "bills relating to civil matters and judicial procedure." And in the case of legislative bills which are objected to by "the government" as unconstitutional if the legislature insist on the bill, as against a veto by the government, it shall be submitted to the Supreme Court, which is to decide upon this question finally. Arts. 90 and 150. See a translation of this constitution by Professor Moses, of the University of California, in the supplement to the *Annals of the American Academy of Political and Social Science,* for January, 1893.

We are much too apt to think of the judicial power of revising the acts of the other departments as our only protection against oppression and ruin. But it is remarkable how small a part this played in any of the debates. The chief protections were a wide suffrage, short terms of office, a double legislative chamber, and the so-called executive veto. There was, in general, the greatest unwillingness to give the judiciary any share in the law-making power. In New York, however, the constitution of 1777 provided a Council of Revision, of which several of the judges were members, to whom all legislative Acts should be submitted before they took effect, and by whom they must be approved. That existed for more than forty

check and correct unconstitutional Acts is so limited, it may
help us to understand why the extent of their control, when
they do have the opportunity, should also be narrow.

It was, then, all along true, and it was foreseen, that much
which is harmful and unconstitutional may take effect without
any capacity in the courts to prevent it, since their whole power
is a judicial one. Their interference was but one of many safeguards, and its scope was narrow.

The rigor of this limitation upon judicial action is sometimes freely recognized, yet in a perverted way which really
operates to extend the judicial function beyond its just bounds.
The court's duty, we are told, is the mere and simple office of
construing two writings and comparing one with another, as
two contracts or two statutes are construed and compared when
they are said to conflict; of declaring the true meaning of each,
and, if they are opposed to each other, of carrying into effect
the constitution as being of superior obligation,—an ordinary
and humble judicial duty, as the courts sometimes describe it.
This way of putting it easily results in the wrong kind of disregard of legislative considerations; not merely in refusing to

years, giving way in the constitution of 1821 to the common expedient of merely
requiring the approval of the executive, or in the alternative, if he refused it, the
repassing of the Act, perhaps by an increased vote, by both branches of the legislature. In Pennsylvania (Const. of 1776, § 47) and Vermont (Const. of 1777, §
44) a Council of Censors was provided for, to be chosen every seven years, who
were to investigate the conduct of affairs, and point out, among other things, all
violations of the constitution by any of the departments. In Pennsylvania this arrangement lasted only from 1776 to 1790; in Vermont from 1777 to 1870. In framing the constitution of the United States, several of these expedients, and others,
were urged, and at times adopted; e.g., that of New York. It was proposed at various times that the general government should have a negative on all the legislation of the States; that the governors of the States should be appointed by the
United States, and should have a negative on State legislation; that a Privy Council
to the President should be appointed, composed in part of the judges; and that the
President and the two houses of Congress might obtain opinions from the Supreme
Court. But at last the convention, rejecting all these, settled down upon the common expedients of two legislative houses, to be a check upon each other, and of an
executive revision and veto, qualified by the legislative power of reconsideration and
enactment by a majority of two-thirds;—upon these expedients, and upon the declaration that the constitution, and constitutional laws and treaties, shall be the supreme law of the land, and shall bind the judges of the several States. This provision, as the phrasing of it indicates, was inserted with an eye to secure the authority of the general government as against the States, i.e. as an essential feature of any
efficient Federal system and not with direct reference to the other departments of the
government of the United States itself. The first form of it was that "legislative Acts
of the United States, and treaties, are the supreme law of the respective States, and
bind the judges there as against their own laws."

to disregard unconstitutional enactments, repeats and strongly reaffirms it:

> I feel so strong a sense of this duty that if a violation of the constitution were manifest, I should not only declare the Act void, but I should think I rendered a more important service to my country than in discharging the ordinary duties of my office for many years. . . . But while I assert this power and insist on its great value to the country, I am not insensible of the high deference due to legislative authority. It is supreme in all cases where it is not restrained by the constitution; and as it is the duty of legislators as well as judges to consult this and conform their acts to it, so it should be presumed that all their acts do conform to it unless the contrary is manifest. This confidence is necessary to insure due obedience to its authority. If this be frequently questioned, it must tend to diminish the reverence for the laws which is essential to the public safety and happiness. I am not, therefore, disposed to examine with scrupulous exactness the validity of a law. It would be unwise on another account. The interference of the judiciary with legislative Acts, if frequent or on dubious grounds, might occasion so great a jealousy of this power and so general a prejudice against it as to lead to measures ending in the total overthrow of the independence of the judges, and so of the best preservative of the constitution. The validity of the law ought not then to be questioned unless it is so obviously repugnant to the constitution that when pointed out by the judges, all men of sense and reflection in the community may perceive the repugnancy. By such a cautious exercise of this judicial check, no jealousy of it will be excited, the public confidence in it will be promoted, and its salutary effects be justly and fully appreciated.[18]

---

[18] This well-known rule is laid down by Cooley (*Const. Lim.*, 6th ed., 216), and supported by emphatic judicial declarations and by a long list of citations from all parts of the country. In Ogden *v.* Saunders, 12 Wheat. 213 (1827), Mr. Justice Washington, after remarking that the question was a doubtful one, said: "If I could rest my opinion in favor of the constitutionality of the law . . . on no other ground than this doubt, so felt and acknowledged, that alone would, in my estimation, be a satisfactory vindication of it. It is but a decent respect due to the . . . legislative body by which any law is passed, to presume in favor of its validity, until its violation of the constitution is proved beyond all reasonable doubt. This has always been the language of this court when that subject has called for its decision; and I know it expresses the honest sentiments of each and every member of this bench." In the Sinking Fund Cases, 99 U.S. 700 (1878), Chief Justice Waite, for the court, said: "This declaration [that an Act of Congress is unconstitutional] should never be made except in a clear case. Every possible presumption is in favor of the validity of a statute, and this continues until the contrary is shown beyond a rational doubt. One branch of the government cannot encroach on the domain of another without danger. The safety of our institutions depends in no small degree on a strict observance of this salutary rule." In Wellington *et al.*, Petitioners, 16 Pick. 87 (1834),

IV. I have accumulated these citations and run them back to the beginning, in order that it may be clear that the rule in question is something more than a mere form of language, a mere expression of courtesy and deference. It means far more than that. The courts have perceived with more or less distinctness that this exercise of the judicial function does in truth go far beyond the simple business which judges sometimes de-

---

Chief Justice Shaw, for the court, remarked that it was proper "to repeat what has been so often suggested by courts of justice, that when called upon to pronounce the invalidity of an Act of legislation [they will] never declare a statute void unless the nullity and invalidity of the Act are placed, in their judgment, beyond reasonable doubt." In Com. *v.* Five Cents Sav. Bnk., 5 Allen, 428 (1862), Chief Justice Bigelow, for the court, said: "It may be well to repeat the rule of exposition which has been often enunciated by this court, that where a statute has been passed with all the forms and solemnities required to give it the force of law, the presumption is in favor of its validity, and that the court will not declare it to be . . . void unless its invalidity is established beyond reasonable doubt." And he goes on to state a corollary of this "well-established rule." In Ex parte M'Collum, I Cow. p. 564 (1823), Cowen, J. (for the court), said: "Before the court will deem it their duty to declare an Act of the legislature unconstitutional, a case must be presented in which there can be no rational doubt." In the People *v.* The Supervisors of Orange, 17 N.Y. 235 (1858), Harris, J. (for the court), said: "A legislative Act is not to be declared void upon a mere conflict of interpretation between the legislative and the judicial power. Before proceeding to annul, by judicial sentence, what has been enacted by the law-making power, it should clearly appear that the Act cannot be supported by any reasonable intendment or allowable presumption." In Perry *v.* Keene, 56 N.H. 514, 534 (1876), Ladd, J. (with the concurrence of the rest of the court), said: "Certainly it is not for the court to shrink from the discharge of a constitutional duty; but, at the same time, it is not for this branch of the government to see an example of encroachment upon the province of the others. It is only the enunciation of a rule that is now elementary in the American States, to say that before we can declare this law unconstitutional, we must be fully satisfied—satisfied beyond a reasonable doubt—that the purpose for which the tax is authorized is private, and not public." In The Cincinnati, etc., Railroad Company, I Oh. St. 77 (1852), Ranney, J. (for the court), said: "While the right and duty of interference in a proper case are thus undeniably clear, the principles by which a court should be guided in such an inquiry are equally clear, both upon principle and authority. . . . It is only when manifest assumption of authority and clear incompatibility between the constitution and the law appear, that the judicial power can refuse to execute it. Such interference can never be permitted in a doubtful case. And this results from the very nature of the question involved in the inquiry. . . . The adjudged cases speak a uniform language on this subject. . . . An unbroken chain of decisions to the same effect is to be found in the State courts." In Syndics of Brooks *v.* Weyman, 3 Martin (La.), 9, 12 (1813), it was said by the court: "We reserve to ourselves the authority to declare null any legislative Act which shall be repugnant to the constitution; but it must be manifestly so, not susceptible of doubt." (Cited with approval in Johnson *v.* Duncan, IB. 539.) In Cotton *v.* The County Commissioners, 6 Fla. 610 (1856), Dupont, J. (for the court), said: "It is a most grave and important power, not to be exercised lightly or rashly, nor in any case where it cannot be made plainly to appear that the legislature has exceeded its powers. If there exist upon the mind of the court a reasonable doubt, that doubt must be given in favor of the law. . . . In further support of this position may be cited any number of decisions by the State courts. . . . If there be one to be found which constitutes an exception to the general doctrine, it has escaped our search."

scribe. If their duty were in truth merely and nakedly to ascertain the meaning of the text of the constitution and of the impeached Act of the legislature, and to determine, as an academic question, whether in the court's judgment the two were in conflict, it would, to be sure, be an elevated and important office, one dealing with great matters, involving large public considerations, but yet a function far simpler than it really is. Having ascertained all this, yet there remains a question—the really momentous question—whether, after all, the court can disregard the Act. It cannot do this as a mere matter of course, —merely because it is concluded that upon a just and true construction the law is unconstitutional. That is precisely the significance of the rule of administration that the courts lay down. It can only disregard the Act when those who have the right to make laws have not merely made a mistake, but have made a very clear one,—so clear that it is not open to rational question. That is the standard of duty to which the courts bring legislative Acts; that is the test which they apply,—not merely their own judgment as to constitutionality, but their conclusion as to what judgment is permissible to another department which the constitution has charged with the duty of making it. This rule recognizes that, having regard to the great, complex, ever-unfolding exigencies of government, much which will seem unconstitutional to one man, or body of men, may reasonably not seem so to another; that the constitution often admits of different interpretations; that there is often a range of choice and judgment; that in such cases the constitution does not impose upon the legislature any one specific opinion, but leaves open this range of choice; and that whatever choice is rational is constitutional. This is the principle which the rule that I have been illustrating affirms and supports. The meaning and effect of it are shortly and very strikingly intimated by a remark of Judge Cooley,[19] to the effect that one who is a member of a legislature may vote against a measure as being, in his judgment, unconstitutional; and, being subsequently placed on the bench, when this measure, having been passed by the legislature in spite of his opposition, comes before him judicially, may there

---

[19] *Const. Lim.,* 6th ed., 68; cited with approval by Bryce, *Am. Com.,* 1st ed., I, 431.

find it his duty, although he has in no degree changed his opinion, to declare it constitutional.

Will any one say, You are over-emphasizing this matter, and making too much turn upon the form of a phrase? No, I think not. I am aware of the danger of doing that. But whatever may be said of particular instances of unguarded or indecisive judicial language, it does not appear to me possible to explain the early, constant, and emphatic statements upon this subject on any slight ground. The form of it is in language too familiar to courts, having too definite a meaning, adopted with too general an agreement, and insisted upon quite too emphatically, to allow us to think it a mere courteous and smoothly transmitted platitude. It has had to maintain itself against denial and dispute. Incidentally, Mr. Justice Gibson disputed it in 1825, while denying the whole power to declare laws unconstitutional.[20] If there be any such power, he insisted (page 352), the party's rights "would depend, not on the greatness of the supposed discrepancy with the constitution, but on the existence of any discrepancy at all." But the majority of the court reaffirmed their power, and the qualifications of it, with equal emphasis. This rule was also denied in 1817 by Jeremiah Mason, one of the leaders of the New England bar, in his argument of the Dartmouth College case, at its earlier stage, in New Hampshire.[21] He said substantially this: "An erroneous opinion still prevails to a considerable extent, that the courts . . . ought to act . . . with more than ordinary deliberation, . . . that they ought not to declare Acts of the legislature unconstitutional unless they come to their conclusion with absolute certainty, . . . and where the reasons are so manifest that none can doubt." He conceded that the courts should treat the legislature "with great decorum, . . . but . . . the final decision, as in other cases, must be according to the unbiassed dictate of the understanding." Legislative Acts, he said, require for their passage at least a majority of the legislature, and the reasons against the validity of the Act cannot ordinarily be so plain as to leave no manner of doubt. The rule, then, really requires the court to surrender its jurisdiction. "Experience shows

---

[20] Eakin *v.* Raub, 12 S. & R. 330.
[21] Farrar's Rep. Dart. Coll. Case, 36.

that legislatures are in the constant habit of exerting their power to its utmost extent." If the courts retire, whenever a plausible ground of doubt can be suggested, the legislature will absorb all power. Such was his argument. But notwithstanding this, the Supreme Court of New Hampshire declared that they could not act without "a clear and strong conviction;" and on error, in 1819, Marshall, in his celebrated opinion at Washington, declared, for the court, "that in no doubtful case would it pronounce a legislative Act to be contrary to the Constitution."

Again, when the great Charles River Bridge Case [22] was before the Massachusetts courts, in 1829, Daniel Webster, arguing, together with Lemuel Shaw, for the plaintiff, denied the existence or propriety of this rule. All such cases, he said (p. 422) involve some doubt; it is not to be supposed that the legislature will pass an Act palpably unconstitutional. The correct ground is that the court will interfere when a case appearing to be doubtful is made out to be clear. Besides, he added, "members of the legislature sometimes vote for a law, of the constitutionality of which they doubt, on the consideration that the question may be determined by the judges." This Act passed in the House of Representatives by a majority of five or six.

We could show, if it were proper, that more than six members voted for it because the unconstitutionality of it *was* doubtful; leaving it to this court to determine the question. If the legislature is to pass a law because its unconstitutionality is doubtful, and the judge is to hold it valid because its unconstitutionality is doubtful, in what a predicament is the citizen placed! The legislature pass it *de bene esse;* if the question is not met and decided here on principle, responsibility rests nowhere. . . . It is the privilege of an American judge to decide on constitutional questions . . . Judicial tribunals are the only ones suitable for the investigation of difficult questions of private right.

But the court did not yield to this ingenious attempt to turn them into a board for answering legislative conundrums. Instead of deviating from the line of their duty for the purpose of correcting errors of the legislature, they held that body to its own duty and its own responsibility. "Such a declaration," said Mr. Justice Wilde in giving his opinion, "should

---

[22] 7 Pick. 344.

never be made but when the case is clear and manifest to all intelligent minds. We must assume that the legislature have done their duty, and we must respect their constitutional rights and powers." Five years later, Lemuel Shaw, who was Webster's associate counsel in the case last mentioned, being now Chief Justice of Massachusetts, in a case [23] where Jeremiah Mason was one of the counsel, repeated with much emphasis "what has been so often suggested by courts of justice, that . . . courts will . . . never declare a statute void unless the nullity and invalidity are placed beyond reasonable doubt."

A rule thus powerfully attacked and thus explicitly maintained, must be treated as having been deliberately meant, both as regards its substance and its form. As to the form of it, it is the more calculated to strike the attention because it marks a familiar and important discrimination, of daily application in our courts, in situations where the rights, the actions, and the authority of different departments, different officials, and different individuals have to be harmonized. It is a distinction and a test, it may be added, that come into more and more prominence as our jurisprudence grows more intricate and refined. In one application of it, as we all know, it is constantly resorted to in the criminal law in questions of self-defence, and in the civil law of tort in questions of negligence,—in answering the question what might an individual who has a right and perhaps a duty of acting under given circumstances, reasonably have supposed at that time to be true? It is the discrimination laid down for settling that difficult question of a soldier's responsibility to the ordinary law of the land when he has acted under the orders of his military superior. "He may," says Dicey, in his *Law of the Constitution*,[24] "as it has been well said, be liable to be shot by a court-martial if he disobeys an order, and to be hanged by a judge and jury if he obeys it. . . . Probably," he goes on, quoting with approval one of the books of Mr. Justice Stephen, ". . . it would be found that the order of a military superior would justify his inferiors in executing any orders for giving which they might fairly suppose their superior officer to have good reasons. . . . The only line that presents itself to my mind is that a soldier

---

[23] Wellington, Ptr., 16 Pick. 87.
[24] 3d ed., 279–81.

should be protected by orders for which he might reasonably believe his officer to have good grounds." [25] This is the distinction adverted to by Lord Blackburn in a leading modern case in the law of libel.[26] "When the court," he said, "come to decide whether a particular set of words . . . are or are not libellous, they have to decide a very different question from that which they have to decide when determining whether another tribunal . . . might not unreasonably hold such words to be libellous." It is the same discrimination upon which the verdicts of juries are revised every day in the courts, as in a famous case where Lord Esher applied it a few years ago, when refusing to set aside a verdict.[27] It must appear, he said, "that reasonable men could not fairly find as the jury have done. . . . It has been said, indeed, that the difference between [this] rule and the question whether the judges would have decided the same way as the jury, is evanescent, and the solution of both depends on the opinion of the judges. The last part of the observation is true, but the mode in which the subject is approached makes the greatest difference. To ask 'Should we have found the same verdict,' is surely not the same thing as to ask whether there is room for a reasonable difference of opinion." In like manner, as regards legislative action, there is often that ultimate question, which was vindicated for the judges in a recent highly important case in the Supreme Court of the United States,[28] viz., that of the reasonableness of a legislature's exercise of its most undoubted powers; of the permissible limit of those powers. If a legislature undertakes to exert the taxing power, that of eminent domain, or any part of that vast, unclassified residue of legislative authority which is called, not always intelligently, the police power, this action must not degenerate into an irrational excess, so as to become, in reality, something different and forbidden,

---

[25] It was so held in Riggs *v.* State, 3 Cold. 85 (Tenn., 1886), and United States *v.* Clark, 31 Fed. Rep. 710 (U.S. Circ. Ct., E. Dist. Michigan, 1887, Brown, J.). I am indebted for these cases to Professor Beale's valuable collection of *Cases on Criminal Law* (Cambridge, 1893). The same doctrine is laid down by Judge Hare in 2 Hare, *Am. Const. Law,* 920.

[26] Cap. & Counties Bank *v.* Henty, 7 App. Cas., p. 776.

[27] Belt *v.* Lawes, Thayer's Cas. Ev. 177, n.

[28] Chic. &c. Ry. Co. *v.* Minnesota, 134 U.S. 418. The question was whether a statute providing for a commission to regulate railroad charges, which excluded the parties from access to the courts for an ultimate judicial revision of the action of the commission, was constitutional.

—e.g., the depriving people of their property without due process of law; and whether it does so or not, must be determined by the judges.[29] But in such cases it is always to be remembered that the judicial question is a secondary one. The legislature in determining what shall be done, what it is reasonable to do, does not divide its duty with the judges, nor must it conform to their conception of what is prudent or reasonable legislation. The judicial function is merely that of fixing the outside border of reasonable legislative action, the boundary beyond which the taxing power, the power of eminent domain, police power, and legislative power in general, cannot go without violating the prohibitions of the constitution or crossing the line of its grants.[30]

It must indeed be studiously remembered, in judicially applying such a test as this of what a legislature may reasonably think, that virtue, sense, and competent knowledge are always to be attributed to that body. The conduct of public affairs must always go forward upon conventions and assumptions of that sort. "It is a *postulate*," said Mr. Justice Gibson, "in the theory of our government . . . that the people are wise, virtuous, and competent to manage their own affairs." [31] "It would be indecent in the extreme," said Marshall, C. J.,[32] "upon a private contract between two individuals to enter into an inquiry respecting the corruption of the sovereign power of a State." And

---

[29] Compare Law and Fact in Jury Trials, 4 Harv. Law Rev. 167, 168.

[30] There is often a lack of discrimination in judicial utterances on this subject, —as if it were supposed that the legislature had to conform to the judge's opinion of reasonableness in some other sense than that indicated above. The true view is indicated by Judge Cooley in his *Principles of Const. Law*, 2d ed., 57, when he says of a particular question: "Primarily the determination of what is a public purpose belongs to the legislature, and its action is subject to no review or restraint so long as it is not manifestly colorable. All cases of doubt must be solved in favor of the validity of legislative action, for the obvious reason that the question is legislative, and only becomes judicial when there is a plain excess of legislative authority. A court can only arrest the proceedings and declare a levy void when the absence of public interest in the purpose for which the funds are to be raised is so clear and palpable as to be perceptible to any mind at first blush." And again, on another question, by the Supreme Court of the United States, Waite, C. J., in Terry *v.* Anderson, 95 U.S. p. 633 "In all such cases the question is one of reasonableness, and we have therefore only to consider whether the time allowed in this Statute [of Limitations] is, under all the circumstances, reasonable. Of that the legislature is primarily the judge; and we cannot overrule the decision of that department of the government, unless a palpable error has been committed." See Pickering Phipps *v.* Ry. Co., 66 Law Times Rep. 721 (1892), and a valuable opinion by Ladd, J., in Perry *v.* Keene, 56 N.H. 514 (1876).

[31] Eakin *v.* Raub, 12 S. & R., p. 355.

[32] Fletcher *v.* Peck, 6 Cr. p. 131.

so in a court's revision of legislative acts, as in its revision of a jury's acts, it will always assume a duly instructed body; and the question is not merely what persons may rationally do who are such as we often see, in point of fact, in our legislative bodies, persons untaught it may be, indocile, thoughtless, reckless, incompetent,—but what those other persons, competent, well-instructed, sagacious, attentive, intent only on public ends, fit to represent a self-governing people, such as our theory of government assumes to be carrying on our public affairs,—what such persons may reasonably think or do, what is the permissible view for them. If, for example, what is presented to the court be a question as to the constitutionality of an Act alleged to be ex post facto, there can be no assumption of ignorance, however probable, as to anything involved in a learned or competent discussion of that subject. And so of the provisions about double jeopardy, or giving evidence against one's self, or attainder, or jury trial. The reasonable doubt, then, of which our judges speak is that reasonable doubt which lingers in the mind of a competent and duly instructed person who has carefully applied his faculties to the question. The rationally permissible opinion of which we have been talking is the opinion reasonably allowable to such a person as this.

The ground on which courts lay down this test of a reasonable doubt for juries in criminal cases, is the greatest gravity of affecting a man with crime. The reason that they lay it down for themselves in reviewing the civil verdict of a jury is a different one, namely, because they are revising the work of another department charged with a duty of its own,—having themselves no right to undertake *that* duty, no right at all in the matter except to hold the other department within the limit of a reasonable interpretation and exercise of its powers. The court must not, even negatively, undertake to pass upon the facts in jury cases. The reason that the same rule is laid down in regard to revising legislative acts is neither the one of these nor the other alone, but it is both. The courts are revising the work of a co-ordinate department, and must not, even negatively, undertake to legislate. And, again, they must not act unless the case is so very clear, because the consequences of setting aside legislation may be so serious.

If it be said that the case of declaring legislation invalid is different from the others because the ultimate question here is one of the construction of a writing; that this sort of question is always a court's question, and that it cannot well be admitted that there should be two legal constructions of the same instrument; that there is a right way and a wrong way of construing it, and only one right way; and that it is ultimately for the court to say what the right way is,—this suggestion appears, at first sight, to have much force. But really it begs the question. Lord Blackburn's opinion in the libel case [33] related to the construction of a writing. The doctrine which we are now considering is this, that in dealing with the legislative action of a co-ordinate department, a court cannot always, and for the purpose of all sorts of questions, say that there is but one right and permissible way of construing the constitution. When a court is interpreting a writing merely to ascertain or apply its true meaning, then, indeed, there is but one meaning allowable; namely, what the court adjudges to be its true meaning. But when the ultimate question is not that, but whether certain acts of another department, officer, or individual are legal or permissible, then this is not true. In the class of cases which we have been considering, *the ultimate question is not what is the true meaning of the constitution, but whether legislation is sustainable or not.*

It may be suggested that this is not the way in which the judges in fact put the matter; e.g., that Marshall, in McCulloch *v.* Maryland,[34] seeks to establish the court's own opinion of the constitutionality of the legislation establishing the United States Bank. But in recognizing that this is very often true, we must remember that where the court is sustaining an Act, and finds it to be constitutional in its own opinion, it is fit that this should be said, and that such a declaration is all that the case calls for; it disposes of the matter. But it is not always true; there are many cases where the judges sustain an Act because they are in doubt about it; where they are not giving their own opinion that it is constitutional, but are merely leaving untouched a determination of the legislature; as in the case where a Massachusetts judge concurred in the opinion of his brethren that a

[33] Cap. & Count. Bank *v.* Henty, 7 App. Cas. 741.
[34] 4 Wheat. 316.

legislative Act was "competent for the legislature to pass, and was not unconstitutional," "upon the single ground that the Act is not so clearly unconstitutional, its invalidity so free from reasonable doubt, as to make it the duty of the judicial department, in view of the vast interests involved in the result, to declare it void." [35] The constant declaration of the judges that the question for them is not one of the mere and simple preponderance of reasons for or against, but of what is very plain and clear, clear beyond a reasonable doubt,—this declaration is really a steady announcement that their decisions in support of the constitutionality of legislation do not, as of course, import their own opinion of the true construction of the constitution, and that the strict meaning of their words, when they hold an Act constitutional, is merely this,—not unconstitutional beyond a reasonable doubt. It may be added that a sufficient explanation is found here of some of the decisions which have alarmed many people in recent years,—as if the courts were turning out but a broken reed.[36] Many more such opinions are to be expected, for, while legislatures are often faithless to their trust, judges sometimes have to confess the limits of their own power.

It all comes back, I think, to this. The rule under discussion has in it an implied recognition that the judicial duty now in question touches the region of political administration, and is qualified by the necessities and proprieties of administration. If our doctrine of constitutional law—which finds itself, as we have seen, in the shape of a narrowly stated substantive principle, with a rule of administration enlarging the otherwise too restricted substantive rule—admits now of a juster and simpler conception, that is a very familiar situation in the development of law. What really took place in adopting our theory of constitutional law was this: we introduced for the first time into the conduct of government through its great departments a judicial sanction, as among these departments,—not full and

---

[35] *Per* Thomas, J., the Opinion of Justices, 8 Gray, p. 21.

[36] "It matters little," says a depressed, but interesting and incisive writer, in commenting, in 1885, upon the Legal Tender decisions of the Supreme Court of the United States, "for the court has fallen, and it is not probable it can ever again act as an effective check upon the popular will, or should it attempt to do so, that it can prevail." The "Consolidation of the Colonies," by Brooks Adams, 55 *Atlantic Monthly*, 307.

complete, but partial. The judges were allowed, indirectly and in a degree, the power to revise the action of other departments and to pronounce it null. In simple truth, while this is a mere judicial function, it involves, owing to the subject-matter with which it deals, taking a part, a secondary part, in the political conduct of government. If that be so, then the judges must apply methods and principles that befit their task. In such a work there can be no permanent or fitting modus vivendi between the different departments unless each is sure of the full co-operation of the others, so long as its own action conforms to any reasonable and fairly permissible view of its constitutional power. The ultimate arbiter of what is rational and permissible is indeed always the courts, so far as litigated cases bring the question before them. This leaves to our courts a great and stately jurisdiction. It will only imperil the whole of it if it is sought to give them more. They must not step into the shoes of the law maker, or be unmindful of the hint that is found in the sagacious remark of an English bishop nearly two centuries ago, quoted lately from Mr. Justice Holmes [37]:

Whoever hath an absolute authority to interpret any written or spoken laws, it is he who is truly the lawgiver, to all intents and purposes, and not the person who first wrote or spoke them.[38]

---

[37] By Professor Gary in 6 Harv. Law Rev. 33, n., where he justly refers to the remark as showing "that gentlemen of the short robe have sometimes grasped fundamental legal principles better than many lawyers."

[38] Bishop Hoadly's Sermon preached before the King, March 31, 1717, on "The Nature of the Kingdom or Church of Christ."

CHAPTER THREE

The Judicial Process in
Constitutional Law

Charles A. Beard's essay, with which this volume began, was concerned with the historical origin of the doctrine of judicial review in the United States; James B. Thayer's contribution was to extend the matter a step further by inquiring what the legitimate scope of the judicial power should be, in the light of precedent and political theory.

Thomas Reed Powell's paper, which is reprinted in the following pages, introduces still another interrogative theme—the problem of what it is that courts actually do when they practice their function of constitutional interpretation. What is "the nature of the judicial process" in constitutional cases? However, as we shall see, this query is closely related to the one propounded by Professor Thayer. For the conclusion we reach about the nature of the judicial operation may help us in determining what ought to be the limits of its scope.

The question of how courts go about their business is extraordinarily subtle and complex, and the literature dealing with the subject is so vast that no attempt can be made here to "summarize" the problem (For a staggering assemblage of ideas and references, see *The Province and Function of Law* by Julius Stone, Cambridge [1950].) Nevertheless, it is worth observing, by way of introduction to Professor Powell's essay, that some judges and scholars have cherished a quite different view of the judicial process than the one he sets forth. Roscoe Pound has said that according to the 19th-century theory judges were supposed to proceed on the basis of "eternal legal conceptions involved in the very idea of justice and containing potentially an exact rule for every case to be reached by an absolute process of logical deduction." (Juristic Science and the Law, 31 Harvard Law Review 1047, 1048). We can fairly doubt that even in the nineteenth century all men were so naive as this; but there is no denying that the view Dean Pound describes was widespread and persistent. Marshall himself gave it classic expression in Osborne *v.* Bank of the United States (9 Wheat. 738, 866 [1824]) when he insisted that judges have no will but simply exist to give effect to "the will of the law." The idea is that judges do and should, as Cardozo has said, march "to pitiless conclusions under the prod of a remorseless logic which is supposed to leave them no alternative" (Benjamin N. Cardozo, *Growth of the Law* [1924] p. 66); in other words that the judicial process is strictly logical, impersonal, and exact. The durability of this notion is evinced by the words of Mr. Justice Roberts in 1935:

When an act of Congress is appropriately challenged in the courts as not conforming to the constitutional mandate, the judicial branch of the government has only one duty; to lay the article of the Constitution which is invoked beside the statute which is challenged and to decide whether the latter squares with the former. (United States *v.* Butler, 297 U.S. 1, 62)

The countervailing view—that judges consider the practicalities of the situation as well as logic, that the judicial process cannot be "mechanistic" and exact—began to be aired in the 19th-century, as Powell's quotation from Holmes' *Common Law* attests. The assault on the old dogmas and the analysis of the way the judicial process actually does operate was carried forward by a host of judges and scholars, including Brandeis,

Cardozo, Holmes, and Pound; and Professor Powell's essay was an important incident in this general offensive.

Powell argues that our constitutional judges try, as Jefferson said he was doing in the Declaration of Independence, to "express the common sense of the subject"; and he further insists that the common sense of the judges, far from being the recondite and exact science of Pound's 19th-century theorists, is pretty much the sort of thing any man might arrive at, if confronted by a similar task. He leaves undecided the issue of whether the courts *should* have this authority to impose their common sense on us, though he seems to imply that we might as well leave the responsibility in the judges' hands, since no other agency is likely to discharge it any better.

Describing the judicial process in constitutional law as a quest for common sense is a particularly happy way of summarizing in a single portmanteau phrase the elaborate analyses of modern jurisprudence. We can pass this point without further comment, since it is hard to imagine that editorial elaboration could improve upon Powell's own development of it. But a few queries may be in order on the other issues he raises.

Powell himself concedes that he may have overstated the similarities between the common sense of judges and the common sense of anyone else. Certainly it is essential that the similarities be recognized so as to scotch the illusion that constitutional doctrine is either mysteriously wonderful or mysteriously wicked. But there is something to be said about the differences as well, and these differences may bear importantly on the question Powell leaves open—whether the courts are really the best agencies to determine constitutional common sense.

Much has been written in recent years to document the insight that judges are human beings. It would be unfortunate if this accumulated biographical data obscured the fact that they are also judges, trained as American lawyers and practicing, whether at bar or bench, a craft that is heavily laden with technicalities. The lawyer-judge in America is likely to be a specialist; yet the common sense evaluations that the courts must make concerning governmental affairs call for a broad, general knowledge of economics, politics, history, international relations, and a host of other subjects not commonly included in the American law school curriculum. The appearance of an occasional exception like Brandeis on the Supreme Court bench does not vitiate the point that he *is* an exception, and we may thus legitimately ask whether the common sense of judges is the most nearly adequate kind of common sense that a democracy has available to it. Was the issue presented in the Lochner case, for example, the sort of issue that Mr. Justice Peckham and his fellow jurists were well-equipped to handle? Or would that delicate assessment of social needs and industrial conditions have been more appropriately delegated to men who were versed in such matters, rather than in the specialized intricacies of the law?

A rejoinder to all this might be that ideal personnel requirements are easy enough to concoct in an armchair, but that it is quite another thing to create an actual, working tribunal. The Supreme Court, one might say, is admittedly less than perfect; but it is idle to dwell on its limitations unless the critic can suggest another agency that could do the work better. And it is equally meaningless to offer such a suggestion without taking account of the American political context. The national tradition has imposed on judges the duty of interpreting the Constitution, and no arbitrary transfer of their authority to someone else would be politically feasible even if it were theoretically desirable. As Professor Powell points out, America has governed the lawyers; and America has also created, sanctioned, and governed the Supreme Court. You do not cavalierly reallocate the functions of an institution so organically related to the growth and existence of the national body politic.

This is quite true. But the question of how good judicial common sense may be is nevertheless a real one, not unhistorical, not merely academic. For, as Professor Thayer pointed out, there is a conception of judicial self-effacement which has an honorable genealogy in America, the very conception which Mr. Justice Harlan was calling upon when he dissented in the Lochner case, i.e. the tradition that courts should defer to the legislative judgment except when statutes are invalid beyond reasonable doubt. And the deficiencies of judicial common sense may be relevant in deciding whether this view or the contrary, self-assertive attitude exemplified by Peckham should guide the Supreme Court. In short, it is not a question of whether some new and ideally qualified agency should be manufactured out of whole cloth to regale us with its superior brand of common sense. It is a question of whether the common sense of judges is inherently so limited that we are justified in asking that its range be restricted and in preferring, in most instances, the common sense expressed in the legislative power. That power enjoys quite as solid a mooring in the American tradition as does the judiciary, and when legislators are able and willing to draw on expert staff assistance they may be better qualified than judges to weigh the practicalities which Professor Powell rightly asserts to lie at the heart of most constitutional problems.

The Logic and Rhetoric of Constitutional Law

by Thomas Reed Powell *

*Journal of Philosophy, Psychology
and Scientific Method*, Volume
15, Page 654 (1918)

My title is a theft from Charles A. Beard's brilliant essay in the *New Republic* on "Political Science in the Crucible." And what I shall say about it is doubtless the fruit of similar larceny from other thinkers. For most of us who labor in the vineyard of learning originate but little. And the few who originate seldom read papers before The American Political Science Association. So I shall not profess to be bringing before you thoughts that have sprung full armed from my own mind. In so far as I can trace their background I acknowledge indebtedness to Roscoe Pound and to John Dewey. And yet I must acquit them of any responsibility for my particular contentions; for the application is my own, and not only may power be lost in its transmission, but, even worse, it may be misdirected.

In the opening sentence of the essay referred to, Beard says

* (1880–1955) Professor of Law, Harvard University Law School, 1920–49.

that "political science in the United States has always been under bondage to the lawyers." This he finds due mainly "to the nature of our system of government, which places constitutionality above all other earthly considerations in the discussion of public measures." "The elucidation of our national issues," he continues, "has called for the lawyer's technology and rhetoric, although they have been at bottom matters of politics and public policy." And he concludes his opening paragraph with the sentence: "The hand is subdued to the dye in which it works, so the mind of men who have speculated on political science in America is subdued to the logic and rhetoric of constitutional law."

I

This prompts me to ask: What is the logic and rhetoric of constitutional law? I shall not trouble much about the rhetoric. Like the world, it is too much with us. Vague phrases which admit of various interpretations, which kindle the emotions, are the greenbacks of our common speech. If we doubt the value behind them, we ask for the gold of the specific and the concrete. Or else all too often we wager against them currency of similar tenor, but backed by other values which we more approve. Beard and the *New York Times* both give us rhetoric. My preference for the rhetoric of Beard is due, not to a literary judgment, but to a confidence in the values that lie behind the felicitous phrase of Beard and to a suspicion that the values behind the editorial oratory of the *Times* have sadly depreciated since the days of Herbert Spencer.

When Beard writes of "the ambulance of capitalism gathering up the wrecks of industrial anarchy," of Sociology wandering "around in the dim vastness of classified emotions," of Political Science "hanging in the vacuum of closed legal speculation," he writes rhetoric, and good rhetoric. But the rhetoric will take the place of specie only for those who trust what lies behind. And what is true of the rhetoric of Beard is true of the rhetoric of constitutional law. If we can personify such an agglomeration as our American constitutional law, and then attribute to it the vice of rhetoric, we must still be lenient: for it is a vice to which we all are prone. Even international affairs succumb to the spell of rhetorical treatment. Man is a rhetorical animal. But his rhetoric he uses to market his notions, not to make them. So it is the factory and not the salesroom that I invite you to explore. It is to the logic behind the rhetoric of constitutional law that I wish to direct your attention.

II

I may give a clue to my thesis by reporting an incident in a debate in the United States Senate. Senator Spooner of Wisconsin had been citing Supreme Court decisions to his purpose. When Senator Tillman of South Carolina was recognized, he complained: "I am tired of hearing what the Supreme Court says. What I want to get at is the common sense of the matter." To which Senator Spooner rejoined: "I too am seeking the common sense of the matter. But, as for me, I prefer the common sense of the Supreme Court of the United States to that of the Senator from South Carolina."

This in a nutshell is my thesis: the logic of constitutional law is the common sense of the Supreme Court of the United States. That common sense may agree with ours, or it may not. In some instances we might prefer Senator Tillman's. This much of comfort we have, at any rate, that, whenever we come upon a decision which is particularly displeasing, we usually find that there is a minority of the court who feel as badly about it as we do. The variety of common sense which is offered by the divergent opinions of different judges is such that no intellectual palate need go without something to its taste.

This division of opinion among the judges of the Supreme Court finds its counterpart in the differences among those who debate in other forums. If the eight judges who sat in Stettler *v.* Oregon were evenly paired on the minimum wage, so were Alvin Johnson and Professor Taussig. Mr. Justice Pitney's views of the Adamson Law were anticipated by three of my friends— a retired dentist, a Professor of English and an instructor in chemistry. They were shocked when I told them that long ago the Supreme Court in Munn *v.* Illinois had decided that the legislature could limit the profits of those who conduct what we call a public utility. It comforted them a little to learn that, if the Adamson Law raised the expenses of the railroads so that their rates did not yield them what the court thought a fair return on their investment, the rates could be raised until the net earnings were reasonably remunerative. Yet to these lay friends of mine the idea that the owner of any kind of a business could not charge what he pleased and pay only such wages as he pleased was novel and abhorrent. And so it is with the other questions that separate the judges of our high tribunal into the familiar camps that shelter five in one and four in the other. Take sampling from the men you talk with at the club and in the Pullman and you will find that their untrained common sense leads them to the same diverse conclusions to which the more highly developed instrument leads the judges.

We often hear that the lawyers have governed America. But it is equally true that America has governed the lawyers. The ideas that lawyers have expressed in the legislature, at the bar and on the bench have not sprung from any mysterious source whose hiding place is revealed only to those who read books in sheep bindings. The doctrine of individualism was not invented by judges. Your Southern school boy is as familiar with the dangers of allowing the federal government to encroach on the reserved powers of the states, as are the judges who annulled the federal Child Labor Law. The "mysteries of constitutional law," which Beard tells us are invoked when other comforts fail, do not seem to me mysteries at all. The rhetoric is not unlike the rhetoric we all use. And the logic behind the rhetoric is the logic with which you and I debate our disagreements.

Immortal principles fly their standards in judicial opinions, yes. But so they do in the common every-day talk of the butcher and banker, of the suffragist and the anti-suffragist, the pacifist and the militarist, the Socialist and the individualist. Arguments from expediency to reinforce the immortal principles will be found in judicial opinions as they are heard on the hustings. And there are judges who find no immortal principles, who conceive their task to be that of making wise adjustments amid competing considerations. "Constitutional Law," says Mr. Justice Holmes, "like other mortal contrivances, has to take some chances." "Difference of degree," observes the same jurist, "is one of the distinctions by which the right of the legislature to exercise the police power is determined." And no one has put better than he the point of view that rejects universals and the absolute. "All rights," he tells us, "tend to declare themselves absolute to their logical extreme. Yet all in fact are limited by the neighborhood of principles of policy which are other than those on which the particular right is founded, and which become strong enough to hold their own when a certain point is reached."

Many men of many minds have sat on our Supreme Bench as they have read papers at meetings of the American Political Science Association or lectured in college classrooms. Judges argue from undisclosed assumptions, as you and I argue from undisclosed assumptions. Judges seek their premises from facts, as you and I strive to do. Judges have preferences for social policies, as you and I. They form their judgments after the varying fashions in which you and I form ours. They have hands, organs, dimensions, senses, affections, passions. They are warmed and cooled by the same winter and summer and by the same ideas as a layman is. If there is a mystery to constitutional law, it is the mystery of the commonplace and the obvious, the mystery of the other mortal contrivances that have to take some chances, that have to be worked by mortal men. The logic behind the rhetoric is the logic of finding out what words mean, what purpose the words were meant to serve. And where the words of the Constitution offer no guide, the logic is that of finding out what is most expedient.

III

It will be apparent how much of our constitutional law is merely getting at the common sense of the matter when we consider how few of the questions of constitutional law are answered by any specific language in the Constitution. When the language is really specific, questions seldom arise. The majority of current decisions have to deal with the clause forbidding the states to deprive any one of life, liberty or property without due process of law, and with the clause granting to Congress the power to regulate commerce among the several states. And most of the questions under the latter clause concern not the power of Congress but the power of the states, about which the Constitution is silent. "Due process of law," though it occurs twice in the Constitution, is left without definition. Important questions respecting the taxing powers of the states and of the United States arise, not under any language of the Constitution, but because the Constitution ordains a federal system of government, and thereby makes possible a clash between state and national interests.

In interpreting the Constitution the courts have the task of applying the general to the particular. Our constitutional clauses are couched in such extremely general language that there is something fictitious in calling the work of the courts a work of interpretation. It is but to a slight extent a literary task. It is to a very large extent the task of weighing competing practical considerations and forming a practical judgment. That this is true in decisions involving the police power is made clear by the judicial recognition of the fact that the question in issue is whether the unwelcome deprivation of liberty or property is reasonable or arbitrary. The judgment of the courts is none the less a practical one because it may be influenced by a general preference for leaving folks unfettered by law, or by an opposing preference for imposing social standards. Those preferences are not unrelated to what is thought to be most desirable in practise.

In determining the scope of state power which touches interstate commerce, the opinions of the Supreme Court make very clear that the problem to be solved in each case is whether the promotion of the local needs of the state justifies the interference with interstate commerce which such promotion entails. Unripe fruits may be forbidden to leave the state, though oil and gas may not. An unimportant inlet of the sea may be dammed, but bridges over important rivers must be high enough for ships to pass under. Interstate trains may be required to slow down and blow whistles, but may not be compelled to make a detour to accommodate the inhabitants of a given city. The formula under which such cases are decided is as flexible as is the distinction between what is reasonable and what is arbitrary. And the practical considerations almost invariably receive chief attention in the judicial opinions.

Under the due-process clause the Supreme Court has held

that a state may restrict the working day to ten hours in mines, but not in bake-shops. Under the commerce clause the states are permitted to tax goods from other states still in the original package, but are forbidden to prohibit their sale. In the absence of any applicable clause in the Constitution, the states are forbidden to tax such part of the capital stock of a corporation as is invested in United States bonds, but are permitted to tax the franchise of the corporation and base the amount on the capital, even though it is invested in United States bonds. Under the clause forbidding the states to impair the obligation of contracts, a creditor of a city may resist a legislative reduction of the city's tax rate, but has no relief against the legislative restriction of the kinds of property subject to municipal taxation.

These contrasted decisions can not be explained by reference to the language of the Constitution. "Due process" is as silent about bakeries as it is about mines. "Obligation of contracts" is as silent about tax rate as it is about exemptions. The controlling considerations in the solution of these problems have been considerations of common sense—none the less common sense because it may not have been your common sense or my common sense, or because the common sense of the majority of the Supreme Court has at times disagreed with that of their dissenting colleagues.

IV

When we turn to the reasons which are given for the constitutional decisions we find them the same kind of reasons that you and I would give for our judgments. In Lochner v. New York which declared unconstitutional a ten-hour law for bakers, Mr. Justice Peckham says that the question is whether the law is a "fair, reasonable, and appropriate exercise of the police power" or an "unreasonable, unnecessary, and arbitrary interference with the right of the individual." He finds it unreasonable because he thinks "there can be no fair doubt that the trade of a baker, in and of itself, is not an unhealthy one to that degree which would authorize the legislature to interfere." Mr. Justice Harlan for the minority says that the question is debatable, and that therefore the court should accept the judgment of the legislature. There is nothing peculiar to constitutional law in this kind of logic. Indeed, if the logic of constitutional law is to be criticized, there is better reason for complaining that it is the kind of logic we all use than for objecting that it is something mysterious.

What is abstruse or mysterious in the opinions of the judges with respect to the constitutionality of the income tax of 1894? The question to be decided was whether such tax was direct or indirect. The majority in the case of Pollock *v.* Farmers Loan & Trust Co. says that a tax on income from land is the same in effect as a tax on the land itself. Since a tax on the land itself is conceded to be a direct tax, the same must be true of a tax on income therefrom. The minority, on the other hand, appeals to precedent to show that only capitation taxes and taxes on land have been regarded as direct taxes. When land is taxed directly, it must contribute to the government, whether it contributes to its owner or not. But to tax the rentals is not to tax the land itself. If the land yields no income, it pays no tax. Therefore a tax on rentals is only indirectly on land, and is thus an indirect tax. These are the main opposing arguments. The question is certainly debatable. And the judges debated it in the same fashion that participants in an intercollegiate contest would debate it. Varying interpretations were put upon quotations from previous authorities. Differing weight was given to various considerations of expediency.

Mr. Justice White was so convinced that the majority was wrong that he filed a long dissenting opinion, notwithstanding his expressed belief that "the only purpose which an elaborate dissent can accomplish, if any, is to weaken the effect of the opinion of the majority, and thus engender want of confidence in conclusions of courts of last resort." But there is no reason why lack of unanimity should engender want of confidence in the courts. Of course, it engenders want of confidence in any notion that constitutional law is some divine voice of which the court is merely the mouthpiece. But the fact that judges disagree, and freely express the reasons for their disagreement, should add to our confidence in their labors rather than detract from it. It indicates that the judgment was reached only after careful consideration and full discussion. We have nine judges instead of one, twelve jurors instead of one, because we know that human judgment is fallible and because we wish by increase of numbers to decrease the margin of error. Though when our passions are strong we sometimes forget that out of a multitude of counsel cometh wisdom, our enterprise of democracy is an expression of our abiding faith that the erring thoughts of individuals are best controlled by the full play of competing opinions. We may therefore lack confidence in the particular conclusions of particular judges, and yet have high regard for the institution that operates, as all human institutions must operate, through the judgments of designated individuals.

V

Some there are who seem to hold that government does not operate through the judgments of individuals. The famous distributing clause of the Massachusetts constitution of 1780 embodies this attitude. The legislative department is forbidden to exercise the executive and judicial powers or either of them; the executive, to exercise the legislative and judicial powers or either of them; and the judicial department, to exercise the legislative or executive powers or either of them: "to the end it may be a government of laws and not of men." This happy phrase is often on the lips of those who profess to think of government as some mechanical contrivance that, once wound up, will run itself. They would undoubtedly be grieved to hear that a philosophic wag had once revised it to read: "to the end it may be a government of lawyers and not of men." They would not care to be reminded that as long ago as March 31, 1717, Bishop Hoadley said: "Whoever hath an absolute authority to interpret any written or spoken laws, it is he who is truly the lawgiver, to all intents and purposes, and not the person who first wrote or spoke them."

Of course the authority of the Supreme Court to interpret the Constitution is by no means an absolute authority. It is limited in part by the language of the Constitution, in part by prevailing sentiments and by existing conditions. Now that the Supreme Court has been at work for over a century, the authority of the present wielders of judicial power is limited to a large extent by the interpretations of their predecessors. The legislative powers of impeachment and of increasing the number of judges, the executive power to select new incumbents of the judicial office, the possibility that an Andrew Jackson in the White House may refuse to execute the order of the court, or that a commander of armed forces may decline to obey a writ of habeas corpus, as Chief Justice Taney discovered when he ordered Merryman to be brought before him—these are all potential restrictions on the actual authority of the Supreme Court. Yet, in determining a great number of the most important questions, there are two or more courses equally open to the Supreme Court, as the constantly recurring division of judicial opinion amply demonstrates. If by some necromancy the majority and the minority opinions in all the great decisions could be transposed our constitutional law would be hardly recognizable.

Even the holders of the mechanical theory recognize that in the past the personal viewpoints of the judges have been influential, if not controlling, factors in the course of judicial decision. Chief Justice Marshall is often and rightly lauded for so "shaping the Constitution" that the power of the national government was unhampered by the residuary powers of the states. The fear of the judges themselves that they shall be discovered to be something more than mere automatons is not so acute as once it was. An able judge of one of our state courts tells me that he is usually able to decide cases as his independent judgment dictates. And he cites me a habit of Coke's to show that this is no new departure. When Coke, he says, had difficulty in adducing precedents for the decisions he wished to reach, he would pen: "As the old Latin maxim saith:" and then he would invent the maxim. In the Yale Law Journal for November, 1917, a judge of the New Hampshire supreme court refers to the time "when the court seems to have thought that it was inspired, or that the rules it formulated were revealed to it," and observes that "the study of the history of the court will show how these rules were in fact formulated, and will, I think, demonstrate that they were made by the court in the same way statutes are made by the legislature." In a later issue of the same journal Mr. Justice Riddell of the Supreme Court of Ontario quotes Lord Bramwell to the effect that "one-third of a judge is a common juror if you get beneath the ermine," and adds that: "The other two-thirds may not be far different." And Mr. Justice Holmes whose judicial opinions teem with wisdom in fine raiment, told us a year ago in the Jensen case that "the common law is not a brooding omnipresence in the sky, but the articulate voice of some sovereign or quasi-sovereign that can be identified." And he says also that he recognizes "that judges do and must legislate," adding, however, that "they can do so only interstitially; they are confined from molar to molecular motions."

Human beings performing a human task—that is the picture thrown on the screen for me by the words "constitutional law." Human beings wondering what to say and how to say it, as I am wondering now, regretting that they lack the time to say it better, to think it through more fully before they write it down. If you hear judges talk about their own decisions and opinions, and criticize or praise the work of their brethren, the mysteries of constitutional law will be revealed. And how could it be made plainer than in every dissenting opinion? If criticism of the courts is a sacrilege, the worst offenders are the courts themselves. Perhaps it is security of tenure that makes them bold. If this is true, it argues well for the grant of security of tenure to all who have the vision and the courage to do something more than echo the platitudes that find acceptance in high places. For dissenting judicial opinions are most valuable equilibrators in the undulating course of the law. They have the modifying influence of the opposition bench in the House of Commons. It is refreshing that the judges themselves have no notion that a sanctity envelops what they write. And the sanctity that lawyers and laymen would sometimes accord to judicial opinions is more lavishly bestowed on those which meet their liking than on those with which they disagree.

VI

In thus emphasizing the common-sense element in the development of the law that is made by judges, I may seem to many to be grossly overstating my case. Others have insisted that judges are slavish adherents to precedent, that they revel in absurd fictions and technicalities, and that they cherish abstractions to the disregard of realities. I will not contend that these plaints are entirely without foundation. But it is a myopic vision which finds these mental traits characteristic of judges or which regards them as the major forces in judicial decision. And the traits are found in many who know Blackstone only as a name. Some of you have doubtless been on committees which disposed of the matter in hand by appeal to precedent or to an abstraction. You may have helped to reject a petition by insisting that it was not properly before you for consideration. But any who have been guilty of such seeming artificiality are well aware that reasons of practical policy actually determined their action. Such is usually true of the seeming artificiality of the law. And the fictions of the law are notoriously the fruit of the desire to achieve some practical end. But even if artificiality is often potent in the mechanics of handling particular cases, it is not characteristic of the gradual shaping and reshaping of the substantive rules of law. If we take a long-time view of the growth and modification of judicial doctrines, we can not escape the realization that beneath the surface the moving forces are the practical judgments of the human beings who wield judicial power.

Lawyer-like and human-like I appeal to authority to support my contention. Over thirty-five years ago Holmes, in his lectures on The Common Law, told us:

> The life of the law has not been logic: it has been experience. The felt necessities of the time, the prevalent moral and political theories, intuitions of public policy, even the prejudices which judges share with their fellow men, have had a good deal more to do than the syllogism in determining the rules by which men should be governed.

And later in the book he reiterates his position:

> On the other hand, in substance the growth of the law is legislative. And this in a deeper sense than that what the courts declare to have always been the law is in fact new. It is legislative in its grounds. The very considerations which judges most rarely mention, and always with an apology, are the secret root from which the law draws all the juices of life. I mean, of course, considerations of what

is expedient for the community concerned. Every important principle which is developed by litigation is in fact and at bottom the result of more or less definitely understood views of public policy; most generally to be sure, under our practise and traditions, the unconscious result of instinctive preferences and inarticulate convictions, but none the less traceable to views of public policy in the last analysis.

It may seem strange to laymen that these forces are even more potent in the judicial interpretation of a constitution reduced to writing than in the evolution of what we call the unwritten law. But this is nevertheless the fact, at least with respect to the interpretation of those clauses of the Constitution which present the chief field for controversy. And those who are competent to speak tell us that the written codes of other peoples are similarly adapted by the judges to the practical situations which call for practical adjustment. Professor Munroe Smith has outlined the process for us in his lecture on Jurisprudence:

> For more than two thousand years it has been an accepted legal principle that, in interpreting the written law, effect should be given, as far as possible, to the spirit and intent of the law. Here again the possibilities of lawfinding under cover of interpretation are very great. A distinguished German jurist, Windscheid, has remarked that in interpreting legislation modern courts may and habitually do "think over again the thought which the legislator was trying to express," but that the Roman jurist went further and "thought out the thought which the legislator was trying to think." Of this freer mode of interpretation Windscheid might have found modern examples. The president of the highest French court, M. Ballot-Beaupré, explained, a few years ago, that the provisions of the Napoleonic legislation had been adapted to modern conditions by a judicial interpretation in "le sens évolutif." "We do not inquire," he said, "what the legislator willed a century ago, but what he would have willed if he had known what our present conditions would be." In English-speaking countries this freer mode of interpretation has always been applied to the unwritten or common law, and it is usually applied to the written law with a degree of boldness which is very closely proportioned to the difficulty of securing formal amendment. Thus the rigidity of our federal constitution has constrained the Supreme Court of the United States to push the interpreting power to its furthest limits. This tribunal not only thinks out the thoughts which

the Fathers were trying to think one hundred and twenty years ago, but it undertakes to determine what they would have thought if they could have foreseen the changed conditions and the novel problems of the present day. It has construed and reconstrued the constitution in "the evolutive sense," until in some respects that instrument has been reconstructed.

VII

Of course in likening the logic and the rhetoric of constitutional law to the logic and the rhetoric of you and me, I am not unaware of differences between an institution and an individual. Constitutional law differs from you and me in that it has a longer history. Its judgments are those of many individuals and not of one alone. It seeks a consistency and a continuity that you and I are free to go without. But even constitutional law changes its mind. In 1895 by vote of five to four the Supreme Court held in Lochner *v.* New York that a state could not limit to ten the daily hours of labor in bake-shops. But the case is no longer law. Very brief is the funeral oration read by the Supreme Court in 1917 over the death of this same and little-lamented Lochner *v.* New York, which is not even mentioned at its own obsequies. Bunting *v.* Oregon, in which the last rites were solemnized, sustained a ten-hour law applying, not to bake-shops alone, but to "mills, factories and manufacturing establishments." In dismissing the contention that the Oregon statute was not necessary or useful for the preservation of the health of employees, Mr. Justice McKenna said briefly: "The record contains no facts to support the contention, and against it is the judgment of the legislature and the supreme court" of the state.

Constitutional law changed its mind about the power of Congress to make government notes legal tender, about its power to levy taxes on incomes from real estate and personal property without apportionment among the states according to population, and about its power to apply to manufacturing corporations its prohibitions against restraint of trade. And in numerous instances where decisions are not directly overruled, they are whittled away by exceptions to avoid results deemed undesirable. Administrative commissions have been allowed to take over function after function previously exercised by the judiciary or by the legislature, though constitutional law still maintains that such commissions can exercise neither legislative nor judicial power. Notwithstanding the biblical warning, much new wine is poured into old bottles. Often the substance changeth though the form doth not. Constitutional law, as well as theology, can reinterpret old doctrines to meet new needs. Genesis can survive Darwin in rigid sheep as well as in limp morocco.

Without knowing anything about the laws of the Medes and the Persians, except by rumor, I am inclined to doubt whether the rumor that they were unchanging is correct. But the rumor establishes at any rate that such fixity as was theirs was eccentric even in those days. If native to them, it is foreign to the law of the Constitution of the United States as laid down by the Supreme Court. In spite of the stabilizing or stratifying effect of the doctrine of stare decisis, constitutional law has less of the idée fixé than many of us. But this is not to deny that in spots it is as stubborn as any of us. But, flexible or stubborn, wise or unwise, doctrinaire or practical, constitutional law is not mysterious, but only human—human as you and I are human, as all government is human.

VIII

This analysis of what seem to me the controlling characteristics of constitutional law is not meant to be applied to constitutional lawyers. For those who have won fame at the bar have been for the most part men whose lives are largely spent in safeguarding private interests against competing public interests. Their private employment is continuous, while the advocates of the public interest serve their brief term and then give way to their successors. Thus there tends to be a persistent bias among lawyers which makes it difficult for them to hold the scales as evenly as do the judges. No one is apt to question the qualifications of Mr. Elihu Root to testify on this point. In his address in 1916 as president of the American Bar Association he says that it is "quite natural that lawyers employed to assert the rights of individual clients and loyally devoted to their clients' interest should acquire a habit of mind in which they think chiefly of the individual view of judicial procedure, and seldom of the public view of the same procedure." And he adds:

There are indeed two groups of men who consider the interests of the community. They are the teachers in the principal law schools and the judges on the bench. With loyalty and sincere devotion they defend the public right to effective service; but against them is continually pressing the tendency of the bar and the legislatures and, in a great degree of the public towards the exclusively individual view.

It is interesting to note that those whom the bar calls great constitutional lawyers are the ones who have been in great cases, irrespective of their success in those cases. Those who may wonder why the obscure attorney general of some sparsely populated state, or some subordinate member of the Department of Justice, so often wins his case against the leaders of the bar may find a clue to the answer in the observation of an able metropolitan attorney. When asked if he thought it fair that his railroad should be represented by a hundred-and-fifty-thousand-dollar man while the people of the United States had only the services of a five-thousand-dollar man, he replied: "Oh, it's not so uneven as that. You see, the Lord is on their side." The remark was not intended to be cynical. It was profound. And it was true, because constitutional law, the distilled and clarified common sense of the judges of our high tribunal, does not "hang in the vacuum of closed speculation," but advances with the march of changing conditions. That is why it is so baffling to many lawyers, as the reason why it is so baffling to many reformers is that it follows conditions rather than leads them.

IX

It may shock some reverential person to hear that law, and especially constitutional law, is not an impersonal and majestic power which moves in some mysterious way its wonders to perform. Those imbued with proper legal piety may think it unbecoming in a great jurist to tell us in a judicial opinion that constitutional law is a human contrivance that has to take chances. As children we used occasionally to think our teacher something other than human—either better or worse. And the same childlike simplicity characterizes the attitude of some who talk about constitutional law. From varied sources constitutional law has received its meed of reverence and of execration. Some deem it holy; others think it sinister. And after all it is merely human. Being human it undoubtedly makes mistakes. Being human it also contributes to the general weal. All will agree that some constitutional law is better than others. But men will forever disagree as to what is good and what is bad. So also will they disagree about what is good and bad in other human contrivances.

If on the whole we do not like the work of our courts, we may assign their tasks to other authorities. But those other authorities would not be always unanimous. Their majorities would not always please the majority of us. Their logic and their rhetoric would differ little from the logic and rhetoric of the courts. They would inevitably have regard for precedent and for the existing scheme of things. For all of us regard these considerations when we make our individual choices. If we do not wish the courts to be trammelled by precedents, we can declare in our constitutions that they shall decide each case according to their independent judgment. But even then their judgments will be influenced by those of their predecessors. The citation of authorities is not confined to courts. We all do it, and why? Because we have respect for the judgments of others.

There is always danger in personification. What is said about Rome or Greece or Germany or England or constitutional law is usually only measurably true. In picking what seems characteristic for the purpose in hand, we neglect the many exceptions and variations. So on general principles I should be somewhat inclined to plead *nolo contendere* to the charge of overstating my case. Yet my thesis seems to me to take care of all possible exceptions and variations. For it is confined to the contention that the logic and rhetoric of constitutional law, however multifarious its manifestations, is not sui generis. Much of it may be peculiar, but it is not peculiar to constitutional law.

CHAPTER FOUR

The Supreme Court and Industrial Society

T HE READER WHO HAS BEEN FOLLOWING THESE ESSAYS CON-
secutively will already be aware that the leitmotiv of one is
likely to be the minor theme of another, that while their broad
concerns can be differentiated, they are seldom unrelated. Thus
Thayer's main preoccupation—the scope of judicial review—is
influenced by his conclusions about the historical roots of the
doctrine, which was the subject of Beard's essay; Powell's views
about the nature of the judicial process are germane to Thayer's
problem of scope; and so on. Max Lerner's brilliant essay, "The
Supreme Court and American Capitalism," is likewise related
to what has gone before, especially to Powell's insights. For
while Lerner's principal interest is to draw parallels between
the ebb and flow of Supreme Court doctrine and the course of
American economic history, he is driven by his inquiry to pose
a final question about judicial motivation which is a natural
sequel to Powell's analysis. Powell argues that judges think and
decide as other men would; Lerner would probably agree, but he
tries to push the matter a step further by asking what factors

do guide the minds of men, including judges, when they make social decisions. What are the constituent elements of the "common sense" the judiciary offers us?

Lerner's treatment of the broad historical relationship between economic institutions and constitutional law speaks eloquently for itself, and there is neither need nor excuse for recapitulating his discussion here. However, it may be worthwhile to underscore the fact that the economic interpretation he advances is not an ingenuous and rigidly deterministic one. He qualifies his exposition artfully, and the qualifications are of a sort that strengthen, rather than attenuate, the argument. He concedes that much of the Court's behavior falls outside the focus of economic causation for one reason or another. He does not, as I read him, view the Court the way a naive Marxist might —as a mere responsive tool of the dominant class; and he explicitly reserves for the judiciary a wide area of choice within the basic framework of capitalist society. What emerges, after his exceptions and elaborations are duly noted, is a three-dimensional portrait of the Supreme Court, profoundly affected by the "economic forces and master trends" of its era, but not necessarily subservient to the particular forces and trends that a doctrinaire observer might think would be controlling.

When Lerner turns to the specific question of "a theory of judicial decision," he maintains the balance and discrimination that make his broader economic analysis rewarding. His fourfold classification of the factors relevant to the judicial process is not the last word that might be said on this complex subject (nor would he, of course, pretend that it was); but it is a perceptive and useful conception, a promising guide for further exploration. Nevertheless, two or three comments seem in order by way of argument or, perhaps, clarification. For one thing, it might be held that he somewhat underrates the function of "pressures" in determining judicial decisions, particularly if we allow the term a somewhat larger meaning than the vulgar corrupt-bargain definition given currency by writers like Gustavus Myers. The Supreme Court has had its moments of stubbornness, but the occasions when it has actually stood firm against a powerful wave of popular sentiment have been comparatively rare. It is hard to believe that pressure in the sense of public opinion played no part in the Court's acceptance of the New Deal in 1937, or in the cases involving free speech and Negro rights in more recent years. Which leads to the further suggestion that Lerner may be hasty when he declares, in passing, that the Court is beyond the reach of democratic control.

Lerner may also give somewhat less weight than is due to the controlling effect of what he calls "technical legal elements" in determining how a judge will decide. As the author says, recent thought had quite rightly emphasized the fact that these factors were more flexible than mythologists had customarily admitted; and this was especially true in the economic fields which were, of course, Lerner's chief concern. By 1935, the due process and commerce clauses had been so variously interpreted that the Court had almost a free choice to approve or disapprove business regulations. But in other areas the range of selection was often a good deal narrower and the force of precedent was thus more compelling. For example, the important question of who has "standing" to challenge the validity of a statute is governed by technical principles that the Court has worked out over the course of its history, and while the Court has sometimes over-ridden such obstacles, it would be going too far to say that their influence on judicial conduct is negligible. Other illustrations could easily be called to mind, not to imply that the "technical legal elements" are the preeminent factor in court behavior, but to suggest that they may have a significant influence nonetheless.

But perhaps the most interesting question raised by Lerner's essay is one that he could not, in the nature of the case, have answered in 1933: how does the construct he outlined fit the pattern of the Court's behavior in the twenty-odd years since he wrote? Admitting that the idea of the Supreme Court as providing "a nexus between our fundamental law and our fundamental economic institutions" has a good deal of historical validity, how apt a description is it of the Court's contemporary function?

The difficulty is that since about 1937 the Supreme Court has increasingly withdrawn from the economic "areas of vital conflict" that concerned it so much in the past. A litigant who would like to argue that a national economic regulation is forbidden by a substantive interpretation of due process, or that Congress has exceeded its commercial powers, is extremely unlikely even to get a hearing before the Supreme Court today. Of course, the Court still deals with economic questions— whether a state regulation has unduly encroached on the sphere of power reserved to the national government, whether as a matter of statutory interpretation Congress intended to regulate a given subject, whether regulatory legislation has provided due procedural safeguards for the persons affected. But these issues, though significant, are not the great fundamental economic issues that face society, e.g. whether the labor and price standards of industry shall be subjected to national control, whether a national social security system shall be established, whether labor unionism shall be promoted or discouraged. Such matters as these are left by the doctrines of the modern Court almost entirely to the other branches of government, although all of them would have deeply concerned the Court of another day.

Does Lerner's analysis explain this contemporary policy of judicial withdrawal from vital economic areas? Perhaps it does to a degree at least, since he points out that modern finance capitalism was still in a fluid state in 1933 and had not yet "articulated a technique to control its new creatures." I suppose it could be argued that this tentative period in capitalist development has simply been extended through the forties and fifties and that the judiciary is still waiting for a "crystallization of capitalist attitudes" to furnish it with a guide.

Alternatively, it might be suggested that the Court has in the past twenty years been spelling out a new role for itself and that it now stands in a new relation to the American system of economic and political institutions. The Court for all its occasional pragmatism has been historically concerned with seeking out and expressing the absolutes of American society. Sometimes in the past it guessed wrong about what those absolutes were and sometimes it wilfully tried to create them by judicial fiat. But broadly speaking the Court's tendency has been to voice the absolutes which would be supported by a fair consensus of American opinion. Until the 1930's and the Great Depression there was a considerable degree of agreement among Americans about the proper relationship between industry and

government, and the Supreme Court, engaged in its characteristic task of pursuing absolutes, was thus at home in the economic
sphere. A certain leeway for choice existed, as Lerner points
out, but the process of selection was channelized by the consensus of American opinion. Is there such a consensus on
economic absolutes today? Is there substantial agreement among
Americans about what government should and should not do to
control the economic order? Or have the hectic events of the
past two decades effectively destroyed most such dogmatisms
in the American mind, replacing them with the highly pragmatic attitude that government should do what it is needful to
do, in order to insure economic plenty? If this has become the
dominant American preconception in the area of political-eco-
nomic relations, then the Court's withdrawal becomes understandable. For such an outlook precludes absolutes by definition;
it shifts the problem of industry and government from the field
of absolute values to the field of interest conflict, i.e., to the
legislative branch; and the Court ceases to be what it was when
Lerner wrote—an important agency of economic control. It by-
passes the great economic issues that confront the nation and,
true to the law of its being, goes looking for other fields where
some absolutes may still remain, perhaps the area of free speech,
perhaps the problem of racial minorities, perhaps the relationship between religion and government. These and several other
relatively untouched constitutional problems the Court has ten-
tatively explored in recent years, trying them on, so to speak,
for size. There seems good reason to believe that the Supreme
Court is still groping to find its new place in the American
system, that it is vacillating, as Lerner maintains it did during
the first three decades of the twentieth century. But the position
it ultimately assumes may turn out to be, for the reason suggested, outside the main battle zones of the industrial order, and
if this is so, the interpretation of the Supreme Court as a reflex
of capitalism will require some drastic revision. A whole-hearted
partisan of the economic interpretation of history might simply
conclude that the Court's departure from the arena of economic
conflict had ended its significance as a vital governmental institution. But an observer less committed to that viewpoint could
believe that the Court's stature was altered but not necessarily

diminished by the transition, that it could still play a significant
part in defining the suppositions of representative democracy.

The Supreme Court and American
Capitalism

Max Lerner[*]

Yale Law Journal,
Volume 42, Page 668 (1933)

The American state has developed two of its institutions to a
degree never before attained—the capitalist form of business
enterprise and the judicial power. At first sight the combination
seems paradoxical, joining in a single pattern an exploitative
type of economic behavior with the objectivity of the judicial
process. But those who have studied the building of the American state know that the paradox lies only on the surface. It is
no historical accident but a matter of cultural logic that a Field
should grow where a Morgan does; and a Brandeis is none the
less organic a product of capitalist society than is a Debs. If the
contrast between the first pair and the second is precipitous, it
is none the less contrast and not contradiction. Between our
business enterprise and our judicial power there is the unity of
an aggressive and cohesive cultural pattern. They seem of the
same fibre; have, both of them, the same toughness, richness,
extravagant growth; hold out at once portent and promise.

Capitalist business enterprise, while it has reached its most
consummate form in the United States,[1] is generic to the whole
western world. But the judicial power—or more exactly, judicial
supremacy—is a uniquely American institution:[2] it could arise

---

[*] (1902–   ), author, lecturer, Professor of American Civilization, Brandeis University, since 1949.

[1] An analysis of the course of American capitalism is included in Section III,
infra.

[2] There have perhaps been states in the past more completely under the judicial sway than America. But that the rule of judges through their veto power over
legislation is the unique American contribution to the science of government has become a truism of political thought.

only in a federal state which attempts, as we do, to drive a wedge of constitutional uniformity through heterogeneous sectional and economic groupings. The core of judicial supremacy is of course the power of judicial review of legislative acts and administrative decisions.[3] And the exercise of that power by the United States Supreme Court has made it "the world's most powerful court"[4] but the focal point of our bitterest political and constitutional polemics.

At the heart of these polemics is the recognition that the real meaning of the Court is to be found in the political rather than the legal realm, and that its concern is more significantly with power politics than with judicial technology. The Court itself of course, in its official theory of its own function, disclaims any relation to the province of government or the formation of public policy: it pictures itself as going about quietly applying permanent canons of interpretation to the settlement of individual disputes. If there is any truth in this position the Court's quietness must be regarded as that of the quiet spot in the center of a tornado. However serene it may be or may pretend to be in itself, the Court is the focal point of a set of dynamic forces which play havoc with the landmarks of the American state and determine the power configuration of the day. Whatever may be true of the function of private law as restricting itself to the settlement of disputes and the channeling of conduct in society, public law in a constitutional state operates to shift or stabilize the balance of social power.

There has been a tendency in some quarters to regard the power function of the Court as the result of an imperialistic expansion by which the justices have pushed their way to a "place in the sun."[5] We still think in the shadow of Montesquieu

---

[3] The literature on judicial review is extensive and polemical. E. S. Corwin, *The Doctrine of Judicial Review* (1914) is still unsurpassed for the history of the doctrine and his article on Judicial Review (1932) 8 *Encyclopaedia of the Social Sciences* 457, is at once sane and penetrating. Boudin, *Government by Judiciary* (1932), in the course of a vigorous attack on the institution, presents a valuable although overaccented examination of the sequence of Supreme Court decisions from the standpoint of the development of the judicial power.

[4] The phrase is that of Felix Frankfurter, "Mr. Justice Brandeis and the Constitution," in Frankfurter, ed., *Mr. Justice Brandeis* (1932) at 125; but the appraisal represented is a general one.

[5] For the most recent and most powerful development of this theme, see Boudin, *op. cit., supra* note 3.

and view the political process as an equation in governmental powers. The growth of the Court's power has, by this conception, taken place at the expense of the legislative and executive departments, and the American state has become the slave of a judicial oligarchy. The literature in which this enslavement is traced and expounded is voluminous, polemical and, even when very able, somewhat dull. It is dull with the dullness of a thin and mechanical leitmotiv—the theory of usurpation, of the deliberate annexation by the Court of powers never intended for it. This theory is part of the general philosophy of political equilibrium which, originating with the eighteenth century philosophies, was reënforced by nineteenth century physics. It holds that the safety of the individual can be assured only by maintaining a balance between the departments of the state. Whatever may have been the validity of such a philosophy in a pre-industrial age, it has become archaic in a period when government is itself dwarfed by the new economic forces. It is as if generals in a besieged city should quarrel over precedence while the enemy was thundering at the gates.

There was, let it be admitted, a period in which the problem of judicial usurpation was a lively issue. Readers of Beveridge's volumes on Marshall [6] are struck by the bitter political tone of the early years of the Court, beginning even with its decision in Chisholm *v.* Georgia.[7] Charge and counter-charge, invective and recrimination were staple, and in the din of party conflict it was no wonder that the still small voice of judicial objectivity was often completely drowned. In such an atmosphere usurpation had meaning and utility. The polity was in its formative stage, and there was little about the constitutional structure that was irrevocably settled. The Revolution had hewn out a new world but, as we who have been contemporaries of another Revolution can well understand, the task of giving that world content and precision of outline still remained. In the jockeying for political position and the general scramble for advantage,

---

[6] *The Life of John Marshall* (1916–20). This was of course due to some extent to the general bitterness of party polemics in a period of political realities. See also Warren, *The Supreme Court in United States History* (1922) for a vivid depiction of a similar effect. Both Beveridge and Warren drew copiously upon newspaper material.

[7] 2 Dall. 419 (U.S. 1793).

every argument counted, and much of the political theory of the day can best be understood in terms of this orientation toward the distribution of power. But what counted even more than theory was the fait accompli. Every new governmental step was decisive for later power configurations, and might some day be used as precedent. And the battles of the giants, Marshall's battles with Jefferson and Jackson, were the battles of men who knew how to use the fait accompli.

The Court has then from the very beginning been part of the power-structure of the state, acting as an interested arbiter of disputes between the branches of the government and between the states and the federal government, and with an increasingly magistral air distributing the governmental powers. But to a great extent the significant social struggles of the first half-century of the new state were waged outside the Court. Each period has its characteristic clashes of interests and its characteristic battlegrounds where those clashes occur. In the pre-industrial period the party formations measured with a rough adequacy the vital sectional, economic and class differences in the country. The party battles of the period had some meaning, and accumulated stresses could find release through changes of party power. The function of the Supreme Court in this scheme lay rather in settling the lines of the polity than in resolving disputes that could not be resolved outside. But when party formations grew increasingly blurred and issues like slavery and industrialism arose to cut across party lines, an attempt was made, notably in the Dred Scott case, to draw the Supreme Court into the struggle over social policy. The attempt was of course disastrous, for the slavery issue reached too deep to the economic and emotional foundations of the life of the day to be resolved by a counting of heads of more or less partisan judges. It is significant that the most direct effect of the Dred Scott decision was the sudden growth to power of a new political party, which should settle the basic question of public policy in the approved manner at the polls. The subsequent resort to war revealed that there might be some issues so basic that they could not be settled at all within the constitutional framework.

The coming of industrialism cut clear across the orientation and function of the Court as it cut across every other phase of American life. The doctrine of judicial review, whatever may have been its precedents and whatever the legalisms of its growth, had become by the middle of the century an integral part of the American political system. But it was not the dominant political institution, nor had it acquired the compelling incidence upon public policy that it has today. Before that could happen there had to be such a shift in the nature of the state that the characteristic clashes of interest would be taken out of the sphere of democratic control. In short only through the building of an extra-democratic structure of reality upon the framework of a democratic theory could the judicial power be given a real vitality or the Supreme Court attain its present towering command over the decision of public policy.

That transformation was effected by the maturing of capitalism with its strange combination of individualism as a pattern of belief and the corporation as a pattern of control. Business enterprise furnished the setting within which the Court was to operate, and in this setting the ramifications of the problems that came up for solution effected a complete change in the meaning and function of the judicial power. That power had always, when exercised, had far-reaching effects upon the process of our national life; even when in abeyance it had been a force to be reckoned with. The Court by expounding and applying the written Constitution had always constituted one of the elements that determined the shape and direction of the real constitution —the operative controls of our society. But the real Constitution became under capitalism merely the modus operandi of business enterprise. Between it on the one hand, and on the other hand the ideals of the American experiment and the phrases in which the eighteenth century had clothed those ideals, there was an ever lengthening gulf: it became the function of the Supreme Court to bridge that gulf. Capitalist enterprise in America generated, as capitalism has everywhere generated, forces in government and in the underlying classes hostile to capitalistic expansion and bent upon curbing it; it became the function of the Court to check those forces and to lay down the lines of economic orthodoxy. For the effective performance of its purposes capitalist enterprise requires legal certainty amidst the flux of modern life,[8] legal uniformity amidst the heterogeneous conditions and opinions of a vast sprawling country, the legal vesting of interests amidst the swift changes of a technological society: to furnish it with these was the huge task which the Supreme Court had successfully to perform. The Court had of course other functions, and may be regarded from other angles. But if we seek a single and consistent body of principles which will furnish the rationale of the judicial power in the last half century, we must find it in the dynamics of American business enterprise.

II

The steady growth in the judicial power and the increasing evidences of its economic affiliations have made the Court one of the great American ogres, part of the demonology of liberal and radical thought.[9] It has served, in fact, as something of a testing-ground for political attitudes of every complexion. The Marxist, making the whole of politics merely an addendum to capitalism, sees the Court as the tool and capitalism as the primary force. The contemporary Jeffersonian, fearful of all centralizing power and zealous for the liberties of the common man, fears Wall Street and the Supreme Court alternately, uncertain as to which is the shadow and which the substance. His cousin the liberal, if he is of a constructive turn, counts on using the machinery of the Court to control in a statesmanlike fashion a developing capitalism which it is futile to turn back; or, if he has lost faith in the efficacy of tinkering with governmental machinery and has become an ethical liberal, he refuses to regard either Big Business or the Supreme Court in them-

---

[8] It is generally accepted that one of the essential elements of law is certainty, and that it is especially essential for the development of capitalism. It encourages accumulation and investment by certifying the stability of the contractual relations. But it is to be conjectured that a speculative period in capitalist development thrives equally or better on uncertainty in the law. And in periods of economic collapse the crystallized certainty of capitalist law acts as an element of inflexibility in delaying adjustments to new conditions.

[9] In America the liberals have been extremely critical of the power of judicial review. In Germany, however, on the question of introducing it, the liberals supported it while the conservative parties opposed it. See C. J. Friedrich, "The Issue of Judicial Review in Germany" (1928) 43 *Pol. Sci. Qu.* 188.

selves important, but looks to the quality of the American experience that flows through them both. The technological liberal, who thinks in blueprints and plans for state planning, regards the Court as the great technical obstruction that his plans must meet, and racks his brain for ingenious ways of avoiding the encounter.

The contemporary indictment of the Court, which furnishes the point of departure for all these shades of opinion, is in the large well known. It holds that the Court's decisions can be better explained by economic bias than by judicial objectivity, and that its trend has been to bolster the status quo. This indictment is itself of course far from objective. It is the expression of an attitude. And that attitude can be best studied in relation to its genesis in the Progressive movement, which ran its brief course between the turn of the twentieth century and the American entrance into the war. To that movement may be traced the current "economic interpretation" of the Court, which links its decisions with the growth of capitalism. The Marxists might of course claim this approach as deriving from their own "materialist" conception, diluted or vulgarized in the course of its transmission to our shores. But whatever the degree of logical identity with Marxist materialism, in its actual historical growth the economic interpretation of the Supreme Court is a native product. It was out of the characteristic social conflicts of the Progressive period that the economic approach to the Court emerged, and from the intellectual dilemmas of the period that it received its formulation. In fact, if one still detects in the attitude of liberal critics of the court an equivocal and confused note, it may be found not wholly alien to the irresoluteness, the divided sense of hostility and the acceptance that lay at the heart of the Progressive movement.

The Progressive period was one of great ferment in thought and gallantry in action.[10] A peculiar emotional intensity surrounded the public life. From the western plains the storm of agrarian Populism had already broken, in the form of state

---

[10] John Chamberlain, *Farewell to Reform* (1932) gives a brilliant survey of "the rise, life and decay of the Progressive mind." 3 Parrington, *Main Currents in American Thought* (1930), left incomplete by the author's death, throws out a few suggestive leads, especially in the Introduction and the last chapter. Hacker and Kendrick, *The United States Since 1865* (1932) gives an excellent account of the period.

granger legislation, an Interstate Commerce Act, and all manner of heterodox currency proposals. The trust-busting offensive, which had opened with the Sherman Act, and had startled Wall Street in Roosevelt's drive against the Northern Securities combine, was moving on to the scrutiny of the Money Trust in the Pujo investigation. In the cities the muckrakers were canvassing the tie-up between political corruption and the "Interests," [11] and more solidly the labor movement was closing up its phalanxes and pressing for social legislation. Intellectually there was a prevailing malaise. The confidence in the national destiny was slipping, as was the faith in the adequacy of the democratic structure. Not since the days of Emerson and John Brown had Americans been forced thus to search their hearts and inquire into the direction of the national drift. The answer of the activists was the liberal revolt in politics against the increasing entrenchment of the illiberal forces. To that revolt the political thinkers made a definite contribution.[12] Probing the principles underlying the American venture they dug beneath the political ideals to their economic basis. They emerged with the discovery that the tie-up with the economic "Interests" applied not only to current politics but to the very fabric of the state; that the august Supreme Court and the still more august Constitution [13] which it expounded and guarded were not, as had been supposed, detached and self-contained; and that between them and the realities of the marketplace there was an unlovely traffic.

This discovery was made not, as the muckrakers and the populists had discovered Corruption and the Interests, through a journalistic foray into contemporary reality, but through a vast historical research. The revaluation of American democ-

---

[11] C. C. Regier, *The Era of the Muckrakers* (1932) gives a detailed account of this movement.

[12] For an interesting analysis of this contribution and the intellectual situation which evoked it, see Parrington, *The Beginnings of Critical Realism in America* (1930) Introductory chapter, xxiii–xxix, and "A Chapter on American Liberalism" at 401–13. Much of the same ground is covered in Parrington's Introduction to J. Allen Smith, *The Growth and Decadence of Constitutional Government* (1930). "Considered historically," he says of the progressive thinkers, "their main contribution was the discovery of the undemocratic nature of the Federal constitution."

[13] For an account of the hold of Constitution-worship on the American mind, see Hamilton, "Constitutionalism" (1931) 4 *Encyclopaedia of the Social Sciences* 255.

racy was pushed back to the Founding Fathers themselves, and with explosive results.[14] To be sure, the dynamite was already at hand, in the temper and intellectual equipment of the period. The "vague terror" which "went over the earth" when "the word Socialism began to be heard" [15] at about this time had to some extent been felt as far away from German Marxism as were the American Centers of academic thought, and the class struggle as well as the materialist interpretation of history was not unheard of. Veblen in 1904 had shown in a chapter [16] of his *Theory of Business Enterprise* that the business influence extended to American law through a carry-over of the eighteenth century natural rights philosophy in the interests of Big Business. Even Turner's theory of a moving frontier, expounded as early as 1893,[17] had suggested how important might be the economic base of political attitudes. But these stray leads of scholarship counted for less than did the felt realities of the day. The air was filled with the clash of group and class economic interests: what easier than to project this clash back to the founding of the Republic?

This was exactly what J. Allen Smith did in 1907 in his *The Spirit of American Government*.[18] It was not a great book, as Veblen's books are great or Turner's essay. There was no titantic outpouring of social analysis in it, no brilliant and clean-cut theory. But it was a courageous book and a dogged one. It hung onto its thesis that the American state had been shaped in its growth by conflicts of interest that were at bottom economic. Smith was followed and buttressed by Charles Beard. In his

---

[14] It should be noted that some of the Fathers themselves were attracted by the idea of economic determination. This is especially true of Madison, whose realistic awareness of the relation between economic interest and political action was striking. See Beard, *Economic Basis of Politics* (1922). In fact it may be said that the contact with Madison's thought became an element which has strengthened the hold of economic determinism in American thought.

[15] Holmes, *Collected Legal Papers* (1920) at 295.

[16] C. viii, "Business Principles in Law and Politics."

[17] "The Significance of the Frontier in American History," reprinted in Turner, *Frontier in American History* (1921). Chamberlain, *op. cit., supra* note 10, has an interesting analysis of the relation of Turner's thesis to the Progressive movement.

[18] For estimates of the place of this book in the thought of its day, see Parrington's Introduction to Smith, *op. cit., supra* note 12; and Walton Hamilton's review of it (1930) 40 Yale L.J. 152.

Economic Interpretation of the Constitution (1913)—a title
which in itself bore witness that a new Higher Criticism had
been born—Beard's search of treasury records, convention debates and contemporary journals turned up formidable evidence
to the effect that the Constitution was an "economic document"
and had been railroaded through by the property interests of
the time who stood to gain by it.[19] The reverberations of these
books were considerable,[20] but whatever the anathema or dis-
cipleship that they stirred up, the venture in historical research
had done its work. Through the attack on the Constitution a
flank attack had been delivered on the Supreme Court.

But the analysis was now extended further, by a host of
scholars and publicists.[21] It was not enough to show that the
Constitution which the Court expounded had not the stainless
objectivity which was claimed for it: the charge was now made
that whatever the origins of the Constitution, the Court was not
really expounding it but that the justices were reading their own
class interests into it. Granted the validity of the historical thesis
of Smith and Beard this was indeed a logical consequence, for it
was not to be supposed that a process operative in the creation
of the Constitution should cease to be operative in its interpretation. Bentley's *Process of Government* (1908), which made an
impression on the scholars of the day, had shown government
not as a formal structure but as a dynamic process twisted and
turned in various directions under the pressure of group interests. This theory of pressures Bentley had applied to the
judicial process as well, and it fitted in with the prevailing
pluralist attack on nineteenth century Austinianism and the new

---

[19] Beard analyzed the "personality interests" as money, public securities, manufactures, and trade and shipping." Beard, *Economic Interpretation of the Constitution* (1913) at 324. See also c. V, "The Economic Interests of the Members of
the Convention." His last chapter contains a clear and forceful statement of his
theses, which have the uncompromising ring of Luther's and were doubtless intended
to be nailed up on all the academic doors of the day. See for a similar analysis of
the first decade of the new state, Beard, *Economic Origins of Jeffersonian Democracy* (1915) especially c. VI, "Security-Holding and Politics."

[20] It is perhaps not without significance that this period represented the impres-
sionable intellectual years of the present generation of American constitutional scholars.

[21] Much of the literature about the judicial power appeared in the decade after
publication of Smith's book, and the writers (Beard, Goodnow, Corwin, McLaugh-
lin, Hadley, Farrand, Boudin, Davis, Haines, Weyl, Warren and others) used as their
point of departure, on one side or the other, the thesis of economic interest.

emphasis given to the reality of economic groupings.[22] The result was a general assumption among the students of the Court that the decisions of the justices could be explained by their economic interests and sympathies—an assumption which rarely went as far as Gustavus Myers did in his uncompromising *History of the Supreme Court* (1912), but was often present as a preconception even where it was not avowed. Most of the discussion in the years immediately preceding the war was concentrated on judicial review.[23] Its incidence and its historical validity were hotly debated, and the issue was even projected into the political campaigns in the form of proposals to strip the Court of its power, or at least determine the conditions under which the power could be exercised.[24]

We can see now that this entire Progressive critique of the connection of the Court with capitalism was itself a phase of capitalist development. It came at the crucial turn in the history of American business when it began to be clear that the system of controls set up by a democratic pre-industrial society were futile under the new conditions of life, and it marked the awakening of the middle class to that fact. Little Business felt itself being crowded out by Big Business, and for a brief moment the farmers, the traders, the unions, and the small bourgeoisie huddled together to check its further career. But as Walton Hamilton has put it, "their best wisdom was the product of a social experience that was passing." [25] Their anti-trust legislation, armed to cope with a situation produced by an exhausted individualism, continued to use the technique of that same individualism. When even that technique was burked by the decisions of the Court, and when more positive attempts at social legislation and government control met with an equal

---

[22] The fusion of these two strains—pluralism and the emphasis on economic realities—in the political thought at the beginning of the war is illustrated in Charles Beard's survey of tendencies, "Political Science in the Crucible" (1917) 13 *New Republic*, Nov. 17, Part II, 3.

[23] The discussion of judicial review of course dates back in a sense to the beginning of the Court's work. In its intense form it may be traced back to the furore that followed the decision in Dred Scott *v.* Sanford, 19 How. 393 (U.S. 1856) and later in Julliard *v.* Greenman, 110 U.S. 421 (1884). It was the latter case that called forth George Bancroft's fiery pamphlet, *A Plea for the Constitution of the United States Wounded in the House of its Guardians* (1886).

[24] The issue was most clearly drawn in La Follette's program.

[25] "The Control of Big Business" (1932) 134 *Nation* 591, 592.

fate,[26] The relation between the Court and Big Business took on an unmistakable clarity for the thinkers who expressed the world of little business.

Perhaps too great a clarity. The intellectual phase of the Progressive movement suffered from the populist tendency of the period toward the personal identification of villainy. Myers, fresh from his investigations of the direct personal corruption of the Tammany braves,[27] and of the unscrupulous careers of some of the builders of great American fortunes,[28] carried over the same mechanical approach to the very different sphere of the judicial process,[29] and tried to show how a reactionary majority opinion might rest on the stock-holdings of the justice who had written it, or on his previous associations as a corporation lawyer. Beard too, on his mettle perhaps against academic hostility, tried to prove more than he had to; and while his investigations into the direct "personal interests" of the framers of the Constitution are a tour de force of historical research, the very concreteness of his approach did much to pave the way for a too mechanical economic interpretation of the Court. The search has been throughout for light on direct pressures and the personal motives of the judges. Even those who are averse to the economic interpretation tend to resolve the whole problem of the judicial process to a matter of personal judicial whim. How unfruitful both these approaches are—the mechanical economic interpretation and the atomistic personal interpretation—I hope to show in the last section of this paper. But before that it will be necessary to inquire to what extent a developing American capitalism did represent an impinging force upon the Court, and how the Court—as a whole and through its various ideological groups—reacted to that impact.

---

[26] The stripping of the Sherman Act of much of its significance, the crippling of the Federal Trade Commission, and the attempts to qualify the powers of the Interstate Commerce Commission are important chapters in American administrative history. See Sharfman, *The Interstate Commerce Commission* (1931); Henderson, *The Federal Trade Commission* (1924); Myron Watkins, The Federal Trade Commission (1932) 32 Col. L. Rev. 272; Keezer and May, *The Public Control of Business* (1930); *The Federal Anti-Trust Laws, A Symposium* (1932).

[27] *The History of Tammany Hall* (1901).

[28] *History of the Great American Fortunes* (1910).

[29] *History of the Supreme Court of the United States* (1912).

III

In itself capitalism is merely the name we give to a system of free individualist enterprise which allows and fortifies the accumulation of wealth.[30] It is thus in essence a scheme of economic organization going back to the beginning of modern times and resting upon legal institutions, the most important of which are private property and contract. Within these limits capitalism has more recently developed on the one hand a set of technological methods and on the other a set of working rules [31] which we call respectively industrialism and business. Both these lines of growth have wrought vast changes in the character of capitalist society. Industrialism in production has brought the factory, the machine process, the large city and the working class, and has given our world the characteristic outer stamp that it bears. Business enterprise has brought the corporation, the credit structure, the investment banker and the marketing mechanism, and has given our world its inner living spirit.[32] In both realms the working rules have changed so rapidly and with such fateful consequence as to merit the designation of "revolution." [33] But these revolutions, however drastic, have not shattered the outlines of the capitalist system. They have merely realized its inherent trends and possibilities.

It is obvious that the large movements of modern law can be understood best in relation to this development of a capitalist society. The ways of life and the property attitudes of this

---

[30] In addition to Marx's classic analysis of capitalism, see Sombart, *Der Moderne Kapitalismus* (4th ed. 1921–27), and *Der Bourgeois*, Eng. trans. (*The Quintessence of Capitalism,* 1915); Hobson, *The Evolution of Modern Capitalism* (1926 ed.); and the writings of Thorstein Veblen, especially *The Theory of Business Enterprise* (1904), and *Absentee Ownership* (1923). The point of departure for Veblen's work is the form capitalism has taken in America. The emphasis of the present article is therefore rather on the Veblenian analysis than on the Marxist.

[31] I take the phrase "working rules" from the suggestive analysis in Commons, *Legal Foundations of Capitalism* (1924).

[32] It is in this contrast between the matter-of-factness of industrialism and the sophisticated and devious business structure imposed upon it, that Veblen finds the central contradiction of capitalism. See his *Theory of Business Enterprise* (1904); *The Instinct of Workmanship* (1914); *Absentee Ownership* (1923).

[33] The revolution in technology has been called the Industrial Revolution; the more recent technological developments have been called by Meakin the "Second Industrial Revolution"; Berle and Means, *The Modern Corporation and Private Property* (1932) speak aptly of the drastic changes in the scale and methods of business as the "corporate revolution."

society while it was still rural and bourgeois have written themselves into the Anglo-American common law. They have written themselves also into American constitutional law, as embodied first in the written document drawn up by a group of "men of substance" acting as spokesmen for the more or less property-conscious American society of the late eighteenth century, and as interpreted by a property-conscious Supreme Court. In all societies the historical function of law has been to elaborate, rationalize and protect the dominant institutions and the accredited ways of life, and the function of public law has been to apply ultimately the coercion of the state toward maintaining the outlines of those dominant institutions.[34] American constitutional law, whatever may be its unique modes of operation and principles of growth, is not exempt from this function.

But here as everywhere the large historical generalization conceals great dangers. To say that American constitutional law rationalizes and gives sanction to American capitalist society is of little value unless the relation between the two is traced historically and with an eye to the evolving character of each. As with all words that have grown to be symbols and are moved about as counters in argument, capitalism has taken on for us a singleness of meaning that beclouds more issues than it illumines. Actually of course it is not only an exceedingly complex institution, reaching out into many domains of what men do and how they think, but it is also a rapidly shifting one. Its tremendous importance for the Supreme Court flows from this fact of its change. For to a static capitalism, however baleful or beneficent, the Court and the nation could eventually work out a harmonious adjustment, balancing somehow the demands of constitutional rules with the interests of constituent groups. But a changing capitalism is continually undoing what is done even before it has been entirely done. Being a growing thing it creates conflicts of interest, problems of control, disorders in the "economic order" while the ink is scarce dry on the statute

---

[34] Maitland's remark, that "our whole constitutional law seems at times to be but an appendix to the law of real property" (*The Constitutional History of England* [1908] at 538) was probably intended mainly to express his sense of the erratic logic of development in history. But it is significant also in showing how the line of development in public law is the legal elaboration and protection of the dominant institutions—in this case property.

or decision which attempted to heal the ravages of some previous change. Its superior mobility over previous systems of economic organization, such as the feudal or slave systems, derives from the fact that it rests on a rapidly moving technological base and appeals to the free and even reckless flow of individual energy. We have as a consequence the characteristic transitionalism of modern western society and that instability of institutional arrangements which gives it its vitality. And in the United States the pace of capitalist development has been extraordinarily rapid, abbreviating the earlier stages upon which the European societies lingered for centuries, and setting the pace for the entire world in the latest stages.

The history of American capitalist development falls roughly into four periods. With due awareness of the danger of schematism, and with an eye especially to their impact upon the problem of legal control, the periods may be described as (1) pre-industrial capitalism, (2) industrial capitalism, (3) monopoly capitalism, and (4) finance capitalism.[35] Pre-industrial capitalism is a catch-all for the various phases of development lying in European history between the commercial Revolution and the early decades of the nineteenth century;[36] in America, between

---

[35] Periodization in modern economic history has varied of course with the point of view adopted (see, for example, works by the Hammonds, Clapham, Weber, Gras, Cunningham). Since capitalism is a Marxist concept, periodization from the point of view of capitalist development has been attempted by the Marxist writers or those deriving from them, and has been tied up intimately with the general development of Marxist theory. Werner Sombart's division of capitalism into Frühkapitalismus, Hochkapitalismus and Spätkapitalismus is well known. Sombart, *op. cit., supra* note 30; also Sombart's article on Capitalism (1930) 3 *Encyclopaedia of the Social Sciences* 195. Marx's own division was between pre-industrial capitalism, industrial capitalism and monopoly capitalism. John A. Hobson, *The Evolution of Modern Capitalism* (1894) follows similar lines. Largely as a result of Hobson's analysis of imperialism in his book of that name, and also as a result of Hilferding *Finanzkapital* (1910) and the logic of events at the outbreak of the war, the Marxists, especially Lenin, *The State and Revolution* (1919), added another stage which they called variously and by its respective aspects "imperialistic capitalism" and "finance capitalism." In American economic history there has been little attempt to lay out a broad analysis of stages, other than that involved in the concept of industrialism. See for representative classifications, Faulkner, *American Economic History* (1924) and Kirkland, *History of American Economic Life* (1932). Commons, *History of Labor* (1926), divides American developments into the custom-order period, the merchant-capitalist or job-capitalist period, the middleman period and the corporation period; his point of view is that of the dependence of the laborer upon shifting entities with the extension of markets and of bargaining power over wider areas.

[36] See for a good account of the European development, J. L. and Barbara Hammond, *The Rise of Modern Industry* (1925).

colonization and the first railroad network in the eighteen forties. It was an economy still basically agricultural, with a growing superstructure of trade and small manufacture. In America as in Europe the juristic importance of this period lies in its having laid the foundations for the capitalist state, hewn out the institution of property, and fashioned the master ideas, such as individualism and natural rights, which were to exercise so tenacious a hold upon the modern mind.

What the pre-industrial period seems so neatly to have settled, industrial capitalism proceeded to unsettle. In America we may block out the four decades from the eighteen forties to the eighties as marking the rise of an industrial society. The machine-process,[37] large-scale industry, a far-flung system of transportation and communication, and an urban way of life represented the principal lines of development. The growth of monopoly, and of a financial structure was not at all absent in this period, but it was accompaniment rather than main theme: its possibilities, scarcely dreamt of, awaited later phases of capitalism. The sectional distribution of industrial development was uneven: until the Civil War it was so completely identified with the northern states to the exclusion of the southern that an only mildly heterodox theory of the Civil War attributes it to this antimony rather than to a struggle over human rights.[38] Large stretches of the West also have remained agrarian to this day. The main drift however toward the creation of an industrial state meant a vast displacement of pre-industrial institutions. The actual meaning and social incidence of property were radically shifted. The gap between the propertied and the propertiless was widened and given significance, and the general lines of economic distribution and social stratification were drawn with the emergence of a capitalist entrepreneur class, a middle-class trading and professional class, and a class of workers of varying degrees of skill. Where the pre-industrial period had laid the property foundations of capitalist society, the industrial period laid its class foundations. But perhaps the outstanding achieve-

---

[37] See Veblen, *op. cit., supra* note 30.

[38] 2 Charles and Mary Beard, *The Rise of American Civilization* (1927) c. XVIII, "The Second American Revolution," which interprets the war as a revolution of the non-industrial south against the industrial north.

ment of the period was its fulfillment of the philosophy of individual initiative and competition as the organizing principles of
economic society. The idea of a triumphant capitalism—the
strongest force in American history—received here its decisive
impetus. Despite the intensifying of class lines, this capitalist
myth—and "myth" is used here neutrally to mean any evocative
idea that patterns men's lives—stirred the energies of rich and
poor and created a united front in the interests of capitalism.[39]
There was as yet relatively little hostility manifested toward the
propertied class by the propertiless: there could scarcely be
hostility toward what every man hoped some day to attain.[40] The
whole of American society was turned into an open state in
which capitalist enterprise was given free movement and bidden
Godspeed.

The period of monopoly capitalism, from the eighties to the
decade before the World War, offers to the historian a striking
dual visage. It was marked by a rapid concentration of economic
power, but also by a disenchantment with capitalism.[41] The period witnessed not only the heightening of the movement for
industrial consolidation, but also the building of a credit and
banking structure, a technique of salesmanship and a set of business mores that all attested to the continuing vitality of capitalism.[42] But the united front was gone. In its place was the "independent" entrepreneur confronting the invincible aggression
of the trusts. The competitive ideal, however neat had been the
conception of it as the dominant control in the economic mechanism, had failed practically in organizing economic life. The
open state was found to be a dangerous program, and some of
the legislatures now began to throw up barricades against its

---

[39] The concept of the "myth" as used here derives from Sorel, *Reflections on
Violence* (1912). Sorel used it of the myth of revolution, but it can be used of
other master-ideas in the history of civilization.

[40] See Hadley, *Undercurrents in American Politics* (1915) lecture II, "The Constitutional Position of the Property Owner." The common man, says Hadley, "was
not ready to declare war against an industrial society that offered him so many inducements to become one of its members."

[41] For an analysis of this disenchantment, written just before the War by one
of the Progressives, and couched in political rather than economic terms, see Walter
Weyl, *The New Democracy* (1912) c. I.

[42] For the classic statement of the outlines of the American business structure
at the end of this period, see Veblen, *Absentee Ownership and Business Enterprise:
The Case of America* (1923).

further extension. Agrarianism, populism, trust-busting, muck-raking, and progressivism grew to alarming strength. They represented, as we have seen, an inner cleavage in the forces that formerly had fought side by side in the advance of capitalism.

The final period—that of finance capitalism, covering the last quarter-century—was marked by a shift of axis in the economic world from industrial organization to financial control. The growth of the giant corporation found its significance not so much in the matter of magnitude as in the separation that it effected between the ownership and the management of industrial enterprise, and the opportunity it gave for the subtleties of corporation finance.[43] Investment banking became the central activity of the higher reaches of economic behavior, and such investment houses as that of Morgan, the symbol of economic power. The attempt to check the monopolistic trend came to seem increasingly hopeless, and attention was transferred to the dangers of financial concentration and banking control of industry.[44] The capitalist myth, so far from receding, received an accession of strength from two decades of mounting prosperity, but its type-figure was now cast not in the image of the entrepreneur but in that of the speculator or the financial promoter. The *bloc* that had been formed in the previous period to stem the growth of the large corporation and the money power found that their task had become archaic, and that the principal concern of the community lay in a fair distribution of profits and risks *within* the corporate and pecuniary structure. The failure of the old controls seemed established by the crisis of 1929, and the search for new controls began along the line of economic planning by the government of some form of autonomous rationalization within the business structure.[45]

These successive shifts of focus in American economic reality have done much to determine the large sweep of American constitutional law. They have done so in a threefold way: by setting the characteristic problems that have appeared for deci-

---

[43] See Berle and Means, *op. cit., supra* note 33.

[44] Brandeis, *Other People's Money* (1914), especially c. IX, "The Failure of Banker-Management."

[45] For the relation of the Supreme Court to the trend of these developments, see E. S. Corwin, "Social Planning under the Constitution" (1932), 26 *American Political Science Review*.

sion before the Supreme Court; by creating the conflicts and the clashes of interests which have given those problems importance for the community; and by fashioning the ideologies which have to a large degree influenced the decisions. Put in another way the impact of American capitalistic development on the Court has been at once to pose the problems and to condition the answers.

The increasing push and thrust of economic problems upon the business of the Supreme Court has been noted by Professors Frankfurter and Landis.[46] Within this larger trend it is interesting to analyze by what dynamics of the economic process the varied range of problems are brought into the area of decision. The ordinary groupings around legal subject matter, or the groupings around clauses in the Constitution or around devices in the Court procedure are not entirely revealing. To know that a case is an injunction case, or that it came under a writ of certiorari, or that it appealed to the due process clause of the Fourteenth Amendment conveys little of the context of emotion and belief that might give it meaning. The groupings might more realistically be built around those clashes of interests within the economic system or clashes of attitude about it out of which the cases proceed.

These clashes of interest are as varied of course as the economic life that they mirror. They are at once evidences of maladjustment and challenges to control. Some are concerned with the organizational aspects of capitalism, others with the incidence of its functioning, still others with the distribution of its flow of income. Thus one may find clashes of interest between workers and employers over wages or hours or working conditions or plans for social insurance; between groups of business-men over trade practices (in the sphere of economic ideology); between consumers and public utility groups over prices and standards; between ownership and control groups within the corporate structure over the division of profits; between agricultural and industrial groups, Big Business and Little Business groups, groups being taxed and the government as taxer; between all sorts of groups who would stand to gain from a particular government

---

[46] *The Business of the Supreme Court* (1927) c. VIII.

policy, such as a grant of direct relief or an issue of legal tender paper, and those who would stand to lose; [47] between the interests of autonomous business control and those of state-enforced competitive enterprise; between the interests of individual enterprise and those of collective control; between those who have a property interest in the status quo and those who have a humanistic interest in changing it.

In short, capitalism pushes ultimately before the Court the clashes of interest that are attendant on the growth of any economic system, with the displacement in each successive phase of elements that had been useful in previous phases, with the antagonisms it generates among those who are bearing its burdens and the rivalry among those who are dividing its spoils, and with the inherent contradictions that it may possess. If it be added to this that modern capitalism is perhaps the least organic system of economic organization the world has seen—"often, though not always, a mere congeries of possessors and pursuers," J. M. Keynes has called it [48]—and that the American social and political structure within which it operates is perhaps more sprawling and heterogeneous than that of any other major capitalist society, some notion may be had of the confusion of interests and purposes out of which it is the task of the Court to bring certainty and uniformity.

The dimensions of the task must however be qualified in several respects. Not every case that comes before the Court involves grave conflicts of interest or broad issues of public policy; it is only the exceptional cases that do. Moreover the pressures and interests summarily analyzed above apply to the entire governmental process in a capitalist state, and not merely to the Court. In fact, the Court does not fight on the front lines but must be considered a reserve force. The brunt of the attack and the task of reconciling the conflicts is met by the legislatures

---

[47] The clash of interest between debtor and creditor groups is clearly expressed in the Legal Tender cases, especially in Mr. Justice Bradley's concurring dissent, 12 Wall. 457, 554, 564 (U.S. 1870): "The heart of the nation must not be crushed out. The people must be aided to pay their debts and meet their obligations. The debtor interest of the country represent its bone and sinew, and must be encouraged to pursue its avocation. . . . But the creditor interest will lose some of its gold! Is gold the one thing needful? Is it worse for the creditor to lose a little by depreciation than everything by the bankruptcy of his debtor"?

[48] Quoted in Tawney, *Religion and the Rise of Capitalism* (1926) at 286.

and the administrative agencies, which are more amenable to democratic control than is a small tribunal holding office for life. It is only what survives the legislative barriers and also the jurisdictional exclusions of the Court,[49] that comes finally to pose its issues. And even of this group not every case involving an important conflict of interests will exact from the Court that intense absorption with its social values and implications which creates the nexus binding the judicial process to the economic system. Many a case which, if it had come later or earlier in the country's development might have been decided differently or constituted a leading case fails at the time to call into play the entire concentration of the Court's social philosophy.[50] For any period neither the Court nor the country can focus its energies on more than a few dominant issues. It is the area that includes these issues—let us call it the "area of vital conflict"—that determines the path of growth in the judicial process and fashions the outlines of constitutional law.

IV

When we turn to the sequence of decision in the history of the Supreme Court do we find in it any of the movement and stir that have marked the growth of American capitalism? To most the question would seem to call for a definite answer in the negative. There is a tendency, whenever economics and the judicial process are brought into relation, to regard the first as the active and the second as the passive element, the first as marking the line of growth and the second as adjusting itself— or rather, failing to adjust itself—to that growth.[51] There is so

---

[49] For the substantive importance of many of these procedural exclusions, see Frankfurter and Landis, *op. cit., supra* note 46; and their annual reviews of the same subject in the Harvard Law Review.

[50] It has been noted that the Court in its present composition is likely to be liberal with regard to cases affecting personal liberties, but conservative with regard to the protection of property rights: see Shulman, The Supreme Court's Attitude Toward Liberty of Contract and Freedom of Speech (1931) 41 Yale L.J. 262. An explanation for this might be sought in the fact that issues of personal liberty are not at present as squarely in the area of vital conflict as are property issues. In time of war or of war hysteria we should expect that inconsistency to be ironed out.

[51] For a clear statement of this theme, see Henderson, *The Position of the Foreign Corporation in American Constitutional Law* (1918) at 3–9, where he speaks of economic change as the "dynamic element" in constitutional development, and formal doctrine as the "static element."

much in legal history which seems to verify this view that our great danger lies in being tempted to regard it as true. The sociologists have built a theory of the "legal lag" on the assumption of its validity,[52] and much of the "liberal" criticism of the Court's decisions attributes to that tribunal a distressing medley of imperviousness and ferocity toward economic reality. The conception is often extended to include the backwardness and inertia of the whole of legal science.

In reality this view embodies only a half-truth and at present the more dangerous half. We may guess that it had its origin and perhaps found its validity in the attempt to bolster the fighting reformist faith of the Progressive movement by building a somewhat ramshackle sociology for legal thought. It dates from the period when a sociological jurisprudence had considerable intellectual appeal, and it seemed to receive confirmation whenever the Court definitely placed obstacles in the path of social legislation. But it tends to obscure the important fact that law is as much a growth as is economics. The principle of growth of a legal doctrine is undoubtedly not that of an economic technique. It is likely to be more tortuous and elusive, and to attain its results rather by indirection than by a steady processional sequence. But legal doctrines do have their life histories.[53] The very fictions they embody are, by the fact of being fictions, vehicles of change. Instead of positing an antithesis between a dynamic economic activity and a static law, it is truer to see the growth of each interwoven with the other and conditioning the other. Just as the meaning of American constitutional law emerges best from the dynamics of American capitalism, so the meaning of capitalism is most securely found in the developing legal institutions of property, liberty and contract, and their aggrandizement through the doctrine of due process.

---

[52] The entire conception of the legal lag, which owes much to Dicey, *Lectures on the Relation between Law and Public Opinion in England during the Nineteenth Century* (1905); Ogburn, *Social Change* (1923); and to American sociological jurisprudence; needs to be re-examined more thoroughly than the limits of this paper will allow.

[53] For a general theory of the life history of legal doctrines, see Walton Hamilton's article on the Judicial Process (1932), 8 *Encyclopaedia of the Social Sciences* 450. See also by the same author, The Ancient Maxim Caveat Emptor (1931) 40 Yale L.J. 1133; and Affectation with Public Interest (1930) 39 Yale L.J. 1089.

The course of Supreme Court decision when viewed thus falls, like the course of capitalist development itself, into fairly well defined periods. It will be well in blocking them out to abstain from ethical designations such as "liberal," "conservative" and "reactionary" which are confusing because of the continual shift of criteria as new forces and alignments come into play.

The line of judicial growth in the first half century of the court lay in a pronounced nationalism as expressed in the subordination of the state legislatures and the protection of vested property rights.[54] Of these the limitation of state power was probably more in the forefront of Federalist consciousness than the protection of property, although the two motives were often fused. But it was more than an article of Federalist faith; it was already a constitutional tradition holding over from the ideology and temper of the Constitutional Convention. There was a prevailing distrust of anything that the states might do in a new society, a distrust which was part of that fear of the people that pursued Federalist thought throughout. State legislatures were deemed dangerous because they had yielded basely to the pressures of the multitude, cutting debts, issuing paper money, cancelling obligations. To prevent such irresponsibility a line of cases, of which Fletcher *v.* Peck [55] and Dartmouth College Trustees *v.* Woodward [56] were the most notable, interpreted the "obligations of contract" clause of the Constitution in a way that has made it of far-reaching economic importance. The Court evidenced thus at the very beginning a concern for property that was to grow in intensity and incorporated it in a doctrine of vested rights which Professor Corwin has noted as one of its first doctrinal creations.[57]

Of course, it is quite easy to read our own property conflicts into the phrases of the day, and make an identification where there is room only for a comparison. Private property was not

---

[54] C. G. Haines, *Revival of Natural Law Concepts* (1930) c. IV is especially full on the growth of judicial doctrine in this early period.

[55] 6 Cranch 87 (U.S. 1810).

[56] 41 Wheat. 518 (U.S. 1819).

[57] E. S. Corwin, The Basic Doctrine of American Constitutional Law (1914) 12 Mich. L. Rev. 247, 275. See for a good general treatment of this period, with an eye to its economic development as well, C. G. Haines, *op. cit., supra* note 54, especially c. IV.

on the defensive in the America of Marshall as it was to be in the successive America's of Field, Peckham, Pitney, and Sutherland. It was part of the rising society and connected with the future of the new state, and the judicial support of it was an expression of the prevailing ideology.[58] It is noteworthy that on the issue of the desirability of social protection of property rights—as distinct from the issue of whether the task was a fit one for the judiciary to perform, and the issue of states rights that was involved—there was little disagreement between the Federalist and Democratic administrations before Jackson. Even the early "populist" outbreaks, like Shays' Rebellion, were not organic revolts against the ominous features of an economic system as was the Populist movement a century later, but were part of the revolutionary unsettlement and the post-war economic impoverishment. And the Jacksonian revolution, with its extension of the suffrage and its frontier democracy, did not materially change the constitutional position of property.[59] On the frontier, as President Hadley has pointed out, property rights had greater sanction and more immediate protection than human rights.[60] One of the striking mélanges of the period, incidentally, is to be found in the manner in which Federalist jurists conscripted the Jeffersonian ideology of natural law in the service of a doctrine of vested rights which restricted the powers of Jeffersonian state legislatures at the same time that it protected property dear to both parties. That Marshall's motivation throughout was national unity in the interests of the smooth functioning of the increasing commercial activity of the country [61] is shown further in his decision in McCulloch *v.* Mary-

---

[58] Hadley, *op. cit., supra* note 40.

[59] Hadley, *id*. at 27.

[60] "The small protection given to the rights of man, as compared with that which was accorded to the rights of property, is a salient feature in the history of the early American state—and continues in its later history as well"—Hadley, *ibid*. He speaks in the same place of the "democratic concern for the interests of the property owner and the democratic unconcern for the interests of humanity."

[61] Boudin, *op. cit., supra* note 3, c. XII, "John Marshall and the Rise of Nationalism," speaks of Marshall as being one of the real leaders of the "Young America" movement and therefore more closely identified with Madison and Clay than with the elder statesmen of the Federalist Party. Mr. Boudin also contends that there is an ideological break in Marshall's career between his earlier and his later opinions, conditioned by this new development. Although Mr. Boudin intends it to show that Marshall was important despite Marbury *v.* Madison, and that he was not the founder of the modern doctrine of Judicial review, the chief importance of this lead

land,[62] in which Congressional control of monetary affairs was upheld, and the decisions interpreting the Commerce Clause,[63] especially Gibbons *v.* Ogden [64] and Brown *v.* Maryland.[65]

The period of judicial nationalism had coincided roughly with the pre-industrial period and expressed its ways of thought and life tolerably well. The second period of the Court's history, extending from the eighteen thirties to the Civil War reflected to a degree the coming of industrial capitalism. It was in its juristic ideas a definitely transitional period, marked by no consistent drive except a disinclination to place obstacles in the way of the forging of an industrial society. The relatively tolerant attitude of the Court toward state legislation in the first two decades of Jacksonian democracy (1830–1850) was followed in the next decade by a reaction against the reckless land and currency activities of the western legislatures.[66] The idea of implied constitutional limitations on the state power was used as a convenient doctrine; but although it followed logically from the sanction that natural law gave to vested rights, and although there was vigorous agitation for it by Story and Kent and later by Cooley, the Court in this period gave only a hesitating allegiance to it.[67] Its attitude was on the whole pragmatic. Industrialism, with its introduction of a system of transportation and a marketing area that cut across state boundaries and shattered the validity of the state-nation concept as a dichotomy, was bringing problems that could not be solved by a single formula. In the interpretation of the commerce clause a series of decisions which, despite the prevalent confusion of purpose, had since Gibbons *v.* Ogden clung to a pragmatic insistence on defining state power in regulating interstate commerce by examining its consequences, was summed up in Cooley *v.* Board

---

for the present discussion lies in its fortifying the view that Marshall, like Clay, Webster and the rest of the nationalist group, was interested in clearing the field for the extension of commerce and industry.

[62] 4 Wheat. 316 (U.S. 1819).

[63] Frankfurter and Freund, "Interstate Commerce" (1932) 8 *Encyclopaedia of the Social Sciences* 220, traces incisively the course of interpretation of the commerce clause in American constitutional law in relation to our economic development.

[64] 22 U.S. 1 (1824).

[65] 25 U.S. 419 (1827).

[66] Haines, *op. cit., supra* note 54, at 97, 98.

[67] Haines, *id.* at c. IV.

of Wardens [68] which in effect opened the way for sustaining state regulation where that would facilitate the progress of industrialism.[69] The slavery issue was the great jarring note of emotional absolutism. It was an unavowed participant in many of the opinions, and by polarizing the emotions of the country it introduced into the decisions of the Court a more marked political bias. But the Dred Scott decision may itself be interpreted in terms of the "sweep of economic forces." [70] It marked a crucial recognition by a land-owning capitalism that the industrial capitalism that was rising in the northern states was more than a principle of economic organization but reached to the fabric of the state, and would have to be combatted with the weapons of constitutional law.

The period of constitutional interpretation that extended from the end of the Civil War to the middle of the eighties presents as interesting and challenging a sequence of decision as any in the Court's history. Since it measures the transition from a competitive industrialism to a monopolistic capitalism, it contains the genesis of many of the problems of regulation that dominate the subsequent history of the Court. Coming also immediately after the Civil War, it marks the convergence of a set of attitudes relating to business enterprise with a set of attitudes relating to Reconstruction—to the confusion of both. Thus in the early part of the period, while the Reconstruction issue was still fresh, the influences which would otherwise have helped shape the course of judicial decision are qualified and confused; and in the latter part, when the economic ideologies reassert themselves, a constitutional amendment intended primarily as a guide for the problem of reconstruction is increasingly pressed into service to bolster a theory of economic statesmanship. Not only do the cases smell of powder but often of the powder of two different battles.

The Fourteenth Amendment, which has laid its hand so heavily upon American constitutional law, seems to have come

---

[68] 53 U.S. 299 (1851).
[69] Frankfurter and Freund, *supra* note 63, at 222.
[70] The phrase is from Charles and Mary Beard, *op. cit., supra* note 38. C. XVII contains a good account of the economic and emotional setting of the Dred Scott decision.

into being with less attendant innocence than had until recently been believed. Professor Kendrick's edition of the Journal of the committee [71] which prepared the amendment indicates that the notion of using a negro rights amendment to restrict state legislative raids upon business interests was not wholly absent from the minds of the members. It did not receive definite expression before the Court, however, until Roscoe Conkling's argument in the San Mateo case.[72] But even clearer was the intent on the part of the Radical Republicans to use the amendment as an entering wedge to effect a complete constitutional subordination of the states to the nation, not so much in the interests of property as in the interests of northern control.[73] The first test of the amendment in the Slaughterhouse case [74] was therefore not a clear-cut decision on the economic issue of regulation that was involved but was oriented toward the political issue, which was more directly in the area of vital conflict of the day. But the most important parts of the decision are the brief of ex-Justice Campbell and Justice Field's dissenting opinion [75] that was based on it. Campbell's line of reasoning, by which the due process clause could be interpreted to support property rights against legislative restriction, was subsequently hammered away at the Court in a series of powerful dissenting opinions by Field [76] and his supporters until their triumph in Allgeyer v. Louisiana.[77] Whatever the orientation of the majority in the case, the Field orientation was economic. It is as if he had a prevision of the future needs of capitalist enterprise and how those needs would be supplied. The second and more crucial test of the Fourteenth Amendment, in Munn v. Illinois,[78] was, because of its setting in

---

[71] B. B. Kendrick, *The Journal of the Joint Committee of Fifteen on Reconstruction, 39th Congress, 1865–1867* (1914).

[72] County of San Mateo v. Southern Pacific Ry. Co., 116 U.S. 138 (1885). For a discussion of this case, see Kendrick, *op. cit., supra* note 71, at 28–36.

[73] Kendrick, *id.* at c. VII, VIII.

[74] Slaughterhouse Cases, 16 Wall. 36 (U.S. 1872).

[75] *Id.* at 83.

[76] Walter Nelles' review of Swisher, *Stephen J. Field* (1930) and (1931), 40 Yale L.J. 998, is a remarkable analysis of the relation between Field's opinions and the forces active in the developing society in which he lived. An adequate treatment of the relation between the Supreme Court and American capitalism must wait upon the publication of such other analytic studies of the other Supreme Court justices.

[77] 165 U.S. 578 (1897).

[78] 94 U.S. 113 (1876); also the Granger cases, 94 U.S. 155 (1876).

the Granger revolt [79] rather than the Reconstruction issue, fought on new ground. The incidence of the monopolistic trends upon the farmers, whose position in a capitalist society is at best anachronistic, had led to the passage of regulatory state legislation. The reaction of the business community to the Waite opinion, with its attitude of judicial toleration of the state acts, and Justice Field's dissent as the expression of that reaction, marked the beginning of a grand peur which seized the property interests and scarcely abated for several decades until they had arrived within the secure confines of Allgeyer v. Louisiana and Lochner v. New York.[80] It was scarcely a coincidence that this epidemic of fear coincided with the publication of Cooley's *Constitutional Limitations*.[81] But the most significant phase of the campaign for a new conception of due process lay in the steady insistence of the counsel for the corporations that the justices owed a duty to the society they lived in to conserve its most sacred institution even in the face of the strict constitutional logic of the situation.[82] This was the first important manifestation of the social animus of the new corporation lawyers and of the effects of their association with the ideology of business.

This period in the Court's history from the Civil War to the first victory of the Field cohorts in the mid-eighties was thus

---

[79] See Solon J. Buck, *The Granger Movement* (1913), and *The Agrarian Crusade* (1920); also Hacker and Kendrick, *op. cit., supra* note 10, Part I.

[80] 198 U.S. 45 (1905).

[81] Haines, *op. cit., supra* note 54, at 122; see also William Seagle, "Thomas M. Cooley" (1931), 4 *Encyclopaedia of the Social Sciences* 356.

[82] A rather remarkable example is contained in Choate's argument in Pollock *v.* Farmers' Loan and Trust Co., 157 U.S. 429, 532, 534, 553 (1895). "I believe that there are rights of property here to be protected; that we have a right to come to this court and ask for this protection, and that this court has a right, without asking leave of the Attorney General or of any counsel, to hear our plea. The act of Congress we are impugning before you is communistic in its purposes and tendencies, and is defended here upon principles as communistic, socialistic—what shall I call them—populistic as ever have been addressed to any political assembly in the world. . . . I have thought that one of the fundamental objects of all civilized government was the preservation of the rights of private property. I have thought that it was the very keystone of the arch upon which all civilized government rests. . . . If it be true . . . that the passions of the people are aroused on this subject, if it be true that a mighty army of sixty million citizens is likely to be incensed by this decision, it is the more vital to the future welfare of this country that this court again resolutely and courageously declare, as Marshall did, that it *has* the power to set aside an act of Congress violative of the Constitution, and that it will not hesitate in executing that power, no matter what the threatened consequences of popular or populistic wealth may be."

one of the fateful periods in our national life. It marked a parting of the ways between a policy of judicial tolerance and one of the further extension of judicial review. The Court stood poised between the agrarian revolt, which had been stirred by the growth of monopolist capitalism, and the business interests whose new militancy concealed their uneasiness. We know of course which policy eventually prevailed and what a difference that has made in our national life. It is relatively easy from the vantage ground of the present to say that a real choice never existed, and that the development of monopoly capitalism made the outcome for the Supreme Court an inevitable one. But inevitability is a summary word that solves too many difficulties. Capitalist development certainly weighted the scales. It set the wider limits outside of which no choice was possible. But within those limits the country had a chance at a choice—and took it.

The doctrine which came to the fore in the mid-eighties and dominated the court for a quarter century was on the economic side a militant expression of laissez-faire and on the legal side a no less militant extension of the economic scope of due process. It seems at first sight surprising that a period which was seeing the individualistic ideal of competition give way to monopoly should call for a laissez-faire policy in its Court decisions. But laissez-faire is to be distinguished from individualism; the latter is a philosophy, the former a mandate.[83] Laissez-faire may conceivably proceed from a cherishing of individualist values, but since it would in such an event have to qualify its imperative claims for freedom from legislative interference by a recognition of the individualist values which are injured by such freedom, its relations are likely to be solely empirical. The change from the individualism at the basis of the previous period of judicial toleration to the laissez-faire-ism of the new restrictive period measured the difference between the two intellectual climates. There was of course a new alignment in the Court; the old minority had become a majority. But it was a new Court in a new society. It was not a sport, but an organic part of a period which has come down in the history of American

---

[83] For the connection between the program of laissez-faire in the American situation, and the theory of natural rights of which it makes use, see Veblen, *The Vested Interests and the Common Man* (1920).

life as thin in its cultural fibre and crass in its political morality. One may hazard that much of the responsibility is to be laid to the disillusioning effect of the competitive breakdown under the pressure of new and unscrupulous business mores.

The period of judicial toleration had, we have noted, been a crucial period, hesitant and divided when confronted by bewildering problems of a new industrialism. The period of judicial restriction was, when confronted by a dangerous revolt against the incidence of the new forms of capitalist enterprise,[84] decisive and militant. And it was in its own way remarkably creative. On every important front of public policy it transformed the existing doctrine with considerable ingenuity [85]—in the field of railroad regulation (Santa Clara County *v.* Southern Pacific R.; [86] Chicago, Milwaukee and St. Paul *v.* Minnesota; [87] Smythe *v.* Ames),[88] business control (Allgeyer *v.* Louisiana), federal taxation (Pollock *v.* Farmers Loan and Trust),[89] regulation of hours (Lochner *v.* New York), social legislation (Employers' Liability Cases),[90] and anti-trust cases (United States *v.*

---

[84] Not least among the causes for the militancy of the possessing classes, reflected in the militancy of the Court, was the influx of immigration and the growth of a labor movement which, while in the main a "business unionism" variety, was often engaged in violent clashes with employers. The fear of the immigrant worker, and the contempt for him have been influential in American history not only in heightening the clash between capitalists and laborers, but in putting behind the former a united body of opinion representing middle class respectability. The Court in its decisions in this period reflected the prevalent Catonian attitude toward the labor movement, which called for its extirpation. I Commons, *op. cit., supra* note 35, at 9, points out however that the courts by blocking labor's way toward reform probably made the trade union movement even more aggressive.

[85] The sequence of steps by which the Fourteenth Amendment was pressed into use for the protection of business interests against legislative regulation seems to have been somewhat as follows: 1) The decision that corporations are "persons" within the meaning of the Amendment; 2) the decision that equal protection of the laws applies to foreign corporations as well as to individuals from outside states; 3) the decision that the due process clause applies to legislative and administrative attempts to regulate rates and other matters connected with the conduct of business enterprise; 4) the decision that liberty of contract is a right of liberty (or of property) within the meaning of the Amendment; 5) the decision that the police power and the public interest doctrine must be narrowly and urgently construed in determining exemption from the due process clause; 6) the decision that the reasonableness of state legislation is not a matter of presumption by the fact that the legislation passed the gauntlet of the legislative process, but is open to examination by the Court.

[86] 118 U.S. 394 (1886).
[87] 134 U.S. 418 (1890).
[88] 169 U.S. 466 (1898).
[89] 157 U.S. 429 (1895).
[90] 207 U.S. 463 (1908).

E. C. Knight Company).[91] It was in this period that the powerful conceptions of contemporary constitutional law—due process,[92] police powers,[93] liberty of contract[94] and the rule of reasonableness[95]—received their real impetus and elaboration.

In the last quarter century the trend of judicial decision has
again become vacillating for lack of some decisive movement
within capitalist enterprise itself to give it firmness and direction. The second decade of the century is generally considered
to have been "liberal," and Muller *v.* Oregon[96] was hailed as a
significant turning-point; the third decade is regarded as a "reactionary" return to normalcy; during the last several years liberals with their ears to the ground have again detected pulsations
of hope. A closer analysis, however, of these three phases of the
period fails to reveal any striking contrasts.[97] Nor do they show
a unified line of growth. At the basis of their failure to achieve
direction lies the character of the finance-capitalist society in
which they have been working. Its pace of change in the field
of both corporate and human relations has been too rapid to
leave the earlier legal rules untouched, but too insecure to furnish a means of transforming them. It has ceased to be merely
a monopoly capitalism, but it has not yet articulated a technique
to control its new creatures, the giant corporation and the expanding credit structure. It has outgrown its complete imperviousness to the plight of the underlying classes, but has not yet
found a way of meeting either their demands or their requirements. The old individualistic controls are clearly a thing of the
past: to cling to them would involve drastic results for the entire economic structure. But pending a discovery of controls

[91] 156 U.S. 1 (1895).
[92] See Haines, *op. cit., supra* note 54, at c. VI; Hough, Due Process of Law—
Today (1919) 32 Harv. L. Rev. 218.
[93] See Freund, *Police Power, Public Policy and Constitutional Rights* (1904).
[94] See Walton Hamilton, "Freedom of Contract" (1931) 6 *Encyclopaedia of the
Social Sciences* 450; Roscoe Pound, Liberty of Contract (1909) 18 Yale L.J. 454;
Shulman, *op. cit., supra* note 50.
[95] See Boudin, *op. cit., supra* note 3; Haines, *op. cit., supra* note 54, at c. VII.
[96] 208 U.S. 412 (1908).
[97] For such analysis, see Boudin, *op. cit., supra* note 54, at c. XXXVIII, XXXIX.
The basis of Boudin's skepticism is partly the failure of the decisions to evidence any
intention on the part of the Court to declare any self-denying ordinances with regard to the judicial power; partly that even in the "liberal" decisions, the Court—
as regards the larger trends of the rule of reasonableness, or any *rule* for future
cases—was timid and even reactionary.

that will replace them the Court has waited for a crystallization of capitalist attitudes.[98] The tentativeness of this period has of course furnished the able and decisive minority group with a golden opportunity to influence the trend of decision. But a minority can work only interstitially,[99] and never against the grain of current economic development. Whether capitalist enterprise can crystallize its new purposes and perfect its techniques sufficiently to give the Court again a clear faith and an articulated ideology remains to be seen.

V

The nexus between the course of Supreme Court decision and the realities of American capitalism [100] poses some crucial problems as to the nature of the judicial process. It is upon this broader question that all our current theoretical interests in American constitutional law converge, for it is here that one approaches the dynamics of growth in the law. Contemporary American thought on this question is in the transitional stage attendant upon having shattered the old absolutes without having yet arrived at new formulations. It has rejected the rhetoric and the traditional mumbo-jumboism with which the reverent generations had invested the fundamental law. It finds it no longer possible to regard the judicial utterances as Delphic,[101] and takes an almost irreverent delight in uncovering the bonds that link Supreme Court justices to other human beings. The myths have fallen away. But the absence of myths does not constitute theory; it is at best merely preparation for it.

---

[98] The critics of the Court have in one respect uniformly done it an injustice. They have not recognized sufficiently the tremendous task that devolves upon the Court—once it is agreed that legislation is to be scrutinized at all—to make the legislation harmonize with the fundamental purposes of a capitalist economy. For these purposes are not always clear, even to industrialists and bankers. And in the confusion of counsel that characterizes present trends within business, the task of the Supreme Court is all the more difficult.

[99] That is, only within the limits set by the dominant institutions.

[100] This brings us back to the problem of the legal lag touched on *supra*. As a matter of fact, it might be said—if it were not so paradoxical—that there is less lag in the conservative decisions than in the liberal criticism of them—lag, that is, with regard to economic reality, and not with regard to enlightened opinion. It is often difficult for liberal minds to understand that the reality does not necessarily conform to their view of it.

[101] For the "discovery theory" of law, see Corwin, The "Higher Law" Background of American Constitutional Law (1928) 42 Harv. L. Rev. 149, 153.

It will be well to distinguish two aspects of contemporary thought on the Supreme Court and its economic relations. One has to do with the function that the Court decisions perform, the other with the forces determining them. The prevailing view of the function of the Court is thoroughly realistic. It sees the Court as a definite participant in the formation of public policy, often on matters of far-reaching economic and social importance. Viewed thus the Court through its power to veto legislation has also the power to channel economic activity. In that sense it has been often called a super-legislature, exercising powers tantamount to the legislative power, but more dangerously since it is not subject to the same popular control. The main contention here is sound, although the particular formulation it is given is often overstressed. Whether we shall call the Court a super-legislature or a super-judiciary has in reality only a propagandist relevance. Except from the standpoint of a separation-of-powers ideal or a shattering of intellectual myths it is of little import. But what is of great import is the fact that the Court has become through its exercise of the judicial power in the intricate context of contemporary capitalist society, a crucial agency of social control. As such it is part of our fabric of statesmanship and should be judged in terms of its incidence upon American life.

The second aspect of the problem relates to an adequate theory of judicial decision. The contemporary trend is to regard each judge as acting upon his own economic beliefs and his own preferences as to social policy, and as rationalizing or deliberately manipulating his legal views into conformity with his social views. This represents of course an extreme revulsion against the traditional view of the judge as objectively expounding a body of law that has some superior truth-sanction. It looks toward a complete and perhaps unfruitful atomism: tel juge, tel jugement. It would hold that the course of judicial decision is the sum of the personal choices of the judges, and that the policy of the Court is determined at any time by the chance concatenation of nine arbitrary wills. Side by side with this there is another trend toward a sort of environmentalism or economic determinism. While holding to the atomistic view of the judicial process, it emphasizes in each judge not the volitional and whimsical elements but the non-volitional and determined. It examines his early life, education, economic affiliations and property interests, and by a selective process with which every biographer is acquainted it shows the inevitable flow of what he is from what he has been. Both these approaches stress the compelling reality of the judge's views of social policy as over against his adherence to legal rules in determining his decision; in this respect they mark a change from the tendency a decade or more ago to make the antithesis one between logic and experience, between a mechanical adherence to stare decisis and a realistic awareness of the changing needs of the day.

Such a theory of the judicial process obviously contains much that is sound and fruitful along with elements that tend to be merely impressionistic. Its atomism derives probably from influences similar to those which led Justice Cardozo to focus his analysis of the Nature of the Judicial Process on the individual judge and the individual decision. Cardozo's discussion of the various intellectual procedures open to the judge comes dangerously close to a new Benthamism by which the isolated judge balances the compulsions of logic against the claims of philosophy and both against the persuasions of sociology. By a similar Benthamism in the current atomistic view the judge is made a lightning calculator not of competing intellectual methods but of his own desires and devices. Both views are helpful through their insistence that whatever influences the judicial decision must pass through the mind of the judge. But they do not take sufficient account of the fact that his mind is itself largely a social product, and that he is a judge within an economic system and an ideological milieu. Their influence is operative even when he is not applying the "method of sociology," or using law consciously as an instrument for social ends.

For the problem of the relation of capitalism to the Supreme Court the construction of a theory of judicial decision is of crucial importance. If the historical analysis presented in the last two sections is valid, much in the development of American constitutional law is explainable in terms of a developing capitalism. Such an influence, to be effective, would have had to be operative somehow on the minds of the judges, through whom alone constitutional law grows. But how? In what form and through what agencies have the effects of economic development been transmitted to the minds of the judges? The easiest answer of course would lie in a theory of pressures. But while this might be valid for some of the lower reaches of the American judiciary, it has no meaning at all for these men, who are placed by their exalted and permanent positions beyond the reach of corruption, as they are placed also beyond that of democratic control. A theory of interests is likely to be more valid. The judge is a member of an economic class, of a social grouping, of a geographical section. He shares their interests and will, even if unconsciously, direct his policy-forming function to their advantage. But unless this theory is broadened to include general ideological influences as well as direct interests, it will suffer from the oversimplified and mechanical interpretation that has been applied to the framing of the Constitution.

An adequate theory of the judicial process in the Supreme Court would have to take account of a number of factors. (1) The Court works first of all with a set of traditional and technical legal elements. It must stay within the framework of a Constitution, confine itself to the facts and issues of actual cases brought before it, observe and create for itself a body of procedure. It must maintain so much continuity with its own past decisions as to achieve the necessary minimum of legal certainty, and so much consistency with its own past reasoning as to make the body of constitutional law a somewhat orderly intellectual system. In the process it creates concepts and develops doctrines, such as due process, liberty of contract and police power, giving them thereby a directive force over its future decisions. There has been a tendency in recent thought to treat all these legal factors in the judicial process less as rules than as techniques—fairly flexible and accordingly subservient to the more deeply rooted purposes of the judges. (2) The Court works within a cultural and institutional framework which the justices share with their fellow citizens. They live in and are sworn to preserve a society which is the end-product of a historical growth but is also changing under their very fingers. This society is dominated by its capitalist system of economic organization and is therefore best viewed as a capitalist society. Its institutions and modes of thought are partly incorporated in the

Constitution, partly in the body of constitutional law, but are mainly resident in the life of the society itself. (3) The Court works in a world of ideas which the justices share with their fellow-men. These ideological elements—conceptions of human nature, human motive, social possibility and ethical values—may be "preconceptions" and therefore submerged in consciousness, or they may be avowedly held and deliberately applied. Many of them, such as the competitive ideal and the right of property, proceed from the economic world, those that do not, such as human nature, individualism and natural law, have nevertheless a definite bearing on economic problems; all of them are social products and are affected by changes in the social and economic structure. (4) There are personal and intellectual differences between the judges—differences of background, philosophy, social convictions and sympathies.

Of these factors the second and third groups—the world of social fact and the world of social idea—include and are conditioned by the nature of our economic life. The selection that any particular judge makes of them will constitute what Thomas Reed Powell has called the "logic" of his decision; the selection that he makes of the first group of factors—the legal tradition and technology—will constitute the "rhetoric" by which he supports and rationalizes his decision.[102] For an explanation of the main trend of constitutional decision we may therefore look to the institutional and ideological elements [103] that exercise their compulsive force on the minds of the judges,[104] and to the

---

[102] See T. R. Powell, "The Logic and Rhetoric of Constitutional Law" (1918) 15 *Journal of Philosophy, Psychology and Scientific Method* 645. This essay was one of the most important in shifting American juristic thought. The accepted theory of the judicial process had been that the judge was like the oracle of Jupiter at Dodona who, upon being presented with the problem that called for decision, stupefied himself with vapors and listened to the dim voices that came to him: or, in other words, that the judge brought to bear ancient lights to illumine modern instances. Professor Powell's emphasis was that the judge brought to bear his current outlook to manipulate the ancient rules.

[103] In constructing an explanation of how those ideological influences operate on the minds of the judges, we shall have to remember that the judges are in this respect no different from ordinary men. The formation of opinion through the operation of "stereotypes," elaborated by Graham Wallas, and also by Walter Lippman, *Public Opinion* (1930) would apply here also.

[104] Perhaps nowhere has this truth been more forcefully stated than in Justice Peckham's remarks about Lord Hale, in connection with Hale's statement of the "public interest" doctrine . . . "his views as to the policy and propriety of laws

changes wrought in these elements principally by economic development. For an explanation of the groupings within the Court, we may look to the variations in outlook and belief as between the individual members.

This raises a question about the Court which is as important for social action as for juristic theory. What technique can be employed for shifting and controlling the trend of the Court's decisions? What are the chances, for example, that the Court will reverse the secular trend of its decisions during the past half century and adopt an attitude toward private property that will tolerate experiments in the direction of a controlled and articulated economy? The contemporary emphasis on the judge's capacity to make his rhetoric march to the tune of his social beliefs has as corollary the view that the crucial concern, whether of liberals or conservatives, should be the selection of the right judges—a sort of eugenics program for the judicial process. It seems clear, however, that such a view is over optimistic. It stops at the judge and does not push its analysis to what it is that determines his view of life. The judge's convictions and social preferences run in terms of the current ideologies of his day; through those ideologies the operative economic forces and master trends of the period find their way into the Court's decisions. In such a sense it has been said that a period deserves whatever Supreme Court it gets—because it has created the judges in its own ideological image. A period in which capitalist enterprise is on the aggressive and the individualistic ideal sweeps everything before it is not likely to read anything but an individualistic philosophy into its constitutional law. A period like the present in which the individualistic ideal has been undermined by worldwide economic collapse is likely to be increasingly tol-

---

involving an interference with the private concerns of the subject were, of course, colored by the general ideas as to the proper function of government then existing. This great magistrate, it will be remembered, was a firm believer in the existence of witchcraft, and presided at the trials of old women accused of such crime, and condemned them to death on conviction thereof. I do not mention this as any evidence against the ability, integrity or learning of this upright man and able lawyer; but it is entirely conclusive of the truth of the statement that all men, however great and however honest, are almost necessarily affected by the general belief of their times, and that Lord Hale was not one of the few exceptions to this rule." People *v.* Budd, 117 N.Y. 1, 46 *et seq.*, 22 N.E. 670, 682 (1889).

erant of departures from an absolute conception of liberty or property.[105]

This does not involve, however, a rigorous determinism, either economic or ideological. The judicial process is not, as a too mechanical view might hold, powerless in the clutch of capitalist circumstance. The current institutions and ways of thought of a period determine only the larger outlines which the constitutional law of the period is likely to take. Within that framework there is room for a fairly wide selection and variation of emphasis. The Supreme Court effects a nexus between our fundamental law and our fundamental economic institutions. But by its very position as an agency of control it is powerful to change the contours of those institutions. The same constitutional fabric that contains the absolute individualism of Justice Sutherland gives scope also to the humanistic individualism of Justice Holmes, and the social constructivism of Justice Brandeis. The judicial process in the Supreme Court is no exception to the order of things everywhere. Within the limits set by its nature and function it can be carried on with creativeness and purpose or it can become merely a form of submission to the current drift.

---

[105] This is how I understand also E. S. Corwin's delightful Presidential address before the American Political Science Association, *op. cit., supra* note 45.

PART TWO

The Modern Constitution

CHAPTER FIVE

The Modern Court and Economic Legislation

T HIRTY YEARS AGO NO THOUGHTFUL LEGISLATOR WOULD HAVE proposed a new development in economic regulation without training a weather eye on the United States Supreme Court. Today he would almost be wasting his time if he expended more than a jot of it worrying about judicial review, unless the measure he advocated threatened to burden interstate commerce. Such is the measure of the revolution in constitutional doctrine which has taken place since the brave days when the Court was doing its impressive best to scuttle the New Deal.

Robert L. Stern's essay on "the problems of yesteryear" is a concise record of that revolution and an assessment of its outcome in revised constitutional standards. Those who were acquainted with the Court of the past but have neglected to follow its perambulations in recent years would no doubt be more startled by this essay than by any in the present volume, startled to realize how far the judiciary has retreated from its old position as a supervisor of the relation between government and the economy, how little is left of the prohibitory "rules" which once laid so many statutes low.

What does remain of yesterday's formidable negativisms? What limits does today's Court impose on economic legislation? Stern puts his finger on the threadbare remnants of judicial control in the fields of substantive due process and national commerce power. As for due process, the Court will approve any law which *might* have had a rational basis in the minds of the legislators who framed it. On its face, this standard may seem to constitute a potential restriction on lawmakers; in fact, the Court's willingness to infer a rational basis has been so great that it is hard to imagine a law unreasonable enough to earn judicial disapproval. Like its relative, the "beyond-rational-question" principle propounded by Thayer, this rubric is theoretically susceptible of a proscriptive interpretation. But the probability that it will be so interpreted by the present Court seems so far-fetched that we must regard substantive due process, at least for the time being, as no limitation at all on governmental power.

This conclusion is equally clear with respect to the commerce power of Congress. Under the criteria Stern spells out, Congress can reach just about any commercial subject it is likely to want to reach, untroubled by the fact that the Court of another era would have regarded many such subjects as purely local in character. As in the due process cases, there is a hint that some regulations might go too far, that some intrastate activities might be exempt from federal control because their effect on interstate commerce was not "substantial." But the Court has yet to discover an example of this exemption, and the strong inference seems to be that the constitutional distinction between intrastate and interstate commerce no longer has practical meaning.

The exception to all this can be found, as Stern points out, in the Court's continued supervision of state laws that threaten to interfere with national commerce. Yet even the cases in this field can be easily enough reconciled with the due process and national commerce power developments. For the Court has steadily adhered to the doctrine that Congress may, if it likes, preclude the states from any and all interferences with interstate commerce, or, by the same token, may permit interference that would otherwise be objectionable. In areas where Congress has not made such a declaration, the Court continues to perform its traditional function of "federal umpire." But it holds to that function only by congressional default; here, as elsewhere in economic matters, the Court acknowledges the superior authority of the legislative branch.

What is to be said for and against this policy of judicial self-abnegation in the economic sphere? On the affirmative side, we might single out for special consideration two arguments, both of which are at least inferentially raised by Mr. Stern's essay. In the first place, there is the point usually attributed to Mr. Justice Stone in United States *v.* Carolene Products Co., 304 U.S. 144, 152–3, n.4 (1938), i.e., that economic regulation requires less searching scrutiny than legislation that restricts the "political processes" simply because the persons adversely affected by economic regulation are free to work for its repeal. The beleaguered business man can take his case to the bar of public opinion rather than to the courts; the member of an oppressed political minority may find such a forum closed to him. Second, there is the related argument, implicit in most of the commerce and due process cases of recent years, that the judiciary is an inappropriate agency for making the complex economic judgments which regulatory policy involves. The Court's retreat from such mechanical tests as the "direct-indirect" standard in commerce cases and its adoption of more pragmatic formulae is really an admission that "technical legal conceptions" (which are, after all, the judiciary's stock-in-trade) are inadequate to control commercial relations. If technical legal criteria are to be superseded by practical evaluations about economics, it is difficult to see the Court as much more than a not-very-well-qualified third branch of the legislature. Recognizing that its competence in this field is highly problematic, the Court has contented itself with standards so broadly framed and tolerantly applied that they leave the whole matter to the discretion of the legitimate legislative power. If that power errs, it can be called to account by the people, spurred on by the normal processes of democratic government.

On the other hand, it can be argued that economic rights must be granted some measure of protection in every just political order. And to the suggestion that such rights are sufficiently protected by the free electoral process one might reply by quoting Mr. Justice Jackson's words:

> The very purpose of a Bill of Rights was to withdraw certain subjects from the vicissitudes of political controversy, to place them beyond the reach of majorities and officials and to establish them as legal principles to be applied by the courts. (West Virginia State Board of Education *v.* Barnette, 319 U.S. 624, 638 [1943].)

Admittedly, the judiciary is not likely to be over-burdened with expertise in the economic field, and it is therefore seemly that the judicial veto be sparingly employed. The constitutional distinction between interstate and intrastate commerce probably had to be sacrificed to meet the exigencies of the 20th-century. But, expert or not, the Supreme Court has inherited the task of defining the personal rights which are beyond the reach of officialdom. And while it may be proper to treat economic rights differently from others, that is no justification for failing to treat them at all. One of the principal concerns of the law, we are often told, is to establish distinctions of degree; but since 1937 the Supreme Court has appeared to deny that such distinctions are possible, holding, by implication, that there is no logical stopping place between the excessive concern for economic freedom of the Old Court and the almost total lack of concern suggested by the modern due process standards.

The Problems of Yesteryear—Commerce and Due Process

by Robert L. Stern *

Vanderbilt Law Review,
Volume 4, Page 446 (1951)

Less than fifteen years ago, there were constitutional problems important enough to stir the country, to threaten the sanctity of the Supreme Court. These were the culmination of at least three

* (1908–   ), Lawyer, author; Office of the Solicitor General, U.S. Department of Justice, 1941– .

decades of judicial controversy, in which the pressure of events brought criticism of the Court's decisions, both in noteworthy dissenting opinions and outside, to a new height. Fifteen years later, there still are difficult and important constitutional problems, and there still is criticism of the Supreme Court's decisions —though on a relatively minor scale. But the issues which rocked more than the legal world in the 1930's and in the period preceding have disappeared. A glance backwards to see what happened to them may help give perspective to the significance of the problems of the current day.

The crucial issue prior to 1937 was whether the Constitution prohibited government—state and Federal—from interfering with the free play of economic forces (outside of the field of public utilities)—no matter how great the public need. Federal legislation dealing with other phases of national or interstate industry than transportation was on important occasions found to invade the powers reserved to the states.[1] State laws were frequently found invalid because they impinged on the field of interstate commerce committed by the Constitution to the Federal Congress.[2] And the due process clauses of the Fifth and Fourteenth Amendments were held to bar both state and federal governments from regulating such economic factors as prices, wages, and labor relations in businesses "not affected with a public interest."[3]

---

[1] Carter *v.* Carter Coal Co., 298 U.S. 238, 56 Sup. Ct. 855, 80 L. Ed. 1160 (1936); United States *v.* Butler, 297 U.S. 1, 56 Sup. Ct. 312, 80 L. Ed. 477 (1936); Railroad Retirement Board *v.* Alton R.R., 295 U.S. 330, 55 Sup. Ct. 758, 79 L. Ed. 1468 (1935); Schechter Corp. *v.* United States, 295 U.S. 495, 55 Sup. Ct. 651, 79 L. Ed. 1570 (1935); United Mine Workers *v.* Coronado Coal Co., 259 U.S. 344, 42 Sup. Ct. 570, 66 L. Ed. 975 (1922); Hammer *v.* Dagenhart, 247 U.S. 251, 38 Sup. Ct. 529, 62 L. Ed. 1101 (1918); Hopkins *v.* United States, 171 U.S. 578, 19 Sup. Ct. 40, 43 L. Ed. 290 (1898); United States *v.* E. C. Knight Co., 156 U.S. 1, 15 Sup. Ct. 249, 39 L. Ed. 325 (1895).
[2] E.g., DiSanto *v.* Pennsylvania, 273 U.S. 34, 47 Sup. Ct. 267, 71 L. Ed. 524 (1927); Leisy *v.* Hardin, 135 U.S. 100, 10 Sup. Ct. 681, 34 L. Ed. 128 (1890). The cases up to 1932 are collected in Gavit, *The Commerce Clause* 551–6, Appendix E (1932).
[3] Morehead *v.* New York ex rel. Tipaldo, 298 U.S. 587, 56 Sup. Ct. 918, 80 L. Ed. 1347 (1936); New State Ice Co. *v.* Liebmann, 285 U.S. 262, 52 Sup. Ct. 371, 76 L. Ed. 747 (1932); Williams *v.* Standard Oil Co., 278 U.S. 235, 49 Sup. Ct. 115, 73 L. Ed. 287 (1929); Ribnik *v.* McBride, 277 U.S. 350, 48 Sup. Ct. 545, 72 L. Ed. 913 (1928); Tyson & Brother *v.* Banton, 273 U.S. 418, 47 Sup. Ct. 426, 71 L. Ed. 718 (1927); Adkins *v.* Children's Hospital, 261 U.S. 525, 43 Sup. Ct. 394, 67 L. Ed. 785 (1923); Charles Wolff Packing Co. *v.* Court of Industrial Relations, 262 U.S. 522, 43 Sup. Ct. 630, 67 L. Ed. 1103 (1923); Adams *v.* Tanner,

There were, of course, cases which ran counter to these general trends [4] and which seemed to offer hope that the Court would relax its restrictions. But as late as 1936 the Court was still holding that labor relations in the coal industry only affected interstate commerce "indirectly," and therefore were not subject to the power of Congress,[5] that the amount of cotton produced in the United States was only of local concern and therefore not subject to federal control; [6] and that the fixing of minimum wages for women violated the due process clause.[7] These decisions, and the doctrines for which they stand, now seem antediluvian. Although they hardly can be said to be of great antiquity, they have a much less modern ring and infinitely less authority than Gibbons *v.* Ogden,[8] decided in 1824.

As all who remember the spring of 1937 in the Supreme Court will recall, the great reversal in constitutional adjudication took place prior to any change in the personnel of the Court—shortly after President Roosevelt announced his plan to add six new Justices to the Supreme Court. This is not the occasion to explore the details of that fascinating period, a story which has often been told elsewhere.[9] Suffice it to say that as new Justices began ascending the bench during the following terms, the principles of

---

244 U.S. 590, 37 Sup. Ct. 662, 61 L. Ed. 1336 (1917); Coppage *v.* Kansas, 236 U.S. 1, 35 Sup. Ct. 240, 59 L. Ed. 441 (1915); Adair *v.* United States, 208 U.S. 161, 28 Sup. Ct. 277, 52 L. Ed. 436 (1908); Lochner *v.* New York, 198 U.S. 45, 25 Sup. Ct. 539, 49 L. Ed. 937 (1905).

[4] *Commerce cases:* Local 167 *v.* United States, 291 U.S. 293, 54 Sup. Ct. 396, 78 L. Ed. 804 (1934); Coronado Coal Co. *v.* United Mine Workers, 268 U.S. 295, 45 Sup. Ct. 551, 69 L. Ed. 963 (1925); Chicago Board of Trade *v.* Olsen, 262 U.S. 1, 43 Sup. Ct. 470, 67 L. Ed. 839 (1923); Stafford *v.* Wallace, 258 U.S. 495, 42 Sup. Ct. 397, 66 L. Ed. 735 (1922); Standard Oil Co. *v.* United States, 221 U.S. 1, 31 Sup. Ct. 502, 55 L. Ed. 619 (1911); Swift & Co. *v.* United States, 196 U.S. 375, 25 Sup. Ct. 276, 49 L. Ed. 518 (1905. *Due process cases:* Nebbia *v.* New York, 291 U.S. 502, 54 Sup. Ct. 92, 78 L. Ed. 940 (1934); O'Gorman & Young *v.* Hartford Fire Ins. Co. 282 U.S. 251, 51 Sup. Ct. 130, 75 L. Ed. 324 (1931); Texas & New Orleans R. R. *v.* Brotherhood of Railway Clerks, 281 U.S. 548, 50 Sup. Ct. 427, 74 L. Ed. 1034 (1930).

[5] Carter *v.* Carter Coal Co., 298 U.S. 238, 56 Sup. Ct. 855, 80 L. Ed. 1160 (1936).

[6] United States *v.* Butler, 297 U.S. 1, 56 Sup. Ct. 312, 80 L. Ed. 477 (1936).

[7] Morehead *v.* New York ex rel. Tipaldo, 298 U.S. 587, 56 Sup. Ct. 918, 80 L. Ed. 1347 (1936).

[8] 9 Wheat. 1, 6 L. Ed. 23 (1824).

[9] E.g., Jackson, *The Struggle for Judicial Supremacy* (1941); Stern, The Commerce Clause and the National Economy, 1933–1946, 59 Harv. L. Rev. 645, 883 (1946).

the 1937 decisions came to be firmly entrenched. The four original dissenters—Justices Van Devanter, Sutherland, Butler, and McReynolds—were quickly reduced to the latter two by voluntary retirement, and then to none. And although the new Court in turn has divided into groups sometimes labeled—accurately or inaccurately—as "conservative" and "liberal," there has seldom been any difference of opinion as to any of the old fighting issues. For a time, cases requiring interpretation of the doctrines finally accepted in 1937 continued to reach the Court. These cases enabled the Court to flesh out the content of the newly accepted— if not newly invented [10]—doctrines. But in recent years fewer and fewer such cases have been heard by the Court, both because most lawyers have probably realized the futility of waging the useless battle any longer, and because, except in very unusual situations, the Court refuses to hear most such cases when attorneys do attempt to bring them up. Only cases on the periphery of the "new" doctrines are now likely to arouse the interest of the Court.

A brief discussion of the principles which the Court now applies, and of the cases since 1937, will indicate both the extent to which the subjects are no longer regarded as controversial and the locality of the present borderline of uncertainty.

1. *Substantive Due Process*

In a series of decisions prior to 1930, the Supreme Court had held that the "liberty" guaranteed by the due process clause included liberty to contract, and that except in "business affected with a public interest," governmental interference with such essential economic relationships as prices and wages was an infringement of that liberty.[11] Since the validity of many restrictions upon the freedom of business men was sustained,[12] the only general rule which could be drawn from the decisions was that types of

---

[10] Some of the "new" doctrines can be traced back to John Marshall. See p. 171 *infra*.

[11] See cases cited in note 3 *supra*.

[12] E.g., the antitrust laws, zoning laws, banking and insurance laws, laws relating to conservation, workmen's compensation, health and safety, laws designed to protect the public against deception and fraud.

regulation of which the Court sufficiently disapproved were unconstitutional.

Although the Nebbia case in 1934,[13] in which Mr. Justice Roberts joined Chief Justice Hughes and Justices Brandeis, Stone, and Cardozo in sustaining a New York statute fixing minimum prices for milk, seemed to presage a departure from this rule, Morehead v. Tipaldo,[14] in 1936, saw Mr. Justice Roberts joining the conservative Justices to nullify the New York minimum wage law, on the disputable ground that overruling of Adkins v. Children's Hospital[15] had not been specifically requested. In 1937, however, he rejoined the liberal Justices to overrule the Adkins case and uphold the validity of the Washington minimum wage legislation in West Coast Hotel Co. v. Parrish.[16] On the same day and two weeks later the provisions of the Railway Labor Act and the National Labor Relations Act, requiring employers to bargain exclusively with the representatives chosen by a majority of the employees, were held not to violate the due process clause[17]—decisions clearly inconsistent with Adair v. United States[18] and Coppage v. Kansas[19] decided in 1908 and 1915.

The 1937 decisions declared that regulatory legislation would not be found to violate the due process clause merely because it restricted economic liberty. Only restrictions which were in fact arbitrary, or not reasonably related to a proper legislative purpose, it was suggested, would be held unconstitutional in the future. Subsequently, in the Carolene Products case, the Court, through Mr. Justice Stone, stated:

[T]he existence of facts supporting the legislative judgment is to be presumed, for regulatory legislation affecting ordinary commercial transactions is not to be pronounced unconstitutional unless in the light of the facts made known or generally assumed it is of

[13] Nebbia v. New York, 291 U.S. 502, 54 Sup. Ct. 505, 78 L. Ed. 940 (1934).
[14] 298 U.S. 587, 56 Sup. Ct. 918, 80 L. Ed. 1347 (1936).
[15] 261 U.S. 525, 43 Sup. Ct. 394, 67 L. Ed. 785 (1923).
[16] 300 U.S. 379, 57 Sup. Ct. 578, 81 L. Ed. 703 (1937).
[17] Virginian Ry. v. System Federation No. 40, 300 U.S. 515, 57 Sup. Ct. 592, 81 L. Ed. 789 (1937); National Labor Relations Board v. Jones & Laughlin Steel Corp., 301 U.S. 1, 57 Sup. Ct. 615, 81 L. Ed. 893 (1937).
[18] 236 U.S. 1, 35 Sup. Ct. 240, 59 L. Ed. 441 (1915).
[19] 208 U.S. 161, 28 Sup. Ct. 277, 52 L. Ed. 436 (1908).

such a character as to preclude the assumption that it rests upon some rational basis within the knowledge and experience of the legislators. . . .

[B]y their very nature such inquiries, where the legislative judgment is drawn in question, must be restricted to the issue whether any state of facts either known or which could reasonably be assumed affords support for it. . . .[20]

Since it is difficult to conceive of any statute for which some rational basis may not be found, this test means that the due process barrier to substantive legislation as to economic matters has been in effect removed—although it still stands in theory against completely arbitrary legislative action.

As might be expected, under this doctrine no statutes have been held violative of the due process clause on grounds of substantive irrationality since 1937. In 1939 and 1940, the Court sustained federal statutes fixing prices of milk and coal,[21] in 1941 the minimum wage provisions of the Fair Labor Standards Act,[22] and in 1944 the general price and rent provisions of the Emergency Price Control Act.[23] Olsen v. Nebraska,[24] which upheld a state law regulating the fees fixed by employment agencies, explicitly repudiated "the philosophy and approach of the majority" of the Court in the pre-Nebbia price fixing cases. And Lincoln Union v. Northwestern Iron Co.,[25] in sustaining state laws prohibiting the closed shop, made it clear that this principle would be applied to laws restricting the freedom to contract of employees as well as employers. In other cases, the Court has disposed summarily of the contention that statutes were in violation of the due process clause because they interfered with economic freedom or were otherwise unreasonable.[26]

---

[20] United States v. Carolene Products Co., 304 U.S. 144, 152, 154, 58 Sup. Ct. 778, 82 L. Ed. 1234 (1938).
[21] United States v. Rock Royal Co-Op., 307 U.S. 533, 59 Sup. Ct. 993, 83 L. Ed. 1446 (1939); Sunshine Anthracite Coal Co. v. Adkins, 310 U.S. 381, 60 Sup. Ct. 907, 84 L. Ed. 1263 (1940).
[22] United States v. Darby, 312 U.S. 100, 61 Sup. Ct. 451, 85 L. Ed. 609 (1941).
[23] Yakus v. United States, 321 U.S. 414, 64 Sup. Ct. 660, 88 L. Ed. 834 (1944); Bowles v. Willingham, 321 U.S. 503, 64 Sup. Ct. 641, 88 L. Ed. 892 (1944).
[24] 313 U.S. 236, 61 Sup. Ct. 862, 85 L. Ed. 1305 (1941).
[25] 335 U.S. 525, 69 Sup. Ct. 251, 93 L. Ed. 212 (1949).
[26] Cities Service Oil Co. v. Peerless Oil & Gas Co., 340 U.S. 179, 186, 71 Sup. Ct. 215 (1950); Railway Express Agency v. United States, 336 U.S. 106, 109, 69 Sup. Ct. 463, 93 L. Ed. 533 (1949); Sage Stores v. Kansas, 323 U.S. 32, 36, 65

Although there is no longer doubt as to how the Court will decide cases of this sort, it cannot be said that the Court has limited the due process clause to procedural matters and repudiated the concept of due process as a bar to sufficiently arbitrary or irrational substantive legislation—although Mr. Justice Black's opinion in the Lincoln Union case looks strongly in that direction. The Court has certainly not so stated in express terms, and the opinions still continue to examine legislation under attack to see whether it has a rational basis or is "substantially related to a legitimate end sought to be attained." [27] But, as the Court recently declared, "a pronounced shift of emphasis . . . has deprived the words 'unreasonable' and 'arbitrary' of the content" which they formerly held.[28] The self-abnegation with which the Court now applies the rationality test may, as a practical matter, make it unnecessary for the Court to decide whether it must reconsider the basic doctrine.

Recent decisions have given the due process clause broad scope in protecting against state action the rights guaranteed by the First Amendment and also other "fundamental" rights contained in the first eight amendments.[29] Certainly the rights to freedom of speech, press, and religion are not "procedural" in the ordinary sense. The due process clause would thus seem still to be interpreted as embodying a restriction which is substantive rather than procedural—but in an orbit entirely different from that of the older cases. Significantly, in the field of civil liberties, the test is not whether there is a rational basis for legislation. Instead, since the due process clause is held to embody the content of the First Amendment, the legislation may be required to sustain the heavier burden imposed upon laws

Sup. Ct. 9, 89 L. Ed. 25 (1944); Carolene Products Co. *v.* United States, 323 U.S. 18, 29, 65 Sup. Ct. 1, 89 L. Ed. 15 (1944); Railroad Commission *v.* Rowan & Nichols Oil Co., 311 U.S. 570, 61 Sup. Ct. 343, 85 L. Ed. 358 (1941); Railroad Commission *v.* Rowan & Nichols Oil Co., 310 U.S. 573, 60 Sup. Ct. 613, 84 L. Ed. 1368 (1940), *as amended,* 311 U.S. 614, 61 Sup. Ct. 66, 85 L. Ed. 390 (1940); Mayo *v.* Lakeland Highlands Canning Co., 309 U.S. 310, 318, 60 Sup. Ct. 517, 84 L. Ed. 774 (1940).

[27] E.g., Cities Service Oil Co. *v.* Peerless Oil & Gas Co., 340 U.S. 179, 186, 71 Sup. Ct. 215 (1950).

[28] Daniel *v.* Family Security Life Ins. Co., 336 U.S. 220, 225, 69 Sup. Ct. 550, 93 L. Ed. 632 (1949).

[29] For an apt exposition of this, see Freund, *On Understanding the Supreme Court,* c. 1 (1949).

restricting First Amendment freedoms.[30] These problems are beyond the scope of this paper. They are suggested here only because of their bearing upon the presently unanswerable question as to the extent to which the due process clauses have been deprived of force as restrictions upon substantive law.

II. *State Power to Regulate Interstate Commerce* [31]

Since Gibbons *v.* Ogden,[32] and Cooley *v.* Board of Wardens,[33] it has been established that under the commerce clause some subjects of regulation are within the exclusive power of Congress, and that even in the absence of a showing of congressional intention some types of state laws are invalid. This has not meant that the states were deprived by the commerce clause of all power to enact measures affecting, or even directly regulating, interstate commerce. But at some point, when the national, as compared to the local, interest in the subject was sufficiently great, when the practical burden on interstate commerce became sufficiently clear, the Court has always drawn a line beyond which the states could not go.

The test applied in drawing this line has been expressed in various ways. In the Cooley case, the first authoritative formulation of the accepted doctrine, the Court declared:

Now the power to regulate commerce, embraces a vast field, containing not only many, but exceedingly various subjects, quite unlike in their nature; some imperatively demanding a single uniform rule, operating equally on the commerce of the United States in every port; and some, like the subject now in question, as imperatively demanding that diversity, which alone can meet the local necessities of navigation.

Either absolutely to affirm, or deny that the nature of this

---

[30] See Nietmotko *v.* Maryland, 340 U.S. 268, 71 Sup. Ct. 325 (1951); Kunz *v.* New York, 340 U.S. 290, 71 Sup. Ct. 312 (1951); Feiner *v.* New York, 340 U.S. 315, 71 Sup. Ct. 303 (1951); Kovacs *v.* Cooper, 336 U.S. 77, 69 Sup. Ct. 448, 93 L. Ed. 513 (1949); Saia *v.* New York, 334 U.S. 558, 68 Sup. Ct. 1148, 92 L. Ed. 1574 (1948), 2 Vand. L. Rev. 113, Thomas *v.* Collins, 323 U.S. 516, 65 Sup. Ct. 315, 89 L. Ed. 430 (1945), in which the prior authorities are collected and discussed.

[31] [This footnote omitted—ed.]

[32] 9 Wheat. 1, 6 L. Ed. 23 (1824).

[33] 12 How. 299, 13 L. Ed. 996 (1852).

power requires exclusive legislation by Congress, is to lose sight of the nature of the subjects of this power, and to assert concerning all of them, what is really applicable but to a part. Whatever subjects of this power are in their nature national, or admit only of one uniform system, or plan of regulation, may justly be said to be of such a nature as to require exclusive legislation by Congress.[34]

In some cases, this doctrine is regarded as "predicated upon the implications of the commerce clause itself," in others "upon the presumed intention of Congress, where Congress has not spoken." [35] Whatever the theory, the result is the same.

In the years preceding 1937, the Court, without ever openly abandoning the Cooley test, used many other expressions—such as whether the state law was a "burden," or a "substantial" or "undue" burden, on commerce, whether the effect on commerce was "direct" or "indirect," whether the regulation was or was not imposed "on" interstate commerce itself. It was difficult, if not impossible, to tell—at least with any certainty—whether these expressions merely constituted different methods of stating the Cooley doctrine, or whether the Court was applying different tests. The only generalization which could be drawn from the numerous decisions and expressions was, approximately in the words of my mentor on this subject,[36] that the states may regulate interstate commerce some, but not too much. Under this not very definite test, a great many state laws were held invalid.[37]

The principal change since 1937 has not been in the formula but in its application. For a number of years thereafter no non-discriminatory [38] state regulations fell afoul of the commerce

---

[34] 12 How. at 319.

[35] Southern Pacific Co. *v.* Arizona, 325 U.S. 761, 768, 65 Sup. Ct. 1515, 89 L. Ed. 1915 (1945), citing cases; California *v.* Zook, 336 U.S. 725, 728, 69 Sup. Ct. 841, 93 L. Ed. 1005 (1949).

[36] Professor Thomas Reed Powell of Harvard Law School.

[37] See the compilation in Appendix E to Gavit, *The Commerce Clause* 550–56 (1932). This tabulation shows that during the decade 1921–1930, 38 state laws (both tax and regulatory) were found invalid under the commerce clause. Between 1941 and 1950 there were ten such decisions, of which five involved state taxes. Of the remaining five cases, three were concerned with statutes which would be regarded as discriminating against interstate commerce (see p. 162 *infra*). The remaining two cases are the Southern Pacific and Morgan cases, discussed immediately below in the text.

[38] As to laws discriminating against interstate commerce, see p. 162 *et seq.*

clause. Justice Black expressed the view that the Cooley doctrine itself went too far in limiting state power; he preferred the theory of Chief Justice Taney that only Congress, and not the courts, could invalidate stage legislation.[39] There was doubt as to whether the Court would find any nondiscriminatory state law in conflict with the commerce clause itself.

Southern Pacific Co. *v.* Arizona,[40] decided in 1945, and Morgan *v.* Virginia,[41] in 1946, not only resolved the doubt, but marked a definite reassertion of the principle of the Cooley case. In doing so, the Court, speaking through Chief Justice Stone and following the thoughts expressed in his earlier opinions,[42] made explicit the considerations which would guide it in applying that principle. The test was a practical one, in which the actual effect upon interstate or national interests was weighed against the local or state interest involved. State laws limiting the number of cars on railroad trains and requiring the segregation of passengers in interstate busses were found to impinge upon commerce in fields in which national uniformity .was essential. In the one instance the make-up of trains, and in the other the seating arrangement in busses was subject to disturbance at every state line if differing state regulations were permissible. On the other hand, state laws having a lesser impact upon interstate transportation, such as a requirement that cabooses be placed at the end of freight trains,[43] were upheld. The competing national interest has not been deemed sufficiently clear to prevent the states from fixing prices for natural gas and milk sold within a state for outside consumption, even though the direct effect was to raise prices for extrastate consumers.[44]

---

[39] See opinions of Mr. Justice Black, dissenting in Southern Pacific Co. *v.* Arizona, 325 U.S. 761, 784, 65 Sup. Ct. 1515, 89 L. Ed. 1915 (1945); concurring in Morgan *v.* Virginia, 328 U.S. 373, 386, 66 Sup. Ct. 1050, 90 L. Ed. 1317 (1946); dissenting in Hood & Sons *v.* DuMond, 336 U.S. 525, 545, 553, 69 Sup. Ct. 657, 93 L. Ed. 865 (1949). For Taney's views, see Frankfurter, *The Commerce Clause Under Marshall, Taney and Waite,* c. 2 (1937).

[40] 325 U.S. 761, 65 Sup. Ct. 1515, 89 L. Ed. 1915 (1945).

[41] 328 U.S. 373, 66 Sup. Ct. 1050, 90 L. Ed. 1317 (1946).

[42] E.g., DiSanto *v.* Pennsylvania, 273 U.S. 34, 44, 47 Sup. Ct. 267, 71 L. Ed. 524 (1927) (dissent).

[43] Terminal Railroad Ass'n *v.* Brotherhood of Railroad Trainmen, 318 U.S. 1, 63 Sup. Ct. 420, 87 L. Ed. 571 (1943).

[44] Cities Service Oil Co. *v.* Peerless Oil & Gas Co. 340 U.S. 179, 71 Sup. Ct. 215 (1950); Milk Control Board *v.* Eisenberg, 306 U.S. 346, 59 Sup. Ct. 528, 83 L. Ed. 752 (1939).

Whether the decisions last cited would be applied to commodities generally, which did not present the problems peculiar to natural gas and milk, cannot be foretold.

The recent cases seem to integrate the "need for uniformity" principle of the Cooley case and the "undue burden" formula appearing in later decisions with the statements requiring the weighing of conflicting local and national interests. In some sentences in the opinions, the first two concepts are stated in the alternative. Thus, in the Southern Pacific case, the Court declared that the states lack "authority to impede substantially the free flow of commerce from state to state, or to regulate those phases of the national commerce which, because of the need of national uniformity, demand that their regulation, if any, be prescribed by a single authority." [45] In the Morgan case, these two ideas—if they are two—are interwoven in Mr. Justice Reed's statement that "state legislation is invalid if it unduly burdens that commerce in matters where uniformity is necessary." [46] In California v. Zook,[47] the balancing of state and national interests is treated as a more accurate statement of the Cooley rule: "if a case falls within an area in commerce thought to demand a uniform national rule, state action is struck down. If the activity is one of predominantly local interest, state action is sustained. More accurately, the question is whether the state interest is outweighed by a national interest in the unhampered operation of interstate commerce." [48] These cases—and others [49] —recognize that the Court exercises a practical judgment in balancing the national interest against the local interest in each case.

Most recently, in December 1950, a unanimous Court, speaking through Mr. Justice Clark in Cities Service Gas Co. v. Peerless Oil & Gas Co.,[50] restated the governing principle as follows:

---

[45] 325 U.S. at 767.

[46] 328 U.S. at 377.

[47] 336 U.S. 725, 69 Sup. Ct. 841, 93 L. Ed. 1005 (1949).

[48] 336 U.S. at 728.

[49] Bob-Lo Excursion Co. v. Michigan, 333 U.S. 28, 37–40, 68 Sup. Ct. 358, 92 L. Ed. 455 (1948); Union Brokerage Co. v. Jensen, 322 U.S. 202, 211, 64 Sup. Ct. 967, 88 L. Ed. 1227 (1944); Illinois Natural Gas Co. v. Central Ill. Pub. Serv. Co., 314 U.S. 498, 506, 62 Sup. Ct. 384, 86 L. Ed. 371 (1942).

[50] 340 U.S. 179, 71 Sup. Ct. 215 (1950).

It is now well settled that a state may regulate matters of local concern over which federal authority has not been exercised, even though the regulation has some impact on interstate commerce. . . . The only requirements consistently recognized have been that the regulation not discriminate against or place an embargo on interstate commerce, that it safeguard an obvious state interest, and that the local interest at stake outweigh whatever national interest there might be in the prevention of state restrictions.[51]

It is likely—though not at all certain—that the Court will apply the same test whether the direct impact of the state law burdening interstate commerce is upon interstate or intrastate transactions. In Parker *v.* Brown,[52] the question presented was whether California regulation of the intrastate marketing of the bulk of the national crop of raisins before they were processed for interstate sale and shipment was prohibited by the commerce clause. The Court, speaking through Mr. Justice Stone, held that whether the proper rule was the "mechanical test" applied in some earlier cases, under which a state law was invalid if it regulated interstate—but not intrastate—commerce, or the balance of interest rule based upon an "accommodation of the competing demands of the state and national interest involved," [53] the state law was valid. But the reference to the first test as "mechanical" strongly suggests that the Court thought such an approach an artificial one, which it would not favor if forced to a choice. The Parker decision cannot properly be appraised without reference to the fact that California's program had been approved and financed by the Secretary of Agriculture pursuant to congressional agricultural policy. The Court has subsequently cast some doubt as to whether, apart from this factor, the decision would have been the same.[54] And indeed, it is certainly arguable that the national commercial interest should prevent a state producing most of a commodity distributed throughout the nation from limiting the quantity produced or marketed in order

---

[51] 340 U.S. at 186–87.
[52] 317 U.S. 341, 63 Sup. Ct. 307, 87 L. Ed. 315 (1943).
[53] 317 U.S. at 362.
[54] Hood & Sons *v.* DuMond, 336 U.S. 525, 537, 69 Sup. Ct. 657, 93 L. Ed. 865 (1949), 3 Vand. L. Rev. 113.

to raise the price to consumers.[55] But, at least where the state is seeking to conserve a limited national resource, the state's authority seems to be definitely established.[56]

Both the Southern Pacific and the Morgan cases significantly rejected the contention that a state may avoid the limitations of the general doctrine of the Cooley case by "simply invoking the convenient apologetics of the police power," [57] in the former as a means of preventing accidents, and in the latter to avert possible friction between races. Although a great many cases have upheld state laws relating to safety, even as applied to interstate transportation,[58] the Court pointed to other safety regulations held invalid when the burden upon interstate commerce became unduly great.[59] State regulation of the weight and width of motor trucks on interstate highways, which concededly "materially interfered with interstate commerce," [60] was differentiated on the ground that the highways were built, maintained, and policed by the states and were, therefore, of peculiar local concern, or, more accurately, constituted a subject over which "the state has exceptional scope for the exercise of its regulatory power." [61]

The conclusion to be drawn from these recent cases is that the Court has returned to the historical Cooley doctrine, but has articulated more candidly than in the older cases what it takes into consideration in applying that principle. It is probably also true that, with respect to most subjects, a heavier burden than formerly is placed upon the party seeking to establish that the state legislation improperly burdens interstate commerce.

The discussion up to this point has assumed that the state legislation involved does not discriminate against interstate com-

---

[55] See p. 163 *infra.*
[56] Cities Service Gas Co. *v.* Peerless Oil & Gas Co. 340 U.S. 179, 71 Sup. Ct. 215 (1950); Champlin Refining Co. *v.* Corporation Commission, 286 U.S. 210, 52 Sup. Ct. 559, 76 L. Ed. 1062 (1932); see Note, 64 Harv. L. Rev. 642 (1951).
[57] Southern Pacific case, 325 U.S. at 780; Morgan case, 328 U.S. at 380; quoting from Mr. Justice Holmes in Kansas City Southern Ry. *v.* Kaw Valley Drainage Dist., 233 U.S. 75, 79, 34 Sup. Ct. 564, 58 L. Ed. 857 (1914).
[58] See cases collected in Southern Pacific, 325 U.S. at 779, and in Morgan, 328 U.S. at 378-9.
[59] *Ibid.*
[60] Southern Pacific Co. *v.* Arizona, 325 U.S. 761, 783, 65 Sup. Ct. 1515, 89 L. Ed. 1915 (1945).
[61] *Ibid.* The leading cases distinguished were South Carolina Highway Dep't *v.* Barnwell Bros., 303 U.S. 177, 58 Sup. Ct. 510, 82 L. Ed. 734 (1938); and Maurer *v.* Hamilton, 309 U.S. 598, 60 Sup. Ct. 726, 84 L. Ed. 969 (1940).

merce. Even Mr. Justice Black seems to agree that a state law imposing greater burdens on interstate commerce than on local commerce is repugnant to the commerce clause.[62] State laws designed to keep a resource or to favor a business within the state, to benefit that state at the expense of other states, have also consistently been held invalid, at least when the injury to other states was substantial.[63] A recent example is the South Carolina statute held invalid in Toomer *v.* Witsell,[64] which required vessels catching shrimp in South Carolina waters to unload, pack and stamp their catch at a South Carolina port before shipment to other states. A California law designed to exclude indigent immigrants from other states would also seem to fall in the same category.[65] Such statutes can be regarded as discriminatory—though the results in the cases are also justifiable under the "uniformity" or "undue burden" theories discussed above.

In Hood & Sons *v.* Du Mond,[66] decided in 1949, the Court divided sharply as to whether in order to prevent depletion of the supply available within the state, and to avoid destructive competition, New York could refuse to permit a Massachusetts local distributor to open an additional receiving plant from which milk could be taken from New York. The majority treated the case as one in which a state was favoring home consumers and competitors against those in other states, and thus condemned the New York regulation as discriminating against, as well as burdening, interstate commerce. The majority opinion of Mr. Justice Jackson declares that the basic historical purpose of the commerce clause was to prevent each state from seeking economic advantage at the expense of the other states.[67] The four dissenting Justices asserted that the Court's decision was a de-

---

[62] See his dissent in Hood & Sons *v.* DuMond, 336 U.S. 525, 549, 556, 69 Sup. Ct. 657, 93 L. Ed. 865 (1949), in which he refers to Best & Co. *v.* Maxwell, 311 U.S. 454, 61 Sup. Ct. 334, 85 L. Ed. 275 (1940), an opinion in which he joined, and his earlier dissent in Gwin, White & Price *v.* Henneford, 305 U.S. 434, 446, 455, 59 Sup. Ct. 325, 83 L. Ed. 272 (1939). *But cf.* his dissents in Toomer *v.* Witsell, 334 U.S. 385, 407, 68 Sup. Ct. 1157, 92 L. Ed. 1460 (1948); and Dean Milk Co. *v.* Madison, 340 U.S. 349, 357, 71 Sup. Ct. 295 (1951).

[63] See cases cited in Hood & Sons *v.* Du Mond, 336 U.S. 535–37, 69 Sup. Ct. 657, 93 L. Ed. 865 (1949).

[64] 334 U.S. 385, 403, 68 Sup. Ct. 1157, 92 L. Ed. 1460 (1948).

[65] Edwards *v.* California, 314 U.S. 160, 62 Sup. Ct. 164, 86 L. Ed. 119 (1941).

[66] 336 U.S. 525, 69 Sup. Ct. 657, 93 L. Ed. 865 (1949), 3 Vand. L. Rev. 113.

[67] 336 U.S. at 532–39.

parture from the fundamental principle of the Cooley case. Mr. Justice Black thought the decision a reinvigoration of the Court's former tendency improperly to restrict the authority of the states to regulate business.[68] Mr. Justice Frankfurter believed that further inquiry into the facts was essential to determine how the competing state and national interests should be balanced.[69]

It is true that the opinion of Mr. Justice Jackson, for the Court, does not follow the Cooley approach, or even cite any of the cases in which the doctrine has been approved and applied. But since he himself, along with most of the Justices who joined with him, had joined in the leading opinions accepting the Cooley principle, it is doubtful if he, or they, regarded the Hood decision as an abandonment of the basic doctrine. It seems much more likely, in view of the language of the opinion and the facts of the case, that the majority believed that the case came within the exceptional category for discriminatory state regulations, and also that such an assertion of state power, from its very nature, imposed a burden on interstate commerce which was necessarily "undue," since it was precisely the type of regulation which the framers meant most clearly to prohibit.[70] Although the case may have been a close one on its facts, it seems clear

---

[68] See *id*. at 562–64, particularly.

[69] *Id*. at 576.

[70] "The material success that has come to inhabitants of the states which make up this federal free trade unit has been the most impressive in the history of commerce, but the established interdependence of the states only emphasizes the necessity of protecting interstate movement of goods against local burdens and repressions. We need only consider the consequences if each of the few states that produce copper, lead, high-grade iron ore, timber, cotton, oil, or gas should decree that industries located in that state shall have priority. What fantastic rivalries and dislocations and reprisals would ensue if such practices were begun! Or suppose that the field of discrimination and retaliation be industry. May Michigan provide that automobiles cannot be taken out of that State until local dealers' demands are fully met? Would she not have every argument in the favor of such a statute that can be offered in support of New York's limiting sales of milk for out-of-state shipment to protect the economic interests of her competing dealers and local consumers? Could Ohio then pounce upon the rubber-tire industry, on which she has a substantial grip, or retaliate for Michigan's auto monopoly?

"Our system, fostered by the Commerce Clause, is that every farmer and every craftsman shall be encouraged to produce by the certainty that he will have free access to every market in the Nation, that no home embargoes will withhold his exports, and no foreign state will by customs duties or regulations exclude them. Likewise, every consumer may look to the free competition from every producing area in the Nation to protect him from exploitation by any. Such was the vision of the Founders; such has been the doctrine of this Court which has given it reality." 336 U.S. at 538–9.

that it was not meant to be the forerunner of any new general doctrine. The subsequent Cities Service case, decided in the following year by a unanimous Court, including, of course, Mr. Justice Jackson, reaffirms the Cooley doctrine and states:

> The vice in the regulation invalidated by Hood was solely that it denied facilities to a company in interstate commerce on the articulated ground that such facilities would divert milk supplies needed by local consumers; in other words, the *regulation discriminated against interstate commerce*.[71]

The most recent case on the subject is both interesting and significant. Madison, Wisconsin, required all milk consumed within the city to be pasteurized within five miles of the center of the town. This excluded milk from the Dean Milk Company's pasteurization plants in Illinois, 65 and 85 miles away. Although the ordinance doubtless favored local business, its avowed and undenied purpose was to facilitate inspection by the local health department; it was certainly more convenient and economical for Madison not to send its inspectors far afield. In Dean Milk Co. *v.* Madison,[72] decided January 15, 1951, the Court, speaking through Mr. Justice Clark, held the ordinance to be an unlawful discrimination against interstate commerce. The Court assumed that, apart from the discrimination, the subject lay within the sphere of state regulation, despite its effect upon interstate commerce. But it concluded that, "an economic barrier protecting a major local industry against competition from without the state" was not permissible "even in the exercise of [a city's] unquestioned power to protect the health and safety of its people, if reasonable non-discriminatory alternatives, adequate to conserve legitimate local interests, are available."[73] The Court then found that "reasonable and adequate alternatives are available,"[74] since Madison could charge the cost of inspection of distant milk plants to the pasteurizer, or could rely on inspection by local officials in other areas whose standards of inspection were so graded by the United States Public Health Service

---

[71] Cities Service Gas Co. *v.* Peerless Oil & Gas Co. 340 U.S. 179, 188, 71 Sup. Ct. 215 (1950). [Italics supplied.]

[72] 340 U.S. 349, 71 Sup. Ct. 295 (1951).

[73] 340 U.S. at 354.

[74] *Ibid.*

as to enable Madison to determine whether its own standards were satisfied. Both Madison and Wisconsin health officials had testified in the case that this system gave consumers adequate protection. The court concluded that to permit Madison to adopt a regulation of this sort when "not essential for the protection of local health interests . . . would invite a multiplication of preferential trade areas destructive of the very purpose of the Commerce Clause." [75]

Mr. Justice Black, with Justices Douglas and Minton concurring, dissented on the grounds that a good faith health regulation applicable both to interstate and intrastate pasteurizers was not a discrimination against interstate commerce, and that in any event, the Court should not "strike down local health regulations unless satisfied beyond a reasonable doubt" that the available substitutes "would not lower health standards." [76]

The Dean Milk decision, seemingly for the first time, applies to a local law found to discriminate against interstate commerce the technique of balancing the respective local and national interests employed in other cases in which local regulations are said to burden commerce, though with a reversed presumption. In the absence of discrimination, the Court tends to sustain the state action unless interference with commerce is clear and the local interest not very substantial; where there is discrimination, the Dean case holds, it must appear that there is no other reasonable method of safeguarding a legitimate local interest.[77] Where a state law has no other purpose than to favor local industry, this balancing of interest approach probably will not be used, inasmuch as the purpose of the state regulation would be illegitimate.

The early cases invalidating state laws requiring local inspection in such a way as to exclude products from distant sources —Minnesota v. Barber [78] and Brimmer v. Rebman [79]—had adopted a less flexible approach. But where no discriminatory purpose is apparent, and where both interstate and intrastate imports

---

[75] *Id.* at 356.
[76] *Id.* at 357, 359.
[77] See Braden, Umpire to the Federal System, 10 U. of Chi. L. Rev. 27, 30 (1942).
[78] 136 U.S. 313, 10 Sup. Ct. 862, 34 L. Ed. 455 (1890).
[79] 138 U.S. 78, 11 Sup. Ct. 213, 34 L. Ed. 862 (1891).

from over five miles away are excluded, it is not too clear whether the regulation can properly be said to "discriminate" against interstate commerce. And even if such a regulation be properly classified as discriminatory for commerce clause purposes, the local need might be so overpowering as to completely outweigh, for the particular situation, the national interest in a market not restricted by state lines.[80] It is thus reasonable in such cases to employ the same practical approach as when a state law interferes with but does not technically discriminate against interstate commerce. The justification for shifting the burden is that an actual prohibition of all interstate but not of all local trade is, on its face, what the commerce clause was designed to prevent, and therefore to be countenanced only when the local need in the particular case can plainly be shown to be greater than the interest in nation-wide free trade upon which the economy and welfare of this nation largely rest.

Basic to the Court's premise is the view, with which the minority seem to disagree, that a local regulation which prohibited both interstate and intrastate trade—shipments from pasteurization plants more than five miles from the city—discriminated against interstate commerce. With respect to this, the majority merely stated, "It is immaterial that Wisconsin milk from outside the Madison area is subjected to the same proscription as that moved in interstate commerce. Cf. Brimmer *v.* Rebman, 138 U.S. 78, 82–83 (1891)."[81] Brimmer *v.* Rebman does appear to be directly in point, since the state law there involved prohibited the sale of all meat slaughtered more than one hundred miles from the place of sale, unless locally inspected, while not requiring the inspection of other meat. As a matter of semantics, however, it cannot be said with certainty that a state regulation of this sort is "discriminatory." It excludes some intrastate trade, along with the interstate; on the other hand, it excludes all interstate. Nevertheless, the purpose of the commerce clause would be effectively frustrated by a multitude of munic-

---

[80] Thus, if pasteurized milk should become unsafe for human consumption in the time necessary to transport it more than a specified distance, the local interest in protecting the health of its people would seem to overbalance, even from the standpoint of the nation as a whole, the advantages of interstate trade in milk from more distant points.

[81] 340 U.S. at 354 n.4.

ipal trade barriers of this sort, even though they discriminated against some intrastate trade along with the interstate. Accordingly, it seems reasonable for the Court to treat such regulations as discriminatory—or at least to require their proponents to justify them by proof of actual and serious local necessity, as distinct from local economic advantage and convenience.

The principles and cases heretofore discussed have been concerned with the effect of the commerce clause itself upon state laws, in the absence of any federal regulation. Since the Constitution vests the power to regulate interstate commerce in the Congress, there cannot be—or at least there should not be [82] —any doubt as to the overriding authority of Congress to determine what the states may or may not regulate in the field subject to congressional control. The Southern Pacific case states in express terms that Congress "may either permit the states to regulate the commerce in a manner which would otherwise not be permissible . . . or exclude state regulation even of matters of peculiarly local concern which nevertheless affect interstate commerce" (citing cases).[83] In 1949, in California *v.* Zook,[84] the Court reiterated that "despite theoretical inconsistency with the rationale of the Commerce Clause as a limitation in its own right, the words of the Clause—a grant of power [to Congress]—admit of no other result." [85] These statements as to the supremacy of the congressional will when Congress breaks its silence were amplified in the exhaustive opinion of Mr. Justice Rutledge, speaking for a unanimous Court, in Prudential Insurance Co. *v.* Benjamin,[86] which sustained the authority of Congress to permit the states to regulate interstate commerce in insurance.

---

[82] Writers have found logical difficulty in reconciling the conception of the commerce clause as forbidding state action by its own force with the power of Congress to consent to otherwise invalid state regulation. See Biklé, The Silence of Congress, 41 Harv. L. Rev. 200 (1927); Powell, The Validity of State Legislation Under the Webb-Kenyon Law, 2 So. L.Q. 112 (1917); Dowling, Interstate Commerce and State Power—Revised Version, 47 Col. L. Rev. 547, 552–60 (1947). But "The Supreme Court has not been concerned in its opinions with the theoretical difficulties." Rutledge, *A Declaration of Legal Faith* 64 n.26 (Univ. of Kan. Press, 1947).

[83] 325 U.S. at 769.

[84] 336 U.S. 725, 69 Sup. Ct. 841, 93 L. Ed. 1005 (1949).

[85] 336 U.S. at 728.

[86] 328 U.S. 408, 66 Sup. Ct. 1142, 90 L. Ed. 1342 (1946).

This paper will not deal with the problem of supersedure or "occupancy of the field"—that is, when state regulation is invalidated or superseded by congressional action under the commerce clause (or any other clause). Although this is often regarded as a constitutional question, since there is no doubt as to the supremacy of federal legislation the issue in each case relates to the intention of Congress, actual or presumed. The problem is thus more akin to statutory construction than to the constitutional matters considered in this symposium. In each case the question to be determined is whether a state law is inconsistent with what Congress has said, or with the accomplishment of the purpose of Congress, or with what can be deduced as to what Congress intends when the federal statute is not explicit. It seems sufficient here to cite the leading recent cases on the subject for the reader who might wish to explore the matter further.[87]

III. *The Commerce Power of Congress*

The burning issue of the 1930's was the extent of the regulatory power of Congress under the commerce clause. Long prior to that time, in the Shreveport Rate case [88] and many others, the Court had recognized that under the commerce power, Congress could regulate intrastate transactions which were sufficiently related to interstate commerce, which affected it "directly" but not "indirectly." [89] But the development of this

---

[87] International Union of Automobile Workers *v.* O'Brien, 339 U.S. 454, 70 Sup. Ct. 781, 94 L. Ed. 978 (1950); United Automobile Workers *v.* Wisconsin Employment Relations Board, 336 U.S. 245, 69 Sup. Ct. 516, 93 L. Ed. 651 (1949); California *v.* Zook, 336 U.S. 725, 69 Sup. Ct. 841, 93 L. Ed. 1005 (1949); Bethlehem Steel Co. *v.* New York State Labor Board, 330 U.S. 767, 67 Sup. Ct. 1026, 91 L. Ed. 1234 (1947); Rice *v.* Santa Fe Elevator Co., 331 U.S. 218, 67 Sup. Ct. 1146, 91 L. Ed. 1447 (1947); First Iowa Hydro-Electric Co-op *v.* Federal Power Commission, 328 U.S. 152, 66 Sup. Ct. 906, 90 L. Ed. 1143 (1946). See note, "Occupation of the Field" in Commerce Clause Cases, 1936–1946: Ten Years of Federalism, 60 Harv. L. Rev. 262 (1946). And see Amalgamated Ass'n. of Street, Elec. Ry., & M.C. Employees *v.* Wisconsin Employment Relations Board, 340 U.S. 383, 71 Sup. Ct. 359 (1951).

[88] Houston E. & W. T. Ry. *v.* United States, 234 U.S. 342, 34 Sup. Ct. 833, 58 L. Ed. 1341 (1914).

[89] Local 167 *v.* United States, 291 U.S. 293, 54 Sup. Ct. 396, 78 L. Ed. 804 (1934); Coronado Coal Co. *v.* United Mine Workers, 268 U.S. 295, 45 Sup. Ct. 551, 9 L. Ed. 963 (1925); Chicago Board of Trade *v.* Olsen, 262 U.S. 1, 43 Sup. Ct. 470, 67 L. Ed. 839 (1923); Stafford *v.* Wallace, 258 U.S. 495. 42 Sup. Ct. 397, 66 L. Ed. 735 (1922); Railroad Comm'n of Wisconsin *v.* Chicago B. & Q. R.R.,

principle was blocked by an opposing doctrine that certain activities, notably those occurring in the process of producing commodities to be shipped in commerce, were "local" by their very nature, and thus exclusively subject to state authority under the Tenth Amendment.[90] The Court reconciled this theory with the "affecting commerce" doctrine by finding that no matter how close the actual factual relationship, production affected commerce only "indirectly." This line of decisions reached its climax, and conclusion, in the Carter Coal case in 1936,[91] which held that labor relations in the coal industry only had an indirect effect upon interstate commerce, even though a coal strike might halt not only all interstate shipments of coal but a large proportion of the interstate movement of everything else as well.

The well-known story of how, in the following term, the Court abandoned this approach and has since given full scope to the power of Congress to regulate intrastate activities which in fact had a substantial relationship to interstate commerce has been told elsewhere.[92] There is no occasion for repeating it here.

The test presently applied has been stated in various ways. Wickard *v.* Filburn [93] declared that "even if appellee's activity be local and though it may not be regarded as commerce, it may still whatever its nature, be reached by Congress if it exerts a *substantial economic effect* on interstate commerce, and this ir-

---

257 U.S. 563 42 Sup. Ct. 232, 66 L. Ed. 373 (1922); United States *v.* Patten, 226 U.S. 525, 33 Sup. Ct. 141, 57 L. Ed. 333 (1913); Southern Ry. *v.* United States, 222 U.S. 20, 32 Sup. Ct. 2, 56 L. Ed. 72 (1911); Swift & Co. *v.* United States, 196 U.S. 375, 25 Sup. Ct. 276, 49 L. Ed. 518 (1905).

[90] See cases cited in note 1, *supra;* Utah Power and Light Co. *v.* Pfost, 286 U.S. 165, 52 Sup. Ct. 548 76 L. Ed. 1038 (1932); Industrial Ass'n *v.* United States, 268 U.S. 64, 45 Sup. Ct. 403, 69 L. Ed. 849 (1925); Oliver Iron Mining Company *v.* Lord, 262 U.S. 172 43 Sup. Ct. 526, 67 L. Ed. 929 (1923); Heisler *v.* Thomas Colliery Co., 260 U.S. 245, 43 Sup. Ct. 83, 67 L. Ed. 237 (1922); Kidd *v.* Pearson, 128 U.S. 1, 9 Sup. Ct. 6, 32 L. Ed. 346 (1888); Veazie *v.* Moor, 14 How. 567, 14 L. Ed. 545 (1852). Although many of these cases involve state legislation, they were treated as authoritative with respect to the power of Congress during the period in question.

[91] Carter *v.* Carter Coal Co., 298 U.S. 238, 56 Sup. Ct. 855, 80 L. Ed. 1160 (1936).

[92] See particularly, the discussion in Mandeville Island Farms *v.* American Crystal Sugar Co., 334 U.S. 219, 229–35, 68 Sup. Ct. 996, 92 L. Ed. 1328 (1948); Wickard *v.* Filburn, 317 U.S. 111, 119–25, 63 Sup. Ct. 82, 87 L. Ed. 122 (1942); Stern, The Commerce Clause and the National Economy, 1933–1946, 59 Harv. L. Rev. 645, 883 (1946).

[93] 317 U.S. 111, 63 Sup. Ct. 82, 87 L. Ed. 122 (1942).

respective of whether such effect is what might at some earlier time have been defined as 'direct' or 'indirect.' " [94] Mr. Justice Jackson's opinion also quotes from the opinion of Mr. Justice Stone in United States *v.* Wrightwood Dairy Co., that "the reach of that power extends to those intrastate activities which *in a substantial way* interfere with or obstruct the exercise of the granted power." [95] The Mandeville Farms case refers to "practical impeding effects" upon commerce,[96] and also declared that: "The essence of the affectation doctrine was that the exact location of this line made no difference, if the forbidden effects flowed across it to the injury of interstate commerce or to the hindrance or defeat of congressional policy regarding it." [97]

These statements still appear to treat the test as one of degree, which does not substantially differ in terms from the former "direct-indirect" formula, except that the standard of judgment is not the same and all non-factual artificial restrictions upon application of the test have been removed. But in these opinions, as well as others, the Court has not relied primarily on these quantitative formulas but has gone back to basic constitutional principles first enunciated by Chief Justice Marshall. In the Mandeville case, Mr. Justice Rutledge pointed out that "the 'affectation' approach was actually a revival of Marshall's 'necessary and proper' doctrine," [98] that is, of the necessary and proper clause of the Constitution itself. The classical expression in McCulloch *v.* Maryland,[99] that "let the end be legitimate, let it be within the scope of the Constitution, and all means which are appropriate, which are plainly adapted to that end, which are not prohibited, but consistent with the letter and spirit of the Constitution, are constitutional," is plainly the source of the statement by Mr. Justice Stone in the Darby [100] and Wrightwood Dairy cases,[101] reiterated by Mr. Jus-

---

[94] 317 U.S. at 125. [Italics supplied.]
[95] *Id.* at 125, quoting from United States *v.* Wrightwood Dairy Co., 315 U.S. 110, 119, 62 Sup. Ct. 523, 86 L. Ed. 726 (1942). [Italics supplied.]
[96] 334 U.S. 219, 233, 68 Sup. Ct. 996, 92 L. Ed. 1328 (1948).
[97] 334 U.S. at 232.
[98] *Id.* at 232.
[99] 4 Wheat. 316, 421, 4 L. Ed. 579 (1819).
[100] United States *v.* Darby, 312 U.S. 100, 121, 61 Sup. Ct. 451, 85 L. Ed. 609 (1941).
[101] United States *v.* Wrightwood Dairy, 315 U.S. 110, 119, 62 Sup. Ct. 523, 86 L. Ed. 126 (1942).

tice Jackson in Wickard *v.* Filburn,[102] that the commerce power "extends to those activities intrastate which so affect interstate commerce, or the exertion of the power of Congress over it, as to make regulation of them appropriate means to the attainment of a legitimate end, the effective execution of the granted power to regulate interstate commerce."

Other leading decisions have returned to the language of Chief Justice Marshall in Gibbons *v.* Ogden,[103] and have emphasized the function of the commerce clause as the practical instrument by which multi-state problems, not susceptible of solution by any single state, were to be subjected to the authority of the only governmental agency capable of dealing with them. In the insurance case, United States *v.* South-Eastern Underwriters [104] the Court, speaking through Mr. Justice Black,[105] declared, quoting from Gibbons *v.* Ogden, that "Commerce is interstate, he said, when it 'concerns more States than one.' . . . No decision of this Court has ever questioned this as too comprehensive a description of the subject matter of the Commerce Clause." [106]

In the case sustaining the validity of the so-called death sentence provision for public utility holding companies, North American Co. *v.* SEC,[107] the Court reaffirmed this practical concept, saying—

> This broad commerce clause does not operate so as to render the nation powerless to defend itself against economic forces that Congress decrees inimical or destructive of the national economy. Rather it is an affirmative power commensurate with the national needs. . . . And in using this great power, Congress is not bound by technical legal conceptions. Commerce itself is an intensely practical matter. *Swift & Co. v. United States,* 196 U.S. 375, 398. . . . To deal with it effectively, Congress must be able to act in terms of

---

[102] 317 U.S. 111, 124, 63 Sup. Ct. 82, 87 L. Ed. 122 (1942).

[103] 9 Wheat. 1, 6 L. Ed. 23 (1824).

[104] 322 U.S. 533, 64 Sup. Ct. 1162, 88 L. Ed. 1440 (1944).

[105] Although this was a 4 to 3 decision, the dissents did not relate to the constitutional issue, or to the constitutional principles set forth in the majority opinion. See Polish National Alliance *v.* NLRB, 322 U.S. 643, 64 Sup. Ct. 1196, 88 L. Ed. 1509 (1944).

[106] 322 U.S. at 551.

[107] 327 U.S. 686, 66 Sup. Ct. 784, 90 L. Ed. 945 (1946).

economic and financial realities. The commerce clause gives it authority so to act. . . . Once it is established that the evil concerns or affects commerce in more states than one, Congress may act. . . .[108]

Since the North American opinion also states that the commerce "power permits Congress to attack an evil directly at its source provided that the evil bears a *substantial* relationship to interstate commerce," [109] it is apparent that the Court does not regard the general principle enunciated in that case as inconsistent with the need for determining the question of degree referred to in some of the other recent cases—whether or not the relationship of the intrastate transaction or regulation to interstate commerce is sufficiently substantial. Indeed, no formulation of a test which requires the exercise of judgment in drawing a line can avoid the necessity for determining such questions of degree. But the cases since 1937 demonstrate not only that the Court will examine the question before it pragmatically, but that it will accord the greatest of weight to the congressional determination that the relationship to interstate commerce is sufficiently close.

The relationship between the intrastate transaction and interstate commerce may take a number of forms. The simplest is actual interference with the physical movement of goods interstate, such as may result from a strike caused by an unfair labor practice or a boycott in violation of the Sherman Act.[110] A physical effect may be that of floods in a nonnavigable tributary upon navigation, or other commercial activities, downstream.[111] Where there is a physical commingling of interstate and intrastate products and activities, the whole may be regulated.[112] And the same is true of economic commingling in a

---

[108] 327 U.S. at 705–06.

[109] *Id.* at 705.

[110] Consolidated Edison Co. *v.* NLRB, 305 U.S. 197, 221–22, 59 Sup. Ct. 206, 83 L. Ed. 126 (1938); NLRB *v.* Jones & Laughlin Steel Corp., 301 U.S. 1, 57 Sup. Ct. 615, 81 L. Ed. 893 (1937); Local 167 *v.* United States, 291 U.S. 293, 54 Sup. Ct. 396, 78 L. Ed. 804 (1934).

[111] Oklahoma ex rel. Phillips *v.* Guy F. Atkinson Co., 313 U.S. 508, 61 Sup. Ct. 1050, 85 L. Ed. 1487 (1941).

[112] Currin *v.* Wallace, 306 U.S. 1, 59 Sup. Ct. 379, 83 L. Ed. 441 (1939); Mulford *v.* Smith, 307 U.S. 38, 59 Sup. Ct. 648, 83 L. Ed. 1092 (1939).

market in which interstate and intrastate transactions are inseparable.[113] The effect may be upon interstate competition, by di-
verting the interstate flow from one competitor to another as
through unlawful restraint in violation of the antitrust laws,[114]
or substandard labor conditions forbidden by the Fair Labor
Standards Act,[115] or where an intrastate price cutter could take
business away from an interstate competitor whose prices were
fixed.[116] The relationship between the supply of a commority
available for interstate shipment and the amount produced
permits regulation of the quantity manufactured or grown,
as in the statutes fixing agricultural quotas.[117] Intrastate practices
affecting interstate prices, such as the cornering of a market or
the control of the intrastate price for raw materials or processes,
are proper objects of federal regulation.[118] Intrastate acts which
result in interstate shipments of noxious or unsafe articles,[119] or
of products which will cause economic or other injury in the
state of destination, may be controlled.[120] The Public Utility
Holding Company Act is in part justified as a means of preventing evils which are spread and perpetuated through the channels
of interstate commerce.[121] More generally, intrastate transactions

---

[113] United States *v.* Wrightwood Dairy Co., 315 U.S. 110, 62 Sup. Ct. 523,
86 L. Ed. 726 (1942); Houston, E. & W. T. Ry. *v.* United States, 234 U.S. 342,
34 Sup. Ct. 833, 58 L. Ed. 1341 (1914).

[114] Federal Trade Commission *v.* Morton Salt Co., 334 U.S. 37, 68 Sup. Ct.
822, 92 L. Ed. 1196 (1948); International Salt Co. *v.* United States, 332 U.S. 392,
68 Sup. Ct. 12, 92 L. Ed. 20 (1947); Local 167 *v.* United States, 291 U.S. 293,
54 Sup. Ct. 396, 78 L. Ed. 804 (1934).

[115] United States *v.* Darby, 312 U.S. 100, 122, 61 Sup. Ct. 451, 85 L. Ed. 609
(1941).

[116] United States *v.* Wrightwood Dairy Co. 315 U.S. 110, 62 Sup. Ct. 523, 86.
L. Ed. 726 (1942).

[117] Wickard *v.* Filburn, 317 U.S. 111, 63 Sup. Ct. 82, 87 L. Ed. 122 (1942).

[118] United States *v.* Women's Sportswear Ass'n, 336 U.S. 460, 69 Sup. Ct.
714, 93 L. Ed. 805 (1949); Mandeville Island Farms *v.* American Crystal Sugar
Co., 334 U.S. 219, 68 Sup. Ct. 996, 92 L. Ed. 1328 (1948); Chicago Board of
Trade *v.* Olsen, 262 U.S. 1, 43 Sup. Ct. 470, 67 L. Ed. 839 (1923); United States *v.*
Patten, 226 U.S. 525, 33 Sup. Ct. 141, 57 L. Ed. 333 (1913).

[119] E.g., Meat Inspection Act, 34 Stat. 1260 (1908, 21 U.S.C.A. §§ 71 *et seq.*
(1927).

[120] United States *v.* Darby, 312 U.S. 100, 61 Sup. Ct. 451, 85 L. Ed. 609
(1941); Kentucky Whip & Collar Co. *v.* Illinois Cent. R.R., 299 U.S. 334, 57 Sup.
Ct. 277, 81 L. Ed. 270 (1937).

[121] North American Co. *v.* SEC, 327 U.S. 686, 66 Sup. Ct. 784, 90 L. Ed. 945
(1946); American Power & Light Co. *v.* SEC, 329 U.S. 90, 67 Sup. Ct. 133, 91 L.
Ed. 103 (1946).

may be regulated when reasonably necessary to the control of interstate movements,[122] or to the effectuation of the purpose for which such movements may be controlled.[123]

A brief reference to some of the recent decisions will show how these principles have been applied.

The original Labor Board cases of 1937 [124] established the power of Congress to regulate labor relations in factories which receive raw materials and ship the goods they produce into other states. Subsequent cases held the Act applicable to processors of products grown within the state but shipped outside [125] and to a small manufacturer who delivered finished products within the state to their owner for shipment.[126] The Sherman Act has also been held to reach conbinations of contractors in a single city who raised prices for manufacturing operations on goods assembled and shipped interstate by local jobbers.[127] It was in this case that Mr. Justice Jackson stated: "If it is interstate commerce that feels the pinch, it does not matter how local the operation which applies the squeeze." [128]

The leading case under the Fair Labor Standards Act held it applicable to a manufacturer of a raw material for sale in interstate commerce, both on the ground that the regulation of wages at the factory helped keep goods made under substandard conditions out of commerce and because such conditions in themselves affect interstate competition.[129] The statute was subsequently held to extend to employees in a building tenanted principally by corporations producing for interstate com-

---

[122] United States *v.* Darby, 312 U.S. 100, 61 Sup. Ct. 451, 85 L. Ed. 609 (1941).
    [123] United States *v.* Sullivan, 332 U.S. 689, 68 Sup. Ct. 331, 92 L. Ed. 297 (1948); McDermott *v.* Wisconsin, 228 U.S. 115, 33 Sup. Ct. 431, 57 L. Ed. 754 (1913).
    [124] NLRB *v.* Jones & Laughlin Steel Corp., 301 U.S. 1, 57 Sup. Ct. 615, 81 L. Ed. 893 (1937); NLRB *v.* Fruehauf Trailer Co., 301 U.S. 49, 57 Sup. Ct. 642, 81 L. Ed. 918 (1937); NLRB *v.* Friedman–Harry Marks Clothing Co., 301 U.S. 58, 57 Sup. Ct. 642, 81 L. Ed. 921 (1937).
    [125] Santa Cruz Fruit Packing Co. *v.* NLRB, 303 U.S. 58 Sup. Ct. 656, 82 L. Ed. 954 (1938).
    [126] NLRB *v.* Fainblatt, 306 U.S. 601, 59 Sup. Ct. 668, 83 L. Ed. 1014 (1939).
    [127] United States *v.* Women's Sportswear Manufacturers Ass'n, 336 U.S. 460, 69 Sup. Ct. 714, 93 L. Ed. 805 (1949).
    [128] 336 U.S. at 464.
    [129] United States *v.* Darby, 312 U.S. 100, 61 Sup. Ct. 451, 85 L. Ed. 609 (1941).

merce,[180] to watchmen and window cleaners in factories producing for commerce even when employed by an independent contractor,[131] to a contractor who drilled oil wells for others with knowledge that any oil produced would move interstate,[132] to employees of a small newspaper with a regular circulation of 45 copies, or one half of one per cent, outside the state.[133]

Perhaps the most sweeping of all the cases holding activity in the field of production subject to the commerce power is Wickard v. Filburn,[134] which sustained the allocation of wheat quotas even to farmers who consumed their own crops in the form of food, livestock feed and seed. More recently, the Sherman Act was held to reach a scheme by manufacturers in a single state to fix the prices paid farmers in the same state for their beets, on the ground that the prices so fixed would inevitably affect the interstate price of refined sugar.[135]

All of these cases involved transactions occurring before commerce began. The Court has also held that the federal power extends to intrastate acts after commerce has ceased. When, in United States v. Sullivan,[136] a retail druggist was prosecuted for selling improperly labeled pills which, though previously shipped in interstate commerce, had been purchased by him within the state and held for nine months, the court disposed of the commerce question summarily by reference to the early case of McDermott v. Wisconsin.[137] That case had barred Wisconsin from substituting for the federal interstate label its own label for use by the retail store, on the ground that the purpose of the regulation of interstate labeling would be frustrated if the label were removed before the product reached the ultimate

---

[180] Kirschbaum Co. v. Walling, 316 U.S. 517, 62 Sup. Ct. 1116, 86 L. Ed. 1638 (1942).

[131] Martino v. Michigan Window Cleaning Co. 327 U.S. 173, 66 Sup. Ct. 379, 90 L. Ed. 603 (1946); Walton v. Southern Package Corp., 320 U.S. 540, 64 Sup. Ct. 320, 88 L. Ed. 298 (1944).

[132] Warren-Bradshaw Drilling Co. v. Hall, 317 U.S. 88, 63 Sup. Ct. 125, 87 L. Ed. 83 (1942).

[133] Mabee v. White Plains Publishing Co., 327 U.S. 178, 66 Sup. Ct. 511, 90 L. Ed. 607 (1946).

[134] 317 U.S. 111, 63 Sup. Ct. 82, 87 L. Ed. 122 (1942).

[135] Mandeville Island Farms Co. v. American Crystal Sugar Co., 334 U.S. 219, 68 Sup. Ct. 996, 92 L. Ed. 1328 (1948).

[136] 332 U.S. 689, 68 Sup. Ct. 331, 92 L. Ed. 297 (1948).

[137] 228 U.S. 115, 33 Sup. Ct. 431, 57 L. Ed. 754 (1913).

consumer. The National Labor Relations Act has also been held to reach large retail stores;[138] for reasons of policy the Board has refrained from bringing cases against smaller retail outlets.[139] At the time this was written, the Supreme Court had before it the application of the Taft-Hartley Act to union restraints in local building operations where some of the building materials have come from without the state.[140] The antitrust laws have also been held to reach a scheme to fix retail prices when the means adopted reach beyond state boundaries.[141]

The courts have also recognized the inseparability of interstate industry by sustaining regulatory provisions which in isolation seem to have little to do with interstate commerce. An extreme example is Egan *v.* United States,[142] which upheld the provision of the Public Utility Holding Company Act prohibiting registered holding companies (by which is meant companies engaged in interstate commerce, *inter alia*) from making contributions to persons running for state or local political office. The court of appeals reasoned that Congress could rationally conclude that such expenditures might affect or burden interstate commerce through their impact upon rates, and might also demonstrate a lack of economy in management and operation which would be injurious to investors and consumers; [143] the Supreme Court denied certiorari.[144] The Court has also removed the pre-existing barrier—or at least what many persons thought was a barrier—to the exercise of the commerce power over the

---

[138] Loveman, Joseph & Loeb *v.* NLRB, 146 F.2d 769 (5th Cir. 1945); J. L. Brandeis & Sons *v.* NLRB, 142 F.2d 977 (8th Cir. 1944), *cert. denied,* 323 U.S. 751 (1944); NLRB *v.* M. E. Blatt Co., 143 F. 2d 268 (3d Cir. 1943), *cert. denied,* 323 U.S. 774 (1944); NLRB *v.* J. L. Hudson Co., 135 F.2d 380 (6th Cir. 1943), *cert. denied,* 320 U.S. 740 (1943); NLRB *v.* Kudile, 130 F.2d 615 (3d Cir. 1942), *cert. denied,* 317 U.S. 694 (1943); NLRB *v.* Suburban Lumber Co., 121 F.2d 829 (3d Cir. 1941), *cert. denied,* 314 U.S. 693 (1941).

[139] See NLRB announcement, October 3, 1950, 19 U.S.L. Week 2147 (1950).

[140] NLRB *v.* Local 74, 181 F.2d 126 (6th Cir. 1950), *cert. granted,* 340 U.S. 902 (1950); International Brotherhood of Electrical Workers *v.* NLRB, 181 F.2d 34 (2d Cir. 1950), *cert. granted,* 340 U.S. 902 (1950); NLRB *v.* Denver Building & Construction Trades Council, 186 F.2d 326 (D.C. Cir. 1950), *cert. granted,* 340 U.S. 902 (1950). All of these cases were argued on February 26 and 27, 1951.

[141] United States *v.* Frankfort Distilleries, 324 U.S. 293, 65 Sup. Ct. 661, 89 L. Ed. 951 (1945).

[142] 137 F.2d 369 (8th Cir. 1943), *cert. denied,* 320 U.S. 788 (1943).

[143] *Id.* at 374–75.

[144] 320 U.S. 788 (1943).

world of finance by holding that insurance companies were engaged in interstate commerce.[145]

These cases, which indicate roughly the present scope of the power of Congress under the commerce clause, justify two general observations. Industry organized on a national scale, all the operations of which are inevitably economically interrelated, will not be compartmentalized into interstate and local segments, the former subject exclusively to federal control and the latter exclusively to state regulation. The Court no longer construes the Constitution as requiring a division for governmental purposes of what is in fact inseparable.[146]

The cases also demonstrate that it is unnecessary to judge merely the effect on commerce of the individual transaction or person involved in the particular case. The amount of wheat produced by a single farmer, or a single sale of drugs by a retailer, obviously would not affect interstate commerce substantially, or even noticeably. But Congress is entitled to take into account the total effect of many small transactions. "The total effect of the competition of many small producers may be great." [147] In Wickard v. Filburn,[148] the Court noted: "That appellee's own contribution to the demand for wheat may be trivial by itself is not enough to remove him from the scope of federal regulation where, as here, his contribution, taken together with that of many others similarly situated, is far from trivial."

It may be true that the application of the principles now approved by the Supreme Court may leave only minor aspects of our economy free from the regulatory power of Congress. The reason for this, however, is not legal but economic. If, in fact, the interstate and intrastate features of American business are inseparable, it would be crippling to require an artificial separa-

---

[145] United States v. South-Eastern Underwriters, 322 U.S. 533, 64 Sup. Ct. 1162, 88 L. Ed. 1440 (1944); Polish National Alliance v. NLRB, 322 U.S. 643, 64 Sup. Ct. 1196, 88 L. Ed. 1509 (1944).

[146] See particularly, Mandeville Island Farms v. American Crystal Sugar Co., 334 U.S. 219, 68 Sup. Ct. 996, 92 L. Ed. 1328 (1948); Wickard v. Filburn, 317 U.S. 111, 63 Sup. Ct. 82, 87 L. Ed. 122 (1942).

[147] United States v. Darby, 312 U.S. 100, 123, 61 Sup. Ct. 451, 85 L. Ed. 609 (1941).

[148] 317 U.S. 111, 127–28, 63 Sup. Ct. 82, 87 L. Ed. 122 (1942). See also Polish National Alliance v. NLRB, 322 U.S. 643, 648, 64 Sup. Ct. 1196, 88 L. Ed. 1509 (1944); North American Co. v. SEC, 327 U.S. 686, 710, 66 Sup. Ct. 784, 90 L. Ed. 945 (1946).

tion for purposes of governmental control. This was the vice of the older, now discarded, authorities.

The expansion of the power of Congress does not mean that there is nothing left for the states to regulate. Congress need not exercise its authority over all aspects of our national economy, and, of course, it has not done so. Some of its legislation is in aid of the authority of the states. It is not at all unlikely—if a guess may be ventured—that the amount of state commerce regulation has expanded along with the federal, rather than the reverse. For along with the growth of federal power has come a greater reluctance to find state legislation in conflict with the commerce clause. In his lectures before the University of Kansas in 1947, Mr. Justice Rutledge concluded:

[J]ust as in recent years the permissible scope for congressional commerce action has broadened, returning to Marshall's conception, the prohibitive effect of the clause has been progressively narrowed. The trend has been toward sustaining state regulation formerly regarded as inconsistent with Congress' unexercised power of commerce. . . .

Nevertheless, the general problem of adjustment remains. It has only been transferred to a level more tolerant of both state and federal legislative action. On this level a new or renewed emphasis on facts and practical considerations has been allowed to work. . . .

But the scope of judicial intervention has been narrowed by the more recent trends, affecting both the affirmative and the prohibitive workings of the clause. Greater leeway and deference are given for legislative judgments, national and state, formally expressed. Larger emphasis is put on scrutiny of particular facts and concrete consequences, with an eye on their practical bearing for creating the evils the commerce clause was designed to outlaw. Correspondingly, less stress . . . is placed upon large generalizations and dogmatism inherited from levels of debate time has lowered. More and more the controlling considerations of policy implicit in thinking, judgment, and decision are brought into the open.[149]

These principles have also governed the application of the due process clause to the regulation of economic relationships. It is because of the greater leeway given legislative judgments

---

[149] Rutledge, *A Declaration of Legal Faith,* 68–70 (Univ. of Kan. Press (1947).

that the commerce and due process clauses have ceased to arouse
as much controversy as formerly. There are, of course, and
presumably always will be, peripheral issues, some of undoubted
importance, for the courts to decide. But, apart from these, in
this vital field of constitutional adjudication, there is seldom any
longer much doubt as to what the Court will do. As a consequence, many of the problems of yesteryear are hardly problems today.

▄▄

CHAPTER SIX

A "Constitution of Powers" and Modern Federalism

WRITERS ON CONSTITUTIONAL LAW NEVER TIRE OF ADMON-
ishing their readers to beware of the delusion that constitutional questions are a judicial monopoly; yet the delusion
endures the onslaughts of scholarship and common sense with
the usual pertinacity of folklore. And one of the dangers we
incur through our devotion to this myth is that important
changes in the Constitution may take place nearly unnoticed by
the populace or even by its elected representatives. The people
and the legislators have well-recognized and heavy responsibilities
to meet without bothering themselves about a subject that is
traditionally the concern of someone else and is in any case
supposed to be almost impossibly recondite. We should not be
surprised that they spend little time poring over the United States
Reports (which record the Supreme Court's doings) and skip
lightly past the journalists' accounts of constitutional decisions,
even if they happen to subscribe to one of the very few newspapers that report such matters adequately. Nevertheless, this
popular neglectfulness, however understandable, does mean that

constitutional mutations of real consequence may develop while, so to speak, no one—or almost no one—is looking.

One who *has* been looking for a long time now is Edward S. Corwin, the author of "The Passing of Dual Federalism." Since the first decade of the 20th-century when his writings began to appear, Corwin's figure has been dominant in the field of constitutional scholarship and he has perhaps advanced our understanding of American constitutionalism more than any man now living. It behooves us then to pay attention when he takes a broad look at the trends of modern constitutional development, as he does in this essay. Robert L. Stern's discussion of "Problems of Yesteryear" concerned the new and generally permissive attitude of the modern judiciary towards problems of economic control. Corwin is here interested in painting with a wide brush the modern constitutional landscape, which the current judicial outlook approximately reflects. He is trying to perceive, through the welter of judicial decisions, legislative actions, and executive orders, the main outlines of the Constitution as it is today.

His conclusions are arresting and may well be disturbing to a reader who has been proceeding on the comfortable assumption that the Constitution is a relatively stable entity and that he need only bestir himself to think about it when formal amendments are proposed. Corwin thinks that three major shifts in the character of America's organic law have occurred in the comparatively few years spanned by the current generation: the replacement of a "Constitution of Rights" by a "Constitution of Powers"; the augmentation within the national government of the authority of the President; and the modification of the federal system in the direction of national consolidation. Those who are interested in pursuing the first two of these points are referred to Professor Corwin's *A Constitution of Powers in a Secular State* (1951); and *The President: Office and Powers* (1948). It is the third great alteration—the decline of "dual federalism"—which chiefly concerns him in this essay.

The term "dual federalism" was devised by Corwin himself to describe the complex relationship between the nation and the states, in the American system, and it has become part of the standard coinage of a generation of constitutional scholars. Its meaning, as he says in this essay, is summarized by the four "axioms" of nation-state relationship that he sets forth; and the measure of our divergence from former constitutional moorings is indicated by the submergence of these axioms in modern constitutional law. That they have largely receded from view seems plain enough and Corwin traces the main developments in their gradual disappearance.

Among many comments that might be made about all this, two seem especially imperative. In the first place, it may be desirable to underline again a point that is clearly suggested by Corwin's essay, but which he does not emphasize: that the meaning of the Constitution is profoundly influenced by the actual course of legislative and executive action, that constitutional interpretation is *not* a judicial monopoly. One way of appraising the material Stern and Corwin deal with would be to say that a great range of constitutional issues have been shifted from the judicial to the legislative-executive level. They are still—or ought to be—issues, but the drift of recent history has devolved the responsibility for considering them on the Congress and the President. The Supreme Court's function in these areas is now confined, as Corwin says, to ratifying the history that Congressional practice chooses to make.

If we do regard the matter thus, we are forced to a reassessment of the traditional legislative function in America, a reassessment that implies a far greater concern among Congressmen for constitutional questions and a greater sophistication about them. Certainly it is reasonable to ask that, if legislators are to shape the Constitution, they be aware that they are doing so and be both able and willing to deal with constitutional problems as an element in the process of legislative decision. One has a feeling that the great transitions Corwin records were achieved with a minimum of reflection about them by the body most responsible for their occurrence—the Congress of the United States. Would the Social Security Act of 1935, for example, have been written as it was if those who drafted and passed the law had asked themselves, not only is this Social Security program a desirable reform, but do we approve the change in the constitutional system, that its passage implies? Quite possibly, an affirmative answer would have been returned even if this query had been posed, but it does seem fair to demand that the process of executive-legislative constitutional decision be made explicit. Students of public administration are properly scandalized if a man is given responsibility for doing a job without the corresponding authority. But surely it is equally illogical and more dangerous to assign authority without responsibility.

That brings us to a second, closely related issue suggested by Corwin's analysis. The author himself neither condemns nor condones the constitutional changes he has described; in this essay at least his only interest is to chart their course. But the reader is left free to ask whether these departures from old guideposts were either desirable or necessary, whether the Constitution that seems to have emerged from the alarms and excursions of the past few decades is what America wants. To propound the question in Corwin's own frame of reference: do we want a federalism in which the national government's powers are almost unrestricted, its purposes unconfined, its ascendancy over the states indubitable, and its relation to the states one of paternal collaboration? It may be a little late to be raising such a question, but better late than never is a good principle in public law, as elsewhere.

An answer should not be lightly ventured. It would be difficult indeed to draw up a list of national governmental purposes which would allow government freedom to do what public opinion may insistently demand and at the same time would impose some meaningful limitations. It would be equally hard to compile a list of powers which the government ought to be restricted to in fulfilling those demands. And surely any system of constitutional rules that failed to take account of popular expectations would be pointlessly unrealistic. Nor is it easy to see how federalism can return to the old relationship of "equality" and "tension" unless we ignore "the unifying forces of modern technology" to which Mr. Justice Frankfurter refers in the quotation on the last page of Corwin's essay. Yet the idea that governmental purposes and societal needs are something less than coterminous may still have some merit in America. And there may remain something to be said for local vitality as a protection against tyranny and as an alternative to static national uniformity.

But whatever the conclusion that may be arrived at, one point

seems clear—that there is nothing at all to be said for letting
the question be answered by default. We may have advanced in
the past few years to a "new federalism," as Corwin contends.
Our commitment to it may be irrevocable, even if it seemed
desirable to retrace our steps. Nevertheless, it is still important
that we realize what has happened, that we understand the role
Congress and the Presidency have played in bringing it about,
and that we take careful stock of the constitutional values that
have been vitiated as well as those which have been elevated to
a new place. There is no reason to believe that the constitution-
making process Corwin describes will cease with the present
generation. And it is still possible to hope that the evolutions of
the future can be attended by the popular awareness and informed discussion that their high seriousness deserves.

The Passing of Dual Federalism

by Edward S. Corwin *

Virginia Law Review,
Volume 36, Page 1 (1950)

Within the generation now drawing to a close this nation has
been subjected to the impact of a series of events and ideological
forces of a very imperative nature. We have fought two world
wars, the second of which answered every definition of "total
war," and have submitted to the regimentation which these
great national efforts entailed. We have passed through an economic crisis which was described by the late President as "a
crisis greater than war." We have become the exclusive custodian
of technology's crowning gift to civilization, an invention capable of blowing it to smithereens, and we greatly hope to retain
that honorable trusteeship throughout an indefinite future. Meantime we have elected ourselves the head and forefront of one of
two combinations of nations which together embrace a great
part of the Western World and in this capacity are at present

---

* (1878–   ), Professor of Jurisprudence, Princeton University, 1918–46,
emeritus since 1946.

involved in a "cold war" with the head of the opposing combination; and as one phase of this curious and baffling struggle we find ourselves driven to combat at obvious risk to certain heretofore cherished constitutional values, the menace of a hidden propaganda which is intended by its agents to work impairment of the national fiber against the time when the "cold war" may eventuate in a "shooting war." Lastly, though by no means least, the most widespread and powerfully organized political interest in the country, that of organized labor, has come to accept unreservedly a new and revolutionary conception of the role of government. Formerly we generally thought of government as primarily a policeman, with an amiable penchant for being especially helpful to those who knew how to help themselves. By the ideological revolution just alluded to, which stems from the Great Depression and the New Deal, it becomes the duty of government to guarantee economic security to all as the indispensable foundation of constitutional liberty.

Naturally, the stresses and strains to which the nation has been subjected by these pressures have not left our Constitutional Law unaffected. In general terms, our system has lost resiliency and what was once vaunted as a Constitution of Rights, both State and private, has been replaced by a Constitution of Powers. More specifically, the Federal System has shifted base in the direction of a consolidated national power, while within the National Government itself an increased flow of power in the direction of the President has ensued. In this article I shall deal with the first of these manifestations of an altered constitutional order.

I

The medium by which social forces are brought to bear upon constitutional interpretation, by which such forces are, so to speak, rendered into the idiom of Constitutional Law, is Judicial Review, or more concretely, the Supreme Court of the United States. This of course is a commonplace. The nature, on the other hand, of the materials with which the Court works is often a more recondite matter; and it is definitely so in the present instance.

Thus, for one thing, the Court has not been called upon, in

adapting the Federal System to the requirements of Total War
and other recent exigencies, to assimilate new amendments to the
constitutional structure, as was the case after the Civil War. The
period in question witnessed, it is true, the adopting of no fewer
than four such amendments, the 18th, 19th, 20th and 21st; and
the first of these, the Prohibition Amendment, contemplated a
considerable augmentation of national power at the expense of
the States—so much so, indeed, that some people argued that it
transcended the amending power itself. Although the Supreme
Court in due course rejected that contention, the controversy
continued for some thirteen or fourteen years, when it was terminated in the same abrupt and drastic manner as that in which
it had been precipitated, namely, by constitutional amendment.
By repealing outright the 18th Amendment, the 21st Amendment restored the *status quo ante* so far as national power was
concerned. Nor is the 19th Amendment establishing woman suffrage, or the 20th, changing the dates when a newly elected
President and a newly elected Congress take over, relevant to
our present inquiry.

Nor again has judicial translation of the power requirements
of national crisis into the vocabulary of Constitutional Law been
effected for the most part by affixing new definitions to the
phraseology in which the constitutional grants of power to the
National Government are couched. One thinks in this connection
especially of the "commerce clause." The phrase "commerce
among the States" was held by the Court five years ago to embrace the making of insurance contracts across State lines,[1] but
the ruling in question—negligible in itself so far as our purpose
goes—was presently considerably diluted in effect by act of Congress.[2] Such expansion of the commerce power as is of relevance
to this inquiry has been a *secondary*, even though important,
consequence of other more immediate factors of constitutional
interpretation.

Finally, the *structural* features of our Federal System still remain what they have always been, to wit: 1. A written Constitu-

---

[1] United States *v.* South-Eastern Underwriters Ass'n, 322 U.S. 533, 64 Sup.
Ct. 1162, 88 L. Ed. 1441 (1944).
[2] 59 Stat. 33, 34 (1945), 15 U.S.C. §§ 1011–1015 (1946); see Prudential
Ins. Co. *v.* Benjamin, 328 U.S. 408, 66 Sup. Ct. 1142, 90 L. Ed. 1342 (1946).

tion which is regarded as "law" and "supreme law"; 2. As in all federations, the union of several autonomous political entities or "States" for common purposes; 3. The division of the sum total of legislative powers between a "general government," on the one hand, and the "States," on the other; 4. The direct operation for the most part of each center of government, acting within its assigned sphere, upon all persons and property within its territorial limits; 5. The provision of each center with the complete apparatus, both executive and judicial, for law enforcement; 6. Judicial review, that is, the power and duty of all courts, and ultimately of the Supreme Court of the Union, to disallow all legislative or executive acts of either center of government which in the Court's opinion transgress the Constitution; 7. An elaborate and cumbersome method of constitutional amendment, in which the States have a deciding role.

Not only have these features of the American Federal System never been altered by constitutional amendment in any way that requires our attention, none has within recent years been *directly* affected by judicial interpretation of the words of the Constitution in a way that need interest us. So far as the form and actual phraseological content of the Constitutional Document are concerned, Professor Dicey's dictum that federalism implies "a legally immutable Constitution," or one nearly immutable, has been fully realized in the American experience.[3]

In just what fashion then has the shift referred to above of our Federal System toward consolidation registered itself in our Constitutional Law in response to the requirements of war, economic crisis, and a fundamentally altered outlook upon the purpose of government? The solution of the conundrum is to be sought in the changed attitude of the Court toward certain postulates or axioms of constitutional interpretation closely touching the Federal System, and which in their totality comprised what I mean by Dual Federalism. These postulates are the following: 1. The national government is one of enumerated powers only; 2. Also the purposes which it may constitutionally promote are few; 3. Within their respective spheres the two centers of government are "sovereign" and hence "equal"; 4. The

---

[3] A. V. Dicey, *Introduction to the Study of the Law of the Constitution* 142 (7th ed. 1903).

relation of the two centers with each other is one of tension rather than collaboration. Here I shall sketch briefly the history of each of these concepts in our Constitutional Law and show how today each has been superseded by a concept favorable to centralization.

II

In settling the apportionment of powers between the central and local governments of a Federal System any one of several principles is conceivably available, two of them being illustrated by the great Anglo-American federations. In the United States, as in the Australian Commonwealth, the principle originally adopted was that the National Government should possess only those powers which were conferred upon it in more or less definite terms by the Constitutional Document, while the remaining powers should, unless otherwise specified, be "reserved" to the States; or in the vocabulary of Constitutional Law, the National Government was a government of "enumerated powers," while the States were governments of "residual powers." On the other hand, in the case of the Dominion of Canada, which was established in the near wake of our Civil War, the reverse principle was followed. For taking counsel from that event, the founders of the Dominion thought to avoid yielding too much to "States Rights." Yet surprisingly enough, when "New Deal" programs were being tested judicially under the two constitutions a decade and a half ago, it was the United States Constitution which proved to be, in the final upshot, the more commodious vehicle of national power, the reason being that the draughtsmen of the British North America Act, besides generally using more precise language than did the Framers, designated certain of the powers which they assigned the Canadian provinces as "exclusive," with the result of rendering them logically restrictive of the powers of the Dominion—or at least the Judicial Committee of the House of Lords so ruled.[4] As we shall see presently, there was a long period of approximately a hundred years when the foes of national power in this country achieved a comparable result

---

[4] Illuminating in this connection is Professor W. P. M. Kennedy's *Essays in Constitutional Law* 105–22, 153–57 (1934).

through their interpretation of the Tenth Amendment—one which the Supreme Court has definitely discarded only within recent years.

Today the operation of the "enumerated powers" concept as a canon of constitutional interpretation has been curtailed on all sides. Nor in fact did it ever go altogether unchallenged, even from the first.

Article I, section 8, clause 1 of the Constitution reads:

> The Congress shall have power to lay and collect taxes, duties, imposts and excises, to pay the debts and provide for the common defense and general welfare of the United States . . .

What is "the general welfare" for which Congress is thus authorized to "provide," and in what fashion is it authorized to provide it? While adoption of the Constitution was pending some of its opponents made the charge that the phrase "to provide for the general welfare" was a sort of legislative joker which was designed, in conjunction with the "necessary and proper" clause, to vest Congress with power to provide for whatever it might choose to regard as the "general welfare" by any means deemed by it to be "necessary and proper." The suggestion was promptly repudiated by advocates of the Constitution on the following grounds. In the first place, it was pointed out, the phrase stood between two other phrases, both dealing with the taxing power—an awkward syntax on the assumption under consideration. In the second place, the phrase was coordinate with the phrase "to pay the debts," that is, a purpose of money expenditure only. Finally, it was asserted, the suggested reading, by endowing Congress with practically complete legislative power, rendered the succeeding enumeration of more specific powers superfluous, thereby reducing "the Constitution to a single phrase."

In the total this argument sounds impressive, but on closer examination it becomes less so, especially today. For one thing, it is a fact that in certain early printings of the Constitution the "common defense and general welfare" clause appears separately paragraphed, while in others it is set off from the "lay and collect" clause by a semicolon and not, as modern usage would require, by the less awesome comma. To be sure, the

semicolon may have been due in the first instance to the splat-
tering of a goose quill that needed trimming, for it is notorious
that the fate of nations has often turned on just such minute
points.

Then as to the third argument—while once deemed an
extremely weighty one—it cannot be so regarded in light of the
decision in 1926 in the case of Myers v. United States.[5] The
Court held that the opening clause of Article II of the Constitution which says that "the executive power shall be vested in a
President of the United States," is not a simple designation of
office but a grant of power, which the succeeding clauses of the
same article either qualify or to which they lend "appropriate
emphasis." Granting the soundness of this position, however,
why should not the more specific clauses of Article I be regarded
as standing in a like relation to the "general welfare" clause
thereof? Nor is this by any means all that may be said in favor
of treating the latter clause as a grant of substantive legislative
power, as anyone may convince himself who chooses to consult
Mr. James Francis Lawson's minute and ingenious examination of
the subject.[6]

Despite these considerations, or such of them as he was aware
of, the great Chief Justice Marshall in 1819 stamped the "enumerated powers" doctrine with his approval. This was in his
opinion in McCulloch *v.* Maryland,[7] where, in sustaining the
right of the National Government to establish a Bank, he used
the following expressions:

> This government is acknowledged by all to be one of enu-
> merated powers. The principle, that it can exercise only the powers
> granted to it, would seem too apparent to have required to be en-
> forced by all those arguments which its enlightened friends, while
> it was depending before the people, found it necessary to urge. That
> principle is now universally admitted.[8]

At the same time, however, Marshall committed himself to
certain other positions in that same opinion which in their total

---

[5] 272 U.S. 52, 47 Sup. Ct. 21, 71 L. Ed. 160 (1926).
[6] The three preceding paragraphs are drawn largely from Corwin, *Twilight
of the Supreme Court* 152–54 (1934).
[7] 4 Wheat. 316, 4 L. Ed. 579 (U.S. 1819).
[8] *Id.* at 405, 4 L. Ed. at 601.

effect went far in the judgment of certain of his critics to render the National Government one of "indefinite powers." One of these was the dictum that "the sword and the purse, all external relations, and no inconsiderable portion of the industry of the nation, are entrusted to its government." Another was his characterization of "the power of making war," of "levying taxes," and of "regulating commerce," as "great, substantive and independent" powers. A third was his famous and for the purposes of the case, decisive construction of the "necessary and proper" clause as embracing "all [legislative] means which are appropriate" to carry out "the legitimate ends" of the Constitution.[9]

Approaching the opinion from the angle of his quasi-parental concern for "the balance between the States and the National Government," Madison declared its central vice to be that it treated the powers of the latter as "sovereign powers," a view which must inevitably "convert a limited into an unlimited government" for, he continued "in the great system of political economy, having for its general object the national welfare, everything is related immediately or remotely to every other thing; and, consequently, a power over any one thing, not limited by some obvious and precise affinity, may amount to a power over every other." "The very existence," he consequently urged, "of the local sovereignties" was "a control on the pleas for a constructive amplification of national power."[10]

So also did Marshall's most pertinacious critic, John Taylor of Caroline, pronounce the Chief Justice's doctrines as utterly destructive of the constitutional division of powers between the two centers of government.[11] A third critic was the talented Hugh Swinton Legaré of South Carolina, who in 1828 devoted a review of the first volume of Kent's *Commentaries* to a minute and immensely ingenious analysis of Marshall's most celebrated opinion. "That argument," he asserted, "cannot be sound which necessarily converts a government of enumerated into one of indefinite powers, and a confederacy of republics into a gigantic

---

[9] *Id.* at 421, 4 L. Ed. at 605.

[10] 8 *Writings of James Madison* 447–53 (Hunt ed. 1908); 2 *Letters and Other Writings of James Madison* 143–47 (Phila. 1867).

[11] Taylor, *Construction Construed and Constitutions Vindicated* 9–28 *passim*, 77–89 *passim* (1820).

and consolidated empire." Nor did one have to rely on reasoning alone to be convinced of this; one needed only to compare the Constitution itself as expounded in *The Federalist* with the actual course of national legislation. For thus, he wrote:

> He will find that the government has been fundamentally altered by the progress of opinion—that instead of being any longer one of enumerated powers and a circumscribed sphere, as it was beyond all doubt intended to be, it knows absolutely no bounds but the will of a majority of Congress—that instead of confining itself in time of peace to the diplomatic and commercial relations of the country, it is seeking out employment for itself by interfering in the domestic concerns of society, and threatens in the course of a very few years, to control in the most offensive and despotic manner, all the pursuits, the interests, the opinions and the conduct of men. He will find that this extraordinary revolution has been brought about, in a good degree by the Supreme Court of the United States, which has applied to the Constitution—very innocently, no doubt, and with commanding ability in argument—and thus given authority and currency to, such canons of interpretation, as necessarily lead to these extravagant results. Above all, he will be perfectly satisfied that that high tribunal affords, by its own shewing, no barrier whatever against the usurpations of Congress—and that the rights of the weaker part of this confederacy may, to any extent, be wantonly and tyrannically violated, under colour of law, (the most grievous shape of oppression) by men neither interested in its destiny nor subject to its controul, without any means of redress being left it, except such as are inconsistent with all idea of order and government.[12]

These words purported one hundred and twenty years ago to be history; they read today much more like prophecy.

What is the standing today of the "enumerated powers" doctrine as a postulate of constitutional interpretation? Even so recently as 1939 the doctrine received the endorsement of a standard work on Constitutional Law in these words: "The courts in construing the scope of the grants of power to the several organs of the federal government by the federal Constitution do so on the assumption that the people of the United States intended to confer upon them only such powers as can be derived

---

[12] 2 *The Southern Review* 72–113, No. 1 (1828); 2 *Writings of Hugh Swinton Legaré* 102, 123–33 (1846).

from the terms of the express grants of power made to them in that Constitution." [13]

In point of fact, the doctrine, when applied to Marshall's three "great, substantive and independent powers," that over external relations, the power to levy taxes and, *subaudi*, the power to expend the proceeds, and the power of commercial relations, had become a very shaky reliance. As to the first of these, indeed, it had been directly repudiated by the Court; and while as to the other two fields, it was still valid in a certain sense, its restrictive potentialities had, for reasons which will soon appear, become practically nil.

III

We turn now to the second of the above postulates. The question raised is whether it was the intention of the Framers of the Constitution to apportion not only the powers but also the purposes of government between the two centers, with the result of inhibiting the National Government from attempting on a national scale the same ends as the States attempt on a local scale? In view of the latitudinarian language of the Preamble to the Constitution, an affirmative answer to this question might seem to encounter ineluctable difficulties. For all that, it has at times received countenance from the Court. Even in the pages of *The Federalist* can be discerned the beginnings of a controversy regarding the scope of Congress's taxing power which was still sufficiently vital 150 years later to claim the Court's deliberate attention, although the substance of victory had long since fallen to the pro-nationalist view.[14] In brief the question at issue was this: Was Congress entitled to levy and collect taxes to further objects not falling within its other powers to advance? Very early the question became dichotomized into two questions. First, was Congress entitled to lay and collect tariffs for any but revenue purposes; secondly, was it entitled to expend the proceeds from its taxes for any other purpose than to provision the government in the exercise of its other enumerated powers, or

---

[13] Rottschaefer, *Handbook of American Constitutional Law* 11 (1939).
[14] *The Federalist*, Nos. 30, 34, 41.

as Henry Clay once put the issue, was the power to spend the *cause* or merely the *consequence* of power?

The tariff aspect of the general question was, for instance, debated by Calhoun, speaking for the States Rights view, and by Story in his *Commentaries* by way of answer to Calhoun.[15] Yet not until 1928 did the Court get around to affix the stamp of its approval on Story's argument, and then it did so only on historical grounds. Said Chief Justice Taft for the unanimous Court:

> It is enough to point out that the second act adopted by the Congress of the United States July 4, 1789 . . . contained the following recital:
>
> "Sec. 1. Whereas it is necessary for the support of government, for the discharge of the debts of the United States, and the encouragement and protection of manufactures, that duties be laid on goods, wares and merchandises imported:
>
> "Be it enacted . . ."
>
> In this first Congress sat many members of the Constitutional Convention of 1787. This court has repeatedly laid down the principle that a contemporaneous legislative exposition of the Constitution when the founders of our government and framers of our Constitution were actively participating in public affairs, long acquiesced in, fixes the construction to be given its provisions. . . . The enactment and enforcement of a number of customs revenue laws drawn with a motive of maintaining a system of protection since the Revenue Law of 1789 are matters of history.[16]

In short, the constitutional case against the tariff went by default; and substantially the same is true also of the restrictive conception of the spending power. The classical statement of the broad theory of the spending power is that by Hamilton, in his *Report on Manufactures* in 1791. Reciting the "lay and collect taxes" clause of Article I, section 8 he says:

The phrase is as comprehensive as any that could have been used, because it was not fit that the constitutional authority of the Union to appropriate its revenues should have been restricted within narrower limits than the "general welfare," and because this necessarily embraces a vast variety of particulars which are susceptible neither

---

[15] See *Commentaries* § 1090.
[16] Hampton & Co. *v.* United States, 276 U.S. 394, 411, 48 Sup. Ct. 348, 353, 72 L. Ed. 624, 631 (1928).

of specification nor of definition. It is therefore of necessity left to the discretion of the National Legislature to pronounce upon the objects which concern the general welfare, and for which, under that description, an appropriation of money is requisite and proper. And there seems to be no room for a doubt that whatever concerns the general interests of learning, of agriculture, of manufactures, and of commerce, are within the sphere of the national councils *as far as regards an application of money.*[17]

Endorsed contemporaneously by Jefferson, stigmatized by him on further reflection, rebutted by Madison in his veto of the Bonus Bill in 1806, rejected by Monroe in the early years of his Presidency, endorsed by him in his famous message of May 4, 1822, Hamilton's doctrine has since the Civil War pointed an ever-increasing trend in Congressional fiscal policy. Yet even as recently as 1923 we find the Court industriously sidestepping the constitutional question and displaying considerable agility in doing so. I refer to a brace of suits in which Massachusetts and a citizen thereof, a Mrs. Frothingham, sought independently to challenge Congress's right to vote money in aid of expectant mothers. It was no function of a State, the Court instructed Massachusetts, to interpose in behalf of the constitutional rights of its citizens, who, being also citizens of the United States, could rely on getting adequate protection against the National Government from the National courts. Thus, at long last was John C. Calhoun's doctrine of State interposition answered. Turning then to Mrs. Frothingham, the Court informed her that her interest as a taxpayer was much too trivial to entitle her to the interposition of the national courts.[18]

Twelve years later, however, in the A.A.A. case, the Court at last came to grips with the constitutional issue, which it decided in line with the Hamiltonian thesis. Said Justice Roberts for the Court:

Since the foundation of the Nation sharp differences of opinion have persisted as to the true interpretation of the phrase, ["lay and collect taxes to . . . provide for . . . the general welfare"]. Madison asserted it amounted to no more than a reference to the other powers

---

[17] 4 *Works of Alexander Hamilton* 151 (Federal ed. 1904).
[18] Massachusetts *v.* Mellon, 262 U.S. 447, 43 Sup. Ct. 597, 67 L. Ed. 1078 (1923).

enumerated in the subsequent clauses of the same section; that, as the United States is a government of limited and enumerated powers, the grant of power to tax and spend for the general national welfare must be confined to the enumerated legislative fields committed to the Congress. In this view the phrase is mere tautology, for taxation and appropriation are or may be necessary incidents of the exercise of any of the enumerated legislative powers. Hamilton, on the other hand, maintained the clause confers a power separate and distinct from those later enumerated, is not restricted in meaning by the grant of them, and Congress consequently has a substantive power to tax and to appropriate, limited only by the requirement that it shall be exercised to provide for the general welfare of the United States. Each contention has had the support of those whose views are entitled to weight. This court has noticed the question, but has never found it necessary to decide which is the true construction. Mr. Justice Story, in his Commentaries, espouses the Hamiltonian position. We shall not review the writings of public men and commentators or discuss the legislative practice. Study of all these leads us to conclude that the reading advocated by Mr. Justice Story is the correct one. While, therefore, the power to tax is not unlimited, its confines are set in the clause which confers it, and not in those of § 8 which bestow and define the legislative powers of the Congress. It results that the power of Congress to authorize expenditure of public moneys for public purposes is not limited by the direct grants of legislative power found in the Constitution.[19]

In short, the Court once more ratified the history that Congressional practice had made.

The theory that the enumerated powers may be validly exercised for certain limited purposes only was first passed upon in relation to the commerce power in 1808 under Jefferson's Embargo Act. The proposition offered the Court—the United States District Court for Massachusetts—was that the power of Congress to regulate foreign commerce was only the power to adopt measures for its protection and advancement, whereas the Embargo destroyed commerce. The Court rejected the argument. Pointing to the clause of Article I, section 9, which interdicted a ban on the slave trade till 1808, the judge remarked: "It was perceived that, under the power of regulating commerce,

---

[19] United States *v.* Butler, 297 U.S. 1, 65, 56 Sup. Ct. 312, 319, 80 L. Ed. 477, 488 (1936).

Congress would be authorized to abridge it in favor of the great principles of humanity and justice." [20]

One hundred and ten years later the same argument was revived and revamped in opposition to the congressional embargo on interstate commerce in child-made goods, and this time it prevailed. The act, said the Court, was not a commercial regulation, but a usurpation of the reserved power of the States to protect the public health, safety, morals, and general welfare.[21] And when the Congress next sought to use its taxing power against firms employing child labor, the Court, adopting the narrow purpose concept of the taxing power *ad hoc*, frustrated that attempt too.[22] We shall now see how this course of reasoning has since toppled to the ground along with other supporting canons of interpretation.

IV

Our third postulate is addressed particularly to this question: By what rule are collisions between the respective powers of the two centers of government supposed by the Constitution to be determined? In answer two texts of the Constitution itself compete for recognition, Article VI, clause 2, which reads as follows:

> This Constitution, and the laws of the United States which shall be made in pursuance thereof, and all treaties made, or which shall be made, under the authority of the United States, shall be the supreme law of the land; and the judges in every State shall be bound thereby, anything in the Constitution or laws of any State to the contrary notwithstanding.

and the Tenth Amendment, which says:

> The powers not delegated to the United States by the Constitution, nor prohibited by it to the States, are reserved to the States respectively, or to the people.

---

[20] United States *v.* The William, 28 Fed. Cas. No. 16,700, at 421 (D. Mass. 1808).

[21] Hammer *v.* Dagenhart, 247 U.S. 251, 38 Sup. Ct. 529, 62 L. Ed. 1101 (1918).

[22] Bailey *v.* Drexel Furniture Co., 259 U.S. 20, 42 Sup. Ct. 449, 66 L. Ed. 817 (1922).

It was quite plainly the intention of the Federal Convention that National laws, otherwise constitutional except for being in conflict with State laws, should invariably prevail over the latter; [23] or, as Madison later phrased the matter, State power should be "no ingredient of national power." [24] This was also Marshall's theory. Indeed, the principle of "national supremacy" was in his estimation the most fundamental axiom of constitutional interpretation touching the federal relationship, one even more vital to the Union and more unmistakably ordained by the Constitutional Document itself than the doctrine of "loose construction," loosely so-called by his critics.

"If," said he in McCulloch *v.* Maryland, "any one proposition could command the assent of mankind, one might expect it would be this—that the government of the Union, though limited in its powers, is supreme within its sphere of action." Nor did the Tenth Amendment affect the question. In omitting from it the word "expressly," its authors had—and apparently of deliberate purpose—left the question whether any particular power belonged to the general government "to depend on a fair construction of the whole instrument." [25] Counsel for Maryland, Luther Martin, agreed—the Tenth Amendment was "merely declaratory." [26]

Yet when, five years later the Court came to decide Gibbons *v.* Ogden,[27] in which the question was whether a New York created monopoly was compatible with legislation of Congress regulating the coasting trade, Marshall was confronted with a very different set of ideas by counsel for the local interest. "In argument," Marshall recites, "it had been contended that if a law, passed by a State in the exercise of its acknowledged sovereignty, comes into conflict with a law passed by Congress in pursuance of the Constitution, they affect the subject, and each other, like equal opposing powers." This contention Marshall answered as follows:

---

[23] See 1 *Records of the Federal Convention* 21–22 (Farrand ed. 1911).
[24] 2 Annals of Congress col. 1891 (1790–91). See Corwin, *Commerce Power Versus States Rights* 117–72 (1936).
[25] 4 Wheat. 316, 405, 4 L. Ed. 579, 601 (U.S. 1819).
[26] *Id.* at 374, 6 L. Ed. at 593.
[27] 9 Wheat. 1, 6 L. Ed. 23 (U.S. 1824).

But the framers of our constitution foresaw this state of things, and provided for it, by declaring the supremacy not only of itself, but of the laws made in pursuance of it. The nullity of any act, inconsistent with the constitution is produced by the declaration that the constitution is the supreme law. The appropriate application of that part of the clause which confers the same supremacy on laws and treaties, is to such acts of the State Legislatures as do not transcend their powers, but, though enacted in the execution of acknowledged State powers, interfere with, or are contrary to the laws of Congress made in pursuance of the constitution, or some treaty made under the authority of the United States. In every such case, the act of Congress, or the treaty, is supreme; and the law of the State, though enacted in the exercise of powers not controverted, must yield to it.[28]

Whence came the notion of National-State "equality," and what effect did it have on the Court's jurisprudence? The germ of it is to be found in the theory of the Constitution's origin developed in the Virginia and Kentucky Resolutions, that it was a compact of "sovereign" states, rather than an ordinance of "the people of America." The deduction from this premise that the National Government and the States, both being "sovereign," faced each other as "equals" across the line defining their respective jurisdictions, was made by John Taylor of Caroline in his critique of the decision in McCulloch v. Maryland. But earlier, the Virginia Court of Appeals had contributed to Taylor's system of constitutional interpretation the notion that under the "supremacy" clause itself, the State judiciaries were the constitutionally designated agencies for the application of the principle of supremacy.[29] It followed that the Supreme Court no more than Congress was able to bind the "equal" States, nor could they on the other hand bind Congress or the Court.

The notion of National-State equality became in due course a part of the constitutional creed of the Taney Court, but stripped of its anarchic implications and reduced to the proportions of a single thread in a highly complicated fabric of constitutional exegesis. It was early in this period that the concept of the Police Power emerged. This, broadly considered, was

---

[28] *Id.* at 210, 6 L. Ed. at 73.
[29] See Hunter *v.* Martin, 4 Munf. 1, 11 (Va. 1814), *rev'd,* Martin *v.* Hunter's Lessee, 1 Wheat. 304, 4 L. Ed. 97 (U.S. 1816).

simply what Taney termed "the power to govern men and things" defined from the point of view of the duty of the State to "promote the happiness and prosperity of the community"; more narrowly, it was a certain central core of this power, namely the power of the States to "provide for the public health, safety, and good order." Within this latter field at least, the powers reserved to the States by the Tenth Amendment were "sovereign" powers, "complete, unqualified, and exclusive." Yet this did not signify that the States, acting through either their legislatures or their courts, were the final judge of the scope of these "sovereign" powers. This was the function of the Supreme Court of the United States, which for this purpose was regarded by the Constitution as standing outside of and over both the National Government and the States, and vested with authority to apportion impartially to each center its proper powers in accordance with the Constitution's intention. And the primary test whether this intention was fulfilled was whether conflict between the two centers was avoided.[30] In Judge Cooley's words, "The laws of both [centers] operate within the same territory, but if in any particular case their provisions are in conflict, one or the other is void," that is, void apart from the conflict itself.[31]

Thus the principle of national supremacy came to be superseded by an unlimited discretion in the Supreme Court to designate this or that State power as comprising an independent limitation on national power. In only one area was the earlier principle recognized as still operative, and that was the field of interstate commercial regulation. This field, indeed, was not properly speaking a part of the "reserved powers" of the States at all; it belonged to Congress's enumerated powers. The States, however, might occupy it as to minor phases of commerce unless and until Congress chose to do so, in which case Article VI, paragraph 2 came into play and conflicting state legislation was superseded.[32]

While, as we have seen, the Police Power was defined in the first instance with the end in view of securing to the States a

---

[30] On this system of constitutional interpretation, see especially New York *v.* Miln, 11 Pet. 102, 9 L. Ed. 648 (U.S. 1837); see also License Cases, 5 How. 504, 527–37, 573–74, 588, 613, 12 L. Ed. 256, 266–71, 287–88, 294, 305 (U.S. 1847) *passim.*

[31] Cooley, *Principles of Constitutional Law* 152 (3d ed. 1898).

[32] Cooley *v.* Board of Wardens, 12 How. 299, 13 L. Ed. 996 (U.S. 1851).

near monopoly of the right to realize the main *objectives* of government, the concept came later to embrace the further idea that certain *subject-matters* were also segregated to the States and hence could not be reached by any valid exercise of national power. That production, and hence mining, agriculture, and manufacturing, and the employer-employee relationship in connection with these were among such subject-matters was indeed one of the basic postulates of the Court's system of Constitutional Law in the era of *laissez faire*.[33] The decisions in both the first Child Labor case and the A.A.A. case were largely determined by this axiom; and as late as 1936, Justice Sutherland's opinion in the Bituminous Coal case gave it classic expression.[34] The question before the Court concerned the constitutionality of an attempt by Congress to govern hours and wages in the soft coal mines of the country. Said Justice Sutherland for the Court:

> In addition to what has just been said, the conclusive answer is that the evils are all local evils over which the federal government has no legislative control. The relation of employer and employee is a local relation. At common law, it is one of the domestic relations. The wages are paid for the doing of local work. Working conditions are obviously local conditions. The employees are not engaged in or about commerce, but exclusively in producing a commodity. And the controversies and evils, which it is the object of the act to regulate and minimize, are local controversies and evils affecting local work undertaken to accomplish that local result. Such effect as they may have upon commerce, however extensive it may be, is secondary and indirect. An increase in the greatness of the effect adds to its importance. It does not alter its character.[35]

This entire system of constitutional interpretation touching the Federal System is today in ruins. It toppled in the Social Security Act cases and in N.L.R.B. *v.* Jones & Laughlin Steel Corporation, in which the Wagner Labor Act was sustained.[36] This was in 1937 while the "Old Court" was still in power. In 1941 in United States *v.* Darby,[37] the "New Court" merely per-

---

[33] See Corwin, *Commerce Power Versus States Rights* 175–209 (1936).

[34] Carter *v.* Carter Coal Co. 298 U.S. 238, 56 Sup. Ct. 855, 80 L. Ed. 1160 (1936).

[35] *Id.* at 308, 56 Sup. Ct. at 871, 80 L. Ed. at 1187.

[36] 301 U.S. 1, 57 Sup. Ct. 615, 81 L. Ed. 893 (1937).

[37] 312 U.S. 100, 61 Sup. Ct. 451, 85 L. Ed. 609 (1941).

formed a mopping-up operation. The Act of Congress involved was the Fair Labor Standards Act of 1938, which not only bars interstate commerce in goods produced under sub-standard conditions but makes their production a penal offense against the United States if they are "intended" for interstate or foreign commerce. Speaking for the unanimous Court, Chief Justice Stone went straight back to Marshall's opinions in McCulloch *v.* Maryland and Gibbons *v.* Ogden, extracting from the former his latitudinarian construction of the "necessary and proper" clause and from both cases his uncompromising application of the "supremacy" clause.[38]

Today, neither the State Police Power nor the concept of Federal Equilibrium is any "ingredient of national legislative power," whether as respects subject-matter to be governed, or the choice of objectives or of means for its exercise.

V

Lastly, we come to the question whether the two centers of government ought to be regarded as standing in a competitive or cooperative relation to each other. The question first emerged at the executive and judicial levels. In Article VI, paragraph 3 the requirement is laid down that members of the State legislatures, their executive and judicial officers shall take an oath, or make affirmation, to support the Constitution, thus testifying, as Hamilton points out in *Federalist* 27, to the expectation that these functionaries would be "incorporated into the operations of the National Government," in the exercise of its constitutional powers. In much early legislation, furthermore, this expectation was realized. The Judiciary Act of 1789 left the State courts in exclusive possession of some categories of national jurisdiction and shared some others with it. The Act of 1793 entrusted the rendition of fugitive slaves in part to national officials and in part to State officials, and the rendition of fugitives from justice from one State to another exclusively to the State executives. Certain later acts empowered State courts to entertain criminal

---

[38] *Ibid.* See also United States *v.* Carolene Products Co., 304 U.S. 144, 58 Sup. Ct. 778, 82 L. Ed. 1234 (1938); Mulford *v.* Smith, 307 U.S. 38, 59 Sup. Ct. 648, 83 L. Ed. 1092 (1939).

prosecutions for forging paper of the Bank of the United States
and for counterfeiting coin of the United States; while still others
conferred on State judges authority to admit aliens to national
citizenship and provided penalties in case such judges should
utter false certificates of naturalization—provisions which are still
on the statute books.[39]

The subsequent rise, however, of the States Rights sentiment
presently overcast this point of view with heavy clouds of doubt.
From the nationalist angle Marshall stigmatized the efforts of
Virginia and those who thought her way to "confederatize the
Union"; and asserting in McCulloch *v.* Maryland the administrative independence of the National Government, he there laid
down a sweeping rule prohibiting the States from taxing even to
the slightest extent national instrumentalities on their operations.
"The power to tax is the power to destroy," said he; and whatever a State may do at all it may do to the utmost extent.[40]

But when a few years later the Taney Court took over, the
shoe was on the other foot. In 1842, the State of Pennsylvania
was sustained by the Court, speaking by Marshall's apostle Story,
in refusing to permit its magistrates to aid in enforcing the fugitive slave provisions of the Act of 1793. Said Story:

. . . the national government, in the absence of all positive provisions
to the contrary, is bound through its own proper departments, legislative, executive, or judiciary, as the case may require, to carry into effect all the rights and duties imposed upon it by the Constitution.[41]

And in Kentucky *v.* Dennison, decided on the eve of the Civil
War, the "duty" imposed by this same act on State governors
to render up fugitives from justice on the demand of the executives of sister States, was watered down to a judicially unenforcea-
ble "moral duty." Said the Chief Justice: ". . . we think it
clear, that the Federal Government, under the Constitution, has
no power to impose on a State officer, as such, any duty whatever, and compel him to perform it; . . ."[42]

---

[39] For references, see Corwin, *Court Over Constitution* 135–36 and notes (1938).
[40] See 4 Wheat. 316, 427–31, 4 L. Ed. 579, 606–7 (U.S. 1819); Brown *v.*
Maryland, 12 Wheat. 419, 439, 6 L. Ed. 678, 685 (U.S. 1827).
[41] Prigg *v.* Commonwealth of Pennsylvania, 16 Peters 539, 616, 10 L. Ed.
1060, 1089 (U.S. 1842).
[42] 24 How. 66, 16 L. Ed. 717, 729 (U.S. 1861).

Nor was even this the end, for as late as 1871 the Court laid down the converse of Marshall's doctrine in McCulloch v. Maryland, holding that, since the States enjoyed equal constitutional status with the National Government, what was sauce for the one was sauce for the other too, and that therefore a national income tax could not be constitutionally applied to State official salaries.[43]

The doctrine of tax exemption was the climactic expression of the competitive theory of Federalism, and is today largely moribund in consequence of the emergence of the *cooperative* conception. According to this conception, the National Government and the States are mutually complementary parts of a *single* governmental mechanism all of whose powers are intended to realize the current purposes of government according to their applicability to the problem in hand. It is thus closely intertwined with the multiple-purpose conception of national power and with recent enlarged theories of the function of government generally. Here we are principally interested in two forms of joint action by the National Government and the States which have developed within recent years, primarily through the *legislative* powers of the two centers.

Thus in the first place the National Government has brought its augmented powers over interstate commerce and communications to the support of local policies of the States in the exercise of their reserved powers. By the doctrine that Congress's power to regulate "commerce among the States" is "exclusive," a State is frequently unable to stop the flow of commerce from sister States even when it threatens to undermine local legislation. In consequence Congress has within recent years come to the assistance of the police powers of the States by making certain crimes against them, like theft, racketeering, kidnapping, crimes also against the National Government whenever the offender extends his activities beyond state boundary lines.[44]

Justifying such legislation, the Court has said:

Our dual form of government has its perplexities, state and Nation having different spheres of jurisdiction . . . but it must be

---

[43] Collector v. Day, 11 Wall. 113, 20 L. Ed. 122 (U.S. 1871).
[44] For references, see Corwin, *Court Over Constitution* 148–50 and notes (1938).

kept in mind that we are one people; and the powers reserved to the states and those conferred on the nation are adapted to be exercised, whether independently or concurrently, to promote the general welfare, material and moral.[45]

It is true that in the Child Labor case of 1918 this postulate of constitutional interpretation seemed to have been discarded, but the logic of United States *v.* Darby, restores it in full force.

Secondly, the National Government has held out inducements, primarily of a pecuniary kind, to the States—the so-called "grants-in-aid"—to use their reserved powers to support certain objectives of national policy in the field of expenditure. In other words, the greater financial strength of the National Government is joined to the wider coercive powers of the States. Thus since 1911, Congress has voted money to subsidize forest-protection, education in agricultural and industrial subjects and in home economics, vocational rehabilitation and education, the maintenance of nautical schools, experimentation in reforestation and highway construction in the States; in return for which cooperating States have appropriated equal sums for the same purposes, and have brought their further powers to the support thereof along lines laid down by Congress.[46]

The culmination of this type of National-State cooperation to date, however, is reached in The Social Security Act of August 14, 1935. The Act brings the national tax-spending power to the support of such States as desire to cooperate in the maintenance of old-age pensions, unemployment insurance, maternal welfare work, vocational rehabilitation, and public health work, and in financial assistance to impoverished old age, dependent children, and the blind. Such legislation is, as we have seen, within the national taxing-spending power. What, however, of the objection that it "coerced" complying States into "abdicating" their powers? Speaking to this point in the Social Security Act cases, the Court has said: "The . . . contention confuses motive with coercion. . . . To hold that motive or temptation is equivalent to coercion is to plunge the law in endless difficulties." [47] And

---

[45] Hoke *v.* United States, 227 U.S. 308, 322, 33 Sup. Ct. 281, 284, 57 L. Ed. 523, 527 (1913).

[46] Corwin, *op. cit., supra* note 44, at 157–63.

[47] Steward Machine Co. *v.* Davis, 301 U.S. 548, 589, 57 Sup. Ct. 883, 892, 81 L. Ed. 1279, 1292 (1937).

again: "The United States and the state of Alabama are not alien governments. They co-exist within the same territory. Unemployment is their common concern. Together the two statutes before us [the Act of Congress and the Alabama Act] embody a cooperative legislative effort by state and national governments, for carrying out a public purpose common to both, which neither could fully achieve without the cooperation of the other. The Constitution does not prohibit such a cooperation." [48]

It has been argued, to be sure, that the cooperative conception of the federal relationship, especially as it is realized in the policy of the "grants-in-aid," tends to break down State initiative and to devitalize State policies. Actually, its effect has often been the contrary, and for the reason pointed out by Justice Cardozo in Helvering *v.* Davis,[49] also decided in 1937; namely, that the States, competing as they do with one another to attract investors, have not been able to embark separately upon expensive programs of relief and social insurance.

The other great objection to Cooperative Federalism is more difficult to meet, if indeed it can be met. This is, that "Cooperative Federalism" spells further aggrandizement of national power. Unquestionably it does, for when two cooperate it is the stronger member of the combination who calls the tunes. Resting as it does primarily on the superior fiscal resources of the National Government, Cooperative Federalism has been, to date, a short expression for a constantly increasing concentration of power at Washington in the instigation and supervision of local policies.

VI

But the story of American federalism may also be surveyed from the angle of the diverse interests which the federal "contrivance" —to use Dicey's apt word—has served. Federalism's first achievement was to enable the American people to secure the benefits of national union without imperilling their republican institutions. In a passage in his *Spirit of the Laws* which Hamilton quotes

---

[48] Carmichael *v.* Southern Coal & Coke Co., 301 U.S. 495, 526, 57 Sup. Ct. 868, 880, 81 L. Ed. 1245, 1262 (1937).

[49] 301 U.S. 619, 57 Sup. Ct. 904, 81 L. Ed. 1307 (1937).

in *The Federalist*, Montesquieu had anticipated this possibility in general terms. He said:

> It is very probable that mankind would have been obliged at length to live constantly under the government of a single person, had they not contrived a kind of constitution that has all the internal advantages of a republican, together with the external force of a monarchical government. I mean a Confederate Republic.[50]

In fact, the founders of the American Federal System for the first time in history ranged the power of a potentially great state on the side of institutions which had hitherto been confined to small states. Even the republicanism of Rome had stopped at the Eternal City's walls.

Then in the century following, American federalism served the great enterprise of appropriating the North American continent to western civilization. For one of the greatest lures to the westward movement of population was the possibility which federalism held out to the advancing settlers of establishing their own undictated political institutions, and endowing them with generous powers of government for local use. Federalism thus became the instrument of a new, *a democratic, imperialism*, one extending over an "Empire of liberty," in Jefferson's striking phrase.

Then, about 1890, just as the frontier was disappearing from the map, federalism became, through judicial review, an instrument of the current *laissez faire* conception of the function of government and a force promoting the rise of Big Business. Adopting the theory that the reason why Congress had been given the power to regulate "commerce among the several states" was to prevent the states from doing so, rather than to enable the National Government to pursue social policies of its own through exerting a positive control over commerce, the Court at one time created a realm of no-power, "a twilight zone," "a no-man's land" in which corporate enterprise was free to roam largely unchecked. While the economic unification of the nation was undoubtedly aided by this time of Constitutional Law, the benefit was handsomely paid for in the social detriments which attended it, as became clear when the Great Depression descended on the

[50] *The Federalist*, No. 9 at 48 (Lodge ed. 1888).

country. Finally, by the constitutional revolution which once went by the name of the "New Deal" but now wears the label "Fair Deal," American federalism has been converted into an instrument for the achievement of peace abroad and economic security for "the common man" at home. In the process of remolding the Federal System for these purposes, however, the instrument has been overwhelmed and submerged in the objectives sought, so that today the question faces us whether the constituent States of the System can be saved for any useful purpose, and thereby saved as the vital cells that they have been heretofore of democratic sentiment, impulse, and action.

And it was probably with some such doubt in mind that Justice Frankfurter wrote a few years ago, in an opinion for the Court:

> The interpenetrations of modern society have not wiped out state lines. It is not for us to make inroads upon our federal system either by indifference to its maintenance or excessive regard for the unifying forces of modern technology. Scholastic reasoning may prove that no activity is isolated within the boundaries of a single State, but that cannot justify absorption of legislative power by the United States over every activity.[51]

---

[51] Polish National Alliance *v.* NLRB, 322 U.S. 643, 650, 64 Sup. Ct. 1196, 1200, 86 L. Ed. 1509, 1516 (1944). The following striking contrast between the United States of 1789 and the United States of 1942 is from the pen of Professor William Anderson in "Federalism—Then and Now," 16 *State Government* 107–12 (May, 1943):

Then *a small area, with a small and sparse population, mainly agricultural and poor.* Now *one of the world's great nations in both area and population, largely urban and highly industrial, with tremendous national wealth.*

Then *largely a debtor people and an exporter of raw materials.* Now *a great creditor nation and large exporter of manufactured as well as agricultural goods.*

Then *meager and slow transportation facilities, and even poorer provisions for communication.* Now *an equipment of railroads, steamship lines, highways, trucks and buses, air transport, and communications of all kinds unexcelled by any nation and undreamed of in the past.*

Then *state citizenship, state and local loyalties, interstate suspicions and tariffs, localized business, and considerable internal disunity.* Now *a nation, with national citizenship, primarily national loyalties, a nationwide free market, and nationally organized business, agriculture, labor, professions, press, and political parties.*

Then *an upstart and divided people, an international weakling, threatened from north and south, with very poor defense arrangements, and*

These be brave words. Are they likely to determine the course of future history any more than Madison's similar utterance—130 years ago—has done to date?

---

looking out over the Atlantic at an essentially hostile world. Now a great world power, an international leader, with a powerful army and navy, and with strong friends and interests (as well as enemies) across both Atlantic and Pacific.

Then inactive, negative, laissez-faire *government with very few functions, and with only business leaders favoring a national government, and they desiring only to give it enough vigor to protect commerce, provide a nationwide free home market, and a sound currency and banking system. Now* active, positive, collectivist *government, especially at the national level, rendering many services with the support of powerful labor and agricultural elements, while many business leaders have reversed their position.*

Then local law enforcement *with state protection of the liberties guaranteed in bills of rights. Now increasing* national law enforcement *and national protection of civil liberties even against state and local action.*

Then practically no employees of the national government and very few state and local employees. Now a national civil service of normally over a million persons reaching into every county of the country, plus extensive state and local civil services.

Then small public budgets at all levels. Now public budgets and expenditures, especially for the national government, that reach astronomical figures.

Then (before 1789) no national taxes at all for decades after 1789, only customs and excise taxes on a very limited scale, with state and local governments relying almost entirely on direct property taxes. Now tremendously increased and diversified taxes at both national and state levels, with a national government rising swiftly to a dominating position with respect to all taxes except those directly on property.

Then (before 1788) state grants to the Congress of the United States for defense and debt purposes. Now grants-in-aid by the national government to the states in increasing amounts and with steadily tightening national controls over state action.

^^^^^^^^^^^^^^^^^^^^^^^^^^^^^^^

CHAPTER SEVEN

International Agreements and Constitutional Amendments

IN EDWARD S. CORWIN'S "THE PASSING OF DUAL FEDERALISM" it was suggested that constitutional changes of great moment may occur even though no formal amendment has been passed and even though the courts' ostensible standards of judgment have been very little altered. The subject here treated by Professor Sutherland—the power to make international agreements —raises a quite different set of issues. For in this field we have seen during recent years a concerted effort to amend the Constitution explicitly, to redefine in accordance with the procedures of the amending clause the scope of the "treaty power." The proposal has evoked a perfect deluge of discussion, some learned and rational, some not. At least no one can complain that the issue is escaping the attention of the nation, and whichever way the matter is decided, we can be sure that this constitutional problem will have been fully aired in the forum of American opinion. Whether such an airing will insure understanding is perhaps another matter, but at least scholars and publicists can feel that a lot of stones have been turned.

For the student of constitutional law the proposal to restrict the treaty power obviously involves two nice questions. The first is the question of where the authority to make international agreements stands today: how far does it reach? Wherein is it limited? what are the legal uncertainties that becloud this field? If we propose to restrict something it first becomes necessary that we know what the something is, and Professor Sutherland has dedicated the first part of his analysis to a description of the treaty power's historical roots and an examination of its scope in modern constitutional law. The essay speaks for itself here, and it is enough in these prefatory remarks to lay some special emphasis on a couple of generalized conclusions: that the treaty power does apparently enable the federal government to grasp some subjects it could not reach under other clauses of the Constitution; and that the exact limitations on the power must in some instances be defined by "educated guesses" (to use a phrase employed by Professor Sutherland in a subsequent article: "The Bricker Amendment, Executive Agreements, and Imported Potatoes," 67 Harvard Law Review 281, 285 [1953]). These guesses may have been pushed a few inches nearer certitude by the holdings in United States *v.* Capps, 204 F. 2d 655 (1953) and Seery *v.* United States 127 F. Supp. 601 (1955) (see Sutherland's "The Flag, the Constitution, and International Agreements" 68 Harvard Law Review 1374 [1955]). But the fact remains that only a temerarious legal scholar would flatly declare that an executive agreement is voided by a prior statute, or that a treaty or even an executive agreement is voided by the Bill of Rights. Uncertainties in the field are further multiplied by the possibility that the Supreme Court will avoid reviewing treaty-power controversies on the ground that they raise a "political question" (see, for example, Foster *v.* Neilson, 2 Peters 253 [1829]).

The second question, of course, is whether, given the legal situation, the proposed amendments are desirable. It is probably fair to say that the great weight of scholarly opinion is opposed to the suggested restrictions. Senator Wiley reported in 1954 that queries sent to law school deans and professors of constitutional law throughout the country had elicited only one response favoring the "Bricker Amendment." (100 Cong. Rec. 71 [Jan. 7,

1954].) On the other hand, the House of Delegates of the American Bar Association, as Sutherland points out, has voted to recommend an amendment specifically subordinating the treaty power to the rest of the Constitution and limiting the force of treaties as internal law.

Before these conflicting opinions can be fully assessed, it would seem necessary to ask whether we can identify any general considerations that might be relevant whenever an amendment proposal is made. How should a citizen go about deciding that an amendment ought, or ought not, to be added to the Constitution? A preliminary answer might be that the proposed amendment should implement a value that is shared by a heavy majority of Americans and that most of them believe to be a legitimate concern of government. On a strictly ethical plane it could be argued that some values merit protection whether or not they are supported by this national consensus; but there is good reason to doubt that it would serve any purpose to express these values in constitutional terms, for it is notorious that a Constitution is seldom much better than the people who live under it. Nor would it make good common sense to embody the American veneration for Motherhood in a constitutional amendment, simply because most Americans, while cherishing this value very highly, would presumably feel that it had little to do with politics.

Apparently the values which the proposed amendments seek to protect are local autonomy, the separation of powers, and the general premise that all governmental power should be subject to concrete limitations: the worriers seem to fear that treaties and executive agreements will be used to impose a national code of law on the sovereign states, that the President and the Senate or the President alone may use these devices to formulate national legislation without the formality of consulting Congress-as-a-whole, and that this "legislation" might transcend the limitations imposed on government when it acts under its other delegated powers. Which, if any, of these values are really primary in the contemporary American value hierarchy is perhaps a subject for debate. The nation seems to have endured with a good deal of equanimity the shifting of power towards the central government that has marked the political history of the past twenty-five years; and there has been no universal outcry against the concomitant increase in presidential authority. But it may be that the earnest convictions of the amenders can end this seeming apathy, and it is, of course, perfectly appropriate for them to try to do so. As for the fear that the treaty power might override such limitations as those found in the Bill of Rights, there is some reason to doubt that this would be constitutionally possible, although there is certainly also some margin for legal conjecture.

Whatever may be thought about these matters, what other factors should be taken into account when a constitutional amendment is proposed? When a governmental power is being called into question, one pertinent consideration might be whether the power is peculiarly liable to abuse. If we wish to be absolutely safe from governmental tyranny, the best prescription would be to grant government no authority at all, since any power may be abused. But for reasons that are sufficiently plain this course has been deemed impracticable, and we have been forced to the second-best expedient of inhibiting authority at the points where the greatest danger is thought to lie. The power of appointment, for example, was thought to be a potential menace, so the President's discretion was hedged by the requirement of Senate participation. Does the power to make "international agreements" belong in a similar category? The sometimes convenient limitations of space require that the answer be left to the reader's private speculation, but one or two comments can be offered. For one thing, it should be borne in mind that the Congress has the undoubted power to revoke by supervening legislation many of the malfeasances that the Senate and the President, or the President alone, might commit. For another thing, in calculating those putative misdeeds, some attention must be paid to plausibility. No clause of the Constitution that I know of would prevent Congress from denying naturalization to all applicants with red hair, but there seems no pressing need to amend the Constitution so as to guard against this remote contingency. Real and fairly immediate dangers are worth fretting about, but judges as well as other folk have sometimes allowed themselves to conjure up a parade of unlikely "judicial horribles" that might theoretically ensue unless their interpretation of the Constitution is adhered to. To this line of argumentation the rejoinder was given a good many centuries ago: "Sufficient unto the day is the evil thereof." It is hard enough to provide in a constitution against what government might reasonably be expected to do; it would be quite impossible to forfend all the dangers that a fertile imagination could envision.

Still another consideration that might be reckoned with in evaluating amendment proposals is the question of whether the subject is an "appropriate" one for constitutional limitation. It is a commonplace that a constitution is not a legal code and that the minor problems of governance are best left to the future. The nature of a constitution requires, as John Marshall once said, "that only its great outlines should be marked, its important objects designated, and the minor engredients which compose those objects be deduced from the nature of the objects themselves." (McCulloch *v.* Maryland 4 Wheaton 316 [1819].) But the larger question is whether the power being considered, assuming its importance, can be adequately exercised under close restrictions, or whether, going further, restrictions can be devised that would not throw the baby out with the bathwater. If the power deals with a subject that is especially complex or especially suppositious, or both, the case for restricting that power may be doubtful indeed, simply because it is impossible to be sure that the general principles embodied in the limitations will fit the cases to which they must apply. The national government's power over interstate commerce, for example, involves the almost incalculable intricacies of commercial relations in an advanced industrial community, and the difficulty of contriving general rules to circumscribe such a power is amply attested by the history of the commerce clause. To quote Marshall again, it is patently unwise that such power be too straitly confined in an "attempt to provide by immutable rules, for exigencies which, if foreseen at all, must have been seen dimly, and which can be best provided for as they occur." (McCulloch *v.* Maryland 4 Wheaton 316 [1819].) Whether the treaty power should be so regarded may, again, be left to the reader, but his attention should be called to the elaborate mosaic of international arrangements compendiously described by Professor Sutherland under the heading "The Effect

of the Proposed Amendments on Present Practices." Surely there
is an element of risk in trusting our descendants as Professor
Sutherland suggests, but it cannot be said too often that government itself is a risky enterprise. And it is always possible that a
limitation designed to guarantee safety may, by shackling discretion, create more inconveniences and perils than it forestalls.

▲▲▲▲▲▲▲▲▲▲▲▲▲▲▲▲▲▲▲▲▲▲▲▲▲▲▲▲▲▲▲▲▲▲▲▲

Restricting the Treaty Power
by Arthur E. Sutherland, Jr. *

Harvard Law Review,
Volume 65, Page 1305 (1952)

I. *Proposals for Constitutional Amendment*

Today, as in 1789, many people in the United States see possible
danger in the Government's power to enter into agreements with
foreign nations. On February 26, 1952, the House of Delegates
of the American Bar Association resolved to recommend to the
Congress a constitutional amendment restricting the making of
treaties.[1] The Journal of that Association has recently carried a
series of forceful articles calling attention to the perils seen by
their authors in the present potentialities of international agreement.[2] A 1951 Pulitzer Prize was awarded to a series of editorials
in the New Orleans *States,* on "Government by Treaty," which

---

* (1902–   ), Professor of Law, Harvard University Law School.
[1] *N.Y. Times,* Feb. 27, 1952, p. 8, col. 4. The proposed amendment reads:

> *A provision of a treaty which conflicts with any provision of this Constitu-
> tion shall not be of any force or effect. A treaty shall become effective as
> internal law in the United States only through legislation by Congress
> which it could enact under its delegated powers in the absence of such
> treaty.*

[2] Deutsch, The Treaty-Making Clause: A Decision for the People of America,
37 A.B.A.J. 659 (1951); Fleming, Danger to America: The Draft Covenant on
Human Rights, 37 A.B.A.J. 739, 816 (1951); Ober, The Treaty-Making and
Amending Powers: Do They Protect Our Fundamental Rights?, 36 A.B.A.J. 715
(1950); Holman, Treaty Law-Making: A Blank Check for Writing a New Constitution, 36 A.B.A.J. 707 (1950).

ended in a call for a restrictive constitutional amendment.[3] At least three state legislatures have sent to the United States Senate drafts of or recommendations for similar measures.[4] A distinguished federal Circuit Judge has advocated such amendments in a book published in 1952.[5] Since July, 1951, a Senator and three members of the House of Representatives have introduced proposed amendments affecting the treaty power.[6] On February 7,

---

[3] *N.Y. Times,* May 8, 1951, p. 1, col. 2. The editorials appeared in the New Orleans *States* from December 11 to 18, 1950; this paper had run similar series in March 1949 and April 1950.

The concluding editorial called for constitutional amendment to: "Forbid the invasion of domestic law by treaty unless specifically authorized by Act of Congress; Forbid the Congress to make treaties effective by laws not otherwise authorized by the Constitution; and Forbid any fundamental change in our form of government as now constituted by the device of treaty ratification."

[4] These were the legislatures of Colorado, 97 Cong. Rec. 1353 (Feb. 19, 1951), California, 97 Cong. Rec. 6186 (June 4, 1951), and Georgia, 98 Cong. Rec. 1076 (Feb. 18, 1952).

The Colorado resolution, after referring with alarm to the *Fujii* case, see note 41 *infra,* urged an amendment which would prevent change in the federal or state constitutions by treaty. The California resolution would prohibit any change by treaty or executive agreement in the form of the Federal Government, state sovereignty, express limits on congressional powers, guarantees of individual liberties, or the independence of the judiciary; treaty ratification would require two-thirds of the entire Senate membership. The Georgia resolution would eliminate self-executing treaties, prevent enlargement by treaty of congressional powers, and prohibit change by treaty or executive agreement in the structure of the Federal Government, the express limitations on the Congress, or the reserved powers of the states.

[5] Allen, *The Treaty as an Instrument of Legislation* (1952). Judge Allen proposes amendments "providing in substance that: (1) Any treaty which directly and substantially interferes with the domestic jurisdiction is invalid except where the subject matter presents a truly international problem which requires international action to handle it. (2) Any treaty which conflicts with or contradicts the Constitution of the United States is invalid." *Id.* at 105.

[6] On September 14, 1951, Senator Bricker of Ohio introduced Senate Joint Resolution 102 which proposed to substitute a new paragraph in place of the second paragraph of Article VI of the Constitution. 97 Cong. Rec. 11, 592. On February 7, 1952, Senator Bricker introduced a new Joint Resolution containing a revised form of his constitutional amendment. 98 Cong. Rec. 921; Sen. Jt. Res. 130, 82nd Cong., 2d Sess. (1952). The proposed amendment would read:

    Sec. 1. No treaty or executive agreement shall be made respecting the rights of citizens of the United States protected by this Constitution, or abridging or prohibiting the free exercise thereof.

    Sec. 2. No treaty or executive agreement shall vest in any international organization or in any foreign power any of the legislative, executive, or judicial powers vested by this Constitution in the Congress, the President, and in the courts of the United States respectively.

    Sec. 3. No treaty or executive agreement shall alter or abridge the laws of the United States or the Constitutions or laws of the several States unless,

1952, when Senator Bricker of Ohio introduced a new version of his amendment intended to impose restrictions on making international agreements and to limit their effect, he mentioned fifty-six other Senators on whose behalf as well as his own he proposed his joint resolution.[7] He spoke of the complex issues of international and constitutional law involved, of the patient and mature deliberation needed for their study, and said that one of the purposes of introducing this resolution was to focus attention on a constitutional defect and to stimulate discussion.[8] This paper is written as a small contribution to the consideration so invited.

The several current proposals for restrictive amendment set forth, with varying phraseology, a number of constitutional changes; the underlying principles of them all were earnestly considered as early as Washington's day.[9] Of course this does not

---

and then only to the extent that, Congress shall so provide by act or joint resolution.

Sec. 4. Executive agreements shall not be made in lieu of treaties.

Executive agreements shall, if not sooner terminated, expire automatically 1 year after the end of the term of office for which the President making the agreement shall have been elected, but the Congress may, at the request of any President, extend for the duration of the term of such President the life of any such agreement made or extended during the next preceding presidential term.

The President shall publish all executive agreements except that those which in his judgment require secrecy shall be submitted to appropriate committees of the Congress in lieu of publication.

[Two additional sections provide congressional enforcement power and a seven-year ratification period.]

Joint Resolutions proposing different forms of amendments were introduced by Congressman Burdick of North Dakota, see 97 Cong. Rec. 7778 (July 3, 1951); Congressman McDonough of California, see 97 Cong. Rec. A5883 (Sept. 17, 1951); and Congressman Phillips of California, see 97 Cong. Rec. 11,847 (Sept. 19, 1951). The McDonough amendment would make treaties and executive agreements void "to the extent that they abrogate or interfere with any of the rights guaranteed to citizens of the United States by the Constitution." Congressman Phillips would forbid treaties "abridging any of the rights and freedoms recognized in this Constitution," would terminate the life of executive agreements not later than six months after the term of the President making the agreement (subject to congressional extension), and would require that all executive agreements be either published or, if requiring secrecy, submitted to appropriate committees of the Congress. The Burdick amendment, however, resembles that passed by the House in 1945. See note 12 *infra.* The Committees on Federal Legislation and on International Law of the Association of the Bar of the City of New York, in a carefully documented printed report, recommended in May, 1952, that the Association oppose the Bricker amendment.

[7] 98 Cong. Rec. 920 (Feb. 7, 1952).
[8] *Id.* at 921.
[9] See notes 18 and 19 *infra.*

by any means foreclose their renewal. Their rejection in the eighteenth century does not establish their lack of merit in the middle of the twentieth. Conceivably a changed political balance within the United States and an accompanying tendency toward centralized federal government, which might be promoted by the use of the treaty power,[10] could call for some constitutional counterweight. Conceivably the division of the world into two armed camps could prompt the United States to make hasty and intemperate foreign alliances of various sorts, and to guard against this, additional restrictions on treaty-making could be thought desirable.[11] National sentimentality, freshly stimulated, might conceivably lead us into well-meant but ill-considered multilateral engagements; we could be thought to need new constitutional protection against our own good will. But our national and international situation can also be read to indicate the opposite conclusion—that agreements with other nations should not be impeded, or perhaps even that they should be facilitated.

While most of the current proposals for amendment are intended to place additional restrictions on the making of treaties and other international agreements and to diminish their domestic effect, a larger number of recent congressional resolutions for changes in the treaty clauses of the Constitution have contemplated the elimination of the present two-thirds rule for approval of a treaty, on the ground that this requirement renders treaty-making too difficult and places too much veto power in the hands of a minority of Senators.[12] Many such proposals have at the same

---

[10] Senator Bricker, explaining his proposed amendment to the Senate on February 7, 1952 said: "By misuse of the treaty power it is possible for the President and the Senate to transfer to Washington all the powers reserved to the States by the Tenth Amendment. I do not see how any such abuse can be prevented." 98 Cong. Rec. 925.

[11] For examples of Senatorial apprehension at a proposed defensive treaty of alliance, see the debates on the North Atlantic Treaty, 95 Cong. Rec. 8812–9916 (1949).

[12] In the 78th Congress, 1st Session, 1944, House Joint Resolutions Nos. 6 and 31 proposed amendments to permit approval of treaties by simple majority of each house, and House Joint Resolution 64 proposed to require only "advice and consent of the Senate." At the second session of the same Congress, House Joint Resolutions Nos. 238, 246, 264 and 320 proposed approval of treaties by simple majority of both houses, which means majority of a quorum, not of total membership. In the first session of the 79th Congress, House Joint Resolution 60, proposing to require only "the advice of both Houses of Congress," was passed by the House. 91 Cong. Rec. 4368 (1945). The committee report refers to eight other House Joint Resolu-

time contemplated extending to the House of Representatives a share in approving treaties. In 1944, when the House Committee on the Judiciary held hearings on seven proposed constitutional amendments, six of these would have permitted the President to make treaties with the concurrence of a majority of the members present in each house; one would have required only the concurrence of the Senate, with no two-thirds provision.[13]

Following the 1944 hearings, the Committee reported its approval of House Joint Resolution 320,[14] which read:

Hereafter treaties shall be made by the President by and with the advice of both houses of Congress.

The resolution made no further progress until the following year, when, reintroduced by Congressman Sumners as House Joint Resolution 60, it was again approved by the Judiciary Committee. The 1944 committee report was reissued in 1945.[15] It stated that the two-thirds rule had been adopted in the eighteenth century to protect sectional interests against discriminatory treaties, not because of any fundamental theory of government.[16] It stressed the necessity for the rapid conduct of international affairs by the United States and the tendency of the two-thirds rule to increase

tions which it describes as similar. H.R. Rep. No. 139, 79th Cong., 1st Sess. (1945). Congressman Burdick's House Joint Resolution 282 in the present Congress calls for the advice and consent of a simple majority of both houses.

For older proposals, see Ames, "Amendments to the Constitution" in 2 Am. Hist. Ass'n, *Ann. Rep.* 267–69 (1896); see also *Proposed Amendments to the Constitution of the U.S.,* Dec. 6, 1926–Jan. 3, 1947 (U.S. Gov't Printing Office 1947).

John Hay, when Secretary of State under McKinley, found the two-thirds rule an irksome obstacle to the settlement of Alaskan boundary questions. He wrote to Joseph H. Choate, our ambassador in London, in 1899: "Now the irreparable mistake of our Constitution puts it in the power of one-third of the Senate to meet with categorical veto any treaty negotiated by the President, even though it may have the approval of nine-tenths of the people of the nation." Quoted in Dennett, *John Hay* 237 (1933).

[13] See note 12 *supra.*

[14] H. Jt. Res. 320, 78th Cong., 2d Sess., was introduced by Congressman Sumners of Texas, Chairman of the House Judiciary Committee. The report is No. 2061 of that Congress.

[15] H.R. Rep. No. 139, 79th Cong., 1st Sess. (1945).

[16] The same might be said for the Supremacy Clause of Article VI, which was intended to meet the problems of British claims and land titles—problems which have long since disappeared. But the proponents of the present amendments would not abandon the two-thirds rule on the ground that New England no longer fears for her fish nor the river country for New Orleans; both the Supremacy Clause and the two-thirds rule have their modern uses. For a discussion of sectional influence in the 1787 Conventions, see Warren, The Mississippi River and the Treaty Clause of the Constitution, 2 Geo. Wash. L. Rev. 271 (1934).

the use of executive agreements. It urged the advantage of participation by the House, which must in most cases support international agreements with legislation, and which with the Senate can legislate its domestic abrogation. In the original and the reissued report, the Committee stated its opinion that the people favored the resolution. Following the favorable action of the Judiciary Committee in 1945, the House passed Joint Resolution 60.[17] It made no progress in the Senate.

The amendments now proposed in limitation of the treaty power can be grouped in five classes. Perhaps the most conspicuous would expressly prohibit any impairment, by treaty or executive agreement, of the constitutional immunities of citizens or other persons among us.[18] Several of the proposals go the whole way to make treaties subordinate to the entire Constitution. These proposals, and the comments which accompany them, indicate apprehension lest some treaty supersede the Bill of Rights and other limits on governmental mistreatment of the individual, and empower the Congress to enact a long train of abuses and usurpations.

Another provision, common to several proposals, would eliminate the self-executing feature which a treaty may have under the Supremacy Clause of Article VI of the Constitution, by providing that an international agreement should only have the force of internal law in the United States when the Congress shall enact a statute so providing. Some of the proposals go further and restrict any such statute to the powers constitutionally delegated to the Congress, preventing the use of treaties to invade the reserved powers of the states.[19]

---

[17] See note 12 *supra*.

[18] The Bricker, McDonough and Phillips amendments so provide. The American Bar Association and Allen amendments subordinate treaties to the whole of the Constitution. The New Orleans *States* would prohibit "any fundamental change" in our form of government. The Colorado, California and Georgia resolutions contain similar language to eliminate the predominance of treaties over the Constitution.

Conflict between treaties and the Bill of Rights was of course not argued in the Constitutional Convention of 1787 or in the state ratifying conventions. The Bill of Rights was not in existence. But the public men of the time understood perfectly well that the treaty power, if abused, could do serious harm to their rights. The localism of the day made the supremacy of treaties over state laws a principal worry of the Fathers. See I Farrand, *Records of the Federal Convention* 54, 164 (rev. ed. 1937); 2 *id.* at 29; 3 *id.* at 113, 548; 4 Elliot, *Debates* 436 (2d ed. 1836).

[19] Treaty-law would be limited to the delegated powers by the Bar Association, New Orleans *States,* California, Georgia, Colorado and Allen proposals. The Bricker

A third proposal would require assent to treaties by a larger representation in the Senate than is now prescribed by Article II, Section 2. It reflects a fear, as old as the Constitution itself, that thirty-three ill-advised Senators and a misguided President could bind us to a treaty which a wider selection of elected officials would have had the wisdom to reject, and contemplates the increase in the required proportion of the Senate to two-thirds of its entire membership, raising the required minimum of Senatorial votes from thirty-three to sixty-four.[20]

An ancient distrust of entangling alliances, intensified by a renewed realization of the supremacy of treaty law over pre-existing internal law, has produced a proposal to prohibit vesting in any international organization or any foreign power any of the legislative, executive, or judicial powers of the United States— an adverse reaction to the rather widespread discussion of the virtues of renouncing some national sovereignty in the interests of hoped-for international concord.[21]

The increasing use of executive agreements, which sometimes look like treaties binding without Senatorial concurrence, explains pending proposals to prohibit the use of such agreements "in lieu of treaties"[22] (a somewhat difficult standard), to limit

---

resolution leaves the treaty power supreme over federal and state law provided it be implemented by Act of Congress—and subject to the limitation against impairment of constitutional rights of citizens, and subject to a prohibition against vesting power in an international body. Essentially this second category of amendments is similar to the first—they evidence the same fear voiced by Monroe in the Virginia ratifying convention, that a president and a few Senators could legislate away cherished rights. See 3 Elliot, *Debates* 221 (2d ed. 1836); 4 *id.* at 118–19; see also notes 1 and 6 *supra*.

[20] See the California proposal, described at note 4 *supra*.

[21] see § 2 of the Bricker amendment, quoted in note 6 *supra*. The point where a difference in degree becomes a difference in kind always presents a puzzle. World government, a League of Nations, or the United Nations was not an issue in our eighteenth century foreign policy. But the possibility of international confederations was obviously in the minds of the draftsmen of the Constitution, for in Article I, Section 10, the states were permitted to enter into agreements or compacts with foreign powers if Congress consented, but were unconditionally forbidden to enter into any "Treaty, Alliance or Confederation," a prohibition not imposed on the central government. Distrust of foreign entanglements was prominent in Washington's Farewell Address of 1796.

[22] See § 4 of the Bricker amendment, quoted in note 6 *supra*, and §§ 2 and 3 of the Phillips amendment, 97 Cong. Rec. 11, 847 (Sept. 19, 1951). Hamilton, in No. 75 of *The Federalist Papers*, expresses a distrust of presidential treaty-making unchecked by the Senate, which goes beyond any recent public utterances. He envisages

their effective life to a relatively short period after the end of the term of the President who negotiates them, and to require the President either to publish them or submit them to appropriate committees of the Congress. The Yalta Agreement has acquired unhappy connotations; mention of the Potsdam Agreement conjures up visions of Soviet obstinacy in Germany. A sort of guilt by association has attached to all executive agreements.

The decision of the Congress and the American people to accept any of these proposals should be made only after thorough examination, with the most informed and dispassionate judgment as to their probable effect, certainly not in rancor at past policies or men. We are in a period of disillusionment and bitterness, worse than that which followed the war of 1917-1918. But we could take little satisfaction in the discovery, a decade or a generation hence, that the United States, by restricting its competence to make international engagements, had impulsively cut off its nose to spite its face.

II. *The Background of the Proposals*

A. ORIGINS AND DEVELOPMENT OF THE TREATY POWER

From the moment of its difficult birth, the new United States felt essentially the same conflicts of interest that plague it today. It needed allies to help it face foreign hostility; it needed reconciliation with its enemies and a chance to earn a peaceful living; but at the same time its people feared alien influence in their internal affairs. The men of 1787 resented the assertion of foreign claims to lands within their borders. They resented the prospect that claims against American citizens, held by foreign creditors, subjects of an enemy nation, might survive a war in which Americans had succeeded. Localism, then as now, was more apparent in state legislatures than in the national government; a consider-

---

some poor man, raised to the presidency, selling his national trust for riches, by means of a presidential treaty.

It is worth noting that Senator Bricker makes his prohibition against the use of executive agreements in lieu of treaties apply alike to agreements made by the president alone and agreements authorized by the Congress.

For Senatorial resentment at certain recent agreements, notably those at Yalta and Potsdam, see 98 Cong. Rec. 926 (Feb. 7, 1952).

able body of state law imposed disabilities on alien inheritance of land;[23] and a Virginia statute of 1777 provided for the discharge, by payment to state officials, of debts owed to enemy aliens.[24]

The three treaties with France signed on February 6, 1778,[25] gave us a military ally and, among other limitations on local law, gave to the nationals of both countries a right of inheritance to "goods moveable and immovable." The loose federal structure of the United States at the time must have made somewhat doubtful the effect of this provision on lands in any states which restricted inheritance by aliens. The Congress ratified the three treaties on May 4, 1778, but Virginia separately ratified the first two the following year.[26] The power of the Federal Government to affect the interests of the states by treaties was thus among the earliest problems of foreign relations that faced the United States.

The treaty with the Netherlands signed at the Hague on October 8, 1782,[27] provided for liberty of worship by the nationals of the respective countries in the other's territories and for reciprocal rights of inheritance—again affecting the internal law of the states.

The Treaty of Peace of 1783, which ended the Revolutionary War,[28] attempted to provide satisfactorily for the solution of the problems of debts owed to British creditors, and of British claims to lands in the United States. The provision for debts was terse:

---

[23] For New York, see Pratt, Present Alienage Disabilities under New York State Law in Real Property, 12 Brooklyn L. Rev. 1, 15 (1942); for Pennsylvania, Lessee of Jackson *v.* Burns, 3 Binn. 75 (Pa. 1810); the situation in Virginia is explained in Martin *v.* Hunter's Lessee, 1 Wheat. 304 (U.S. 1816).

[24] See Ware *v.* Hylton, 3 Dall. 199 (U.S. 1796).

[25] 8 Stat. 6, 12 (1778); 17 Stat. 795 (1778); 2 Miller, *Treaties and Other International Acts of the United States* 3, 35, 45 (1932).

[26] 2 *id.* at 30. On June 17, 1779, Gerard, the French Minister, wrote from Philadelphia to the Count de Vergennes that the Virginia action had somewhat offended the Congress, as that body thought it contrary to its own prerogatives. See 4 Doniol, *Histoire de la Participation de la France à l'Etablissement des Etats-Unis d'Amerique* 155, 165, 167 (1886).

[27] 8 Stat. 32 (1782); 2 Miller, *op. cit., supra* note 25 at 59. The guarantee of freedom of worship was notable at a time when a number of the states still retained established churches. See Sutherland, Due Process and Disestablishment, 62 Harv. L. Rev. 1306, 1323 (1949). The Treaty with Sweden of 1783, 8 Stat. 60, 2 Miller, *op. cit., supra* note 25, at 123, and that with Prussia of 1785, 8 Stat. 84, 2 Miller, *op. cit., supra* note 25, at 162, also contains reciprocal guarantees of inheritance and of freedom of worship.

[28] 8 Stat. 54 (1782); 2 Miller, *op. cit., supra* note 25, at 96.

It is agreed that Creditors on either side, shall meet with no lawful Impediment to the Recovery of the full value in Sterling Money of all bona fide Debts heretofore contracted.[29]

Future confiscation of loyalist lands was forbidden.[30] Where lands had already been confiscated, more difficult questions appeared, as the claims of purchasers had now intervened. Instead of declaring invalid any titles so created, the treaty required the Congress to recommend to the several states provision for the restitution of confiscated British estates.

This hopeful exhortation proved insufficient. During the Constitutional Convention delegates repeatedly said that experience had shown a tendency in the states to violate the national treaties.[31] Madison's Preface speaks of disregard of the authority of the Confederation by violations of the existing treaties with France and Holland, and of the Treaty of Peace of 1783; [32] and when the Supremacy Clause was being formulated, Madison secured the addition of phraseology to express the intention that existing as well as future treaties be law in the several states and their courts.[33] And to quiet fears of New England lest a treaty hamper her fisheries, and of the West lest a treaty close the Mississippi, the two-thirds rule was adopted to give some degree of minority protection.[34]

In 1777 the State of Virginia had enacted a law much like a modern statute setting up an alien property custodian.[35] It provided in substance that any citizen of Virginia who owed money to a British subject might pay the debt to an officer of the State of Virginia and thereby obtain a discharge. On April 26, 1780, a Virginia business house called Hylton and Co. paid a portion of such a debt to the appropriate Virginia officer. After the adoption of the Federal Constitution, the administrator of the British creditor sued Hylton and Co. in the federal circuit court for Virginia

---

[29] Art. 4.
[30] Art. 6.
[31] I Farrand, *Records of the Federal Convention* 164, 316 (rev. ed. 1937); 3 *id.* at 113.
[32] 3 *id.* at 548.
[33] 2 *id.* at 417.
[34] See note 16 *supra* and *Hearings before Subcommittee No. 3 of the House Committee on the Judiciary on H. Jt. Res. 6, etc.,* 78th Cong. 2d Sess. (1944).
[35] For the circumstances and litigation here discussed see *Ware v. Hylton,* 3 Dall. 199 (U.S. 1796).

upon their obligations, including that portion which Hylton thought had been discharged by payment to the Virginia public officer. In the circuit court Hylton successfully pleaded the payment as a discharge, and the disappointed creditor brought error in the Supreme Court of the United States. John Marshall (not yet a judge) argued for the Virginia debtor that nothing in the new Constitution revived the debt already paid under Virginia law, but the Supreme Court reversed the lower federal court and held that Hylton must pay over again, this time to the British creditor. Under the newly-adopted Constitution, the treaty with England prevailed over the laws of Virginia.[36]

Other difficulties arose over land titles. Lord Fairfax was the owner of a great tract of land in what was known as the northern neck of Virginia.[37] His title came from grants made to his predecessors by Charles II and James II. When Fairfax died in 1781, he devised 300,000 acres of this land to the Reverend Denny Martin, who was and remained a subject of George III. Virginia, pursuant to certain statutes providing for the escheat of lands owned by British subjects, granted the land on April 30, 1789, to a man named Hunter. In 1791 Hunter, claiming under Virginia, brought ejectment against Martin in the Virginia courts. In 1794, while the case was pending, the Jay treaty confirmed all royal land titles. The Court of Appeals of Virginia in 1796 nevertheless found in favor of the Virginia grantee, Hunter; but the disappointed British subject, Martin, brought error in the Supreme Court of the United States, which reversed and held that the treaty prevailed over the Virginia title. The state authorities, much irritated, refused to carry out the decision and it was necessary for Lord Fairfax's devisee to go back to the Supreme Court a second time before he could get his judgment enforced.[38]

---

[36] The Supreme Court rejected an argument that a subject of Great Britain was in no position to rely on the treaty because, in violation of it, British troops continued to garrison Detroit and Niagara, and supplied Indians with munitions to keep up hostilities.

Thomas Jefferson is said to have paid some debts once to the Virginia officer, and then, as a result of the principle established in Ware *v.* Hylton, over again to British creditors. Malone, *Jefferson the Virginian* 260 (1948).

[37] For the circumstances and litigation here discussed see Fairfax's Devisee *v.* Hunter's Lessee, 7 Cranch 603 (U.S. 1813).

[38] Martin *v.* Hunter's Lessee, 1 Wheat. 304 (U.S. 1816). See note 41 *infra* for an attempted application of the principle of this case to the United Nations Charter.

The self-executing feature of treaties under Article VI of the United States Constitution was thus no matter of ill-considered whim. The draftsmen found it necessary, and the Supreme Court enforced it. The disadvantages of enabling the President and Senate to legislate for the entire nation were drawn to the attention of the Constitutional Convention, of the state ratifying conventions, and of the people of the nation. Their choice was made deliberately as one of the necessary adjustments between reserved state power and national policy—one of many such compromises essential to the creation of a federal nation.

The decision might have been the other way if our situation and federal structure had been different; in many nations of the world, treaties are not self-executing.[39] Canadian treaties do not prevail over those laws which are peculiarly within the competence of the Provinces. In *Attorney General for Canada* and *Attorney-General for Ontario*[40] the Judicial Committee of the Privy Council passed on the validity of three acts of the Parliament of Canada passed pursuant to conventions adopted by the International Labor Organization of the League of Nations and ratified as treaties by the Dominion of Canada. The three statutes, the "Weekly Rest in Industrial Undertakings Act," the "Minimum Wages Act," and the "Limitation of Hours of Work Act," came within the classes of subjects assigned by Section 92 of the British North America Act exclusively to the legislatures of the Provinces. The only possibility of their being *intra vires* the Dominion Parliament was through an extension of the Dominion powers by the force of the international conventions. When the test case reached the Privy Council, Lord Atkin, announcing its judgment, said:

It would be remarkable that while the Dominion could not initiate legislation, however desirable, which affected civil rights in the Province, yet its Government, not responsible to the Provinces nor controlled by Provincial Parliaments, need only agree with a foreign country to enact such legislation, and its Parliament would be forthwith clothed with authority to affect Provincial rights to the full ex-

---

[39] See Myers, "Treaty and Law under the Constitution," 26 *Dep't State Bull.* 371 (1952).
[40] [1937] A.C. 326 (P.C.).

tent of such agreement. Such a result would appear to undermine the constitutional safeguards of Provincial constitutional autonomy.

The Judgement of the Privy Council was that the Act in each case was *ultra vires* the Dominion Parliament. To implement such a treaty, legislation would have to be handled by cooperation of the Dominion and the Provinces.

If the choice of the United States Constitutional Convention of 1787 had been to limit the effect of treaties as in modern Canada, enactment of a series of statutes by each of the states of the Union would have been necessary in order to carry out a great many of our treaties. The Federal Government has frequently undertaken international obligations which themselves change the local law of the states. Litigation concerning the effect of treaties has concerned the inheritance of land contrary to state real property law,[41] the right of an alien to engage in pawnbroking

---

[41] Hauenstein *v.* Lynham, 100 U.S. 483 (1880); see Geofroy *v.* Riggs, 133 U.S. 258 (1890); see also Fairfax's Devisee *v.* Hunter's Lessee, 7 Cranch 603 (U.S. 1813).

In 1946 the Supreme Court held that such a treaty concerning inheritances, made with Germany in 1923, survived the war of 1941–1945. Clark *v.* Allen, 331 U.S. 503 (1947).

The United Nations Charter is a multilateral treaty containing certain language indicating that it is an objective of the signatories that all persons shall have fundamental freedoms without regard to race, sex, language or religion. Preamble, Arts. 1, 2, 55, 56. For many years California has had a statute barring from the ownership of real property an alien ineligible to citizenship. In the case of Fujii *v.* State, 217 P.2d 481, *rehearing denied,* 218 P.2d 595 (1950), a California District Court of Appeal held that the United Nations Charter was predominant over the local law of California, and that Fujii, though a Japanese national ineligible to citizenship, was entitled to hold his land despite the alien land law. (It is worth noting that Japan was not a signatory to the Charter.)

An appeal was taken to the Supreme Court of California, but in the meantime the opinion of the intermediate appellate court occasioned much comment in state legislatures, in Congress and by scholars in the field of international law. Judge Hudson felt that it was based on a mistaken idea that these provisions were self-executing, and pointed out that there was venerable precedent in the United States for the construction of some treaties as non-self-executing, citing Foster *v.* Neilson, 2 Pet. 253 (U.S. 1829). See *Charter Provisions on Human Rights in American Law,* 44 Am. J. Int'l L. 543 (1950). Professor Quincy Wright approved of the decision. See National Courts and Human Rights—The Fujii Case, 45 Am. J. Int'l L. 62 (1951). The prospect of the Charter as a self-executing treaty occasioned some alarm. Senator Bricker said in the Senate, "If the Fujii case should eventually be affirmed by the United States Supreme Court, or if the principle announced therein should be sustained, literally thousands of Federal and State laws will automatically become invalid. . . . Obviously something must be done to prevent treaties from having such far-reaching and unintended consequences." See 98 Cong. Rec. 925 (Feb. 7, 1952). The Colorado legislature urged the United States Senate to amend the Constitution to avoid the effects of the decision which, it found, disclosed a "peril to the very fundamentals of American law and liberty, and the entire theory

despite a local ordinance [42] and the right of an alien to pay no more inheritance tax than a national of the United States; [43] but the most discussed case of a treaty extending the area of federal legislative competence arose over the right to go duck-hunting.

In 1913, Congress passed a statute regulating the shooting of migratory birds. The federal courts in Arkansas and Kansas held it unconstitutional on the ground that the Constitution delegates no game-protecting powers to the Federal Government. [44] In order to achieve the desired protection the United States thereupon entered into a treaty with Great Britain which provided that reciprocal legislation should provide closed shooting seasons in the United States and Canada. [45] Subsequently, in 1918, the Congress passed a statute to give effect to that treaty. [46] Missouri, still resisting, brought an action to enjoin a federal game warden named Holland from enforcing the statute. Thus arose the celebrated Missouri *v.* Holland. [47] When this case reached the Supreme Court, Mr. Justice Holmes, delivering the majority opinion, found that the treaty power prevailed over the distribution of functions between state and nation in the Constitution, and that the migratory bird treaty enabled the Congress to legislate for matters which would otherwise be entirely within state control.

Presumably the founding fathers had not considered the prospect of a treaty permitting federal restrictions on wild-fowling; but they had foreseen the possibility of federal restriction by treaty of offshore fishing; Missouri *v.* Holland is not so very radical an extension of the federal powers contemplated in 1787. However, on the part of those who favor the elimination of

---

of popular government, a peril which certainly the founding fathers never contemplated and which must be obviated at the earliest possible moment; . . ."

However, in affirming the Fujii case, the California Supreme Court gave as its opinion that the provisions were not self-executing, and did not supersede the California land laws; instead the Supreme Court of California rested its decision on the Fourteenth Amendment. See *N.Y. Times,* April 18, 1952, p. 1, col. 2, and *id.,* April 20, 1952, p. 25, col. 1; 38 Adv. Cal. 817 (1952).

[42] Asakura *v.* Seattle, 265 U.S. 332 (1952).

[43] Nielsen *v.* Johnson, 279 U.S. 47 (1929).

[44] United States *v.* Shauver, 214 Fed. 154 (E.D. Ark. 1914); United States *v.* McCullagh, 221 Fed. 288 (D. Kan. 1915).

[45] 39 Stat. 1702 (1916).

[46] Migratory Bird Treaty Act, 40 Stat. 755 (1918).

[47] 252 U.S. 416 (1920).

the supremacy of treaties over the retained powers of the states, it might be argued that the conditions which gave rise to the Supremacy Clause passed with the settlement of British debts and the quieting of the other controversies arising from the War of Independence. One can only judge this by considering whether today's national needs are for more states' rights or for a stronger Federal Government.

B. THE TREATY POWER AND THE CONSTITUTIONAL GUARANTEES AGAINST GOVERNMENT OPPRESSION

The Supremacy Clause is unqualified in terms. It contains no provision limiting the predominance of treaties over the Constitution to such matters as merely alter the distribution of legislative power between the states and the Federal Government; there is no express exception leaving supreme over any treaties such constitutional limitations on governmental power as those controlling criminal trials in Article III. A reasonable argument can be made from the circumstances surrounding the adoption of the Supremacy Clause that original constitutional limitations intended for the protection of the citizen cannot be abrogated by treaty, for civil liberties are entirely outside the reason for the Supremacy Clause, the desire to protect British claims to land and credits. The same argument applies with even greater force to the Bill of Rights and the post-Civil War amendments. As the Supreme Court has never actually held either a treaty or an executive agreement invalid,[48] the limits on the federal power to make international agreements are still uncertain. The court has, however, suggested *obiter* a number of times that the treaty power cannot be utilized to cancel provisions of the Federal Constitution which expressly prohibit various types of action by the United States. Mr. Justice Field in a much quoted dictum said in 1890:

The treaty power, as expressed in the Constitution, is in terms unlimited except by those restraints which are found in that instrument against the action of the government or of its departments, and those

---

[48] The extent to which courts will undertake to review acts of the executive in the field of foreign policy is not clear. See Chicago & Southern Air Lines, Inc. *v.* Waterman S.S. Corp., 333 U.S. 103, 111 (1948).

arising from the nature of the government itself and of that of the States. It would not be contended that it extends so far as to authorize what the Constitution forbids, or a change in the character of the government or in that of one of the States, or a cession of any portion of the territory of the latter, without its consent.[49]

President Coolidge and the Senate evidently thought that a treaty could prevail over at least one amendment. In 1924 the United States entered into a treaty with Great Britain which allowed British ships to bring intoxicating liquor under seal into waters of the United States[50] although the Supreme Court of the United States had held during the preceding year that the Eighteenth Amendment prohibited such importation.[51] A sensible argument could be made that the prohibition amendment resembled more closely the commercial and real-property legislation which the Supremacy Clause was intended to affect than it resembled provisions of the Bill of Rights, and that the treaty of 1924 was valid while a treaty purporting to establish, say, press censorship would not be. In the only case[52] which challenged the 1924 treaty, however, the standing of the plantiffs, who were a mariner, a secretary of an incorporated Masters' and Mates' Association, and others interested in American shipping, which suffered by the competition of more attractive British ships, was held insufficient to sustain an adjudication on the validity of the treaty.

C. TREATIES AND SUPERVENING STATUTES

The Supreme Court has clearly established the supremacy of a congressional statute subsequent and contrary to a treaty. The Chinese Exclusion Case[53] concerned the right of re-entry into the United States of a Chinese who had been lawfully a resident of this country for some time, who had returned to visit China

---

[49] Geofroy *v.* Riggs, 133 U.S. 258, 267 (1890). See also Missouri *v.* Holland, 252 U.S. 416, 433 (1920); United States *v.* Minnesota, 270 U.S. 181, 207 *et seq.* (1926).

[50] 43 Stat. 1761 (1924).

[51] Cunard S.S. Co. *v.* Mellon, 262 U.S. 100 (1923).

[52] Milliken *v.* Stone, 16 F.2d 981 (2d Cir.), *cert. denied,* 274 U.S. 748 (1927).

[53] Chae Chan Ping *v.* United States, 130 U.S. 581 (1889). See also Head Money Cases, 112 U.S. 580 (1884). The supremacy of a later statute is restated in Moser *v.* United States, 341 U.S. 41, 45 (1951).

and who, under the provisions of a treaty between China and the United States, was entitled to return to this country. A few days before he arrived at San Francisco, the Congress, prompted by irritation against oriental people on the West Coast, passed a statute abrogating the right of re-entry. The Supreme Court held that the unfortunate Chinese was not entitled to re-enter the United States. The statute of the Congress, so far as it constituted a command to American immigration officers, had over-ridden and nullified the treaty.

Such a unilateral piece of legislation can not, of course, wipe out the Chinese claim; Congress cannot legislate for China. Our international obligations remain unaffected in such a case, and we run the risk of whatever reprisals the offended nation may care to take. The position of the United States after such congressional action appears to be very similar to that of Great Britain in any case where her executive has made a treaty with a foreign power, and Parliament subsequently fails to implement the treaty with legislation. If the treaty requires domestic legislation, the Crown must induce Parliament to legislate.

If Parliament declines to do so, the Crown will not ratify the treaty; if by imprudence the Crown has already ratified the treaty, the United Kingdom is bound by it (for the Crown is internationally omnipotent in the matter of treaties), and the Crown must do its best to extricate the country from an embarrassing situation.[54]

D. EXECUTIVE AGREEMENTS

The United States conducts some of its foreign affairs by agreements made by the executive alone without Senatorial concurrence. Federal agreements other than treaties are not mentioned in the Constitution, although Article I, Section 10, while entirely forbidding the several states to enter into any "Treaty, Alliance, or Confederation," permits any state, if Congress consents, to enter into an "Agreement or Compact . . . with a foreign Power," showing that at the time of the adoption of the Constitution, the existence of international agreements other than treaties was recognized. It seems necessary from time to time

---

[54] McNair, *Treaties* 7, 8 (1938).

in a nation's affairs to make quick and confidential compacts with friendly powers. The difficulty is to define the limits of the competence to make such engagements; to determine when Senatorial concurrence is necessary, if that determination be possible in any way other than ad hoc in each instance, for reasons of policy.

Executive agreements, sometimes authorized by the Congress in advance, and sometimes not, have been used by the United States throughout its history. Washington's Postmaster General made an agreement for mail service with the Deputy Postmaster General of Canada.[55] In 1817, by an interchange of notes between Charles Bagot, Minister of Great Britain, and Richard Rush, Acting Secretary of State of the United States, an agreement was made limiting the naval forces to be maintained on the Great Lakes and Lake Champlain.[56] The Secretary of the Navy gave the necessary orders to carry out the agreement; but nearly a year later, after Mr. Bagot had expressed to John Quincy Adams, then Secretary of State, some interest in the question whether the agreement, "which he said was a sort of treaty," was to be sent to Congress, President Monroe on April 6, 1818, submitted it to the Senate with a message which included this sentence:

I submit it to the consideration of the Senate, whether this is such an arrangement as the Executive is competent to enter into, or is such an one as requires the advice and consent of the Senate; and, in the latter case, for their advice and consent, should it be approved.[57]

On April 16, 1818, the Senate resolved that it did "approve of and consent to the arrangement" [58] in question—using neither the words "concur" nor "treaty" which would be suggested by Article II, Section 2 of the Constitution, and still leaving some doubt whether the Senate thought its concurrence was necessary.

Though President Monroe had debated the merits and demerits of the treaty clauses in the Virginia ratifying convention

---

[55] McClure, *International Executive Agreements* 38 (1941).
[56] 2 Miller, *Treaties and Other International Acts of the United States* 645 *et seq.* (1931).
[57] *Id.* at 647.
[58] *Id.* at 648.

of 1788,[59] and like his successors in the twentieth century he was
confident that some international agreements were appropriate
for unsupported executive action, he seems to have been uncertain which they were.

As the country has become more concerned with foreign
affairs, the use of executive agreements has rapidly increased. A
noteworthy example of recent times was the Litvinoff Agreement entered into on November 16, 1933, by President Roosevelt and Maxim Litvinoff, People's Commissar for Foreign Affairs, USSR. Made by an informal exchange of notes, this agreement "established normal diplomatic relations with" the Union
of Soviet Socialist Republics as the Government of Russia.[60] In
connection with that recognition the United States accepted an
assignment of certain Russian claims against "American nationals, including corporations, companies, partnerships or associations." Following the Litvinoff Agreement, the United States, as
assignee of the Soviet Government, attempted to enforce in various courts the claims so acquired. In 1942, such a case, United
States *v.* Pink, reached the Supreme Court [61] after a judgment by
the New York Court of Appeals adverse to the claims of the
United States. The principal defendant was the Superintendent
of Insurance of the State of New York who had in his hands
assets of the First Russian Insurance Company. The Russian Insurance Company, establishing a New York branch in 1907, had
deposited certain securities with the Superintendent of Insurance in order to obtain the privilege of doing business in that
State. After the revolution, Russia claimed to have become entitled to its assets by nationalizing the corporation. The United
States, asserting rights under the Litvinoff Agreement, sued the
Superintendent for the assets in his hands. The New York Court
of Appeals held that the law of New York governed the dispo-

---

[59] 3 Elliot's *Debates* 220 *et seq.* (2d ed. 1836).

[60] U.S. Dep't State, *Establishment of Diplomatic Relations with the Union of
Soviet Socialist Republics* (European Series No. 4, 1933).

[61] 315 U.S. 203 (1942). The Litvinoff Agreement had several times before been
considered by the Supreme Court. United States *v.* Belmont, 301 U.S. 324 (1937);
Guaranty Trust Co. *v.* United States, 304 U.S. 126 (1938); Moscow Fire Ins. Co. *v.*
Bank of New York, 280 N.Y. 286, 20 N.E. 2d 758 (1939), *aff'd without opinion
by an equally divided court sub nom.* United States *v.* Moscow Fire Ins. Co., 309
U.S. 624 (1940). The Pink case finally settled the question of the effect of the
agreement on local law.

sition of the assets and that law accorded no effect in New York to the Soviet decrees of confiscation. The Supreme Court, however, held that the executive agreement would prevail over this local policy of the State of New York and would entitle the United States to the fund. The purpose of the agreement was to recognize and validate the claims of Russia, and the absence of Senatorial concurrence did not deprive it of predominance over the contrary state law.

The preparation for and conduct of hostilities in cooperation with other nations is an area in which presidential agreements are particularly frequent. An example is the arrangement made with Great Britain in 1940 for the lease of certain bases to the United States in return for fifty destroyers.[62] The constitutionality of the transaction in the absence of Senatorial concurrence aroused some doubts, but the Attorney General of the United States, then Robert Jackson, gave the President his opinion [63] that the agreement needed no Senate action to support its validity. It rested on the President's power as Commander-in-Chief and his inherent power over foreign relations. The agreement, the Attorney General wrote, made no future commitment on behalf of the United States, and this made Senatorial concurrence unnecessary. He cited as a precedent for his opinion the agreement made by Secretary of State Daniel Webster in 1850,[64] by which the United States acquired Horse Shoe Reef at the entrance to Buffalo Harbor on condition that the United States would engage to erect a lighthouse and maintain a light but would erect no fortifications thereon.[65]

The Congress, ever since it authorized postal agreements in 1792,[66] has from time to time given advance consent by statute for the executive to make international engagements without subsequent Senatorial concurrence. Such congressional-executive agreements are in common use. In 1934, for example, the Con-

---

[62] 54 Stat. 2405 (1940).

[63] 39 Ops. Att'y Gen. 484 (1940).

[64] 1 Malloy, *Treaties* 668 (1910).

[65] Another important executive agreement entered into when the United States was not engaged in warfare, but involving the dispatch of troops to a foreign country for defensive purposes, was the agreement of July, 1941, between the United States and Iceland. 55 Stat. 1547 (1941).

[66] 1 Stat. 232, 239 (1792), reenacted by the following Congress, 1 Stat. 354, 366 (1794). See McClure, *International Executive Agreements* 38 (1941).

gress added to the Tariff Act of 1930 "Part III, Promotion of Foreign Trade" [67] which authorized the president, within pre-scribed limitations, to enter into "foreign trade agreements with foreign governments or instrumentalities." The statute has been extended from time to time, and the executive has negotiated a substantial number of reciprocal agreements providing for re-ductions in tariffs. Of these the best known, perhaps, is the Gen-eral Agreement on Tariffs and Trade of October 30, 1947, a multi-lateral agreement occupying more than 2,000 pages—the whole of Parts 5 and 6 of Volume 61 of the Statutes at Large.

The literature on executive agreements is abundant.[68] Some-times they have been viewed with alarm by those who see in them a dangerous device by which a headstrong executive may evade the control of a two-thirds Senate vote; sometimes they have been praised as quick and convenient means of conducting day-to-day foreign affairs. Two things are certain: they have been used from the earliest days of the independence of the United States; and thoughtful men have during all that time been unable to supply what the Constitution lacks—a clear distinction between what is appropriate matter for executive agreement, and what should be handled by treaty with Senatorial concurrence.

Because of the infinite varieties of agreements now in use, an undertaking to devise a constitutional amendment which will satisfactorily separate the one from the other seems, to say the least, extraordinarily difficult. A provision that executive agree-ments shall not be used "in lieu of treaties," unfortunately leaves the problem of definition untouched. We are as puzzled as Pres-ident Monroe was in 1818. If we knew what was essentially treaty-like, we could define executive agreements by exclusion;

---

[67] 48 Stat. 943 (1934).

[68] McClure, *International Executive Agreements* (1941) treats the subject ex-haustively and contains a full bibliography. The late Professor Borchard expressed objections to the extension of the use of executive agreements in fields customarily covered by treaties requiring Senatorial concurrence. See Borchard, Shall the Execu-tive Agreement Replace the Treaty?, 53 Yale L.J. 664 (1944); the other point of view is given in McDougal and Lans, Treaties and Congressional-Executive or Presi-dential Agreements: Interchangeable Instruments of National Policy, 54 Yale L.J. 181, 534 (1945). See also Borchard, Treaties and Executive Agreements—A Reply, 54 Yale L.J. 616 (1945).

but it is no more possible in our day than in his to define one unknown in terms of another.[69]

III. *The Effect of the Proposed Amendments on Present Practices*

The renewal, in mid-twentieth century, of the historic debates concerning the limitation of the power of the Federal Government to make international agreements can only be evaluated by a study of their present use. Most of the contemporary literature on the subject is devoted to discussion of the possible domestic effect of several projected multilateral treaties originating under the sponsorship of the United Nations: [70] the International Convention on the Prevention and Punishment of the Crime of Genocide, intended to end the calculated extinction of entire racial or other groups, which the President transmitted to the Senate on June 16, 1949; [71] the still somewhat nebulous proposal, found desirable by the International Law Commission of the United Nations, though not by unanimous vote, for the creation of an international criminal court for the trial of genocide and other crimes; [72] the International Covenant on Human Rights still in draft by the Commission on Human Rights of

---

[69] Senator Bricker commented on the problem when he introduced the latest version of his proposed amendment: "I found it very difficult in my own mind to define an executive agreement, or what ought to be an executive agreement, and what ought to be encompassed by a treaty." 98 Cong. Rec. 923 (Feb. 7, 1952). "No attempt is made in the amendment to define the subject matter appropriate for an executive agreement. It is probably impossible to draw a satisfactory line of demarcation even in a statute. It would be unwise to make the attempt in a constitutional amendment." 98 *id.* at 927.

[70] See the articles in the *American Bar Association Journal*, cited in note 2 *supra*. Judge Florence Allen, like these commentators, sees danger for the United States in broad multilateral engagements. See Allen, *The Treaty as an Instrument of Legislation* (1952). The opposite view is expressed by Professor Zechariah Chafee in Federal and State Powers under the UN Covenant on Human Rights [1951], Wis. L. Rev. 389, 623.

[71] 21 *Dep't of State Bull.* 844 (1949).

[72] See Finch, Draft Statute for an International Criminal Court, 46 Am. J. Int'l L. 89 (1952). The Draft Statute is found in 46 Am. J. Int'l L. Supp. 1 (1952). It was drafted by a Special Committee established by the General Assembly. Cf. The Draft Code of Offenses against the Peace and Security of Mankind, 45 Am. J. Int'l L. Supp. 123 (1951) (drafted by the International Law Commission).

the United Nations; the Convention on Freedom of Information, and the Convention on International Transmission of News and Right of Correction.[73] Of these the executive branch has approved only the Genocide Convention, and that has been before the Senate for nearly three years without confirmation.

The adverse criticism of these projected sweeping treaties, earnest and voluminous as it is, can be restated in a few lines: that in the United States we already enjoy constitutionally guaranteed freedoms substantially greater than these treaties undertake to provide, and that by an unintended inversion of effect, instead of increasing our liberties they would diminish them by effecting a downgrading of the Bill of Rights; that the Congress would be authorized to implement the treaties by oppressive legislation heretofore unconstitutional; and that perhaps our citizens would be subject to interference in the United States by representatives of international bodies, or liable here or abroad for novel offenses not forbidden by Congress or the state legislatures, before courts in which our traditional procedure is abandoned. And, it is suggested, even if foreign functionaries do not come into the United States to enforce treaties, might not the entire balance between state and nation be altered by some treaty provision under the doctrine of *Missouri v. Holland*? [74]

These possibilities would be more disturbing if they were more immediate. There is much unfinished business for the United Nations drafting organizations. The State Department has expressed itself as opposed to the Draft Convention on Freedom of Information.[75] The Genocide Convention seems no closer to ratification by the Senate than it was nearly three years ago; and Senator Bricker said to that body on February 7, 1952, when discussing his proposed constitutional amendment:

---

[73] See note 2 *supra* and Chafee, *supra* note 70. For vigorous opposition to the proposals for an international criminal court and to the Convention on the Gathering and International Transmission of News and the Right of Correction, see A.B.A., *Report of Standing Comm. on Peace and Law Through United Nations* (1952). The reports of this committee for the preceding three years also contain strong statements of the arguments against participation by the United States in the Covenant on Human Rights.

[74] Similar fears were expressed in the Senate during the debate on the North Atlantic Treaty. See 95 Cong. Rec. 9631, 9633 (1949) (Sen. Donnell).

[75] See the statement made before the United Nations Economic and Social Council by the United States Deputy Representative on Aug. 24, 1951. 25 *Dep't State Bull.* 504 (1951).

There is not the remotest chance that even one-third of the present Senate would undermine the rights of the American people by voting for any UN Draft Covenant on Human Rights or any other treaty of similar import.[76]

Assuming a change of heart and concurrence by the Senate, one hesitates to expect a ruling by the Supreme Court that treaties expressed as intended to increase freedom from governmental oppression would justify the Congress in passing statutes downgrading the Bill of Rights.[77] And if the Supreme Court were to decide that a treaty required the trial of an accused in some now unconstitutional place or manner, or drastically altered the structure of the government, one would not expect passive acquiescence by a Congress which has complete power to abrogate its domestic effect.

However, the proposed constitutional amendments affecting the treaty power are not limited in their application to these novel and sweeping multilateral undertakings. If one or more of the amendments were to be adopted, the effect on the ordinary yearly grist of international agreements by which the foreign affairs of the United States are carried out would become a matter of immediate and critical importance. The projects for amendment should be examined at least as minutely to determine their impact on the accustomed current business of the nation as to determine their success in inhibiting future agreements of a somewhat speculative nature which presently show no signs of becoming the law of the land.

The last century and three-quarters have seen an impressive increase in our use of all sorts of international agreements. Dur-

---

[76] 98 Cong. Rec. 921 (Feb. 7, 1952).

[77] Judge Allen has expressed her view that such constitutional guarantees as those protecting free speech and press should prevail, but "in view of Missouri *v.* Holland . . . this cannot be assumed." Allen, *op.cit., supra* note 70, at 33. Some worry has arisen over the language of the First Amendment, which is in terms a restriction on lawmaking by the Congress, and an argument could be made that therefore this Amendment does not restrict treaty law. But Professor Chafee upholds the Bill of Rights over treaties. See Chafee, *supra* note 70, at 433 *et seq.* Charles Evans Hughes suggested a different limitation—that treaties must be limited to matters which "pertain to our external relations," and must not "make laws for the people of the United States in their internal concerns through the exercise of the asserted treaty-making power." [1929] Proc. Am. Soc'y Int'l L. 195, 196. See also note 49 *supra.*

ing the first fifty years under the Constitution, only 60 treaties and 27 executive agreements went into effect. During the next half-century the United States entered into 215 treaties and 238 executive agreements. In the half century ending April 30, 1939, 524 treaties and 917 executive agreements went into force.[78] The United States Treaty Series shows 30 treaties, and the Executive Agreement Series shows 432 such agreements for 1940–1945 inclusive. In the State Department's current Treaties and Other International Acts Series, which begins with a few instruments dated 1945, there appear through the early part of the year 1951, 50 treaties and 675 executive agreements. During the decade 1940–1950 the rate of treaty-making seems to have declined a little, while the making of executive agreements has continued to increase.

A large number of the treaties and executive agreements into which the United States may be expected to enter[79] would probably be unaffected by any of the constitutional amendments recently introduced. During the past six years the United States has made over 45 agreements for health and sanitation assistance to other nations in the western hemisphere under the auspices of the Institution of Inter-American Affairs;[80] it has made similar arrangements for educational and cultural assistance.[81] During the same period the United States has made executive agreements to send over thirty military missions to various countries, mostly in Latin America.[82] It has agreed to maintain

---

[78] These figures are taken from McClure, *International Executive Agreements* 4 (1941). The Department of State's Executive Agreement Series lists 506 such agreements (1929–45); the span of time is not such as to permit a check on McClure's figures. The Department's Treaty Series lists 994 treaties (1795–1944), of which 30 are dated after 1939, indicating that the McClure treaty figure may be too low.

[79] One question raised by all the proposed constitutional amendments is the extent of their retrospective effect. Invalidation of an undetermined part of the great existing body of international conventions by a change in the Constitution is certainly not intended, and seems unlikely on its face. However, if any change in the constitutional provisions concerning treaties is contemplated, clear language restricting the effect of the amendments to future transactions is highly desirable.

[80] E.g., 61 Stat. 3651, U.S. Treaties & Other International Acts Series No. 1693 (Dep't State 1947) (Haiti) (this series will hereafter be cited T.I.A.S.); 61 Stat. 3361, T.I.A.S. No. 1673 (Dep't State 1947) (Peru).

[81] E.g., 61 Stat. 3902, T.I.A.S. No. 1749 (Dep't State 1947) (Ecuador); 61 Stat. 2301, T.I.A.S. No. 1549 (Dep't State 1946) (Brazil).

[82] E.g., 61 Stat. 4006, T.I.A.S. No. 1760 (Dep't State 1946) (Chile); 61 Stat. 3306, T.I.A.S. No. 1666 (Dep't State 1947) (Iran).

weather stations abroad.[83] It has made divers arrangements with other countries respecting our military forces abroad,[84] the boundaries of occupied zones,[85] the handling of leased bases and other property,[86] jurisdiction to try members of our forces charged with nonmilitary crimes abroad,[87] agreements for the care of the bodies of war dead,[88] and many other comparable arrangements essential for a nation with an active foreign policy and with military commitments overseas. Most such arrangements would probably be unaffected.

"Probably" unaffected, one says, because the extent of the effect of the proposals for amendment of the Constitution is not clear even respecting such routine agreements as those described. A little uneasiness remains as to whether some of these arrangements might be invalid as executive agreements made "in lieu of treaties," a proscription which, in the proposed resolution thus far most popular in the Senate, makes no distinction between executive agreements authorized in advance by the Congress, and those signed by the President on his own responsibility. Either type is forbidden if used "in lieu of" a treaty; and a distinction which President Monroe in 1818 and Senator Bricker in 1952 found impossible to define [89] would, under this amendment, be written into the Constitution. Furthermore, any agreement with a foreign power for the trial of any of our military personnel abroad, or civilian personnel accompanying the forces, by any tribunal other than one set up by the United States would probably run afoul of one of the proposed amendments for-

---

[83] E.g., 61 Stat. 2858, T.I.A.S. No. 1617 (Dep't State 1947) (Philippines); 61 Stat. 4084, T.I.A.S. No. 1842 (Dep't State 1944) (Cuba).

[84] E.g., 61 Stat. 3755, T.I.A.S. No. 1715 (Dep't State 1947) (authorization for continued stationing of United States troops in China); 61 Stat. 3661, T.I.A.S. No. 1694 (Dep't State 1947) (rights and privileges of United States forces in Italy).

[85] E.g., 61 Stat. 2679, T.I.A.S. No. 1600 (Dep't State 1945) (Austria).

[86] E.g., 60 Stat. 1741, T.I.A.S. No. 1531 (Dep't State 1946) (transfer of defense installations and equipment to Canada); 60 Stat. 1525, T.I.A.S. No. 1509 ("Mutual Aid Settlement" with United Kingdom); 60 Stat. 1707, T.I.A.S. No. 1528 (Dep't State 1946) ("Mutual Aid Settlement" with Australia).

[87] E.g. 61 Stat. 3661, 3664, T.I.A.S. No. 1694 (Dep't State 1947) (Italy). For a grant by treaty to certain North Atlantic Treaty nations of jurisdiction to try military personnel of other signatories, see 65 Harv. L. Rev. 1072 (1952).

[88] E.g., 61 Stat. 3750, T.I.A.S. No. 1713 (Dep't State 1947) (Italy); 61 Stat. 3767, T.I.A.S. No. 1720 (Dep't State 1947) (France); 61 Stat. 3898, T.I.A.S. No. 1748 (Dep't State 1946) (Hungary).

[89] See pp. 233, 237 *supra*.

bidding any treaty or executive agreement to abridge the constitutional rights of citizens of the United States, or to vest in a foreign power or international organization any of the constitutional powers of the United States. Lawmaking, constitutional or other, requires vast foresight if the lawmaker is to imagine all the different situations in which the proposed change will take effect, and thus to appraise its desired or undesired results. On most of the types of agreement just discussed, the amendments would probably have little effect, as far as one man's imagination now carries, but it would be a bold prophet who would make an inclusive and confident prediction.

Elimination of the self-executing character of United States treaties under Article VI of the Constitution and of executive agreements under the Pink case would undoubtedly affect other common arrangements. During the last six years about fifty air transport agreements [90] have been made supplementing the multilateral treaty known as the Convention on International Civil Aviation, signed at Chicago in 1944.[91] The Convention itself contains a number of clauses which purport to make law in the United States, without implementing statutes.

By the Convention, aircraft of one contracting State are granted the right to take on or discharge passengers, cargo, or mail in the others, under certain circumstances; [92] and aircraft of each are entitled to make non-stop flights over the territory of another. In scheduled international airline service, each contracting State (including of course the United States) agrees not to prohibit foreign aircraft from flying over areas where our own international airliners are allowed to fly.[93] Public airports, radio and meteorological services are to be open to the aircraft of all other contracting parties alike; [94] we renounce the privilege of playing favorites. We exempt foreign aircraft and spare parts from seizure, detention, and from claims arising out of patent infringements.[95] The documents of planes engaged in international navigation are prescribed, and this requirement applies to

---

[90] See the index to U.S. Treaty Developments (Dep't State) under Air Transport.
[91] 61 Stat. 1180; ratification advised by Senate July 25, 1946; proclaimed by President March 17, 1947, effective April 4, 1947.

[92] Art. 5.	[94] Art. 15.
[93] Art. 9A.	[95] Art. 27.

our own as well as foreign aircraft.[96] We agree that certificates of airworthiness of foreign contracting States and their certificates of the competency of pilots will be recognized in the United States provided the licensing nation observes minimum standards established by the International Civil Aviation Organization.[97] Each contracting State agrees to bar from its airspace an airline that fails to conform to the decision of prescribed international tribunals.[98] Thus under this convention, domestic law is made without the statutory action of the Congress; and certain disputes under the convention are subject to decision by international bodies, rather than agencies of the United States. If all the proposed amendments were adopted, the first arrangements could still be made by the enactment of congressional legislation implementing the treaty, but under Senator Bricker's amendment the second would be unconstitutional.[99]

Numerous executive agreements, multilateral and bilateral, made in pursuance of the same policy which brought about the Convention on Civil Aviation, also affect local law to some extent. The Air Transport Agreement with Portugal, made December 6, 1945,[100] to pick one of many examples, limits the charges which may be made to Portuguese aircraft for the use of our public airports to whatever is "just and reasonable," provided the charges are no higher than we make to our own planes in similar service—a sort of rate-making by executive agreement. An even more striking example of the internal effect of an international agreement is the grant to a foreign airline of a right to do international business in this country in competition with the international business of a domestic line.[101]

Such an agreement, that with Canada dated June 4, 1949,[102] was challenged before a three-judge federal court in November of that year.[103] The Civil Aeronautics Board was about to issue,

---

[96] Art. 29.
[97] Art. 33.
[98] Art. 87. We thus engage to so bar our own international lines.
[99] Section 2; see note 6 *supra*.
[100] 59 Stat. 1846; see also 61 Stat. 3185 (1947).
[101] See Annex to Portuguese Air Transport Agreement, 59 Stat. 1849 (1945).
[102] T.I.A.S. No. 1934 (Dep't State). See 12 *Dep't State Bull.* 766 (1949). The agreement gave the United States routes across Canada to Alaska and the Orient via Edmonton, and to Europe via Gander, in addition to other benefits.
[103] Colonial Airlines, Inc. *v.* Adams, 87 F. Supp. 242 (D.D.C. 1949).

pursuant to the Canadian Air Agreement, a permit to Trans-Canada Airlines to operate between Montreal and New York in competition with Colonial Airlines. Colonial, considering that its business would be seriously prejudiced, brought an action to enjoin the Board from taking any steps toward the issuing of the permit. The complaint alleged, among other things, that the Canadian Air Agreement had all the elements of a treaty and would be invalid and unconstitutional unless "ratified" by the Senate. The complaint also alleged that an annex to the Agreement made the rates to be charged both by Colonial and Trans-Canada subject to approval of "the appropriate aeronautical authorities of Canada and the United States, whereas no such authority is presently found in the statutes of the United States" and further alleged that as Trans-Canada was owned by the Canadian National Railway, which in turn was wholly owned by the Canadian Government, the rates of Colonial would be subject to the approval of its competitor, and that certification of Trans-Canada, "in view of its enormous monopoly position," would violate the antitrust legislation of the United States.

Annexed to the complaint as an exhibit was an excerpt from a report of hearings before the Senate Committee on Interstate and Foreign Commerce, held five days after the Canadian Agreement had been signed, at which a State Department official was questioned by Senators Brewster and Bricker about that arrangement. Asked why treaties were not used for such bilaterals, his response went little beyond a statement that executive agreements were more flexible.[104]

Colonial Airlines obtained a preliminary injunction on August 27, 1949, but on November 16, 1949, the three-judge court dismissed the complaint.[105] Colonial immediately appealed, and argument was set by the Supreme Court for February 17, 1950; but on February 6, Colonial moved for and obtained an order dismissing its own appeal.[106] The president of the airline said in a statement,

---

[104] Record, p. 59. Colonial Airlines, Inc. *v.* Adams, *infra* note 106.

[105] 87 F. Supp. 242. Goldsborough, J., dissented. Neither the prevailing nor the dissenting opinion discusses the validity of the executive agreement. They treat only the constitutionality of the delegation by Congress to the CAB and the president of power to issue a permit to an airline.

[106] 338 U.S. 947 (1950).

. . . with the increasing gravity of the international situation we have concluded that it would not be right, in the public interest, to challenge the executive power of the government to make executive agreements with foreign powers.[107]

International telecommunications—and indeed all international commerce—present problems similar to those of international aviation. Occurring partly in each of two or more countries, the activity requires international agreement, which must in some measure subject the local law of each country to the provisions of the agreement. The United States in 1949 joined in the International Telecommunication Convention, a multilateral treaty which carried forward the work of the earlier International Telecommunications Union.[108] The United States adhered only to the Radio Regulations which, however, even without implementing legislation bind us in many internal matters—notably the allocation of frequencies. If the proposed amendment concerning self-executing treaties were adopted, Congress could easily replace the eliminated domestic law by statute. Presumably such an agreement would not be forbidden as a treaty or executive agreement "respecting the rights of citizens of the United States protected by this constitution," though the meaning of that expression has not emerged with clarity from the opinions discussing similar phrases.[109]

However, a treaty providing for extradition of one of our citizens seems clearly to affect constitutionally protected rights. The omission from the powers delegated to the Federal Government of any authority to extradite a citizen in the absence of a treaty entitles such a citizen to habeas corpus if extradition is attempted,[110] though once such a treaty is made, the citizen is extraditable,[111] even though the crime was committed before the treaty took effect.[112] Will further treaties providing for extra-

---

[107] *N.Y. Times,* Feb. 6, 1950, p. 41, col. 1.

[108] T.I.A.S. No. 1901 (Dep't State 1947). See De Wolf Telecommunications in the New World, 55 Yale L.J. 1281 (1946); De Wolf, Atlantic City Telecommunications Conferences, 17 *Dep't State Bull.* 1033 (1947).

[109] Slaughter-House Cases, 16 Wall, 36 (U.S. 1873); United States *v.* Williams, 341 U.S. 70 (1951).

[110] Valentine *v.* United States, 299 U.S. 5 (1936).

[111] Charlton *v.* Kelly, 229 U.S. 447 (1913).

[112] See a note on the case of the late Samuel Insull, 31 Mich. L. Rev. 544 (1933). In re de Giacomo, 7 Fed. Cas. 366, No. 3747 (C.C.S.D.N.Y. 1874); see Factor *v.* Laubenheimer, 290 U.S. 276, 304 (1933).

dition of a citizen be constitutionally impossible if the nation adopts Senator Bricker's amendment providing that "no treaty or executive agreement shall be made respecting the rights of citizens of the United States protected by this Constitution, or abridging or prohibiting the free exercise thereof"?

The Senate has been chary of consenting to the ratification, as treaties, of conventions submitted by the International Labor Organization. The United States has been a member of that body since 1934,[113] and in 1948, following the dissolution of the League of Nations, confirmed by treaty its membership in the ILO as a specialized agency of the United Nations.[114] Since it originated in 1919, the Organization has prepared 100-odd draft conventions, 43 of them since the United States became a member.[115] Sixteen of these have been submitted by the President for appropriate action by the Senate. Of those submitted, five have been approved by the Senate, but only three, respectively prescribing a minimum age for seamen,[116] setting standards of competency for ships' officers,[117] and imposing shipowners' liability for sick and injured seamen,[118] have taken effect. The remaining two, providing for annual paid holidays for seamen,[119] and prescribing hours of work on shipboard,[120] will not be in force until similar action is taken by other nations. None of these five conventions raises the problem of Missouri *v.* Holland because Congress has legislative power in maritime matters; each does however make American law in the maritime field, and if the proposed constitutional amendment eliminating the Supremacy

---

[113] 48 Stat. 1182 (1934); see "International Labor Organization," under date June 28, 1919, U.S. Treaty Developments (Dep't State); U.S. Treaty Ser., No. 874 (Dep't State 1934).

[114] 62 Stat. 1672 (1946); see also 62 Stat. 1151 (1948).

[115] See "International Labor Organization," under original date June 28, 1919, U.S. Treaty Developments (Dep't State), for the statistics concerning draft conventions submitted, approved, etc.

[116] 54 Stat. 1705 (1936).

[117] 54 Stat. 1683 (1936).

[118] 54 Stat. 1693 (1939). See, for a discussion of the self-executing character of this treaty, the concurring memorandum of Stone, C.J., in Waterman Steamship Corp. *v.* Jones, 318 U.S. 724, 738 (1943).

[119] See "International Labor Organization," under date June 28, 1919, U.S. Treaty Developments (Dep't State); 83 Cong. Rec. 9025 (1938).

[120] See "International Labor Organization," *supra* note 119; 83 Cong. Rec. 9031–33 (1938).

Clause were adopted similar treaties would have no domestic effect without legislation.

It is possible that such a change would be desirable, or at any rate not seriously harmful to the conduct of our international affairs. Many nations get on perfectly well without self-executing treaties, though the Canadian experience demonstrates that in a federal nation some inconveniences are bound to arise. Even if the Supremacy Clause in our Constitution were altered by the amendments now proposed so as to exclude federal legislation in the Missouri *v.* Holland situation, the present scope of the commerce power is so inclusive in the United States that a great many treaties could be made subject to subsequent federal legislation, without the necessity of recourse to state statutes.[121]

The number and variety of our international engagements is so great that an effort to discuss the effect of each of the proposed amendments on each sort of engagement would only be exhausting. Clearly there are a great many types in common use which would have to be treated differently if the changes were made. The amendment intended to prevent abrogation of the Bill of Rights would have to be carefully qualified to make sure it did not prevent future treaties affecting such commonplace matters as extradition, because of the unintended breadth of its language.[122] The elimination of the self-executing feature by change in the Supremacy Clause could require federal legislation to implement such useful agreements as the ordinary treaties of commerce and navigation.[123] If the implementing statute were required to fit within the delegated powers, in order to eliminate Missouri *v.* Holland, no treaty could thereafter be enacted to provide for reciprocal rights to inherit land, or for similar local matters, unless it depended on subsequent legislation in the forty-eight States. The increase in the proportion of

---

[121] The local activities which are now held to "affect" interstate commerce are surprising. See Wickard *v.* Filburn, 317 U.S. 111 (1942). Would the taking of wildfowl now be held to affect interstate commerce in poultry?

[122] See pp. 245, 246 *supra*.

[123] See for example the treaty of Friendship, Commerce and Navigation between the United States and Italy, proclaimed by President Truman on August 5, 1949, T.I.A.S. No. 1965 (Dept. State). International agreements sometimes regulate surprisingly small details of business; for one affecting the resale of imported potatoes, see United States *v.* Guy W. Capps, Inc., 100 F. Supp. 30 (E.D. Va. 1951).

Senators required for approval raises a policy question that has been eloquently argued both ways for a century and three-quarters. The inclusion of the House in the treaty-making process has appealed to more political scientists and members of the House than Senators, as became clear when the House passed and the Senate took no action on such a resolution in 1945.

The prohibition against vesting any of the legislative, executive, or judicial powers of the United States in any international organization or foreign nation is so sweeping and inclusive as to cover all the governmental powers of the United States. Its effect on a joint military operation like Torch, or the Italian or Normandy campaigns, would be paralyzing if it were applied, which of course would not happen. If obeyed to the letter it would eliminate the ordinary internationally constituted Claims Commission such as that which settled many Mexican–United States disputes,[124] or the United States–Germany Mixed Claims Commission which settled the Black Tom explosion case [125] or any other agreement for arbitration, the outcome of which would depend in part at least on the vote of a foreign arbitrator or umpire. Of course the proposal to render unconstitutional a vesting of any powers of the Government of the United States in "any international organization or foreign nation" was not intended by its sponsors to apply to any such usual arrangement as a Mixed Claims Commission but was meant to prevent the United States from subjecting itself to a world government. The unintended literal applicability to a great number of customary agreements, however, points up the difficulty and hazard of such sweeping changes.

Finally, the prohibition of executive agreements "in lieu of treaties" is unworkably indefinite in its present form; and it is not susceptible of satisfactory clarification, as statesmen from President Monroe to Senator Bricker have acknowledged. The proposed limit on the life of such agreements is not clear. Would a military armistice, unless extended by the Congress, automatically expire a year after the end of the term of the Pres-

---

[124] See Feller, *Mexican Claims Commissions* (1935).
[125] See Mixed Claims Commission, United States and Germany, *Opinions and Decisions in the Sabotage Cases* (1939).

ident whose field commander signed it? [126] Would we expect the other party, then, to have a similar option on that date to start up the war again, or to renew interminable tented negotiations? Or is there in the proposed amendment an unexpressed distinction between executed and executory agreements, such as Attorney General Jackson found when he approved the Destroyer Deal? And is this distinction a clear one; is an armistice executed or executory; and in any event would or could such a prohibition be observed amid the exigencies of a world at war? Or perchance had the present power to make executive agreements better be left as it is?

iv. *An Estimate*

A legislature quite properly serves, among other purposes, as a means of expressing popular emotion. The sovereign American who finds some condition objectionable says that there ought to be a law against it. If the condition is very objectionable, he feels that it ought to be unconstitutional. Many pieces of legislation, originating in indignation or alarm, are thus more resolutions of protest than efficiently designed devices of government. The resounding preamble of the statute is sometimes a mountain in labor. Eloquent recital of grievances is apt to be followed by anticlimactic prescription; enforcement appears inconvenient and is soon forgotten. But the legislation has attained its real end. Popular feeling has found release; warning of evil has gone forth.

Sometimes, of course, mistakes are made in the effective part of the statute—almost inevitable mistakes if the statute has a sweeping effect, as any draftsman of legislation soon finds. No matter how scrupulously the possibilities are canvassed in advance, some circumstance will arise which the draftsman, because of the limitations of human foresight, did not anticipate. Where the legislators' attention is centered on their resentment or alarm, and not on the practical functioning of the governmental change they propose, the chances of malfunction are increased.

[126] Presumably an armistice in the present Korean operations would be signed on behalf of the United Nations, not on behalf of the several States furnishing components to the United Nations command.

Fortunately, in the case of ordinary legislation, correction is generally easy.

Constitutional change is a more serious matter. The Eighteenth Amendment, ratified in a generous spirit of protest at the evils of misused drink but without any conception of the practical problems of application, plagued police and citizens, politicians and courts, for fifteen years. Perhaps the sanctity that hedges the Constitution would even then have prevented its correction were it not for a great wave of political protest that changed many things at once. Proposals to add to the Federal Constitution an amendment imposing a twenty-five percent limit on income taxes express an understandable outcry against high rates; but they demonstrate no workable program for financing the United States of America. If resentment at tax bills should bring about such an amendment, the financial repercussions would probably be surprising; but amending the amendment could be lamentably slow.

Transaction of our foreign affairs by the several forms of international compact has become a complex, varied, and extremely voluminous business. Tariffs, extradition, military bases, economic aid, telecommunication, whaling, automobile traffic—the list of subject matters is endless. These agreements have come to be handled in an understood manner by governmental specialists, while the Congress always retains a corrective domestic control by legislative means, and thirty-three Senators are able to block any treaty, as the League of Nations was blocked, and as for three years the Genocide Convention has been successfully opposed. As a practical matter, except necessarily in the conduct of war, major matters are ordinarily presented to the Senate as treaties, not handled as executive agreements. Political realism requires it. The evils feared by the proponents of the pending amendments seem remote and speculative. To adopt sweeping constitutional changes in a spirit of alarm, or of annoyance at past mistakes of domestic or international policy, is to create certain confusion and delay in our complicated day-by-day foreign affairs, gaining in return only an estimated protection against the suppositious unwisdom of men now unknown, who may come to office years after the amenders have left the scene.

Any lawyer who practices for a time comes to know some testator—self-made, successful, competent, confident—who seeks so to provide by will that his descendants, to the farthest reaches of the Rule against Perpetuities, will be protected against mistakes which the testator has shrewdly avoided. A certain amount of this prescribed control sometimes works well; but the draftsman of wills comes to learn to give a trustee a considerable measure of discretion. The conditions of tomorrow are not those of today, and grandchildren are ultimately protected only by wisdom in their own time.

So, too, for a constitution—some limits on the trustees of the nation work well. But the conditions we will face next year, or that our grandchildren will face fifty years from now, are beyond our present knowing. Wise men have sometimes found difficulty in meeting problems even under today's treaty restrictions. We should do well to trust our descendants at least as far as our ancestors trusted us.

CHAPTER EIGHT

The Power of the President

O NE IMPORTANT DIFFERENCE BETWEEN THE AMERICAN AND British political systems is supposed to rest on the contrast between a "written" and an "unwritten" constitution. Like many such generalizations, this one thins down remarkably under analysis. On the one hand, as every schoolboy knows, substantial portions of the British Constitution are written down as clearly as black-and-white can ever be; and on the other hand, as has been suggested earlier in this volume, unwritten constitutional principles are by no means unknown or unimportant in America. The standard example of an essentially constitutional American form based largely on usage rather than written law is the modern Electoral College. But judicial review itself is another, and more important, illustration of the phenomenon, as we have seen.

An equally good illustration is the modern institution of the Presidency, which is the focus of Edward S. Corwin's concern in his commentary on "the steel seizure case." As Corwin points out, extremely little is said about presidential powers in the written Constitution, and there is surely nothing at all in the document which would lead a reader to suspect that the powerful executive of the twentieth century was being described. Judicial inferences from what the Constitution said, or did not say, have helped some in filling out the meager statements of the Constitution itself, but in large part the President of today is a creature of custom. Presidents have done what they thought was needful; Congress has either tacitly or explicitly approved these doings; and the result is the extraordinarily potent chief executive of present times. The limits of his power are, in many circumstances, ill-defined (far less clear, by the way, than the limits on the authority of the British monarchy). When these shadowlands of presidential prerogative are reached, constitutional law in the orthodox sense is usually of little relevance.

A good many students of American government and public law would probably have been content to leave this situation as it was, arguing that rigid constitutional restrictions on executive power are unrealistic today and that an attempt to define what the President cannot do under the Constitution might, paradoxically, produce a definition so broad as to invite presidential autocracy. However, the Supreme Court felt differently and chose in the Steel Seizure Case to meet the constitutional issue of executive prerogative, to spell out the scope of the President's "inherent powers."

As Corwin makes plain, the constitutional principles that may be drawn from the opinions are not quite those that might appear at first blush. Mr. Justice Black's opinion is identified as the opinion of the Court, and he explicitly denies the President any authority to act, even in an emergency, within the legislative sphere. But language in the opinions of Justices Clark, Frankfurter, Jackson, and Burton leaves room for the inference that they might uphold such executive action if it did not contravene any statute; and when they are added to the three dissenters, there emerges a fairly clear majority in favor of some concept of inherent power. The concern of Corwin's essay is to explore the meanings of the various opinions and to assess the historical justification for the doctrines the opinions reflect.

It may be useful for us, therefore, to address ourselves to another question, one that Corwin does not deal with—whether it was a good idea for the Court to grasp the constitutional issue that was presented to it by the Steel Seizure Case, or whether it should, on the other hand, have left the problem of presidential inherent powers where it found it, in the lap of "custom." Many of the constitutional issues presented to the Court each year are evaded for one reason or another in the actual decision, and the Court has been often criticized either for being too reluctant or too willing to answer the constitutional questions litigants have asked. In the Steel Seizure Case most of the justices were obviously in a mood of willingness that amounts to boldness, and the suggestion has been made that in this situation modest self-restraint would have been a more appropriate judicial spirit. (See especially Paul A. Freund, 66 Harvard Law Review 89 [1952].)

Prior to the question of whether the Court *should* have met the constitutional issue here, is the question of whether it could have avoided doing so. Professor Freund has argued compellingly that there was a good basis for holding that the extraordinary relief of an injunction should have been denied "for want of equity," and those who are interested in pursuing this nice jurisdictional point will find it developed in the essay just cited. For present purposes, it is perhaps enough to say that, whether or not the use of equity powers was improper, it was certainly not required, and the Court could easily have by-passed the constitutional problems of the case.

Leaving aside Freund's analysis of the particular jurisdictional proprieties, what can be said generally in favor of judicial avoidance of constitutional issues like that of presidential power? Quite a lot perhaps. No one, on the Court or off it, has ever been able to describe satisfactorily the precise meaning of the doctrine of "political questions" (I am not aware that anyone has added much to the conflicting explications of Maurice Finkelstein, 37 Harvard Law Review 338 [1923] and 39 Harvard Law Review 221 [1926], and M. L. Fuller, 38 Harvard Law Review 296 [1925]), and it may be that the steel seizure issue does not fall within a technical definition of that term. But it did involve "politics" in the most explosive sense, and the historical occasions when the Court has joined in such a maelstrom of political contention have not made happy reading for the Court's friends. Of course, it may be said that this particular decision was joyously received by the Nation and that the Court in this

instance risked no storm of outraged popular feelings, but quite
the reverse. (See *New York Times*, June 3, 1952, p. 1, cols. 5, 8;
p. 28, col. 1; cited in 66 Harvard Law Review 99, note 5[1952].)
The answer is that a judge is one thing and a courtier another,
and that the decision to take jurisdiction in the Steel Seizure
Case can be defended only on grounds that apply whether the
sovereign is smiling or frowning. It is very easy to imagine a
situation in the future when an exercise of presidential prerogative might be insistently demanded by public opinion, and the
question is whether the Court could then effectively perform its
self-assigned task of sitting in judgment on the matter. At least
one judicious observer has suggested that the Court should "shy
off" when a controversy presented to it involves the "trained
moral sentiment of the judge" on the one hand and "the hyper-
sensitive nerve of public opinion" on the other (Finkelstein, 37
Harvard Law Review 338, 339 [1924]). Surely this was just such
a controversy.

Apart from the explosive factor of public opinion, there is another basis for arguing that this subject would be better left
alone by the Supreme Court. As John Locke pointed out long
ago, the executive branch of government needs discretionary el-
bow-room if it is to operate effectively, and this leeway is all
the more necessary when the executive's decisions relate to foreign affairs. In that field, foreknowledge is exceedingly difficult
to come by, unprecedented situations frequently develop, and
the President must be able to act with dispatch. It is arguable
therefore that the executive power should be exempt from rigid
confinement of a constitutional rule, and that the scope of the
President's emergency authority should be prescribed, not by
the courts, but by the more flexible device of statutory limitations. Whether President Truman's decision to seize the steel
mills was right or wrong, it reflected his conviction that America's international status was imperilled by the threatened strike
and thus was an exercise of what Mr. Justice Sutherland has
called "the very delicate, plenary and exclusive power of the
President as the sole organ of the federal government in the field
of international relations." (United States *v.* Curtiss-Wright, 299
U.S. 304, 320 [1936].) Evidently Congress' right to lay statutory
restrictions on the President when he treads such legislative

ground is conceded unanimously by the Supreme Court; an ample safeguard is available if Congress chooses to apply it. Until Congress does so choose the Court should "*hesitate long before limiting or embarrassing such powers.*" (The emphasis was supplied by Mr. Justice Sutherland quoting this phrase from Mackenzie *v.* Hare, 239 U.S. 299, 311 [1915], *Ibid.*, 322.)

Yet there is, as always, another side. Perhaps it would be better in theory to leave the matter of presidential power to Congress and to trust that the legislators would be jealous enough of usurpation of their function to forfend the threat of executive autocracy. But the Supreme Court was faced here by the plain fact that Congress had taken no action, even though the President had earnestly requested it for guidance. More, although the nation had faced a threatening state of emergency almost continuously since the close of World War II, Congress had so far ignored its responsibility for enacting an Emergency Powers Law which would both endow the President with authority to meet extraordinary situations and ensure that his power was defined and canalized. The members of the Court might well have felt that the executive in modern government is so potent a being that we cannot afford to leave him entirely unfettered and that, failing a congressional definition of his scope, a judicial definition is better than none. It takes a bold judge to arrive at such a conclusion; but it would be a bold critic who felt sure that democracy lost more than it gained by this particular example of judicial audacity.

The Steel Seizure Case: A Judicial Brick Without Straw

by Edward S. Corwin*

Columbia Law Review,
Volume 53, Page 53 (1953)

President Truman's seizure of the steel industry without specific statutory warrant [1] brings to a new pitch a developing reliance on the "Executive Power" which began almost at the inception of the Federal Government. True, this development has not always proceeded at the same pace; while at times it has seemed to be arrested, during the last fifty years its maturation has been virtually uninterrupted. Moreover, the forces, interests and events which have energized the development are today more potent than ever.

The opening clause of Article II of the Constitution reads: "The executive Power shall be vested in a President of the United States of America." The records of the Constitutional Convention make it clear that the purposes of this clause were simply to settle the question whether the executive branch should be plural or single and to give the executive a title.[2] Yet, in the very first Congress to assemble under the Constitution, the opening clause of Article II was invoked by James Madison and others in order to endow the President with power to remove officers whose appointments had been made with the advice and consent of the Senate. Madison's view prevailed,[3] and was finally ratified by the Supreme Court in 1926.[4] The same theory was invoked by Hamilton in support of President Washington's Proclamation of Neutrality upon the outbreak of war between France and Great Britain.[5] This time the Court's acqui-

---

* (1878—), Professor of Jurisprudence, Princeton University, 1918–46, emeritus since 1946.

[1] Youngstown Sheet & Tube Co. v. Sawyer, 343 U.S. 579 (1952).

[2] 2 Farrand, *Records of the Federal Convention* 171, 185 (rev. ed. 1937).

[3] Corwin, *The President: Office and Powers* 102–14, 428 (3d ed. 1948).

[4] Myers v. United States, 272 U.S. 52 (1926).

[5] Corwin, *op. cit., supra* note 3, at 217 *et seq.*, 465, 474–75.

escence was not long delayed. Even in the act of asserting the power of the Court to pass upon the constitutionality of acts of Congress, Chief Justice Marshall said: "By the Constitution of the United States the President is invested with certain important political powers, in the exercise of which he is to use his own discretion, and is accountable only to his country in his political character, and to his own conscience." [6] Even Thomas Jefferson, cousin and congenital enemy of Marshall, had said of the executive power in an official opinion as Secretary of State in 1790: "The Executive [branch of the government], possessing the rights of self-government from nature, cannot be controlled in the exercise of them but by a law, passed in the forms of the Constitution." [7]

Throughout the last half century the theory of presidential power has recruited strength from a succession of "strong" presidents, from an economic crisis, from our participation in two world wars and a "cold" war, and finally from organization of the labor movement. Moreover, the constitutional basis of the doctrine has shifted somewhat since the early nineteenth century. It no longer relies exclusively, or even chiefly, on the opening clause of Article II. To the terminology of political disputation in the Jacksonian period it is indebted for such concepts as "residual," "resultant" and "inherent" powers. Thanks to Lincoln, it is able to invoke the president's duty to "take care that the laws," i.e., all the laws, "be faithfully executed," and his power as commander-in-chief of the armed forces. Of more recent origin is the quite baffling formula of an "aggregate of powers vested in the President by the Constitution and the laws." [8]

The chief constitutional value which overextension of presidential power threatens is, of course, the concept of a "government of laws and not of men"—the "Rule of Law" principle. In 1882 Justice Samuel Miller gave classical expression to this principle in the following words: "No man . . . is so high that he is above the law. . . . All officers of the government . . .

---

[6] Marbury *v.* Madison, 1 Cranch 137, 166 (U.S. 1803).
[7] 5 *Writings of Jefferson* 209 (Ford ed. 1895).
[8] 40 Ops. Att'y Gen. 312, 319 (1944).

are creatures of the law, and are bound to obey it." [9] Yet eight years later this same great judge queried whether the president's duty to "Take care that the laws be faithfully executed is limited to the enforcement of the acts of Congress or treaties . . . [in] their *express terms*," or whether it embraces also "the rights, duties and obligations growing out of the Constitution itself . . . and all the protection implied by the nature of the government under the Constitution?" [10] The answer assumed is evident.

In 1895 the Debs case,[11] a landmark in the judicial history of Article II, was decided. Here the Court held that the United States has at all times the right to enter its courts to ask for an injunction to protect "matters which by the Constitution are entrusted to the care of the nation." The "United States" here meant the President. The significance of the Court's choice of terminology is that it was not basing its holding on the duty of the president "to take care that the laws be faithfully executed," but on a broader principle—national interest.

The procession of "strong" presidents was headed by Theodore Roosevelt, who asserts in his *Autobiography* that the principle which governed him in his exercise of the presidential office was that he had not only a right but a duty "to do anything that the needs of the Nation demanded unless such action was forbidden by the Constitution or by the laws." [12] Although in his book, *Our Chief Magistrate and His Powers*, Ex-President Taft warmly protested against the notion that the president has any constitutional warrant to attempt the role of a "Universal Providence," [13] yet, as Chief Justice, he later relied on the opening clause of Article II as a grant of power.[14] He also interpreted the Debs case as signifying that the national executive may seek an injunction in any case involving a widespread public interest.[15]

As for the influence of the labor movement and the resultant

---

[9] United States *v.* Lee, 106 U.S. 196, 220 (1882).
[10] In re Neagle, 135 U.S. 1, 64 (1889).
[11] In re Debs, 158 U.S. 564 (1895).
[12] Roosevelt, *An Autobiography* 389 (1913).
[13] Taft, *Our Chief Magistrate and His Powers* 144 (1916).
[14] See Myers *v.* United States, 272 U.S. 52, 118 (1926).
[15] See Taft, *The Presidency* 90 *et seq.* (1916).

consolidation of labor's political strength in a few great organizations subject to a highly autocratic leadership, it is sufficient
to mention that, between the anthracite strike of 1902 and the
bituminous coal strike of 1946, presidents intervened in a purely
personal or political capacity in no fewer than twenty-six
strikes.[16] Indeed, President Truman's course of action in dealing
with the bituminous coal situation in 1946 may be regarded as
having both foreshadowed his conduct in the steel strike of
1952 [17] and influenced judicial attitudes in some measure in the
Youngstown (Steel Seizure) case.[18]

THE FACTS OF THE YOUNGSTOWN CASE

To avert a nation-wide strike of steel workers which he believed would jeopardize the national defense, President Truman,
on April 8th, 1952, issued Executive Order 10340 [19] directing the
Secretary of Commerce to seize and operate most of the country's steel mills. The order cited no specific statutory authorization, but invoked generally the powers vested in the president
by the Constitution and laws of the United States. Secretary
Sawyer forthwith issued an order seizing the mills and directing their presidents to operate them as managers for the United
States in accordance with his regulations and directions. The
President promptly reported these events to Congress,[20] conced-
ing Congress' power to supersede his order; but Congress failed
to take action either then or a fortnight later, when the President again raised the problem in a special letter.[21] Of course,
in the Defense Production Act of 1950,[22] the Labor Management
Relations (Taft-Hartley) Act of 1947 [23] and the Selective Service Act of 1948,[24] Congress had in fact provided other procedures for dealing with such situations; and in the elaboration of

---

[16] Corwin, *op. cit., supra* note 3, at 453–54 (figures compiled by Professor Dish-
man of Dartmouth College).

[17] Corwin, *Constitution of Powers in a Secular State* 76 n.20 (1951). See also
id. 62 n.8a.

[18] Youngstown Sheet & Tube Co. *v.* Sawyer, 343 U.S. 579 (1952).

[19] 17 Fed. Reg. 3139 (1952).

[20] 98 Cong. Rec. 3962 (April 9, 1952).

[21] 98 Cong. Rec. 4192 (April 21, 1952).

[22] 64 Stat. 798 (1950), as amended, 50 U.S.C. App. § 2071 (Supp. 1952).

[23] 61 Stat. 136 (1947), as amended, 29 U.S.C. §§ 141–197 (Supp. 1952).

[24] 62 Stat. 604 (1948), 50 U.S.C. App. §§ 451–462 (Supp. 1952).

these statutory schemes it had repeatedly declined to authorize governmental seizures of property to settle labor disputes. The steel companies sued the Secretary in a federal district court, praying for a declaratory judgment and injunctive relief. The district judge issued a preliminary injunction, which the court of appeals stayed. On certiorari to the court of appeals, the Supreme Court affirmed the district court's order by a vote of six to three. Justice Black delivered the opinion of the Court in which Justices Frankfurter, Douglas, Jackson and Burton concurred; Justice Clark expressly limited his concurrence to the judgment of the Court. All these Justices presented what are termed "concurring" opinions. The Chief Justice, speaking for himself and Justices Reed and Minton, dissented.

THE DOCTRINE OF THE OPINION OF THE COURT

The chief point urged in Justice Black's opinion is that there was no statute which expressly or impliedly authorized the President to take possession of the steel mills. On the contrary, in its consideration of the Taft-Hartley Act in 1947, Congress refused to authorize governmental seizures of property as a method of preventing work stoppages and settling labor disputes. Authority to issue such an order in the circumstances of the case was not deducible from the aggregate of the executive powers under Article II of the Constitution; nor was the Order maintainable as an exercise of the president's powers as commander-in-chief of the armed forces. The power sought to be exercised was the lawmaking power. Even if it were true that other presidents have taken possession of private business enterprises without congressional authority in order to settle labor disputes, Congress was not thereby divested of its exclusive constitutional authority to make the laws necessary and proper to carry out all powers vested by the Constitution "in the Government of the United States, or in any Department or Officer thereof." [25]

The pivotal proposition of the opinion is, in brief, that inas-

---

[25] U.S. Const. Art. I, § 8. See Youngstown Sheet & Tube Co. *v.* Sawyer, 343 U.S. 579, 660–61 (1952).

much as Congress could have ordered the seizure of the steel mills, there was a total absence of power in the president to do so without prior congressional authorization. To support this thesis no proof in the way of past opinion, practice or adjudication is offered. Justice Black's attitude toward this matter of authority is, in fact, decidedly cavalier. The closing paragraph of his opinion reads:

The Founders of this Nation entrusted the lawmaking power to the Congress alone in both good and bad times. It would do no good to recall the historical events, the fears of power and the hopes for freedom that lay behind their choice. Such a review would but confirm our holding that this seizure order cannot stand.[26]

The somewhat different truth of the matter is that the framers of the Constitution were compelled to defend their handiwork against the charge that it violated "the political maxim that the legislative, executive, and judicial departments ought to be separate and distinct." [27] To meet this charge Madison sought to show in *The Federalist* that the three departments ought not to be so far separated as to have no control over each other.[28] In his opinion for the Court in Ex parte Grossman,[29] decided 137 years later, Chief Justice Taft adopted the same point of view: the fact that when two departments both operate upon the same subject matter the action of one may cancel that of the other *affords no criterion of the constitutional powers of either*. Rather the question is what does *the pertinent historical record* show with regard to presidential action in the field of congressional power?

---

[26] *Id.* at 589.
[27] *The Federalist*, No. 47 at 245 (Everyman's ed. 1929).
[28] *The Federalist*, No. 48 (Madison).
[29] 267 U.S. 87 (1925). "The Federal Constitution nowhere expressly declares that the three branches of the Government shall be kept separate and independent. All legislative powers are vested in a Congress. The executive power is vested in a President. The judicial power is vested in one Supreme Court and in such inferior courts as Congress may from time to time establish. The Judges are given life tenure and a compensation that may not be diminished during their continuance in office, with the evident purpose of securing them and their courts an indepencence of Congress and the Executive. Complete independence and separation between the three branches, however, are not attained, or intended, as other provisions of the Constitution and the normal operation of government under it easily demonstrate." *Id.* at 119–20.

THE HISTORICAL RECORD

Our history contains numerous instances in which, contrary to the pattern of departmental relationship assumed in the Black opinion, presidential action has occurred within a recognized field of congressional power and has, furthermore, fully maintained its tenancy until Congress adopted superseding legislation. And Congress' right to supersede was not contested. In brief, the mere existence in Congress of power to do something has not, of itself, excluded the president from the same field of power until Congress finally acted. But once this happened, its legislation was forthwith recognized as governing the subject and as controlling presidential action in the area.

An early example of this pattern of departmental relationship is afforded by the case of the Flying Fish,[30] in which Chief Justice Marshall denied that the president had power to order the seizure of a vessel bound from a French port, *because* Congress had acted in the same field of power:

It is by no means clear that the president of the United States whose high duty it is to "take care that the laws be faithfully executed," and who is commander in chief of the armies and navies of the United States, might not, without any special authority for that purpose, in the then existing state of things, have empowered the officers commanding the armed vessels of the United States, to seize and send into port for adjudication, American vessels which were forfeited by being engaged in this illicit commerce. But when it is observed that [an act of Congress] gives a special authority to seize on the high seas, and limits that authority to the seizure of vessels bound, or sailing to, a French port, the legislature seem to have prescribed that the manner in which this law shall be carried into execution, was to exclude a seizure of any vessel not bound to a French port.[31]

Another field which the President and Congress have occupied successively is extradition. In 1799 President Adams, in order to execute the extradition provisions of the Jay Treaty, issued a warrant for the arrest of one Jonathan Robbins. As Chief Justice Vinson recites in his opinion:

---

[30] Little *v.* Barreme, 2 Cranch 170 (U.S. 1804).

[31] *Id.* at 177–78 quoted in Youngstown Sheet & Tube Co. *v.* Sawyer, 343 U.S. 579, 660–61 (1952) (Clark, J., concurring). Justice Clark asked: "I know of no subsequent holding of this Court to the contrary." *Ibid.*

This action was challenged in Congress on the ground that no specific statute prescribed the method to be used in executing the treaty. John Marshall, then a member of the House of Representatives, in the course of his successful defense of the President's action, said: "Congress, unquestionably, may prescribe the mode, and Congress may devolve on others the whole execution of the contract; but, till this be done, it seems the duty of the Executive department to execute the contract by any means it possesses. [32]

Not until 1848 did Congress enact a statute governing extradition cases and conferring on the courts, both State and Federal, the duty of handling them.[33]

The power of the president to act until Congress acts in the same field is also shown in these instances. The first Neutrality Proclamation, issued by President Washington in 1793, was also without congressional authorization.[34] The following year Congress enacted the first neutrality statute,[35] and subsequent proclamations of neutrality have been based on an act of Congress governing the matter. The president may, in the absence of legislation by Congress, control the landing of foreign cables in the United States and the passage of foreign troops through American territory, and has done so repeatedly.[36] Likewise, until Congress acts, he may govern conquered territory[37] and, "in the absence of attempts by Congress to limit his power," may set up military commissions in territory occupied by the armed forces of the United States.[38] He may determine in a manner binding on the courts whether a treaty is still in force as law of the land,

---

[32] Youngstown Sheet & Tube Co. *v.* Sawyer, 343 U.S. 579, 684 (1952), citing 10 Annals of Congress 619 (1948).

[33] Rev. Stat. §§ 5270–79 (1878), as amended, 18 U.S.C. §§ 651–76 (1946).

[34] For the controversy thereby precipitated between Hamilton (Pacificus) and Madison (Helvidius), see Corwin, *The President's Control of Foreign Relations* c. I (1917).

[35] 1 Stat. 381 (1794). The act was the direct outcome of suggestions made by Washington in his message of December 3, 1793. See 1 Richardson, *Messages and Papers of the Presidents* 139 (1896).

[36] 22 Ops. Att'y Gen. 13 (1898); see Tucker *v.* Alexandroff, 183 U.S. 424, 434–35 (1902). An act was passed May 27, 1921, 42 Stat. 8 (1921), 47 U.S.C. § 34 (1946) which requires presidential license for the landing and operation of cables connecting the United States with foreign countries. See Wright, *The Control of American Foreign Relations* 302 n.75 (1922).

[37] Santiago *v.* Nagueras, 214 U.S. 260 (1909).

[38] Madsen *v.* Kinsella, 343 U.S. 341 (1952).

although again the final power in the field rests with Congress.[39] One of the president's most ordinary powers and duties is that of ordering the prosecution of supposed offenders against the laws of the United States. Yet Congress may do the same thing under the "necessary and proper" clause.[40] On September 22, 1862, President Lincoln issued a proclamation suspending the privilege of the writ of habeas corpus throughout the Union in certain classes of cases. By an act passed March 3, 1863, Congress ratified his action and at the same time brought the whole subject of military arrests in the United States under statutory control.[41] Conversely, when President Wilson failed in March, 1917, to obtain Congress' consent to his arming American merchant vessels with defensive arms, he went ahead and did it anyway, "fortified not only by the known sentiments of the majority in Congress but also by the advice of his Secretary of State and Attorney General." [42]

To turn to the specific matter of property seizures, Justice Frankfurter's concurring opinion in the Youngstown case is accompanied by appendices containing a synoptic analysis of legislation authorizing seizures of industrial property and also a summary of seizures of industrial plants and facilities by presidents without definite statutory warrant. Eighteen such statutes are listed, all but the first of which were enacted between 1916 and 1951. Of presidential seizures unsupported by reference to specific statutory authorization he lists eight as occurring during World War I. One he fails to mention is the seizure of the Marconi Wireless Station at Siasconset in the late summer of 1914, as a result of the company's refusal to give assurance that it would comply with naval censorship regulation.[43] To justify these seizures it was deemed sufficient to refer to "the Constitution and laws" generally. For the World War II period he lists eleven seizures in justification of which no statutory authority

---

[39] Charlton *v.* Kelly, 229 U.S. 447 (1913). See also Botiller *v.* Dominquez, 130 U.S. 238 (1889).

[40] See Sinclair *v.* United States, 279 U.S. 263, 289, 297 (1929).

[41] 12 Stat. 755 (1863).

[42] Berdahl, *War Powers of the Executive in the United States* 69 (1921).

[43] Attorney General Gregory's justification of this action, 30 Ops. Att'y Gen. 291 (1914), more or less set the style for similar future opinions.

was cited. The first of these was the seizure of North American Aviation, Inc. of Englewood, California. In support of this action Attorney General Jackson, as Chief Justice Vinson points out in his dissenting opinion, "vigorously proclaimed that the President had the moral duty to keep this Nation's defense effort a 'going concern.' "[44] Said the then Attorney General:

For the faithful execution of . . . [the] laws the President has back of him not only each general law-enforcement power conferred by the various acts of Congress but the aggregate of all such laws plus that wide discretion as to method vested in him by the Constitution for the purpose of executing the laws.[45]

In the War Labor Disputes Act of June 25, 1943,[46] all such seizures were put on a statutory basis. Congress having at last acted on the subject, its expressed will thereafter governed.

In United States *v.* Pewee Coal Co.,[47] the Court had before it the claim of a coal mine operator whose property was seized by the President without statutory authorization, "to avert a nation-wide strike of miners." The company brought an action in the Court of Claims to recover under the Fifth Amendment for the total operating losses sustained during the period in which this property was operated by the United States. The court awarded judgment for $2,241.46 and the Supreme Court sustained this judgment, a result which, by implying the validity of the seizure,[48] supported the Government's position in the Youngstown case.[49]

---

[44] Youngstown Sheet & Tube Co. *v.* Sawyer, 343 U.S. 579, 695 (1952).

[45] 89 Cong. Rec. 3992 (1943).

[46] 57 Stat. 163 (1943).

[47] 341 U.S. 114 (1951).

[48] Such suits are based on the Tucker Act, 24 Stat. 505 (1887), as amended, 28 U.S.C. §§ 41(20), 250 (1)(2), 287 (1946), and are founded upon the Constitution of the United States. "The constitutional prohibition against taking private property for public use without just compensation is directed against the Government, and not against individual or public officers proceeding without the authority of legislative enactment." Hooe *v.* United States, 218 U.S. 322, 335–36 (1910). See United States *v.* North American Co., 253 U.S. 330, 333 (1920). While the above quoted language is doubtless correct as an interpretation of the Tucker Act, it ignores the constitutional obligation of the United States to compensate for acts of "taking" which stem from the president's power, especially his power as commander-in-chief. See United States *v.* Causby, 328 U.S. 256, 267 (1946); notes 58–61 *infra*.

[49] "The relatively new technique of temporary taking by eminent domain is a most useful administrative device: many properties, such as laundries, or coal mines, or railroads, may be subjected to public operation for a short time to meet war or emergency needs, and can then be returned to their owners." United States *v.* Pewee Coal Co., 341 U.S. 114, 119 (1951) (Reed, J., concurring).

The doctrine dictated by the above considerations as regards the exercise of executive power in the field of legislative power was well stated by Mr. John W. Davis, principal counsel on the present occasion for the steel companies, in a brief which he filed nearly forty years ago as Solicitor General. The brief defended the action of the president in withdrawing certain lands from public entry, although his doing so was at the time contrary to express statute. "Ours," the brief reads,

is a self-sufficient Government within its sphere. (Ex parte Siebold, 100 U.S. 371, 395; in re Debs, 158 U.S. 56, 564, 578.) "Its means are adequate to its ends" (McCulloch v. Maryland, 4 Wheat. 316, 424), and it is rational to assume that its active forces will be found equal in most things to the emergencies that confront it. While perfect flexibility is not to be expected in a Government of divided powers, and while division of power is one of the principal features of the Constitution, it is the plain duty of those who are called upon to draw the dividing lines to ascertain the essential, recognize the practical, and avoid a slavish formalism which can only serve to ossify the Government and reduce its efficiency without any compensating good. The function of making laws is peculiar to Congress, and the Executive can not exercise that function to any degree. But this is not to say that all of the *subjects* concerning which laws might be made are perforce removed from the possibility of Executive influence. The Executive may act upon things and upon men in many relations which have not, though they might have, been actually regulated by Congress. In other words, just as there are fields which are peculiar to Congress and fields which are peculiar to the Executive, so there are fields which are common to both, in the sense that the Executive may move within them until they shall have been occupied by legislative action. These are not the fields of legislative prerogative, but fields within which the lawmaking power may enter and dominate whenever it chooses. This situation results from the fact that the President is the active agent, not of Congress, but of the Nation. As such he performs the duties which the Constitution lays upon him immediately, and as such, also he executes the laws and regulations adopted by Congress. He is the agent of the people of the United States, deriving all his powers from them and responsible directly to them. In no sense is he the agent of Congress. He obeys and executes the laws of Congress, not because Congress is enthroned in authority over him, but because the Constitution directs him to do so.

Therefore it follows that in ways short of making laws or disobeying them, the Executive may be under a grave constitutional duty to act for the national protection in situations not covered by the acts of Congress, and in which, even, it may not be said that his action is the direct expression of any particular one of the independent powers which are granted to him specifically by the Constitution. Instances wherein the President has felt and fulfilled such a duty have not been rare in our history, though, being for the public benefit and approved by all, his acts have seldom been challenged in the courts.[50]

SOME LOGICAL CONSIDERATIONS

If the legislative power and executive power are not always mutually exclusive, neither, on the other hand, are the legislative and judicial powers. Replying to the contention in Wayman v. Southard [51] that it was unconstitutional for Congress to delegate to the courts its power to regulate their practice, Chief Justice Marshall answered that while Congress cannot delegate powers which are "strictly and exclusively legislative," the courts do have certain rule-making powers with respect, for example, to the returning of writs and processes and the filing of pleadings which Congress might have retained but which it had the right to confer on the judicial department.[52] Indeed, if the President was forbidden to seize the steel mills by virtue of the fact that Congress could have done so, the right of the Court to "invalidate" the seizure becomes highly questionable; and, as all admitted, Congress could have invalidated the seizure.

Actually the President was exercising the same *kind* of power that he would have exercised had the Taft-Hartley Act, for example, made provision for such a seizure "when necessary to avert a serious strike." The Court's opinion says, however:

The President's order does not direct that a congressional policy be executed in a manner prescribed by Congress—it directs that a presidential policy be executed in a manner prescribed by the President. The preamble of the order itself, like that of many statutes, sets out reasons why the President believes certain policies should be adopted, proclaims these policies as rules of conduct to be followed,

---

[50] Brief for Appellant, pp. 75–77, United States *v.* Midwest Oil Co., 236 U.S. 459 (1915). Assistant Att'y Gen. Knaebel's name was also on the brief.
[51] 10 Wheat. 1 (U.S. 1825).
[52] See *id.* at 42–43.

and again, like a statute, authorizes a government official to promulgate additional rules and regulations consistent with the policy proclaimed and needed to carry that policy into execution.[53]

So what? The same thing can be said of orders of the Interstate
Commerce Commission setting "reasonable rates," something
which Congress can do directly any time it chooses to by-pass
or override the Commission. Besides, the chief factors of the
"national emergency" described in Executive Order 10340 put
into operation "cognate powers" of President and Congress
which may be merged indefinitely in the former at the option
of Congress.[54]

THE CONCURRING OPINIONS

Justice Frankfurter begins the material part of his opinion
with the statement:

we must . . . put to one side consideration of what powers the
President would have had if there had been no legislation whatever
bearing on the authority asserted by the seizure, or if the seizure had
been only for a short, explicitly temporary period, to be terminated
automatically unless Congressional approval were given.[55]

He then enters upon a review of the proceedings of Congress
which attended the enactment of the Taft-Hartley Act, and
concludes that Congress expressed its intention to withhold the
seizure power "as though it had said so in so many words." [56]

Justice Douglas' contribution consists in the argument that
a necessary result of the condemnation provision of the Fifth
Amendment is that the branch of government with "the power
to pay compensation for a seizure is the only one able to authorize a seizure or make lawful one that the President has effected." [57] This contention overlooks such cases as Mitchell *v.*
Harmony,[58] United States *v.* Russell,[59] Portsmouth Harbor Land

---

[53] Youngstown Sheet & Tube Co. *v.* Sawyer, 343 U.S. 579, 588 (1952).
[54] United States *v.* Curtiss-Wright Corp., 299 U.S. 304, 319–29 (1936).
[55] Youngstown Sheet & Tube Co. *v.* Sawyer, 343 U.S. 579, 597 (1952).
[56] *Id*. at 602.
[57] *Id*. at 631–32.
[58] 13 How. 115 (U.S. 1852).
[59] 13 Wall. 623 (U.S. 1871).

& Hotel Co. *v.* United States [60] and United States *v.* Pewee Coal Co.,[61] in all of which a right of compensation was recognized to exist in consequence of a taking of property or damage to property which resulted from acts stemming ultimately from constitutional powers of the president. In United States *v.* Pink,[62] Justice Douglas quoted with approval the following words from *The Federalist:* "All constitutional acts of power, whether in the executive or in the judicial department, have as much . . . validity and obligation as if they proceeded from the legislature." [63] If this is so as to treaty obligations, then all the more must it be true of obligations which are based directly on the Constitution.[64]

Justice Jackson's rather desultory opinion contains little that is of direct pertinence to the constitutional issue. Important, however, is his contention, which seems to align him with Justice Frankfurter, that Congress has "not left seizure of private property an open field but has covered it by three statutory policies inconsistent with this seizure." From this he reasons that ". . . we can sustain the President only by holding that seizure of such strike-bound industries is within his domain and beyond control by Congress." [65] The opinion concludes:

> In view of the ease, expedition and safety with which Congress can grant and has granted large emergency powers, certainly ample to embrace this crisis, I am quite unimpressed with the argument that we should affirm possession of them without statute. . . . But I have no illusion that any decision by this Court can keep power in the hands of Congress if it is not wise and timely in meeting its problems. A crisis that challenges the President equally, or perhaps primarily, challenges Congress. If not good law, there was worldly wisdom in the maxim attributed to Napoleon that "The tools belong to the man who can use them." We may say that power to legislate for emergencies belongs in the hands of Congress, but only Congress itself can prevent power from slipping through its fingers.[66]

[60] 260 U.S. 327 (1922).
[61] 341 U.S. 114 (1951).
[62] 315 U.S. 203, 230 (1942).
[63] *The Federalist*, No. 64, at 330 (Everyman's ed. 1929).
[64] See 40 Ops. Att'y Gen. 250, 253 (1942).
[65] Youngstown Sheet & Tube Co. *v.* Sawyer, 343 U.S. 579, 639–40 (1952).
[66] *Id.* at 653–54.

Justice Burton says that the Taft-Hartley Act, read in the light of its legislative history,[67] significantly fails to provide authority for seizures. He also agrees that "Congress authorized a procedure which the President declined to follow."[68] Justice Clark bases his position directly on Little *v.* Barreme.[69] The President must, he says, follow the procedures laid down in the Taft-Hartley, Selective Service and Defense Production Acts.[70] At the same time he endorses the view, "taught me not only by the decision of Chief Justice Marshall in Little *v.* Barreme, but also by a score of other pronouncements of distinguished members of this bench," that "the Constitution does grant to the President extensive authority in times of grave and imperative national emergency."[71]

DISSENTING OPINION

Chief Justice Vinson launched his dissent, for himself and Justices Reed and Minton, with a survey of the elements of the emergency which confronted the President: the Korean War, the obligations of the United States under the United Nations Charter and the Atlantic Pact, the Appropriations Acts by which Congress voted vast sums to be expended in our defense and that of our European allies, the fact that steel is a basic constituent of war matériel. He reproaches the Court for failing to give consideration to the President's finding of an emergency. According to the Court, he said, "the immediacy of the threatened disaster" is "irrelevant"; and the President, unable to use the executive power to avert the disaster, "must confine himself to sending a message to Congress." The opinion of the Chief Justice musters impressive evidence to show that the steel seizure, considering the emergency involved, fits into the picture of past presidential emergency action. And "plaintiffs admit that the emergency procedures of Taft-Hartley are not mandatory."[72]

---

[67] 93 Cong. Rec. 3835–36 (1947).
[68] Youngstown Sheet & Tube Co. *v.* Sawyer, 343 U.S. 579, 659 (1952).
[69] 2 Cranch 170 (U.S. 1804).
[70] Youngstown Sheet & Tube Co. *v.* Sawyer, 343 U.S. 579, 663–65 (1952).
[71] *Id.* at 662.
[72] *Id.* at 705.

RÉSUMÉ AND EVALUATION

Youngstown will probably go down in history as an outstanding example of the *sic volo, sic jubeo* frame of mind into which the Court is occasionally maneuvered by the public context of the case before it. The doctrine of the case, as stated in Justice Black's opinion of the Court, while purporting to stem from the principle of the separation of powers, is a purely arbitrary construct created out of hand for the purpose of disposing of this particular case, and is altogether devoid of historical verification. Nor do the concurring opinions contribute anything to the decision's claim to be regarded seriously as a doctrine of constitutional law. Their importance consists in the suggestion, cogently urged by Justice Frankfurter and endorsed by Justices Jackson, Burton and Clark, that the President should have heeded the intention of the Taft-Hartley Act. Only Justice Clark, however, guided by Marshall's opinion in the early case of Little *v.* Barreme, had the courage to draw the appropriate conclusion: Congress having entered the field, its ascertainable intention supplied the law of the case. Justice Clark accordingly refused to concur in the opinion of the court, while voting for its decision.

The Chief Justice's dissenting opinion is impressive for its delineation of the emergency and convincing in its summation of evidence regarding presidential emergency power. In view of the attitude of the concurring justices, however, his assertion as to the bearing of Taft-Hartley on the problem before the Court is deceptive. The statement that Taft-Hartley was "not mandatory" is equivocal. Granting that the Act was not intended to require the president to resort to it in preference to permitting the situation to take an uncontrolled course, yet resort to it may very well have been intended as an indispensable preliminary to a seizure. This conclusion is borne out by the fact that when the procedures provided by the act fail, the president is required to submit a report and recommendations to Congress for action. In the opinion of the writer the case was rightly decided, but for wrong reasons. The line of reasoning suggested by Justices Frankfurter, Jackson, Burton and

Clark should have been pursued to its logical end, as by Justice Clark it was.[73]

The question remains whether the record of the case is of value for constitutional law and practice. It is. (1) That the president does possess "residual" or "resultant" powers over and above, or in consequence of, his specifically granted powers to take temporary alleviative action in the presence of serious emergency is a proposition to which all but Justices Black and Douglas would probably have assented in the absence of the complicating issue that was created by the president's refusal to follow the procedures laid down in the Taft-Hartley Act. (2) Such residual powers being conceded, it would follow logically that a seizure of property made by exercise of them would give rise to a constitutional obligation on the part of the United States to render "just compensation" in accordance with the requirements of the Fifth Amendment. (3) It is also fairly evident that the Court would never venture to traverse a presidential finding of "serious" emergency which was prima facie supported by judicially cognizable facts, but would wave aside a challenge to such a finding as raising a "political question." (4) The Court would unquestionably have assented to the proposition that in all emergency situations the last word lies with Congress when it chooses to speak such last word. And the moral from all this is plain: namely, that escape must be sought from "presidential autocracy" by resort not to the judicial power, but to the legislative power—in other words, by resort to timely action by Congress and to procedures for the meeting of emergency situations so far as these can be intelligently anticipated.

And—not to give the thing too fine a point—what seems to be required at the present juncture is a new Labor Disputes

---

[73] The case for the President is not improved by Congress' adoption of the following provision as a part of the Defense Production Act Amendments of 1952, Pub. L. No. 429, 82d Cong., 2d Sess. § 115 (June 30, 1952): "Section 503 of the Defense Production Act of 1950, as amended, is hereby amended by adding at the end thereof the following: 'It is the sense of the Congress that, by reason of the work stoppage now existing in the steel industry, the national safety is imperiled, and the Congress therefore requests the President to invoke immediately the national emergency provisions (sections 206 to 210, inclusive) of the Labor-Management Relations Act, 1947, for the purpose of terminating such work stoppage.' "

Act which ordains procedures for the handling of industry-wide strikes in terms so comprehensive and explicit that the most headstrong president cannot sidestep them without manifest attaint to the law, the Constitution and his own oath of office. "Presidential autocracy," when it is justified, is an inrush of power to fill a power vacuum. Nature abhors a vacuum; so does an age of emergency. Let Congress see to it that no such vacuum occurs.

CHAPTER NINE

~~~~~~

Freedom of Speech

Since the First World War, American constitutional law has been more or less constantly entangled in the problems raised by speech that is alleged to be "subversive" and, on the other hand, by laws that aim to punish such expression. When action by the national government is involved, the question is, of course, whether the affected individual's rights under the First Amendment have been infringed; but since Gitlow *v.* New York (268 U.S. 652) in 1925, freedom of expression has also been protected against state action by the Fourteenth Amendment.

Bibliographically speaking, this field suffers from a kind of embarrassment of riches. The indexes which record the literature of public law abound with references on the subject, but most of the writings to which they refer are, for one reason or another, inappropriate to a volume of this kind. Many of them, though very acute, are restricted to a special aspect of the "subversion problem." Others are too long for inclusion. Zechariah Chafee's *Free Speech in the United States*, which might fairly be called the primary modern classic in the area, is a book rather than an essay and was published in 1941 before the postwar excitement over this constitutional problem began. Perhaps because the subject matter is so vastly complex, there seems to be no single essay that does not encounter these, or other, objections.

It has seemed desirable therefore, to reprint three rather short selections in the field, in the hope that the reader will be enabled at least to savor the complexities of the problem. Professor Chafee's review of Professor Meiklejohn's book accomplishes a double objective. In the first place, it raises some of the questions that are, in a way, prior to any detailed discussion of the First Amendment's meaning—what is the theoretic rationale that underlies the free speech guaranties of the Constitution? Should the defenders of free speech place their heaviest reliance on the argument that a given restriction is undesirable, or on the argument that it is unconstitutional? In the second place, the review brings into juxtaposition two scholarly personalities who eminently deserve representation in a volume of this kind. Chafee probably knows more about this subject than any other living man, and his writings are as engaging as they are wise. Meiklejohn is a distinguished philosopher and educator who has spent a lifetime fighting for freedom of expression and weaving an unforgettable spell over generations of students. Chafee is a lawyer, while Meiklejohn is not; but they can meet, even though to disagree, on the philosophical ground that Meiklejohn's book is concerned with.

After this introduction to some of the underlying premises of constitutional free speech, N. L. Nathanson's perceptive essay brings us directly to the question of their application, to the "Communist trial" and its legal aftermath. Nathanson offers us one view of the issues. The excerpt from Judge Hand's Court of Appeals opinion is perhaps the best and certainly the most authoritative statement yet made on the other side. Judge Hand is among the most distinguished jurists now living, and his opinion in this case was more definitive and will probably be more influential than the subsequent decision of the Supreme Court of the United States (Dennis *v.* United States, 341 U.S. 494 [1951]).

The issues raised by the authors of these selections can be

touched on only lightly in the limitations of this foreword. Professor Meiklejohn's main thesis is presented by Professor Chafee about as fairly as is possible at second hand. The idea that free speech is essential to effective self-government is an important one, and it would be hard to find a more eloquent and persuasive statement of the point than Meiklejohn's. Whether or not the reader follows him in his insistence that this is the *only* philosophic justification for the First Amendment, it will surely be agreed that this is *one* justification, and a very significant one. Professor Chafee does agree, but goes on to urge that a man's private interest in speaking his mind may be as relevant to the First Amendment as the public's need to hear him. The distinction Meiklejohn makes between private and public speech and his corresponding legal differentiation of the First Amendment and the "due process" clause is, in Chafee's judgment, unwarranted and unworkable.

However, this dual distinction is crucial to Meiklejohn's argument, for it must serve as the premise of his second major point—that the free expression protected by the First Amendment is unqualified. He could hardly contend that all speech of whatever kind is immune from any legal limitation, so he erects a special limited category of speech which is, he feels, entitled to absolute protection. One trouble with categories is that they are often averse to staying put, and Chafee points to some of the difficulties involved in keeping this one stationary. But even if the category of "public speech" could be pinned down, Chafee would reject the contention that we can, or should, grant it absolute immunity. He believes, if I understand him, that some line must be drawn "between good public speech and bad public speech" and that the main task of analysis, both for judges and for citizens, is to determine where and how that line shall be drawn.

This query leads us directly to the Nathanson and Hand selections, and to the "clear and present danger" concept. The constitutional idea that goes by that name is the product of an effort by various Supreme Court justices to draw such a line between punishable and non-punishable expression. Its principal draftsmen were Justices Holmes, who first advanced the doctrine in Schenck *v.* United States (249 U.S. 47 [1919]), and

Brandeis, who spelled it out further in Whitney *v.* California (274 U.S. 374 [1927]). Since Herndon *v.* Lowry (301 U.S. 242 [1937]), this test, if it can be called that, has been invoked by the Supreme Court in a number of free speech cases, and Dennis *v.* United States, *supra,* established it as the standard which must be met by the government in defending the constitutionality of most sedition statutes.

However, like most legal formulas, this one has raised as many issues of definition as it has resolved. The phrase "clear and present danger" describes, as Judge Hand says, "a penumbra of occasions, even the outskirts of which are indefinable," and both judges and scholars have been confronted with the delicate task of drawing lines within that penumbra as the specific cases arise. These difficulties are too many to be recounted in full here, but a few, which especially concern Nathanson and Hand, may be singled out, so as to indicate that the job is not an easy one.

In the first place, there is the problem posed by asking the question: clear and present danger of *what?* Holmes said in the Schenck case that speech may be inhibited if it creates a clear and present danger of bringing about "substantive evils that Congress has a right to prevent" (249 U.S. 47, 52). However, in Whitney *v.* California Brandeis qualified this terminology, arguing that prohibition of free speech is justified only if the evil apprehended is "relatively serious" (274 U.S. 357, 377). Though the legislature has an undoubted right to forbid and punish the "substantive evil" of trespass, for example, Congress would not be warranted in muzzling free speech merely to prevent this minor evil. Brandeis did not undertake to define the exact degree of evil that *would* justify such a law, and judges and scholars have been somewhat uncertain about that question ever since. If the evil feared must be as serious as "the immediate overthrow of the government," as counsel contended in the Dennis case, then the clear and present danger rule implies a great—some would think an insanely exaggerated—degree of freedom of speech. But Nathanson rightly points out that the "rule" does not involve such an extreme requirement, and was never meant to by its authors. The fact remains, nevertheless, that the distinction between "trivial" and "relatively serious" evils is an ambiguous one, and that making the distinction plunges the judicial process into formidable difficulties.

Secondly, there is the problem presented by the particular character of the speech we propose to forbid. The trial judge seemed to feel that secret discussion might be less entitled to protection than open discussion. Judge Hand in the Court of Appeals and the Chief Justice in the Supreme Court were evidently impressed by the fact that the discussions for which the defendants had been indicted were linked to a highly disciplined and widespread organization of determined zealots— the Communist Party of the United States. Nathanson's assault upon these points is cogent, but it does not perhaps entirely dispose of their underlying force. Plainly the judges have a feeling, which would probably be shared by many other men, that the advocacy of violence may be more dangerous when it issues from members of an efficient, purposeful, and semiclandestine organization than when it is spoken by an isolated soapbox orator. This feeling is not without a measure of what T. R. Powell called "common sense" in an earlier essay in this volume. But the problem, as always, is to express that common sense in meaningful judicial rhetoric, or, in other words, to take account of these considerations in developing the implications of the clear and present danger rule without reducing the rule to a merely fictitious limitation on government. It cannot be said that the courts have adequately met this problem.

Third, there are some rather thorny difficulties involved in the use of the phrase "*present* danger." Judge Hand holds that the real question is whether the danger is "probable," and that the problem of immediacy enters in only insofar as it affects the judgment of probability. If there is an appreciable time lapse between the speech and its possible violent result, the process of public discussion and education will have a better chance to prevent the result from occurring. But under some conditions these corrective processes may not operate even though they have time to do so, and in such circumstances the danger may be highly "probable" even though it is not "present." Should the government sit still in the face of this probability simply because it will take some time for it to develop into actuality? One answer—and it would presumably be Nathanson's

—can be made in terms of democratic theory, i.e., that a time lapse between advocacy and execution will *always* affect probability. Democracy, so the argument runs, is premised on the faith that public opinion will reject erroneous ideas and render them harmless, so long as there is adequate time and opportunity to discuss those ideas. If this trust in the wisdom of popular judgments is really central to the American credo, then Judge Hand's amendment of the "clear and present danger" phraseology seems highly questionable. On the other hand, insofar as we are disposed to admit that democratic processes sometimes err, his position becomes more defensible. As so often in constitutional law, the legal issue boils down to an ultimate conflict in political philosophy.

Finally, there is the question raised by the whole nature of the courts' assignment under the clear and present danger principle: what sort of objective circumstances should the courts take account of in applying the rule? The problem is not so difficult when the case involves a street-corner orator who seeks to incite a casual crowd to violence, for the circle of relevant considerations will then be comparatively small. But the hazards of the judicial process are greatly enhanced if the case forces the judge to venture on the enormous stage of world politics and to consider, as Judge Hand did, such complex matters as the nature of world Communism, the probable military intentions of the U.S.S.R., and the implications of the Berlin airlift. Justice Jackson pointed out, when the case had reached the Supreme Court, that the appraisal of these imponderables had baffled "the best informed foreign offices and our most experienced politicians." If the clear and present danger principle compels the Court to unravel such mysteries, he said, it requires a prophecy under the pretext of a legal decision, and he would forsake the rule rather than assume a function so foreign to the judicial universe (341 U.S. 494, 570).

These then are some of the perplexities the analyst must contend with if he seeks to draw a line, as Chafee would, between punishable and non-punishable political expression. The impulse is strong to by-pass these quandaries by insisting with Meiklejohn that "public" speech is absolutely immune, or at the other extreme by urging, as Justice Jackson seemed to do, that the government should be free to punish such expression when and how it chooses. But the trouble with these apparently clear-cut resolutions of the dilemma is that they resolve old difficulties by propounding new ones. Much as we would like life and law to be simple, even professors and judges must learn to live with the fact that they are often not.

[BOOK REVIEW]

Free Speech: and Its Relation to Self-Government by Alexander Meiklejohn (NEW YORK: HARPER & BROTHERS, 1948), 107 pages, $2.00

by Zechariah Chafee, Jr.*

Harvard Law Review,
Volume 62, Page 891 (1949)

The first time I saw the author of this book was on an October morning forty-five years ago. With other Brown freshmen, I was emerging from the daily chapel service to find a solid mass of sophomores waiting for us outside the door. A free fight was starting when Dean Meiklejohn suddenly appeared out of nowhere, right in the center of the fray, wearing a stiff derby hat. His good-humored display of authority stopped the fight, but in the process his derby got several bad dents.

Now, with similar pluck, he rushes between two fiercely contending groups of lawyers and tells them they are both wrong. On the one hand, he stands firmly against distinguished members of the American Bar Association, like my old friend Frank Ober, who thinks that the Supreme Court has gone much too far in granting liberties to radicals.[1] Mr. Meiklejohn is opposed to sedition legislation, to FBI dossiers collecting the political and economic opinions of individuals, to the Un-American Committee and its local imitations, to Department of Justice

---

* (1885–1957), Professor of Law, Harvard University Law School, 1919–1957.
[1] See Ober, Communism vs. the Constitution: The Power to Protect Our Free Institutions, 34 A.B.A.J. 645 (1948). See also his references to other opinions in the American Bar Association, *id.* at 747 n.80; the Maryland statute of last June appointing a "little Dies Committee" of which Mr. Ober is chairman, *id.* at 760; and the resolutions by the House of Delegates, 34 A.B.A.J. 281 (1948).

lists of "subversive" organizations, to the President's Loyalty Order.

We are saying that the citizens of the United States will be fit to govern themselves under their own institutions only if they have faced squarely and fearlessly . . . everything that can be said against them. (p. 91)

Yet Mr. Meiklejohn is by no means on the side of lawyers like myself who regard the "clear and present danger" test of Justice Holmes as substantially sound. He spends most of his pages in condemning Holmes and the present Court. Their position, in his opinion, completely misconceives the First Amendment and consequently protects political discussion too little.

. . . the court . . . has persistently ruled that the freedom of speech of the American community may constitutionally be abridged by legislative action. That ruling annuls the most significant purpose of the First Amendment. It destroys the intellectual basis of our plan of self-government. The court has interpreted the dictum that Congress shall not abridge the freedom of speech by defining the conditions under which such abridging is allowable. Congress, we are now told, is forbidden to destroy our freedom except when it finds it advisable to do so. (p. 29)

Once more, the courageous vigor with which Mr. Meiklejohn dashes at contending factions excites my admiration, but his derby is likely to get a good many dents.

This is a timely book. The country seems to be suffering again from an epidemic of hysteria such as it underwent during the "Red Menace" of 1919–1920. Even men who recognize "that the dangers from subversive organizations at the time of World War I were much exaggerated" [2] are so apprehensive of the dangers from subversive organizations today that they are once more seeking to fight objectionable ideas with long prison sentences and heavy pecuniary penalties. If the First Amendment as construed by the Supreme Court prevents such suppression, then they propose to amend the First Amendment in order, so they say, "to preserve the *whole* Constitution." [3]

---

[2] Ober, *supra* note 1, at 742.
[3] *Id*. at 747.

This alarm about our national safety is increased by our recent acquisition of the strongest weapon we have ever possessed—the atom bomb. Instead of making us less fearful, it makes us more fearful, because we are constantly worried about losing the deadly secret. We are like LaFontaine's cobbler, who sang gaily so long as he was poor but was made silent by getting some gold coins.

> *Le sommeil quitta son logis:*
> *Il eut pour hôtes les soucis,*
> *Les soupçons, les alarmes vaines.*
> *Tout le jour il avait l'oeil au guet; et la nuit,*
> *Si quelque chat faisait du bruit,*
> *Le chat prenait l'argent.*

And so the most powerful nation on earth is rapidly losing the confidence which Thomas Jefferson displayed when we had virtually no army and a weak navy and when a hostile government owned the mouth of the Mississippi. That was the moment he chose to declare:

If there be any among us who would wish to dissolve this union or to change its republican form, let them stand undisturbed, as monuments of the safety with which error of opinion may be tolerated where reason is free to combat it.[4]

This courage, many now tell us, is out of date—the United States in 1801 did not have to face Communism and Stalin. But it had to face the French Revolution and Napoleon. The lawyers who drafted the Sedition Act of 1798 and the judges who enforced that law felt that they were stamping out a foreign menace fully as dangerous as the foreign menace which confronts us today. The New York legislators who outlawed five Socialists in 1920 were just as sure that they had ample cause for alarm as are the patriotic citizens who want to outlaw all Communists in 1948. And the principles which Jefferson used to allay such apprehensions in his time are equally valid in our time. Meet unlawful action with action; proceed against spies and real plotters with vigor, as he prosecuted Aaron Burr

---

[4] 1 Richardson, *Messages & Papers of the Presidents* 310 (1897).

and approved the dismissal of Genêt. Meet objectionable ideas from abroad by living up to our own ideas—give increased drawing-power to our great traditions of democracy and freedom.

Therefore, at a time when we are urged to fight the Russian censorship of the press by establishing censorship of the press, to fight a land riddled with secret police by increasing our own secret police, to contend against people who will not talk with foreigners by dismissing the head of the Bureau of Standards because he talked with foreigners, etc., etc., it is refreshing to read language like Mr. Meiklejohn's:

If, then, on any occasion in the United States it is allowable to say that the Constitution is a good document it is equally allowable, in that situation, to say that the Constitution is a bad document. If a public building may be used in which to say, in time of war, that the war is justified, then the same building may be used in which to say that it is not justified. If it be publicly argued that conscription for armed service is moral and necessary, it may likewise be publicly argued that it is immoral and unnecessary. If it may be said that American political institutions are superior to those of England or Russia or Germany, it may, with equal freedom, be said that those of England or Russia or Germany are superior to ours. These conflicting views may be expressed, must be expressed, not because they are valid, but because they are relevant. If they are responsibly entertained by anyone, we, the voters, need to hear them. When a question of policy is "before the house," free men choose to meet it not with their eyes shut, but with their eyes open. To be afraid of ideas, any idea, is to be unfit for self-government. (p. 27)

As an exposition of political wisdom, this and several other passages in the book are admirable. I hope that they will be widely read, for if so they will help counteract the current belief that the way to save freedom is to sacrifice our most cherished liberties.

Mr. Meiklejohn, however, is not content to present the ideas just quoted as desirable policy in the crisis of today. He is writing *sub specie aeternitatis*. He insists that they are forever embodied in the Constitution. His next sentence is: "Any such suppression of ideas about the common good, the First Amendment condemns with its absolute disapproval." Instead of arguing on the level of wisdom and policy, he argues on the level of constitutional prohibitions.

In endeavoring to oppose suppressive measures, I have found it best to keep on the level of wisdom and policy as much as possible. In the situation which now confronts us, we have to start by recognizing that a considerable number of decent people want more suppression of speech and opinions because they are sincerely afraid of the dangers of Communism within the United States. The best practical hope is to persuade them that this danger is smaller than they think—small enough so that the risks of toleration are negligible in comparison to the losses to the American way of life which would inevitably follow from a systematic legal campaign against "dangerous thoughts." The First Amendment comes into the discussion chiefly as a powerful means of persuasion. If persuasion fails, then the First Amendment will be invoked in the courts, but that is a last resort. Once a measure is enacted, a large amount of suppression always occurs before it reaches a test in the courts, and plenty of harm is done even if the law is eventually declared unconstitutional. So the most important thing is to prevent the enactment of an unwise measure if possible. And that enactment is most likely to be prevented if a majority of the legislature and of active members of the public can be persuaded that it is undesirable.

It is much more difficult to conduct the argument on a constitutional level when you are appealing to the public or to a legislative committee. What you are really saying then is that they ought not to pass the measure even though they are not persuaded that it is undesirable. Whatever they think about it, the Supreme Court will annul it and so it will be useless. But this argument will fail unless you can convince your hearers that the Court will in fact be against the measure. In order to do this, you have to turn aside from the reasons about desirability which are part of everybody's thinking and stick to the kind of language which lawyers use. You have to be absolutely sure of your ground, for if other lawyers (on the legislative committee or elsewhere) can raise plausible doubts about the validity of your constitutional position, you will get nowhere.

Herein lies my main objection to Mr. Meiklejohn's book.

He places virtually all his argument against current proposals for suppression on a constitutional position which is extremely dubious. Whereas the supporters of these measures are genuinely worried by the dangers of Communism, he refuses to argue that these dangers are actually small. Instead, his constitutional position obliges him to argue that these dangers are irrelevant. No matter how terrible and immediate the dangers may be, he keeps saying, the First Amendment will not let Congress or anybody else in the Government try to deal with Communists who have not yet committed unlawful acts. It is hopeless to use reasoning like this in order to win votes against the Mundt-Nixon Bill. Such a view may be courageous, but it won't work.

Since Mr. Meiklejohn as a philosopher is not a pragmatist, he would probably reply that what has just been said does not matter. If he is right in his interpretation of the Constitution, then his view is not made wrong by the fact that nobody else agrees with him. He is not trying to frame arguments which will win votes, but is seeking for eternal truth. The earth would still be round although the great majority voted that it was flat.

What a majority of the Supreme Court votes, however, does have considerable bearing on truth in constitutional law. In a sense, the First Amendment is what the Supreme Court says it means. Inasmuch as most of the author's book is an attack on the Court's interpretation of the Constitution, his view of that document is bound to be useless in the practical task of opposing current suppressive measures.

Still, this does not dispose of his constitutional position. We can afford to take a longer view, as he does. On other occasions the Court has taken a view of the Constitution which thoughtful writers considered unsound, and eventually the Court changed and agreed with the writers. The Child Labor Law is a well-known example. Therefore it is worth while to examine Mr. Meiklejohn's view. If his reasons are convincing, perhaps the Court will someday adopt them and reject the clear and present danger test which he attacks. Let us ask, then, whether the First Amendment ought to have the meaning which the author ascribes to it.

Mr. Meiklejohn's basic proposition is that there are two distinct kinds of freedom of speech, protected by quite different clauses of the Constitution. Freedom of speech on matters affecting self-government is protected by the First Amendment and is not open to restrictions by the Government. The Amendment is absolute in its terms: "Congress shall make no law . . . abridging the freedom of speech. . . ." By contrast, private discussion is open to restrictions because it is protected by the Fifth Amendment: ". . . nor shall any person . . . be deprived of . . . liberty . . . without due process of law. . . ." Correspondingly, where state governments are concerned, the due process clause of the Fourteenth Amendment permits limits on private discussion, but public discussion belongs under the absolute prohibition: "No State shall make or enforce any law which shall abridge the privileges or immunities of citizens of the United States . . ."—although it is regrettable, the author says, that this clause did not give the same immunity to public discussion by aliens.[5]

His view of the First Amendment is elaborated in such statements as these:

When men govern themselves, it is they—and no one else—who must pass judgment upon unwisdom and unfairness and danger. And that means that unwise ideas must have a hearing as well as wise ones, unfair as well as fair, dangerous as well as safe, un-American as well as American. . . . The principle of the freedom of speech . . . is a deduction from the basic American agreement that public issues shall be decided by universal suffrage. (pp. 26–27)

Its [the Amendment's] purpose is to give to every voting member of the body politic the fullest possible participation in the understanding of those problems with which the citizens of a self-governing society must deal. When a free man is voting, it is not enough that the truth is known by someone else, by some scholar or administrator or legislator. The voters must have it, all of them. The primary purpose of the First Amendment is, then, that all the citizens shall, so far as possible, understand the issues which bear upon our common life. That is why no idea, no opinion, no doubt, no belief, no counterbelief, no relevant information, may be kept from

---

[5] Pages 59–61. Anybody familiar with the difficulties the Court has had in construing the "privileges and immunities" clause will realize the morass into which this theory would throw every free-speech case involving state legislation. See Chafee, *Free Speech in the United States* 413 n.77 (1941).

them. Under the compact upon which the Constitution rests, it is agreed that men shall not be governed by others, that they shall govern themselves. (pp. 88–89)

At Brown, Mr. Meiklejohn loved to open his logic class by asking: "If I should tell you that I just saw a unicorn running across the campus, how could you prove that I was wrong?" What he has just seen in the First Amendment is a beautiful unicorn.

Is there any historical evidence that the framers of the First Amendment conceived of two freedoms of speech or intended the Amendment to apply only to discussions of matters connected with the process of self-government? [6] Surely they did not link the Amendment with "universal suffrage" as the author insists, because the much-restricted state franchises of 1791 were left completely untouched by the Constitution; the feminine half of the population could hardly vote at all for more than a hundred and twenty-five years after the Bill of Rights was adopted. No doubt, the Zenger trial and the controversy over Wilkes and Junius in England did associate the struggle for freedom of speech to some extent with popular discussion of political questions, but the struggle was also related to the abolition of the censorship of books of any sort. Milton's *Areopagitica* advocated freedom for much else besides political tracts. The First Amendment brackets freedom of speech with freedom of the press, which Mr. Meiklejohn never mentions. If "speech" is limited as he proposes, so is

---

[6] Space does not permit me to criticize adequately the author's conception of self-government in Chapter I. It seems to me a mystical identification of the rulers with the ruled to say "We, the People, . . . by explicit compact, are the government . . ." (p. 13), or ". . . the citizens of this nation shall make and shall obey their own laws . . ." (p. 13), or "Free men . . . governed—by themselves" (p. 14). If it be true that "no man is called upon to obey a law unless he himself, equally with his fellows, has shared in making it" (pp. 10–11), why were women bound by law before the Nineteenth Amendment? By self-government, the framers meant that direct or indirect popular participation in the choice of the federal rulers would produce the best sort of rulers in the long run. But they were constantly thinking of the rulers as human beings set apart and liable to be corrupted by their power. Hence they took much pains to set up several sharply separated groups of human beings to do different tasks and check each other. Just because Mr. Meiklejohn and I voted at every election for one candidate for the House of Representatives, who was often defeated, I refuse to say that the author and I made the law establishing the Dies-Thomas-Rankin Committee, or that what that Committee does is his action or mine.

"press." Yet that is impossible in view of the address of the Continental Congress in 1774 to the people of Quebec, in which freedom of the press, in addition to its political values, is said to be important for "the advancement of truth, science, morality and arts in general." [7] Jefferson's vigorous support of the Philadelphia bookseller, Dufief, when Dufief was arrested for selling a French book on the creation of the world, shows how closely Jefferson connected freedom of the press with freedom of religion and of all thinking. [8] As he said on another occasion, "I have sworn upon the altar of God eternal hostility against every form of tyranny over the mind of man." [9]

Moreover, the framers would hardly have relegated science, art, drama, and poetry to the obscure shelter of the Fifth Amendment, as the book implies, inasmuch as "due process" meant mainly proper procedure until the middle of the nineteenth century. James Madison had no reason to expect that the phrase would eventually be used to upset unreasonable and arbitrary legislative rules of substantive law. Indeed, it was not until 1925 that "liberty" in the Constitution became a safeguard to freedom of speech. [10]

Mr. Meiklejohn's argument that all the freedoms within the First Amendment are not open to any governmental restrictions (pp. 1–2) leans far too heavily on the absolute nature of its language. [11] Even "the free exercise" of religion has been held not to include polygamy [12] or the exhibition of poisonous snakes in church. [13] Especially significant is the contemporaneous evidence that the phrase "freedom of the press" was viewed against a background of familiar legal limitations which men of 1791

---

[7] I Journals of Congress 57 (1800). See Chafee, *Free Speech in the United States* 17, 545 (1941); I Chafee, *Government and Mass Communications* 53 (1947).

[8] Boyd, "Subversive of What?" *Atlantic Monthly*, Aug. 1948, p. 19.

[9] 10 *The Writings of Thomas Jefferson* 175 (Washington ed., 1903). For a more accurate copy of the letter quoted, see *Library of Congress Quarterly Journal of Current Acquisitions*, No. 2, 1944, pp. 3–8.

[10] Gitlow *v.* New York, 268 U.S. 652 (1925).

[11] The Thirteenth Amendment is absolute except as to crime, but involuntary servitude has been lawfully imposed on sailors till the end of the voyage and on millions drafted into the army, even in peace.

[12] Davis *v.* Beeson, 133 U.S. 333 (1890); Reynolds *v.* United States, 98 U.S. 145 (1878).

[13] Lawson *v.* Commonwealth, 291 Ky. 437, 164 S.W. 2d 972 (1942). For a very interesting case involving the use of the mails to extend an extraordinary religion, see United States *v.* Ballard, 322 U.S. 78 (1944).

did not regard as objectionable, such as damage suits for libel. Many state constitutions of this time included guaranties of freedom of speech and press which have been treated as having approximately the same scope as the federal provisions. Some of these, as in Massachusetts, were absolute in terms, while others, as in New York, expressly imposed responsibility for the abuse of the right. The precise nature of the state constitutional language did not matter; the early interpretation was much the same. Not only were private libel suits allowed, but also punishments for criminal libel and for contempt of court. For instance, there were several Massachusetts convictions around 1800 for libels attacking the conduct of the legislature and of public officials.[14] This evidence negatives the author's idea of a firmly established purpose to make all political discussion immune.

The truth is, I think, that the framers had no very clear idea as to what they meant by "the freedom of speech or of the press," but we can say three things with reasonable assurance. First, these politicians, lawyers, scholars, churchgoers and *philosophes*, scientists, agriculturalists, and wide readers used the phrase to embrace the whole realm of thought. Second, they intended the First Amendment to give all the protection they desired, and had no idea of supplementing it by the Fifth Amendment. Finally, the freedom which Congress was forbidden to abridge was not, for them, some absolute concept which had never existed on earth. It was the freedom which they believed they already had—what they had wanted before the Revolution and had acquired through independence. In thinking about it, they took for granted the limitations which had been customarily applied in the day-to-day work of colonial courts. Now, they were setting up a new federal government of great potential strength, and (as in the rest of the Bill of Rights) they were determined to make sure that it would not take away the freedoms which they then enjoyed in their thirteen sovereign states.

Still, the First Amendment has the power of growing to meet new needs. As Marshall said, it is a *Constitution* which we

---

[14] Duniway, *The Development of Freedom of the Press in Massachusetts* 144–46 (1906).

are interpreting. Although in 1791 the Amendment did not mean what Mr. Meiklejohn says, perhaps it ought to mean that now. But the Supreme Court is unlikely to think so in any foreseeable future. The author condemns the clear and present danger test as "a peculiarly inept and unsuccessful attempt to formulate an exception" to the constitutional protection of public discussion (p. 50), but he does not realize how unworkable his own views would prove when applied in litigation.

In the first place, although it may be possible to draw a fairly bright line between speech which is completely immune and action which may be punished, some speech on public questions is so hateful that the Court would be very reluctant to protect it from statutory penalties. We are not dealing with a philosopher who can write what he pleases, but with at least five men who are asked to block legislators and prosecutors. The history of the Court Plan in 1937 shows how sure judges have to be of their ground to do that. Take a few examples. A newspaper charges the mayor with taking bribes. Ezra Pound broadcasts from an Italian radio station that our participation in the war is an abominable mistake. A speaker during a very bad food shortage tells a hungry mass of voters that the rationing board is so incompetent and corrupt that the best way to avoid starvation is to demand the immediate deaths of its members, unless they are ready to resign. Plainly few judges can grant constitutional protection to such speeches.

Even the author begins to hedge. Although his main insistence is on immunity for all speech connected with self-government, as my examples surely are, occasionally he concedes that "repressive action by the government is imperative for the sake of the general welfare," e.g., against libelous assertions, slander, words inciting men to crime, sedition, and treason by words (e.g., p. 18). Here he is diving into very deep water. Once you push punishment beyond action into the realm of language, then you have to say pretty plainly how far back the law should go. You must enable future judges and jurymen to know where to stop. That is just what Holmes did when he drew his line at clear and present danger, and the author gives us no substitute test for distinguishing between good pub-

lic speech and bad public speech. He never faces the problem
of Mark Anthony's Oration—discussion which is calculated to
produce unlawful acts without ever mentioning them.

At times he hints that the line depends on the falsity of
the assertions or the bad motives of the speaker. In the mayor's
case, it is no answer to say that false charges are outside the
Constitution; the issue is whether a jury shall be permitted to
find them false even if they are in fact true. Moreover, in such
charges a good deal of truth which might be useful to the
voters is frequently mixed with some falsehood, so that the
possibility of a damage action often keeps genuine information away from voters. And the low character of speakers and
writers does not necessarily prevent them from uttering whole-
some truths about politics. Witness the *Essays* of Francis Bacon.
Mr. Meiklejohn has a special dislike for paid "lobbyists for special interests" (p. 99). But if discussing public questions with
money in sight is outside the First Amendment, how about
speeches by aspirants to a $75,000 job in Washington or editorials
in newspapers or books on Free Speech? Dr. Johnson declared
that any man who writes except for money is a fool. In short,
the trouble with the bad-motive test is that courts and juries
would apply it only to the exponents of unpopular views. If
what is said happens to be our way, the speaker is as welcome
as an ex-revolutionist to the Un-American Committee.

The most serious weakness in Mr. Meiklejohn's argument
is that it rests on his supposed boundary between public speech
and private speech. That line is extremely blurred. Take the
novel *Strange Fruit*, which was lately suppressed in Massachusetts.[15] It did not discuss any question then before the voters, but
it dealt thoughtfully with many problems of the relations between whites and Negroes, a matter of great national concern.
Was this under the First Amendment or the Fifth? Birth control is the most personal of matters, and yet any discussion of
it raises questions of the desirable size of our population, the
intelligent rearing of children, dependency, immorality, and

---

[15] Commonwealth *v.* Isenstadt, 318 Mass. 543, 62 N.E.2d 840 (1945). See
I Chafee, *Government and Mass Communications* 200–26 (1947).

clerical control of votes. The truth is that there are public aspects to practically every subject. The satisfactory operation of self-government requires the individual to develop fairness, sympathy, and understanding of other men, a comprehension of economic forces, and some basic purpose in life. He can get help from poems and plays and novels. No matter if Shakespeare and Whitehead do seem very far away from the issues of the next election. The author recognizes this when he says that the First Amendment is directed against "mutilation of the thinking process of the community" (p. 26), and when he blames the radio for not cultivating taste, reasoned judgment, integrity, or loyalty, "qualities . . . upon which the enterprise of self-government depends" (p. 104). This attitude, however, offers such a wide area for the First Amendment that very little is left for his private speech under the Fifth Amendment. For example, if books and plays are public speech, how can they be penalized for gross obscenity or libels?

On the other hand, if private speech does include scholarship (as the author suggests, pp. 99–100) and also art and literature, it is shocking to deprive these vital matters of the protection of the inspiring words of the First Amendment. The individual interest in freedom of speech, which Socrates voiced when he said that he would rather die than stop talking, is too precious to be left altogether to the vague words of the due process clause. Valuable as self-government is, it is in itself only a small part of our lives. That a philosopher should subordinate all other activities to it is indeed surprising.

Mr. Meiklejohn's best contribution to the analysis of the First Amendment is his stress on the interest of self-government. Balancing among interests must go on, although he cannot find it in the Constitution (p. 64), but it may very well be that a description of the balancing process should give more attention to self-government than is sometimes done. For this purpose many passages of his book are very useful, notably his account of discussion in a town meeting (pp. 22–27). And his critique of the clear and present danger test, although badly misdirected, will be interesting to legal scholars who do not regard that test as by any means the last word on the whole of free speech in spite of its great value where war and radicalism are concerned.[16]

As for the author's protracted denunciations of Justice Holmes—"the leading hero, or villain, of the plot" (p. 70)— because he failed to give unlimited constitutional protection to speech on public issues, I remember how President Coolidge, when asked what he thought about a muckraking life of George Washington, looked out of the White House window across the Mall and said: "The Monument still stands!" Even if Holmes had agreed with Mr. Meiklejohn's view of the First Amendment, his insistence on such absolutism would not have persuaded a single colleague, and scores of men would have gone to prison who have been speaking freely for three decades. After all, a judge who is trying to establish a doctrine which the Supreme Court will promulgate as law cannot write like a solitary philosopher. He has to convince at least four men in a specific group and convince them very soon. The true alternative to Holmes' view of the First Amendment was not at all the perfect immunity for public discussion which Mr. Meiklejohn desires. It was no immunity at all in the face of legislation. Any danger, any tendency in speech to produce bad acts, no matter how remote, would suffice to validate a repressive statute, and the only hope for speakers and writers would lie in being tried by liberal jurymen.[17] What would happen to unpopular discussion is plainly shown by the Espionage Acts trials in World War I.[18]

The author shows no realization of the long uphill fight which Holmes had to wage in order to give free speech its present protection. First, Holmes worked out a formula which would invalidate a great deal of suppression, and won for it the solid authority of a unanimous Court. Afterwards, again and again, when his test was misapplied by the majority, Holmes restated his position in ringing words which, with the help of Brandeis and Hughes, eventually inspired the whole Court.

This is what Mr. Meiklejohn repeatedly calls a "disaster."

---

[16] Some of the recent thinking on this test is presented in 1 Chafee, *Government and Mass Communication* 49–61 (1947).

[17] See the very able presentation of this view of the First Amendment by Mr. Kimball in Note, 33 Harv. L. Rev. 442 (1920).

[18] These are reviewed in Chafee, *Free Speech in the United States* 51–60 (1941).

He is like the mother in F. D. R.'s story, whose boy was rescued far out from shore by a lifeguard. She went after the lifeguard and scolded him for losing her son's cap.

United States v. Dennis

183 F.2d 201 (1950)

[This case involved an indictment under the "Smith Act," Section 11, Title 18, United States Code, for "wilfully and knowingly" conspiring to organize the Communist Party of the United States as a group to "teach and advocate the overthrow and destruction" of the government "by force and violence," and "knowingly and wilfully to advocate and teach the duty and necessity of overthrowing and destroying" the government "by force and violence." The defendants challenged their conviction on a variety of grounds before the United States Court of Appeals, Second Circuit. Our concern here is with the challenge to the law's constitutionality, and the portion of Judge Learned Hand's decision here reprinted deals only with that question. The trial judge had held that the law applied to the defendants' conduct only if they were found to intend to use violence "as speedily as circumstances would permit it" (the overthrow and destruction of the government) "to be achieved" and had held, as a matter of law, that their conduct, since it did create a "clear and present danger," was constitutionally punishable.]

Coming then to the first point [whether the Act is constitutional as the judge construed it] although the interest which the Amendment was designed to protect—especially as regards matters political—does not presuppose that utterances, divergent from current official opinion, are more likely to be true than that opinion, it does presuppose that official opinion may be wrong, and that one way—and perhaps the best way—to correct or supplement it, is complete freedom of criticism and protest. This may convince the officials themselves, and in any event it may rouse up a body of contrary opinion to which they will yield, or which will displace them. Thus, the interest rests upon a skepticism as to all political orthodoxy, upon a belief that there are no impregnable political absolutes, and that a flux of tentative doctrines is preferable to any authoritative creed. It rests upon a premise as yet unproved, and perhaps incompatible with men's impatience of a suspended judgment when the stakes are high. However, it concerns beliefs alone, not actions, except in so far as a change of belief is a condition upon action.

Nobody doubts that, when the leader of a mob already ripe for riot gives the word to start, his utterance is not protected by the Amendment. It is not difficult to deal with such situations; doubt arises only when the utterance is at once an effort to affect the hearers' beliefs and a call upon them to act when they have been convinced. As a new question it might have been held that the Amendment did not protect utterances, when they had this double aspect: i.e., when persuasion and instigation were inseparably confused. In that view the Amendment would give protection to all utterances designed to convince, but its protection would be conditional upon their not being part of, or coupled with, provocation to unlawful conduct, whether that was remote or immediate. True, one does not become an accessory to a crime who "counsels, commands, induces . . . its commission."[1] unless the crime is committed; but he will be guilty of conspiracy by the mere agreement; and it will not protect him that the objective of the conspiracy is lawful, and only the means contemplated are illegal.[2] Had this view of the Amendment been taken, although the utterances of these defendants so far as they attempted to persuade others of the aims of Communism would have been protected, they would have lost that protection, coupled as they were with the advocacy of the unlawful means. And that is probably in fact true of utterances not political or religious; for it is at least doubtful whether other kinds of utterance, however lawful in so far as they were persuasive only, would retain their privilege if coupled with appeals to unlawful means. One can hardly be-

---

[1] § 2(a) Title 18, U.S.C.A.
[2] Truax *v.* Corrigan, 257 U.S. 312, 327, 42 Sup. Ct. 124, 66 L. Ed. 254, 27 A.L.R. 375.

lieve that one would be protected in seeking funds for a school, if he suggested that they should be obtained by fraud. His privilege would be conditional upon separating the means from the end. However, that may be, it is not true of political agitation and the question is what limits, if any, the advocacy of illegal means imposes upon the privilege which the aims or purposes of the utterer would otherwise enjoy. [The Court here describes and analyzes a series of Supreme Court cases involving freedom of speech since 1919.]

From this wearisome analysis of the decisions of the Supreme Court it has appeared, as we indicated at the outset, that to deprive an utterance of the protection of the Amendment it is not always enough that the purpose of the utterer may include stirring up his hearers to illegal conduct—at least, when the utterance is political. The same utterance may be unprotected, if it be a bare appeal to action, which the Amendment will cover, if it be accompanied by, or incorporated into, utterances addressed to the understanding and seeking to persuade. The phrase, "clear and present danger," has come to be used as a shorthand statement of those among such mixed or compounded utterances which the Amendment does not protect. Yet it is not a vade mecum; indeed, from its very words it could not be. It is a way to describe a penumbra of occasions, even the outskirts of which are indefinable, but within which as is so often the case, the courts must find their way as they can. In each case they must ask whether the gravity of the "evil," discounted by its improbability, justifies such invasion of free speech as is necessary to avoid the danger. We have purposely substituted "improbability" for "remoteness," because that must be the right interpretation. Given the same probability, it would be wholly irrational to condone future evils which we should prevent if they were immediate; that could be reconciled only by an indifference to those who come after us. It is only because a substantial intervening period between the utterance and its realization may check its effect and change its importance, that its immediacy is important; and that, as we have said, was the rationale of the concurrence in Whitney v. People of State of California, *supra*.[3] We can never forecast with cer-

---

[3] 274 U.S. 357, 372, 47 Sup. Ct. 641, 71 L. Ed. 1095.

tainty; all prophecy is a guess, but the reliability of a guess decreases with the length of the future which it seeks to penetrate. In application of such a standard courts may strike a wrong balance; they may tolerate "incitements" which they should forbid; they may repress utterances they should allow; but that is a responsibility that they cannot avoid. Abdication is as much a failure of duty, as indifference is a failure to protect primal rights.

In the case at bar the defence seems to us to kick the beam. One may reasonably think it wiser in the long run to let an unhappy, bitter outcast vent his venom before any crowds he can muster and in any terms that he wishes, be they as ferocious as he will; one may trust that his patent impotence will be a foil to anything he may propose. Indeed, it is a measure of the confidence of a society in its own stability that it suffers such fustian to go unchecked. Here we are faced with something very different. The American Communist Party, of which the defendants are the controlling spirits, is a highly articulated, well contrived, far spread organization, numbering thousands of adherents, rigidly and ruthlessly disciplined, many of whom are infused with a passionate Utopian faith that is to redeem mankind. It has its Founder, its apostles, its sacred texts—perhaps even its martyrs. It seeks converts far and wide by an extensive system of schooling, demanding of all an inflexible doctrinal orthodoxy. The violent capture of all existing governments is one article of the creed of that faith, which abjures the possibility of success by lawful means. That article, which is a common-place among initiates, is a part of the homiletics for novitiates, although, so far as conveniently it can be, it is covered by an innocent terminology, designed to prevent its disclosure. Our democracy, like any other, must meet that faith and that creed on the merits, or it will perish; and we must not flinch at the challenge. Nevertheless, we may insist that the rules of the game be observed, and the rules confine the conflict to weapons drawn from the universe of discourse. The advocacy of violence may, or may not, fail; but in neither case can there be any "right," to use it. Revolutions are often "right," but a "right of revolution" is a contradiction in terms, for a society which acknowledged it, could not stop at tolerating conspiracies to overthrow it, but must include their execution. The question before us, and the only one, is how long a government, having discovered such a conspiracy, must wait. When does the conspiracy become a "present danger"? The jury has found that the conspirators will strike as soon as success seems possible, and obviously, no one in his senses would strike sooner. Meanwhile they claim the constitutional privilege of going on indoctrinating their pupils, preparing increasing numbers to pledge themselves to the crusade, and awaiting the moment when we may be so far extended by foreign engagements, so far divided in counsel, or so far in industrial or financial straits, that the chance seems worth trying. That position presupposes that the Amendment assures them freedom for all preparatory steps and in the end the choice of initiative, dependent upon that moment when they believe us, who must await the blow, to be worst prepared to receive it.

We need not say that even so thoroughly planned and so extensive a confederation would be a "present danger" at all times and in all circumstances; the question is how imminent: that is, how probable of execution—it was in the summer of 1948, when the indictment was found. We must not close our eyes to our position in the world at that time. By far the most powerful of all the European nations had been a convert to Communism for over thirty years; its leaders were the most devoted and potent proponents of the faith; no such movement in Europe of East to West had arisen since Islam. Moreover in most of West Europe there were important political Communist factions, always agitating to increase their power; and the defendants were acting in close concert with the movement. The *status quo*, hastily contrived in 1945, was showing strains and tensions, not originally expected. Save for the unexpected success of the airlift, Britain, France and ourselves would have been forced out of Berlin, contrary to our understanding of the convention by which we were there. We had become the object of invective upon invective; we were continuously charged with aggressive designs against other nations; our efforts to reestablish their economic stability were repeatedly set down as a scheme to enslave them; we had been singled out as the chief enemy of the faith; we were the eventually doomed, but the still formidable, protagonist of that decadent system which it was to supplant. Any border fray, any diplomatic incident, any difference in construction of the modus vivendi—such as the Berlin blockade we have just mentioned—might prove a spark in the tinder-box, and lead to war. We do not understand how one could ask for a more probable danger, unless we must wait till the actual eve of hostilities. The only justification which can be suggested is that in spite of their efforts to mask their purposes, so far as they can do so consistently with the spread of the gospel, discussion and publicity may so weaken their power that it will have ceased to be dangerous when the moment may come. That may be a proper enough antidote in ordinary times and for less redoubtable combinations; but certainly it does not apply to this one. *Corruptio optimi pessima.* True, we must not forget our own faith; we must be sensitive to the dangers that lurk in any choice; but choose we must, and we shall be silly dupes if we forget that again and again in the past thirty years, just such preparations in other countries have aided to supplant existing governments, when the time was ripe. Nothing short of a revived doctrine of *laissez faire*, which would have amazed even the Manchester School at its apogee, can fail to realize that such a conspiracy creates a danger of the utmost gravity and of enough probability to justify its suppression. We hold that it is a danger "clear and present."

The Communist Trial and the Clear-and-Present-Danger Test

by Nathaniel L. Nathanson*

Harvard Law Review,
Volume 63, Page 1167 (1950)

At the close of the Government's case in the recent trial of the leaders of the Communist party for violation of the Smith Act,[1]

---

* (1908–   ), Professor of Law, Northwestern University, since 1945.
[1] The indictment charged in part that the defendants "unlawfully, wilfully, and knowingly, did conspire with each other, and with divers other persons to the Grand

the defense presented, and the trial judge denied, a motion for a directed verdict [2] based on the ground that there had been no showing of a clear and present danger resulting from the defendants' advocacy of Communist doctrines.[3] Colloquy between Judge Medina and one of the defense counsel in the course of the argument on the motion [4] indicates that counsel relied upon the dissenting opinion of Justice Holmes in the Gitlow case,[5] while the judge was inclined to accept the majority opinion as controlling. In response to persistent questioning from the bench as to just what would be "the clear and present danger that is applicable in this case," counsel finally agreed that it would be "the immediate overthrow of the government." "That

---

Jury unknown, to organize as the Communist Party of the United States of America, a society, group, and assembly of persons who teach and advocate the otherthrow and destruction of the Government of the United States by force and violence, and knowingly and wilfully to advocate and teach the duty and necessity of overthrowing and destroying the Government of the United States by force and violence, which said acts are prohibited by Section 2 of the Act of June 28, 1940 [18 U.S.C. § 2385 (Supp. 1949) Smith Act]." *N.Y. Times*, Oct. 14, 1949, p. 14, col. 2.

[2] *N.Y. Times*, May 20, 1949, p. 12, col. 8; *id.*, May 24, 1949, p. 1, col. 2 and p. 13, col. 1.

[3] In his instructions to the jury Judge Medina later commented on this contention thus:

If you are satisfied that the evidence establishes beyond a reasonable doubt that the defendants, or any of them, are guilty of violation of the statute, as I have interpreted it to you, I find as a matter of law that there is sufficient danger of a substantive evil that the Congress has a right to prevent to justify the application of the statute under the First Amendment of the Constitution. N.Y. Times, *Oct. 14, 1949, p. 15, col. 7.*

Judge Medina did not explain further the basis for his finding as a matter of law that there was "sufficient danger of a substantive evil."

[4] *N.Y. Times*, May 21, 1949, p. 6, cols. 2 and 3.

[5] Gitlow *v.* New York, 268 U.S. 652 (1925). The Gitlow case has been distinguished from other recent free speech cases where the clear-and-present-danger test has been applied on the ground that it involved the application of a statute outlawing the advocacy of a particular doctrine which the legislature had found likely to create danger of a serious substantive evil. See particularly Herndon *v.* Lowry, 301 U.S. 242, 256 (1937); Note, 49 Col. L. Rev. 363, 367–70 (1949); Cushman, *Clear and Present Danger in Free Speech Cases* 315 (1948). The validity of this distinction is certainly questionable. The distinction was accepted by the court of appeals in Dunne *v.* United States, 138 F.2d 137 (8th Cir.), *cert. denied*, 320 U.S. 790 (1943), in affirming a conviction for conspiracy to violate the Smith Act, by advocating the overthrow of the government and also insubordination in the armed forces. Perhaps the Court denied certiorari in the Dunne case because it was thought that the complicating factors presented by incitement of insubordination in the armed forces made the record an inappropriate one for reconsideration of the principle of the Gitlow and Whitney cases. Cf. Maryland *v.* Baltimore Radio Show, Inc., 338 U.S. 912 (1950).

being so," said the Judge, "it seems to me it reduces itself to an absurdity because on that theory you couldn't punish anybody for such a conspiracy unless the Government was about to be overthrown and then it would be too late . . . Isn't that so?" Counsel answered: "That is throwing the clear and present danger test out of the window." To this the Judge responded: "Maybe the Gitlow case is controlling."

There is little doubt that the decision in the Gitlow case, if followed, would sustain Judge Medina's ruling.[6] But there are also indications in Judge Medina's charge to the jury which suggest that he was anxious to come as close as he could, consistently with his ruling, to the philosophy expressed in the dissenting opinions of Justices Holmes and Brandeis. The most pertinent parts of the charge are the following:

> You must be satisfied from the evidence beyond a reasonable doubt that the defendants had an intent to cause the overthrow of the Government of the United States by force and violence. . . .
>
> And you must further find that it was the intent of the defendants to achieve this goal of the overthrow or destruction of the Government of the United States by force and violence as speedily as circumstances would permit it to be achieved.
>
> . . . I charge you that it is not the abstract doctrine of overthrowing or destroying organized government by unlawful means which is denounced by this law, but the teaching and advocacy of action for the accomplishment of that purpose, by language reasonably and ordinarily calculated to incite persons to such action.[7]

---

[6] The state statute involved in the Gitlow case was substantially similar to the provisions of the Smith Act involved in the Communist trial. There were no indications of danger of immediate violence and the trial court had refused to charge that the language used must advocate the duty, necessity, or propriety of doing " 'some definite or immediate act or acts' of . . . violence" or must be " 'reasonably and ordinarily calculated to incite certain persons' " to acts of force or violence. 268 U.S. at 661. The fact that in one case an individual was indicted for advocating the forbidden doctrine, whereas in the other a group was indicted for conspiracy to advocate it does not suggest a significant difference. Undoubtedly the Communist leaders did get to the point of advocating Marxist-Leninist principles. This Comment assumes, for the purpose of the discussion only, that this constituted advocacy of the overthrow of the government by force and violence in violation of the statute. The Gitlow case might conceivably be distinguished on the ground that it involved a state statute, but that would hardly be a satisfying ground in the light of other applications of the principles of the First Amendment through the medium of the Fourteenth. Cf. Mr. Justice Jackson's dissent in Terminiello *v.* City of Chicago, 337 U.S. 1, 13 (1949).

[7] *N.Y. Times,* Oct. 14, 1949, p. 15, col. 6.

These instructions, in recognizing that the advocate's intent should be considered in determining whether his words were within the scope of the constitutional protection, bear some resemblance to the clear-and-present-danger test formulated by Justices Holmes and Brandeis. Thus, Justice Holmes in the Abrams case said: "I do not doubt for a moment that by the same reasoning that would justify punishing persuasion to murder, the United States constitutionally may punish speech that produces or is *intended* to produce a clear and imminent danger that it will bring about forthwith certain substantive evils that the United States constitutionally may seek to prevent." [8] Similarly, in the concurring opinion for himself and Justice Holmes, in Whitney v. California, Justice Brandeis wrote: "In order to support a finding of clear and present danger it must be shown either that immediate serious violence was to be expected or was advocated, or that past conduct furnished reason to believe that such advocacy was then contemplated." [9] But this intention of which Holmes and Brandeis spoke was always an intent to create an immediate danger. The instructions which Judge Medina gave required the jury to find only that the defendants intended to accomplish the overthrow of the government "as speedily as circumstances would permit it to be achieved." The difference is significant enough to warrant the conclusion that Judge Medina's instructions were inconsistent with the clear-and-present-danger test as formulated by Holmes and Brandeis, unless there were other circumstances in the facts actually presented which made that test inapplicable.

That there were such circumstances was apparently one of the principal themes of Mr. McGohey's brief argument in opposition to the defendants' motion. Mr. McGohey's picturesque and forceful language was:

> When Holmes spoke about freedom of speech, he said he meant the right of men to get their ideas accepted in the market place of thought. Holmes was talking from the background of a life and an experience where there was the freest possible discussion, in the town meetings of New England, in the public taverns, in the pub-

---

[8] Abrams *v.* United States, 250 U.S. 616, 627 (1919). [Italics supplied.] See also Holmes's dissent in the Gitlow case, 268 U.S. at 672, 673.

[9] 274 U.S. 357, 376 (1927).

lic squares, in the public halls, where men frankly and fearlessly
stated their ideas. He was not talking about the kind of propaganda
speakeasy that we heard about in this case, where persons went to
school under assumed names or using only their first names, coming
through a doctor's or a dentist's office into rooms some place else.
This is not the kind of freedom of speech Holmes said could be protected.[10]

Mr. McGohey's distinction between open and clandestine discussion was reflected to some extent in the following passage
of Judge Medina's charge to the jury:

> No such intent could be inferred from the open and above-
> board teaching of a course on the principles and implications of com-
> munism in an American college or university, where everything is
> open to scrutiny of parents and trustees and anyone who is interested
> to see what is going on. That is why it is so important for you to weigh
> with scrupulous care the testimony concerning secret schools, false
> names, devious ways, general falsification and so on, all alleged to be
> in the setting of a huge and well-disciplined organization, spreading
> to practically every state of the union and all the principal cities and
> industries.[11]

But this instruction is not sufficiently explicit to bring the
jury's verdict to the support of the distinction which Mr. Mc-
Gohey was trying to make. The jury was directed to take into
account the secrecy of the defendants' operations in determining
their intent; but it was not instructed that it could find the defendants guilty only if they had conspired to advocate secretly
the overthrow of the government by force and violence. Since
the indictment charged the offense substantially in the words of
the statute, which makes no distinction between secret and
open advocacy, the jury's verdict established only that the defendants violated the statute as construed by the instructions.[12]
The jury may have believed the crime was committed through

---

[10] N.Y. *Times,* May 21, 1949, p. 6, col. 3.
[11] N.Y. *Times,* Oct. 14, 1949, p. 15, col. 6.
[12] The indictment also added certain specific charges, such as that the defendants would "cause the Party Convention to adopt a Constitution basing said Party
upon the principles of Marxism-Leninism" and that the defendants "would conduct
and would cause to be conducted, schools and classes for the study of the principles of Marxism-Leninism, in which would be taught and advocated the duty and
necessity of overthrowing and destroying the Government of the United States by
force and violence."

the open, rather than the clandestine, activities of the defendants.

But even assuming that the constitutional issue in the Communist case could be narrowed to the right to advocate revolutionary doctrines in private conversations or secret discussion groups, the distinction suggested by Mr. McGohey does not seem sufficiently significant to render inapplicable the principles espoused by Justices Holmes and Brandeis if those principles are accepted as basically sound. The freedom of private discussion, in one's own home, or the home of others, in small and carefully selected groups of intimates, may be just as precious an attribute of the democratic way of life as the right to hire a hall or speak from a soapbox. Freedom of thought in a democratic community depends in large part on the myriads of private conversations in which public opinion is formulated, as well as upon newspaper editorials and public speeches. Indeed it may be said that, at times when social, business, and political pressures all put a premium upon conformity, the right of private, confidential discussion may be even more important to the right of dissent than public discussion. And it is inconceivable to postulate a body of revolutionary doctrine spoken privately in the home becoming a danger to the community without also being the subject of general public discussion, even if the particular proponents of the doctrine do not openly take part in that discussion.

Of course the Government will have to reject this comparison between discussions among friends in private homes and the chain of secret study groups apparently operated by the Communist party for the enlightenment of its members in the principles of Marxism and Leninism. It will perhaps emphasize instead the relation of those study groups to a carefully designed plan to infiltrate members of the party into key positions of labor, business, and government, in order that they may act effectively when the time comes for revolution or for attempting to turn foreign war into civil war. In this view, the study groups are preliminary to the development of secret cells for action, when the hour strikes; the first essential for action is the creation of an organization of devoted disciples, all well instructed in the fundamentals of the party philosophy, upon which the course of action is to be predicated. Assuming that the evidence lends some color of authenticity to this picture, can we say that this is enough to make the clear-and-present-danger rule inapplicable?

The chief objection to this argument is that it attempts to defend the validity of a conviction under the Smith Act on the same basis as if the conviction were for seditious conspiracy. If the factual picture assumed by the argument is correct, the defendants might have been indicted for conspiring "to overthrow, put down, or to destroy by force the Government of the United States, or to levy war against them, or to oppose by force the authority thereof, or by force to prevent, hinder, or delay the execution of any law of the United States." [13] Presumably there might be a gigantic long-term conspiracy, plotted years in advance, the groundwork laid long before the time was ripe for action, but the signals arranged among the conspirators so that they would be ready to spring into action when war, economic collapse, or some natural calamity made the circumstances propitious. If such conspiracy by the particular defendants could have been proved, there would have been no substantial issue of freedom of speech involved. But the important point is that Government did not choose to prosecute the defendants for the crime of seditious conspiracy; it did not assume the heavy burden of establishing the development of a secret plan of action by the defendants either for the purpose of effectuating their professed philosophy through violence, or for assuring the defeat of the United States in the event of an "imperialistic war." Since the Government did not make that choice, it should not be permitted to becloud the issue of the constitutional right to advocate revolutionary doctrine, by reliance upon evidence which—though it may have been extremely effective in lending a darkly conspiratorial or even treasonable color to the defendants' activities—might not have been sufficient, as a matter of law, to establish the crime of seditious conspiracy.[14]

---

[13] 18 U.S.C. § 2384 (Supp. 1949). For comparable seditious conspiracy cases see Albizu v. United States, 88 F.2d 138 (1st Cir. 1937); Bryant v. United States, 257 Fed. 378 (5th Cir. 1919).

[14] This aspect of the Government's case was summarized by Judge Medina as follows: "that plans were deeply laid to place energetic and militant members of the Communist Party in key positions in various industries indispensable to the func-

If the foregoing analysis is valid, it brings us back to the soundness of the Gitlow case and Judge Medina's question: Is it not an absurdity to apply the clear-and-present-danger test to revolutionary doctrine since "on that theory you couldn't punish anybody for such a conspiracy unless the government was just about to be overthrown and then it would be too late"? Before meeting the question directly we must note an important qualification with respect to the assumptions underlying it. The clear-and-present-danger test, as formulated by Justices Holmes and Brandeis, did not require a clear and present danger of successful revolution; they were speaking of an attempt at violent revolution, however foolhardy and doomed to failure such an attempt might be. That is why they included reference to the intent of the advocate as an alternative to objective evidence of the likelihood of an attempt at violence, although Justice Holmes also suggested that intent might not be sufficient if it were obvious that the speaker's efforts were entirely futile because he could not possibly persuade anyone to action.[15] But Justice Holmes meant futile in the sense that no one would be moved to action, not futile in the sense that the revolution could not succeed. The agitator who incites others to risk their lives and fortunes in futile adventures in violence and who subjects law enforcement officers and innocent bystanders to the dangers involved in the suppression of insurrection cannot escape responsibility by asserting that he exercised his constitutional right of freedom of speech, and that the government was never in danger anyway.[16] In short, Justices Holmes and Brandeis were

tioning of the American economy to be ready for action at a given signal, and that such action was to consist of strikes, sabotage, and violence of one sort or another appropriate to the consummation of the desired end, that is to say, the smashing of the machine of state, the destruction of the army and the police force and the overthrow of the Government and what the Communists call 'bourgeois democracy.' " *N.Y. Times,* Oct. 14, 1949, p. 14, col. 8.

[15] Justice Holmes dissenting in Gitlow *v.* New York, 268 U.S. at 673.

[16] It is true that in Whitney *v.* California, Justice Brandeis said: "The fact that speech is likely to result in some violence or in destruction of property is not enough to justify its suppression. There must be the probability of serious injury to the State." 274 U.S. at 378. But he also said in the same opinion: "[Miss Whitney] claimed below that the statute as applied to her violated the Federal Constitution; but she did not claim that it was void because there was no clear and present danger of serious evil, nor did she request that the existence of these conditions of a valid measure thus restricting the rights of free speech and assembly be passed upon by the court or a jury. On the other hand, there was evidence from which the court or jury might have found that such danger existed." *Id.* at 379. It is hardly con-

trying to suggest basic lines of distinction between an appeal to
reason and an incitement to action, recognizing that the two
might overlap, but also taking the position that so long as the
action contemplated by the appeal to reason was sufficiently remote to permit time for counterappeals to reason, the advocacy,
even of the right of violence, should be treated as within the
protection of freedom of speech.[17]

If this be a fair statement of the principle, the government
must stay its hand, not until there is imminent danger of successful revolution, but only until there is danger that some
hardy or even foolhardy souls may sally forth to action under
the influence of the persuasion, exhortation, or incitement with
which we are concerned. But it will doubtless be suggested in
reply that not every revolutionary is so irresponsible as to urge
action before his forces have grown strong enough to afford a
fair chance of success.[18] And if under such circumstances we
adhere to the clear-and-present-danger principle, do we not per-

---

ceivable that Justice Brandeis was talking about the possible overthrow of the government of California or that he meant that the court or jury in each application
of the clear-and-present-danger test should estimate the possible chances of successful revolution. Rather he was talking, as the context, 274 U.S. at 379, indicates,
about the possibility that Miss Whitney's advocacy would substantially contribute to
a wave of terrorism or to "the present serious crimes" which it was alleged the
IWW was conspiring to commit.

The defense counsel submitted several different variations of requested instructions on the clear-and-present-danger test. Some of these were vulnerable to the objection that they required the jury to determine whether there was an immediate
danger of a *successful* attempt to overthrow the government, but there were others
which avoided this pitfall. The defense objected to the "court's refusal to charge
the instructions on clear and present danger which were submitted and because of
the court's omission to charge in any way on that doctrine." Transcript of Record,
p. 16,074.

[17] Meiklejohn, *Free Speech: and its Relation to Self-Government* (1948), apparently assumes that there is some significant difference between Justice Holmes's original formulation of the clear-and-present-danger test and Justice Brandeis' restatement
of it in the Whitney case, for he vigorously berates the first and applauds the second. It seems more likely that Justice Brandeis was only spelling out in greater detail what was implicit in the shorthand of Justice Holmes. For a full critique of
Mr. Meiklejohn's thesis, see Chafee, Book Review, 62 Harv. L. Rev. 891 (1949).

[18] This was, of course, the Government's theory of the true doctrine of the Communist party as advocated by the defendants. The defendants' own explanation of
their doctrine, as summarized by Judge Medina, was that "the capitalist class uses
force and violence to prevent the transition to socialism, and that they justified the
use of force and violence only as a method of preventing an attempted forcible overthrow of a succeeding government which had obtained control in a peaceful manner, or as a method of last resort to enforce the majority will if, at some indefinite future time, because of peculiar circumstances, constitutional or peaceful channels were no longer open." *N.Y. Times,* Oct. 14, 1949, p. 15, col. 2.

mit the advocate of revolution to pick his own time for a trial of strength—a time when it may be too late for the government to take effective measures for its own preservation?

To this fundamental question there is only one fundamental answer—the answer implicit in the clear-and-present-danger test itself. We deliberately subject our government to the rigorous test of toleration of criticism of our basic constitutional processes, because we regard such toleration as our best assurance that the criticism will never be valid.[19] And it is part of the faith expressed in the First Amendment, as interpreted by Holmes and Brandeis, that so long as the criticism is not valid, no substantial proportion of the people can be induced to act upon it. Thus, we expose our government to the apparent risk of successful revolution because we are confident that no government which is worth preserving can be seriously endangered by advocacy of the propriety or necessity of its violent overthrow. That is one of the prophecies, based perhaps upon imperfect knowledge, upon which we have wagered our salvation.[20] Since this is a prophecy based essentially on faith in the democratic process, it may not lie in the mouth of a Communist to base his defense upon it. But by the same token he should welcome his own conviction as proof of the validity of his thesis. That is hardly a good reason why anyone else should welcome it.

---

[19] It is of course also true that a statute outlawing revolutionary doctrine is easily subject to the abuse of being invoked against unpopular minorities who vigorously criticize the existing system without advocating its forcible overthrow—minorities such as the Communist leaders claimed they themselves represented. See Chafee, Free Speech in the United States 177–95 (1941); 1 Chafee, *Government and Mass Communications* c. 14 (1947).

[20] Justice Holmes dissenting in Abrams *v.* United States, 250 U.S. at 630.

CHAPTER TEN

Separation of Church
and State

T HE FIRST AMENDMENT OF THE CONSTITUTION PROVIDES, among other things, that "Congress shall make no law respecting an establishment of religion." During most of our history, this phrase has provoked no great agitation even in the breasts of those whose business it was to ponder the meaning of the fundamental law. National statues respecting religion were comparatively few; those few usually went unchallenged; state laws did not involve the Amendment because its limitations applied only to Congress. In the modern period, however, the Supreme Court has evolved the doctrine that the restrictions of the First Amendment may bind the states as well as the Nation, because a state law infringing freedom of conscience may be a violation of the Fourteenth Amendment, which is aimed at state action. This doctrine has provided the constitutional rationale for challenging state laws that affect religion.

The Supreme Court's embroilment in the matter began with Everson *v*. Board of Education (330 U.S. 1) in 1947. The narrow question of the case was whether state tax money could be used to pay the bus fares of students attending parochial schools, since it was argued that such disbursement of public funds contravened the "no establishment of religion" prohibition. The Court held that it did not, arguing that transporting pupils to school was a public service measure and not an aid to religion. But before reaching this conclusion, Mr. Justice Black, who spoke for the majority, laid down an exceedingly stringent definition of the state's leeway in this field. (The definition was later invoked to forbid the use of public school facilities for religious education. See McCollum *v.* Board of Education, 333 U.S. 203 [1948].) According to the rule he stated, "no tax in any amount, large or small, can be levied to support any religious activities or institutions." (330 U.S. 16). Although Zorach *v.* Clauson (343 U.S. 306 [1952]) did uphold the state's right to release students from school at specified times in order to participate in out-of-school religious instruction programs, the rule against use of tax money for religious purposes was not relaxed in principle.

This rule is, of course, the focus of the controversy that has developed on the subject. The question of whether New Jersey parents can be reimbursed for the bus fares their children pay, or whether Champaign, Illinois, can offer religious instruction in public-school classrooms is secondary to the broader question of whether tax funds can be earmarked to ease the fiscal difficulties of parochial schools in general. The conflict over the issue has been sharp, and sometimes bitter, and because the convictions of both sides are so deeply felt, it has been especially hard to choose an essay to represent the "establishment question." One resolution of the dilemma might have been achieved by selecting for inclusion two essays so as to make sure that both sides were duly represented, but, significant though it is, the establishment question is not important enough to warrant such a disproportionately extended treatment. Another expedient might have been to reprint a "neutral" account of the subject, but it would be too bad thus to devitalize an issue that is naturally so lively.

There is nothing neutral about John Courtney Murray's essay, "Law or Prepossessions." As the reader will quickly see, Father Murray is acutely critical of the Everson and McCollum doctrine, questioning its validity in terms of either history or logic. Whether or not it is ultimately persuasive, the essay accomplishes two purposes important to the objectives of this volume: it raises most of the main issues that have been presented by the church-state-relationship controversy, and it deals with them in terms that can hardly help provoking an intellectual reaction, whether hostile or concurring. An essay as stimulating as this one serves its author's case well, of course; but it also, by a seeming paradox, serves the case of his opponents better than a flat "neutral" treatment could. For it is notorious that thoughtful arguments tend to generate thoughtful rejoinders.

Nevertheless a few words about the other side are included here so as to underline beyond possibility of doubt the fact that there *is* another side and that its arguments must also be met. A great deal has been published in the field during recent years, and the reader who is interested in pursuing the no-state-aid argument farther might begin with Louis Pfeffer's "Church and State: Something Less than Separation," 19 University of Chicago Law Review 1 (1951), which is a frontal assault on the historical position represented by Father Murray and others like J. M. O'Neill and Father Wilfred Parsons. Their contention is that the establishment clause was historically intended only to preclude *preferential* treatment of any particular religion by the state; and, further, they contend, that is what it ought to mean today. According to Pfeffer, acceptance of the limited, "no preference" interpretation "would pervert the First Amendment to an end directly opposite to its purpose" (*Ibid.*, p. 28). The historical points on which these diametrically opposed views turn are too many and complex for fair analysis here, but the flavor of the controversy may be suggested by considering how Pfeffer's treatment bears on several of Father Murray's historical arguments.

The position of Father Murray and of what Pfeffer calls "the O'Neill school" rests in part on a semantic base. The version of the First Amendment originally suggested by Madison, for example, prohibits that "any national religion be established," and Father Murray infers that this would merely have barred the setting up of a national church in preference to others, i.e., the "no preference" doctrine. In the subsequent debates, Madison again referred to the purpose of preventing "a national religion."

and Father Murray draws the same inference about his meaning. Pfeffer argues, however, that the phrases used cannot be limited to the precise meaning Murray assigns to them, that such terminology was employed loosely by some to indicate an objection to all ties between government and religion, and that among those who so employed it was, notably, James Madison himself. By way of verification, Madison used the term "establishment of a national religion" in protesting against the appointment of chaplains to the two houses of Congress (*Ibid.*, p. 17).

Even apart from semantic uncertainties, Pfeffer casts some doubt on the contention that either the prior versions of the First Amendment, the debates in Congress, or the hostility towards the Amendment in the Virginia Senate verify the "no preference" interpretation. Among the prior versions, he points out, was one introduced by Samuel Livermore, which would have forbidden all laws "touching" religion and would thus have explicitly ratified the Everson-McCollum interpretation. He suggests, reasonably enough, that if other prior versions are considered, this one must be considered as well. As for the congressional debates, Pfeffer quotes Justice Rutledge's explanation in the Everson case of Madison's reference to a "national religion," and the result is further to cloud Murray's "perfectly clear" legislative intent. Finally, there is Murray's point that Virginia's dissatisfaction with the Amendment shows that it fell short of the complete separation requirement accepted in Virginia itself. Pfeffer observes that, in spite of the opposition of some of its members, the Virginia legislature ratified the Amendment, and he argues that the pro-amendment majority might well have felt the opponents' misgivings were groundless and that the Amendment accomplished all that even Virginia could ask; in other words, that it *did* decree a "wall of separation."

For a definitive resolution of these scholarly conflicts over the "intent" of the Amendment the reader must make his own way through the labyrinth of data the warring camps have assembled. But he should be warned in advance that he may find at the end of the road something less than serene certainty, unless indeed his prepossessions guide him from the outset. This is not to say that the enterprise is futile. Historical conclusions must often be arrived at by a balancing of data, and there are many well-accepted historical points which cannot be verified beyond a reasonable doubt. But what is acceptable as a scholarly necessity may not be equally acceptable as a constitutional *ipse dixit*, for it matters little to most men "whether Charles the Fat was at Ingelheim or Lustnau on July 1, 887," but it may matter a good deal whether the state shall subsidize parochial schools. And one of the most impressive things about the literature on the subject is the comparative ease with which each partisan demolishes the positive arguments of his opponents and the corresponding difficulty each has in establishing his own interpretation of the Amendment's intent on irrefutable ground. An observer who maintains impartiality is tempted to conclude that neither the Everson-McCollum nor the "no preference" doctrine can be defended with full confidence. The blissful self-assurance with which Justice Black invoked history in the Everson case seems a little artless now; but so does O'Neill's flat dogmatism:

> that the words 'establishment of religion' meant to Madison, Jefferson, the members of the First Congress, the historians, the legal scholars, and substantially all Americans who were at all familiar with the Constitution until very recent years, *a formal, legal union of a single church or religion with government, giving the one church or religion an exclusive position of power and favor over all other churches or denominations.* (J. M. O'Neill, *Religion and Education under the Constitution*, 1949, p. 56.)

To the extent then that the "intent of the framers" is ambiguous the focus of controversy shifts to the question of what the First Amendment *should* mean in the 20th century, whatever it may or may not have meant in the 18th century. The arguments on both sides of this question are formidable, and, again, we can only notice a few of them here.

Murray's objection to the "wall of separation" dogma centers around the argument that it leads to a concept of religious freedom as "sheer immunity" from governmental power. From this primary error, he feels, a series of disastrous results ensue. The negative view of freedom enables those who hold it to ignore the fact that a purely secular compulsory public school system impairs the right of parents to guide the education of their children along religious lines. It causes those who hold it to miss the point that absolute separation is itself a sectarian notion—"a deistic version of fundamentalist Protestantism"—and that it, paradoxically, throws the weight of the Constitution behind the religion of James Madison. It allows those who hold it to worry about the pressures on education that might be generated under a policy of state support for religious training and at the same time to slide merrily over the pressures that already exist *against* religion in the determinedly secular public school atmosphere. These results, Murray feels, are hostile to the democracy whose name they take in vain; and they deprive that democracy of one of its greatest potential sources of strength —the training in ethical values that might be achieved by judicious cooperation between church and public school.

To these arguments, the opposing forces might offer these rejoinders (among others). Parental choice may be in a sense restricted by the "wall of separation" doctrine, but against this restriction we must balance the coercion in favor of religion that would develop if the "wall" were breached. Murray denies (note 7) that any threat to rights was visible in the McCollum case. But Mrs. McCollum argued that her son had been subject to "embarrassment" because of his non-participation in the religious instruction program and that school facilities were therefore being employed to coerce his participation. A similar objection has been made to the "released time" system challenged in Zorach *v.* Clausen; Justice Jackson pointed out that the public school was employed as a kind of "jail" to hold in durance those children who did not attend religious instruction classes.

Second, it might be held that Murray dismisses the "entering-wedge" argument somewhat cavalierly (note 32 *infra*), and that his opponents may find some shred of substance in their fears— that the fairly modest state aids to religion in the Everson, McCollum, and Zorach cases might, if tolerated, open the way to further church involvement in governmental affairs, or, even worse perhaps, to state control over religion. Of course, it is true, as he says, that the entering-wedge argument is never self-evidently valid in whatever context it may be used. The objection to permitting the wedge to enter should be based on a judgment that the particular subject in question is particularly vulnerable to wedges, given the circumstances of modern American society. There is no reason to doubt that the Everson-Mc-Collum doctrine reflects precisely this judgment, and while Murray may disagree with it specifically, his strictures against opening-wedge arguments in general are not entirely apposite.

Finally, the "wall of separation" proponents have made much of the point that the secular public school is a unifying factor in American life and that religious education with its sectarian implications promotes "divisiveness." (See, for example, R. F. Butts, *The American Tradition in Religion and Education,* 1950, p. 212 and *passim.*) Murray argues powerfully that the unity achieved by enforced secularism is a pernicious thing and that the crowning glory of American democracy is not the unification of all in a "standard 'democratic' mass" but the concern for "the equality of *differences.*" It is not an argument to be lightly set aside. Yet it remains true that *both* unity and diversity can lay some claim to a place in the value system of American democracy, and that the choice between them in particular circumstances must frequently be made. The problem of choice is not quite solved by hymning the virtues of the one value to the exclusion of the other. Hard questions—and this is a hard question—are never properly decided that way.

Law or Prepossessions?

by John Courtney Murray[*]

Law and Contemporary Problems,
Volume 14, Page 23 (1949)

The constitutional law written in the Everson[1] and McCollum[2] cases is obviously not what is called learned law; consequently one who is not a lawyer, learned in the law, may speak his mind on it. In fact, to do so is a matter of civic duty, since, as the Journal of the American Bar Association pointed out, these decisions contain "a pronouncement by our Supreme Court on a

---

[*] (1904–   ), S.J., Professor of Theology, Woodstock College, since 1937.
[1] Everson *v.* Board of Education, 330 U.S. 1 (1947).
[2] McCollum *v.* Board of Education, 333 U.S. 203 (1948).

fundamental principle, not only of national policy but of our civilization and way of life." [3] Reasoned civic judgment on such a pronouncement is very necessary. Obviously, as embodying a rule of law, these decisions impose themselves on the collective will as norms of action; but by the same token they present themselves to the individual intelligence as matter for reflection; for law, I take it, ought to be reason and not arbitrary will.

My concern is with the reasoning of the Court in support of its new rule of law—with this reasoning in itself and as it reveals a concept of the problem of separation of church and state. These decisions represent the first formal efforts of the Court to work out an official contemporary philosophy of the political principle enshrined in the "establishment" clause of the First Amendment. Such an essay in philosophy is a much more crucial matter than the simple laying down of pragmatic rules to govern the relations between religion and government; it therefore deserves close scrutiny. No one who knows a bit about the literature on separation of church and state, that for centuries has poured out in all languages, will be inclined to deny that hardly another problem in the religious or political order has received so much misconceived and deformed statement, with the result that the number of bad philosophies in the matter is, like the scriptural number of fools, infinite. As I see it, the original American philosophy that inspired the First Amendment was fundamentally sound; it is therefore important to see that it is not corrupted, under the pretext, for instance, of "development."

A second reason for close scrutiny of the Court's reasoning in these cases derives from the absoluteness of the rule of law that has emerged from them: "no aid of any kind to religion in any form." I have been given to understand that the present Court has a certain horror of absolutes, and is disinclined to give room for them in its jurisprudence; if this is so, it is somewhat ironical that the Court should suddenly have come up with one: "absolute separation of church and state, as an absolute principle." At all events, dogmas that pretend to be absolute must rest on reasons that are themselves absolute, unchallengeably ulti-

[3] 34 A.B.A.J. 483 (1948).

mate. One would like to know therefore what these reasons are in the case.

Moreover, the far-reaching consequences of this absolute doctrine, if it should be logically applied, make it further imperative that the reasons for the doctrine should be unshakably valid. Justice Reed in his McCollum dissent pointed out that the Court's "rigid interpretation" of the First Amendment "conflicts with accepted habits of our people," and is capable of "upsetting practices embedded in our society by many years of experience." [4] Moreover, it is the considered opinion of many that the decision will contribute towards an alteration in the very quality of American society by altering the traditional friendly, cooperative attitude of government toward religious forces, especially in the field of education. It may be that the state is still neutral as between religious belief and unbelief, [5] as Justice Black in the Everson decision said it should be [6] (although to fly through the air between these two trapezes is in itself an act not to be accomplished with the greatest of ease). At all events, the McCollum decision gives rise to a decided impression that the state —to apply the famous Irish phrase—is now neutral *against* religious belief. I understand that one must be chary about drawing out the logical implications of a particular decision; we are constantly being given the soothing assurance, on Holmes's paramount authority, that the life of the law is not logic but experience. However, there can be no complementary assurance of the Court's complete immunity from sudden attacks of logic; it seems to have had one in the McCollum case. It is not therefore comforting to see lying about, ready to the legal hand, a premise of deduction as sweeping and absolute as the McCollum rule.

Finally, the decision seems to mark the assumption by the Court of a new role; I mean a role in the field of educational policy. This is much more delicate ground than, for instance,

---

[4] McCollum *v.* Board of Education, 333 U.S. 203, 256 (1948).

[5] The Court's disclaimer of any intent hostile to religion is of course accepted. It remains to consider the effects of the ruling, and the use that will be made of it, e.g., by anti-religious groups. For my part, I fully agree with the public statement made by a group of the most thoughtful minds in Protestantism: "We believe that, whatever its intention may be, this hardening of the idea of 'separation' by the Court will greatly accelerate the trend toward the secularization of our culture." 8 *Christianity and Crisis* 90 (1948).

[6] Everson *v.* Board of Education, 330 U.S. 1, 18 (1947).

the field of economic policy. To touch education is to lay hands on the child-parent relationship; and this is a far more sensitive zone of right than the one marked out by the relationship between the citizen and his property. If therefore the Court is to venture into this field (in what must seem a rather heavy-footed way), it must at very least have cogent reasons for doing so, as for instance, the protection of clearly threatened rights.[7]

I

Given then the need of good tight reasoning in support of our new constitutional doctrine, it is dismaying to the citizen not to find it. Let me be precise about the issue. It is not a question of the reasons for a constitutional separation of church and state in some general sense, but for the particular rigid, radical, and absolute doctrine laid down in the Everson and McCollum cases. What needs justification is the absoluteness of the doctrine; and at this point the Court fails. Actually, it has advanced two separate lines of reasoning. Taken together, they tend to negate one another; taken singly, neither of them is valid.

In the Everson case the Court undertook to show that "no law in aid of religion" was the original meaning and native intent of the clause, "no law respecting an establishment of religion," as this meaning and intent emerges from its general historical background. Justice Rutledge for the minority took the same line; his opinion differed from that of the Court chiefly by its more extensive allegation of the supposedly unique authority of James Madison, and consequently by the more radical and rigid character of its conclusions.

In the McCollum case this line of argument was severely challenged by appellee.[8] Assembling all the available historical data, he argued that the clause in question natively and originally forbade only laws "respecting" (i.e., favoring or disfavoring) "an establishment of" (i.e., preferential status in law for) "religion" (i.e., the doctrines, practices, or modes of worship of a particular religious group). The historical evidence does not

---

[7] No such threat to any right—personal or property—was visible in the McCollum case.

[8] Brief for Appellees, filed by Messrs. Franklin, Peterson, Rall, and Fisk, pp. 24–100, McCollum *v.* Board of Education, 333 U.S. 203 (1948).

yield the absolute Everson conclusion: "no aid of any kind to religion in any form." In reply, the McCollum decision simply stated that the Court was "unable to accept" appellee's historical argument.[9] It did not go on to say why the argument was unacceptable, whether for the reason that it was bad history or for other reasons, not historical. Nor has one any way of knowing what impression was made on the judges (other than Justice Reed, whose dissent reveals that he was impressed) by a presentation of the historical data far more complete and scientific than their own. At all events, a new line of argument appears in the McCollum case. It does not appear in the opinion of the Court, which is content curtly to reaffirm the sweeping Everson doctrine, without pausing to consider that the grounds had been shot out from under it; the new line appears in the opinion of Justice Frankfurter, in which the original Everson minority concurred.

Justice Frankfurter's concern is not with what the First Amendment meant in 1791, which was the concern of the whole Court in the Everson case, but singly with what the First Amendment meant in 1948. The appeal now is not to the wisdom of the Founding Fathers, led by James Madison, but to the developed wisdom of their children, uttered by Justice Frankfurter. In token of this alteration of viewpoint, the constitutional formula, no "establishment of religion," drops completely out of sight, in favor of the more accordion-like slogan, "separation of church and state." From the Everson opinions it would indeed have seemed that the content even of this latter formula had been defined by the constitutional consensus of the states in 1791. Not so, Justice Frankfurter now says. We have to do here "not with a full-blown principle"[10] but with one historically subject to progressive inflation. Separation of church and state is a "spacious conception";[11] and, contrary to Justice Rutledge's Everson view (in which Justice Frankfurter concurred), its interior reaches of space were not measured out by James Madison and made the native dimensions of the First Amendment. Rather (Justice Frankfurter corrects himself and his colleagues), they

---

[9] McCollum *v.* Board of Education, 333 U.S. 203, 211 (1948).

[10] *Id.* at 217.

[11] *Id.* at 213.

have awaited survey in later ages, and the "metes and bounds" [12] (a phrase of Madison's), so far from being fixed by Madison, are not yet really fixed.

The first Congress did indeed erect a wall of separation between church and state, on Jeffersonian specifications. However, time and "changing conceptions regarding the American democratic society" [13] alter all constitutional blueprints. Always impregnable, the wall has not been immovable; originally high, it has not proved high enough. The Founding Fathers, whose Madisonian masonry Justice Rutledge had viewed as architecturally complete, actually left much building for future masons to do. And the masons have appeared to do it. They have, on Justice Frankfurter's account, progressively walled religion out of the public school, and likewise walled government off from aid to religious education. Finally, in contradiction of Justice Rutledge's Everson thesis, in which the "wholly secular" atmosphere of the public school is a federal "constitutional necessity" [14] by intrinsic exigence of the First Amendment in its native meaning as determined by Madison, Justice Frankfurter now asserts that the "basis of the restriction [of government to purely secular education] is the whole experience of our people." [15]

Here in brief are the two lines of argument presented by the judges to persuade the American people that an absolute doctrine of separation of church and state, as having rigid application in the field of education, is reason and not arbitrary will. In the Everson case the Court in effect said: "Absolute separation always was the meaning of the First Amendment, as determined by the Founding Fathers." In the McCollum case we read in effect: "Absolute separation has become in time the meaning of the First Amendment, as determined by the whole experience of our people."

Well, one asks, which is it? The judges can hardly have it both ways. It is not a question here of two mutually supporting lines of argument; on the contrary, the two lines negate one an-

---

[12] *Id.* at 217.
[13] *Id.* at 214.
[14] Everson *v.* Board of Education, 330 U.S. 1, 59 (1947).
[15] McCollum *v.* Board of Education, 333 U.S. 203, 215 (1948).

other. (Unless it be that lawyers possess some philosopher's stone for dissolving logical inconsistencies that is denied to a mere philosopher?) Moreover, the poor citizen is left at a loss even to know what jurisprudential theory the judges intend to apply in interpreting the First Amendment. Is it to be an appeal to legislative intent—to the meaning of the First Amendment "in the light of its history and the evils it was designed forever to suppress" [16] (the Everson line)? Or is it to be an appeal to some contemporary sociological theory of values (the McCollum line)? If one takes the former line, is the "history" to be written after the manner of Ranke—to explain *wie es eigentlich geschehen ist?* Or after the manner of Voltaire—to play some tricks on the dead? If one takes the latter line, whose values are to be adopted as decisive—Holmes's or Justice Frankfurter's or the common values of an immense section of the American people whose hierarchy of values is not Holmesian?

After reading the three opinions in the McCollum case, Justice Reed dissenting confessed: "I find it difficult to extract from the opinions any conclusion as to what it is in the Champaign plan that is unconstitutional." [17] In addition to that difficulty I have another more fundamental one: after reading the seven opinions in the two cases I find it difficult to extract from them any conclusion as to *why* it was that something in the Champaign plan was declared unconstitutional, whatever it was. Doubtless a legal realist, interested in the psychological elements in the judicial process, could have a field day with the opinions; but one whose concern is for history, rationality, logic, and an ordered system of religious, social, and educational values must inevitably experience bewilderment. He will indeed submit to the "judgment of the doom"; but he will not be convinced that the doom has been pronounced (in the good old legal phrase, that one hopes has not lost all its meaning) *iuste et rationabiliter.*

II

Let us first take the Everson line. The essence of it, as laid down both by the Court and by the dissent, is that James Madison's

---

[16] Everson *v.* Board of Education, 330 U.S. 1, 14–15 (1947).
[17] McCollum *v.* Board of Education, 333 U.S. 203, 240 (1948).

concept of the relations between religion and government, together with the philosophy on which this concept rests, became in 1791 the fundamental law of the land by act of the states ratifying the First Amendment. Two questions arise: First, is this the historical fact? And second, could it have been the historical fact? The answer to both questions is, quite flatly, no. Moreover, I find it extremely difficult to believe that the Court could seriously have meant to answer yes.

Justice Black, for instance, is far too good a historical scholar not to have known that the First Amendment met sharp and serious objection in the Virginia senate, on grounds of its inadequacy in comparison with the Virginia statute, with the result that ratification was held up for nearly two years.[18] Against this historical fact his central argument shatters; for it is derived from a supposed continuity in purpose and identity in meaning between the Virginia statute (the Madisonian idea) and the First Amendment. Again, Justice Rutledge is far too good a legal scholar not to realize that the First Amendment, as an act of the states, did not and could not incorporate the total personal ideology of James Madison. He must further know that any such assumption is contradicted by historical facts—Madison's own words in the Congressional debates, the whole legislative history of the Amendment, and the practical construction given it in subsequent acts of the legislative and judicial branches on both federal and state levels.[19]

Finally, the whole Court must know that, as a piece of history, its argument in the Everson case is one which a considerable body of scholarship finds itself, in Justice Black's words, "unable to accept." [20] When one has performed the very modest feat of scholarship involved in mastering the historical data that determine the meaning of the First Amendment as first formulated and ratified, one is driven to the conclusion that, if Justice Black and Justice Rutledge are essaying history, it is only in the Voltairean sense. The tricks they play on the dead are astonishing. If the Court wishes in 1948 to pour the total Madisonian

---

[18] III Annals of Cong. 54 (1849). See the Historical Note at the end of this article.
[19] See the Historical Note at the end of this article.
[20] McCollum *v.* Board of Education, 333 U.S. 203, 211 (1948).

concept into the First Amendment, it cannot justify this procedure by saying that the total Madisonian concept *was* poured
into it in 1791. The facts invalidate this justification.

I go farther, to the second question. Madison's total concept
could not have been poured into the First Amendment in 1791,
and by the same token it cannot be now. (I make the point,
first, because I suspect that the Court was really saying that
Madison's idea *should* have been the idea of the First Amendment, whether it actually was or not; and secondly, because the
point I shall make leads to the heart of this whole matter: what
is the American philosophy of separation of church and state?)

Justice Rutledge correctly stated the essence of the Madisonian concept and its ultimate premise when he said: "As the
Remonstrance discloses throughout, Madison opposed every
form and degree of official relation between religion and civil
authority. For him religion was a wholly private matter beyond
the scope of civil power either to restrain or support." [21] Correctly too, Justice Rutledge points out that the characteristic of
this concept is its unrelenting absoluteness. But the crucially important thing is the basic reason for this unrelenting absoluteness. In his Remonstrance Madison advances a variety of reasons
for his view, some derived from principle, others from expediency. He appeals to the common-law tradition of the distinction
between ecclesiastical and civil authority; [22] to natural rights, as
he understood the term, after the fashion of John Locke; [23] to
the principle of political equality, which is violated by civic
distinctions on religious grounds; [24] to the exigencies of civic
unity, "moderation and harmony," in a religiously divided society. He also argues from expediency: establishment is not
necessary for religion [25] nor good for it; [26] it is not necessary for
political society nor good for it.[27] Finally, he uses the famous
emotional argument, the entering-wedge argument (nowadays,
the camel's-nose, or the crack-in-the-wall, argument). All these

---

[21] Everson *v.* Board of Education, 330 U.S. 1, 39–40 (1947).

[22] Memorial and Remonstrance Against Religious Assessments, pars. 2, 5. This
document is printed in II *The Writings of James Madison* 183–191 (Hunt ed. 1901–
1910), and also as an Appendix to the opinion of Justice Rutledge in Everson *v*
Board of Education, 330 U.S. 1, 63–72 (1947).

[23] Remonstrance, *supra* note 22, pars. 1, 15.

[24] *Id*. Pars. 4, 9.   [26] *Id*. pars. 7, 12.

[25] *Id*. par. 6.   [27] *Id*. pars. 8–10.

arguments persuaded Madison of the necessity of a constitutional separation of church and state.

My point, however, is that neither singly nor collectively do these arguments yield, as a conclusion, the special concept that was Madison's own. In its distinguishing characteristic of absoluteness, this concept rested, as Justice Rutledge perhaps unwittingly pointed out, on a particular sectarian concept of "religion." For Madison, Justice Rutledge rightly says, "religion was a wholly private matter," [28] and therefore (this reason is by itself adequate to the conclusion and supplants all the rest, as it runs all through the Remonstrance) must be absolutely free from governmental restriction and likewise absolutely "free" from governmental aid. Here is the basic reason—a reason, be it noted, of the theological order—for Madison's unrelenting absolutism. The other arguments, notably the common-law tradition of a duality of jurisdictions (that had indeed been badly obscured by Protestant Reformation theology), forbid restraints on religion. All of them contribute to prove that any governmental aid to religion ought to be ruled by principles of natural right, political equality, and social harmony, and by considerations of the "necessities" and "goods" of both religious and political life. But none of them singly, nor all of them collectively, reach the absolute conclusion: "*No* form or degree of official relations between religion and government, and *no* aid to religion." Only Madison's theological premise supports a conclusion of such comprehensive sweep and utter rigidity.

For Madison, as for John Locke, his master, religion could not by law be made a concern of the commonwealth as such, deserving in any degree of public recognition or aid, for the essentially theological reason that religion is of its nature a personal, private, interior matter of the individual conscience, having no relevance to the public concerns of the state. [29] The state could indeed and should create an interest for itself in the *free-*

---

[28] Everson *v.* Board of Education, 330 U.S. 1, 39 (1947).

[29] Justice Frankfurter in the McCollum case says that "the deep religious feeling of James Madison is stamped upon the Remonstrance." McCollum *v.* Board of Education, 333 U.S. 203, 216 (1948). Possibly; it depends on whether one can attribute depth of religious feeling to one steeped in eighteenth-century deism, which I personally consider a rather superficial and conventional form of religion. At all events, it ought to be added that likewise stamped on the Remonstrance is Madison's radically individualistic concept of religion, that is today quite passé.

dom of religion, as a matter of individual "natural right" that it is bound to guarantee, and as a means to the social harmony amid conflicting creeds that it is bound to protect. But in religion itself the state can have no interest; for by very definition (Madison's personal definition) it has no rank among the civil and social interests that may claim the aid of government. Legislation, therefore, whose purposes or effects would be in the slightest degree an aid to religion, would *ipso facto* be legislation for private purposes and therefore illegitimate. Religion, as a "wholly private" interest, lies behind a wall. In fact; it exists in another world from that of the state. It is, in Justice Rutledge's echo of the Madisonian theology, "the kingdom of the individual man and his God." [30] It is the single duty of government to halt its armies on the threshold of that kingdom, encircling it with legal force, to keep it (in Justice Rutledge's extraordinary phrase) absolutely "free from sustenance, as also from other interferences, by the state." [31] Aid to religion is political interference with what is theologically a private interest. Therefore it is absolutely forbidden.

This is the essence of Madison's concept of separation of church and state. Its ultimate ground is a religious absolute, a sectarian idea of religion. The separation therefore is itself absolute. And no other grounds may be assigned for its absoluteness but its theological premise. I should add too that Madison's principle of separation stands as an absolute in its own right. It need not be sustained by any functional relationship to "free exercise." It forbids all governmental aid to religion even in the demonstrable absence of any coercion of conscience, any inhibition of full religious liberty, any violation of civil equality, any disruption of social harmony. These considerations are secondary, and irrelevant to the principle in as much as it is absolute. They prop the wall, if you will, with some flying buttresses; but the wall itself is built, not by an idea of liberty, but by an idea of religion.[32]

---

[30] Everson *v.* Board of Education, 330 U.S. 1, 57–58 (1947). I take it that atheism is analogously the kingdom of the individual man and his Infinite Blank or Ultimate Doubt or whatever inhabits that kingdom, and has a similar sacredness.

[31] *Id.* at 53.

[32] I dismiss the wedge argument, so called—the notion that the wall must be absolute because, if any little crack is made in it, the crack will inevitably widen

This is the philosophy of separation advanced by the Supreme Court in the Everson case, implicitly by the Court's opinion, explicitly by the dissent, on which the Court fell back in the McCollum case. Justice Rutledge's exposition lacks the hard clarity of Madison's own thought, but the essential thesis is sufficiently clear.

And it is absolutely unacceptable. That is my point. This philosophy could not in 1791, and cannot in 1948, be poured into the First Amendment. The simple reason is that it is an irredeemable piece of sectarian dogmatism. And if there is one thing that the First Amendment forbids with resounding force it is the intrusion of a sectarian philosophy of religion into the fundamental law of the land.[33] We have got here a paradox that would be laughable were it not so serious in its consequences: in the effort to prove that "no establishment of religion" means "no aid to religion" the Supreme Court proceeds to establish a religion—James Madison's.[34] In order to make separation of church and state absolute, it unites the state to a "religion without a church"—a deistic version of fundamentalist Protestantism. In the name of freedom of religion it decrees that the relations of government to religion are to be controlled by the fundamental tenet of secularism—the social irrelevance of religion, its exclusion from the secular affairs of the City and its educa-

---

and the whole wall will come crashing down. Its appeal (in the contemporary camel's-nose form) is highly successful emotionally; but its fallaciousness demonstrates the precarious nature of argument from metaphor. First, it begs the question: is the wall an absolute? Second, it proves too much; would the wedge argument be admitted, for instance, in a labor dispute or in any other case where the question is one of rights (as it is here)? Third, it has the same legal fallaciousness that Holmes recognized when he swept away Marshall's famous dictum in his Panhandle dissent: "The power to tax is not the power to destroy while this Court sits." Panhandle Oil Co. *v.* Knox, 277 U.S. 218, at 223 (1928).

[33] Consider Justice Rutledge's Everson dictum, echoed by Justice Frankfurter in the McCollum case: . . . we have staked the very existence of our country on the faith that complete separation between the state and religion is best for the state and best for religion." Everson *v.* Board of Education, 330 U.S. 1, 59 (1947). First, we have not staked the existence of our country on any "faith," but on a set of rational political principles. Second, if we had staked it on the secularist faith implied in that dictum, it was as reckless a gamble as history ever saw. Third, by what constitutional authority is the Supreme Court empowered to legislate as to what is "best for religion"? I thought church and state were separated here. Judgment on what is best for religion is strictly reserved to the religious conscience; it does not fall to the competence of secular government, which judges only what is best for the state, in consultation with the religious consciences of its citizens.

[34] Justice Frankfurter, too, comes perilously close to establishing the "religion of patriotism."

tional system, its relegation to the private forum of conscience or at best to the hushed confines of the sacristy. Justice Jackson thought up an apt allusion,[35] but he got its reference wrong; actually, it is the philosophizing of the whole Court that reminds one of Byron's Julia, who, in momentary disregard of her original lines and the exigencies of metre, "screaming, 'I will ne'er consent to an establishment of religion,' imposed one on the American people."

The issue here is serious. And, I repeat, it concerns the reasoning of the Court, as it shapes itself into a philosophy of separation. If there is to be a sort of official American philosophy in the matter, promulgated by the Supreme Court, it must be constructed in the absence of all appeal to sectarian dogmas—Madison's as well as anybody else's. I do not deny that the dogma in question is widely held—by educationists like Kilpatrick, Thayer, Hook *et al.;* by jurists in the tradition of Holmes and by jurisprudents of the positivistic schools; by a variety of Protestants; [36] by the secularists en masse; in fact, even an atheist would grudgingly grant that religion is "a wholly private matter." But this dogma is not part of our fundamental law, and no constitutional doctrine can be erected on it. It was repudiated by jurists of the stature of Story and Cooley,[37] standing in a genuine American tradition of great original strength; it is repudiated by an enormous number of American citizens today of all faiths. And what is more important, it is demonstrably false in terms both of religious philosophy and the lessons of political experience. It is therefore intolerable to see it endowed somehow with a constitutional status that it never had and could not have. If today the Court were to take as a premise of argument Madison's particular theory of "natural rights" as deriving from a pre-social "state of nature" (a theory borrowed from Locke), there would be legal howlings. It is not more legitimate to adopt

---

[35] Everson *v.* Board of Education, 330 U.S. 1, 19 (1947).

[36] Certainly not all; the most serious Protestant thinkers were shocked by what one of them, Dr. F. Ernest Johnson, called "the extreme secularism of the minority opinion" in the Everson case. Johnson, "Church, School and Supreme Court," 17 *Religion in Life* 483–484 (1948).

[37] See Corwin, The Supreme Court as National School Board, 14 Law & Contemp. Prob. 3 (1949).

Madison's particular theory of religion in its relation to organized society.

III

Be it noticed that in all this I am arguing only against Madison's (and the Court's) absolutism, on the ground that it can rest only on a religious absolute, a theological premise. Take away this premise, and you can combine Madison's other arguments into a satisfactory theory of separation of church and state—a satisfactory theory because it will not make separation an absolute, and its reasons will be such as to command consensus. The distinction of the ecclesiastical and civil jurisdictions,[38] the immunity of conscience from coercion by civil authority in the free exercise of religion, the principle of political equality, the legitimate demands of political unity in a religiously divided society, the general requirements of the common good (which include the need of society to be a "good" society)—these are proper and adequate materials from which to fashion an acceptable American philosophy of separation of church and state. They were in fact the original materials from which that philosophy was fashioned and made the premise of the First Amendment. Madison's added element, the absolutizing element, was not included.

There were two merits to this original philosophy, both of which perish in the new philosophy of the Court. The first is that separation of church and state, thus put on its proper grounds, appears in its true relation to the free exercise of religion. It appears as instrumental to freedom, therefore as a relative, not an absolute in its own right. As a Congregationalist writer recently put it: "Separation of church and state, then, is simply a means, a technique, a policy to implement the principle of religious freedom. It assumes organic separation but dynamic interaction between church and state; it functions through co-

---

[38] A distinction, be it noticed, that recognizes that there are certain areas of common interest to both state and church, notably education. Moreover, even within these areas there is no "fusion," "commingling," or "confusion" (loose, question-begging terms used by the Court) of the two functions. The distinction remains: there is simply cooperation.

operation without favoritism. As a method, separation of church and state can never be an absolute." [38a]

Precisely at this point—the relation between the establishment clause and the free exercise clause—the Court's reasoning falters badly. In the Everson decision, Justice Black made no attempt to analyze the relation of the two clauses, but simply said: "There is every reason to give the same application and broad interpretation to the 'establishment of religion' clause," [39] as the Court has given to the "free exercise" clause. [40] But the question is not broad or narrow interpretation. It is a problem of functional interpretation: How is an issue of "aid to religion" to be decided in such wise as to make the decision instrumental to "free exercise of religion"? Justice Black seems obscurely to feel the problem, without firmly grasping it, where he says that, despite the "no aid to religion" doctrine, "on the other hand, other language of the amendment commands that New Jersey cannot hamper its citizens in the free exercise of their own religion." [41] He then attempts to balance the requirements of the two clauses, with the aid of the public-welfare-legislation argument. The attempt is commendable; but in the absence of a firm grasp of the problem it is bound to seem fumbling, and, I confess, vulnerable to Justice Jackson's charge of being Julia-like. And again the Madisonian absolutism, which totally separates the problem of aid to religion from that of free exercise, is at fault. One cannot balance an absolute against anything.

Obviously, a firm, realistic grasp of these two problems in their relation puts to the Court a much more severe task. It is much easier to hew one's way out of the difficulty with the axe of Madison's absolutism. The trouble is that the axe then falls on "free exercise," as the McCollum decision, in which the axe was more ruthlessly swung, luminously shows. But this is a perversion of the whole intent and philosophy of the First Amendment. And this is actually what has happened: so far from being instrumental to "free exercise," a means relative to an end, the

---

[38a] Keehn, "Church-State Relations," *Social Action,* Nov. 15, 1948, p. 31.

[39] Everson *v.* Board of Education, 330 U.S. 1, 15 (1947).

[40] Justice Rutledge asserts the same thing, but undertakes to inflict some unusual exegetical torture in order to fit the two clauses to the Procrustean bed of his absolutism.

[41] Everson *v.* Board of Education, 330 U.S. 1, 16 (1947).

"establishment" clause (in the meaning of "no aid to religion") has now assumed the primacy, the status of an absolute, an end-in-itself; and the "free exercise" clause has become subordinate to it. The First Amendment has been stood on its head. And in that position it cannot but gurgle juridical nonsense.

The second great merit of the original American philosophy (pragmatic as it was in the best sense, as a political philosophy, based on sound concepts of freedom, equality, and the common good) is that it would permit an equitable, socially healthy solution to a new American problem for which there is no solution in the new ideological and doctrinaire philosophy of the First Amendment. I mean the educational problem—the relation of religion to public education, and of government to the religious school.[42] The McCollum decision "solves" this problem, in its double aspect, simply by looking the other way and refusing to see it. Or what is worse, without taking a fair look at the problem, the Court comes perilously close to slamming the door on a solution by its sweeping negativism.

With regard to religious schools, the "underlying issue," as a writer in the Harvard Law Review put it, "is brutally simple: are parochial schools to be encouraged or not? Until American society has reached an equilibrium, the judicial decisions will continue to reflect uncertainty." [43] I must put the issue with even more brutal simplicity: the problem of "encouragement" here is not a financial one but a juridical one; it is not a question primarily of "aid" by money but of "aid" by legal recognition. The essential question concerns the juridical status, within the American system of education, of the non-profit school with religious affiliations, that serves a public purpose by educating for the public life of citizenship, without being a "public" school in the narrow sense, because it is only under partial, not total, governmental supervision and control. This problem of juridical status is fundamental, antecedent to all questions of financial

---

[42] Justice Reed in his courageous and thoughtful McCollum dissent is the only member of the Court that seems to have seen the specialty of the field of education, and to have called attention to the fact that in Virginia Jefferson likewise saw it, and did not hold a "no aid" doctrine in that field. This, together with his distinction of the concept of "aid" and his sense of the realities of American history, are outstanding merits of Justice Reed's argument.

[43] Note, 60 Harv. L. Rev. 793, 800 (1947).

support of any kind—questions which cannot in fact be solved except by prior solution of the fundamental problem.

Moreover, this problem is posited today concretely, in a set of particular circumstances. A determinant circumstance is the existence of a powerful and articulate philosophy of "American" education in whose explicit tendency is the denial or diminishing of the juridical status of these schools. The major premise of this philosophy is a concept of the "historic unity" of the American people and a rather mystical concept of "democracy." The minor premise is the "divisiveness" of "segregation" in education on religious grounds; it is a manifestation of "isolationist religious practices," that are "disruptive" of the "democratic community." The conclusion of the philosophy was put, for example, in a resolution of the American Federation of Teachers, which asserts "the basic principle that the interests of the democratic community are best served where children of all component groups of American society are enrolled in a common public school." [44] This is the "rightful" position; any other is to be given only toleration, more or less provisional. The conclusion is further supported by some theorists on grounds that only in the public schools can children be nourished with a robust, quasi-religious faith in the "unifying secularism" of American democracy. [45] And a final rib in the theory is the principle that, although (at least for the moment) the child may not be the creature of the state, the school definitely is. Government is the primary educator; its interests are paramount; in particular, it makes its own interests (democratic unity and "faith" in democracy) the controlling norm of parental interests, by right of superior situation in the hierarchy of social values.

---

[44] *The American Teacher,* Oct. 1947.

[45] The idea as put, for instance, by Mrs. Agnes E. Meyer, is that our society, which is itself secular, has a "tolerance of religious diversity, which alone makes brotherhood possible in our country [the churches, she explains, would by themselves destroy it]. This spiritual unity is the saving grace of democracy and its real defense against totalitarianism or against the divisive influence of sectarianism. Therefore, what can justly be called the unifying mission of secularism has a sanctity all its own," which imparts to the public school, wherein true social salvation is found, a holiness transcendent to any that may attach to the destructively divisive churches. Meyer, "The School, the State and the Church." *Atlantic Monthly,* Nov. 1948, pp. 45, 49, and *passim.* I cite Mrs. Meyer for her significance, not as a thinker, but as the purveyor of a thought that is widely propagandized.

On these ideological grounds, about which clings an aura of mysticism, experiments such as "released time" are opposed or reluctantly submitted to. They are "encroachments" by religion on education; they are a "sectarian invasion" of the public school; or, most damning of all adjectives, they are "divisive." Again, any attempt at rational argument for some measure of financial aid to schools not "public" in the narrow sense is usually met with some variant of the fear-instilling speech of Demetrius of ancient Ephesus: "The temple of the great goddess Diana will count for nothing; she will be shorn of her greatness, the goddess whom Asia and all the world reveres." Whereupon all the silversmiths of Teachers College take up the cry: "Great is Diana of Ephesus! And their uproar filled the whole city." The city is not Ephesus but, of course, Washington, where "the meeting was all in confusion and most of them could not tell what had brought them together;" [46] for indeed the cult of Diana, the Divine Public School, brings together an ill-assorted lot.

Most of them will, of course, concede a formal legality to the existence of religiously affiliated schools. Parents whose religious scruples will not permit their children to drink deep at the genuine well-springs of democracy are "free" to send them to other schools. But the "freedom" here is a simple immunity, on a par with that which government grants to the religious eccentricities of Jehovah's Witnesses, which forbid them to salute the flag. These children forego the great American right to a "public" education, behind which stands all the juridical and financial power of our great democracy; they avail themselves of an immunity, taking refuge behind the famous wall.[47] Or in Justice Rutledge's phrase, they embrace "the greater, the most comprehensive freedom," [48] freedom from all governmental aid.

---

[46] Cf. Acts 19:23–41.

[47] There is a vocabulary in the matter: these schools are "protest" schools, their pupils "withdrawal pupils," who have to get "permission" from the state to attend. The Supreme Court was introduced to the vocabulary in the brief *amicus curiae* of the Civil Liberties Union in the Everson case. The Appellate Division of the Supreme Court of New York got a good whiff of the conclusion of the theory in the Lewis case. Appellant's brief stated: "We may add that no true educator in our judgment could have any real interest in the perpetuity of the parochial school system in this country or faith in the calibre of education dispensed in a sectarian institution of learning." Brief for Appellant, filed by Arthur G. Hays, p. 32, Lewis *v.* Graves, 219 App. Div. 233, 219 N.Y.S. 189 (1927).

[48] Everson *v.* Board of Education, 330 U.S. 1, 58.

What more (the proponents of this philosophy exasperatedly ask) could one want than that?

I deliberately put this contemporary sociological and educational situation with a tinge of rhetorical emotion, because the situation itself is (more than slightly) tinged with emotion. Inevitably; for something fundamentally important is involved here. There is a clash of basic philosophies of education and of democracy. In addition there is a clash of power; for behind the philosophy of education as the agent of a unifying, democratic secularism powerful organized forces are aligned—professional educational associations, for instance, and other groups pursuing ideological interests. And the contention, I repeat, primarily is not over money but over principle, and over money as it gives to the soul of principle a visible, juridical body.[49]

It is into this delicate, troubled situation, marked by a struggle of ideas and forces, that the Everson and McCollum policy decisions and reasoning are projected. And my contention, in contrast to the Harvard writer's implication, is that the Court has not left American society to reach an "equilibrium," and it does not "reflect uncertainty." On the contrary, it weights the scales; it betrays an appalling certainty. One consideration will make this clear; I mean a striking omission in the Court's reasoning.

In the McCollum case there was squarely presented to the Court the issue of parental rights in education. And the Court greeted the presentation with a blank, unseeing stare.[50] Yet the issue is woven all through the facts of the case; the whole Cham-

---

[49] I note here that this is the heart of the Catholic case for the inclusion of religious schools in pending federal aid legislation. There are further reasons, but central is the fact that the first such bill passed will be pattern legislation, not only determinant of future federal programs of aid but also indirectly determinant of the juridical status of parochial schools; their omission from the first program will initially damage them, not financially but juridically. Of the essence of the Catholic case is the contention that these schools are public in every sense save two: the secular education they impart is not secularized, and they are under only partial, not total governmental supervision; but neither of these two characteristics are disqualification from public aid in some just, proportional measure, since they are legitimate expressions of parental rights.

[50] Admittedly, appellee did not adequately present the issue in his brief. The issue was excellently drawn out by appellee before the New York Supreme Court, defending the New York released time program from the attack of Mr. Joseph Lewis, President of the Freethinkers of America. Brief for Appellee, filed by Mr. Charles H. Tuttle, pp. 21–67, Lewis *v.* Spaulding, 193 Misc. 66, 85 N.Y.S.2d 682 (Sup. Ct. Albany Co., Nov. 12, 1948).

paign plan hung suspended on the right of parents to have effective voice in regard to what their schools should do for their children, what role in the community their schools should play. Yet the Court does not betray by so much as a word any awareness of this outstanding fact of the case. It passes the issue by on the other side of the street, grimly pounding the sidewalk of its own absolutism. What is worse, its clear assumptions are that the public school system belongs singly to the state and is under its sole supervision; that its functions are determined solely by the state; that the state's compulsory education machinery grinds away with only the state at the controls; that even the child's time in school is owned by the government; that the child has a "legal duty" to put all this time in on secular subjects, none on religious subjects, apart from the state's sovereign permission, which (the Court says) the state is constitutionally powerless to give.

This silence on the parental right is equivalent in the context to positive statement. It implicitly qualifies the Pierce [51] doctrine; now apparently the child is not a creature of the state —until he crosses the threshold of a public school. Parents have a right to direct the education of their children—limited by the exigencies of a "unifying secularism" that is a constitutional necessity in public education. The Court's silence on the parental right argues that it is not a factor in the case; and this is particularly damaging at the present moment, when this right is under open or veiled or unconscious attack from highly articulate groups. It tends to undermine the juridical status of the parental right in American law. Correlatively, it tends to render exclusive the rights of the state in education. In a moment of delicate balance it weights the scales, as I said, in favor of a philosophy of education of decidedly statist flavor. And the parental right which, as a sheer immunity, is already like the smile on some sort of disembodied educational Cheshire cat, begins to fade under the Court's unseeing stare.

Yet the parental right in education is the very pivotal point of a democratic system. It is, to change the metaphor again, the touchstone of difference between democratic education and the

---

[51] Pierce *v*. Society of Sisters, 268 U.S. 510 (1925).

monolithic systems of cultural totalitarianism, whether on the
Soviet or even on the Third Republic style. When the modern
state with its immense power embarks (as indeed it must) on
the spiritual mission of educating its children, its whole native
tendency (as recent developments in United States educational
theory and practice abundantly show) is toward state monopoly.
And it is only held back on its plunging course toward the extreme of *l'école unique*, symbol of the *Kulturstaat*, by the frail
barrier of the parental right to control and direct the education
of their children. After the McCollum decision this barrier is, I
think, frailer than ever. I sometimes think it is already too frail
a legal barrier to confine the bursting expansionism of the new
educational Leviathan.

One might have thought that a "civil rights Court" would
have been sensitive on this neuralgic point of democratic theory;
instead it is callous to the extreme of complete and utter in-
sensibility. It did not even feel the point as present. It erects
massive barriers to protect the right of Jehovah's Witnesses to
take highly uncivil liberties with the rights of other citizens; it
pursues to the verge of quixotism a hyper-sensitive concern for
individual religious freedom of the most individualistic kind. But
it does not lift a judicial finger to fortify against insidious attack
a right that is the cornerstone of democracy in education—the
parent's last rampart against the "unification" of his child with
other children into a standardized "democratic" mass. It pursues,
this time over the verge of quixotism, a hyper-sensitive concern
for the absoluteness of separation of church and state, with resultant legal damage to a human right that rests on the most
absolute political and religious grounds, and is the foundation of
a social freedom of the most indispensable sort. A right is legally
damaged when, in a case where it appears as central and clamors
for recognition, it meets judicial blindness and deafness.

IV

There is worse. Enter Justice Frankfurter, with the two operative concepts that stand out in his McCollum opinion. The first,
that seems to be basically decisive of his judgment, is a quasi-
mystical one—the public school as "a symbol of our secular

unity," [52] a sort of sacrament (if I may for a moment stay with him on the religious level) of our democracy, which works with a sort of Tridentine efficacy *ex opere operato*, being "designed to serve as perhaps the most powerful agency for promoting cohesion among a heterogeneous democratic people." [53] The public school is, it seems, the educational embodiment of the Great American Absolute, separation of church and state, and like it "one of the vital reliances of our Constitutional system for assuring unities among our people stronger than our diversities." [54] It is the efficacious "symbol of our democracy." [55]

This sounds familiar. Is it not the original Gobitis case [56] redivivus? The promotion of national unity is "an interest inferior to none in the hierarchy of legal values." [57] Only now it is "secular" unity. Justice Frankfurter is still saying, with Holmes, "We live by symbols." Only now the life-giving symbol is not Holmes's flag but Horace Mann's public school. Now too the argument from symbol, which was used to help support the legislative freedom of the Minersville school board, is used to strike down the legislative freedom of the Champaign School Board. The Frankfurter national-unity argument was of course rejected in the Murdock [58] and Barnette [59] cases; but now the stone rejected by the builders of the wall of religious freedom has become the cornerstone in the wall of separation of church and state. And the final piquancy is to see Justice Jackson, who in the Barnette case saw the term of the national-unity argument as the "unanimity of the graveyard," [60] now solemnly unanimous over Justice Frankfurter's new symbol of unanimity. " 'Tis now the very witching time of night, When churchyards yawn . . ." —and yield up old arguments.

One might be tempted to yawn too, were it not that this old argument, which we thought we had "had" is so potentially dangerous in its new setting. First if there is a symbol of de-

---

[52] McCollum *v.* Board of Education, 333 U.S. 203, 217 (1948).
[53] *Id.* at 216.
[54] *Id.* at 231.
[55] *Ibid.*
[56] Minersville School District *v.* Gobitis, 310 U.S. 586 (1940).
[57] *Id.* at 595.
[58] Murdock *v.* Pennsylvania, 319 U.S. 105 (1943).
[59] Board of Education *v.* Barnette, 319 U.S. 624 (1943).
[60] *Id.* at 641.

mocracy in education, it is not the public school as the single "democratic" school; rather it is (or would be) the coexistence of several types of schools, including church-affiliated schools, on a footing of juridical equality, with a consequent proportionately equal measure of state encouragement and support.[61] It would be an educational system pivoting on the parental right as fully operative, not on a doctrinaire concept of "national unity."

Second, the national-unity concept itself needs to be brought down to the earth of reality and divested of all fuzzy mysticism. Our national unity is a political unity, supported by shared sentiments in regard to the demands of freedom, justice, civic charity, and all the political virtues—the virtues of a citizen—as these emerge from sound ethical principles. It involves too a sense of a great common historic past, and a still greater destiny (if we do not fumble it). But it has nothing to do with an artificial, government-promoted levelling of differences, especially religious differences. Still less has it to do with the substitution by governmental policy and pressure of a unified "religion of patriotism," a common quasi-religious "democratic faith," as a value "inferior to none" in American society. Whatever spiritual mission of promoting unity government may have, it is conditioned (and I thought the Murdock and Barnette cases had established this) by its primal duty of promoting justice, guaranteeing an order of rights, insuring the equality of *differences*. Are we at this date to go in for the creation by government, through education, of "the soul of our people," à la Schleiermacher and the German "enlightened despots"?

For my part, I find it disconcerting to see in a Supreme Court opinion the ideology and phraseology proper to a genuinely sectarian philosophy of public education—lightly underlined, if

---

[61] I say "proportionately equal"; I mean that the juridical status of these schools is equal to that of the public school, as an equally valid expression of the parental right. They have therefore an equal right to aid. But not a right to equal aid; only to a proportionate measure of aid—the proportion to be determined according to the canons of distributive justice which are applied under consideration of a number of juridical and factual elements in a given context. In my personal opinion, total support of parochial school education (the good old camel behind the nose!) is neither a right nor a desideratum. At the other extreme, to declare that this type of education, because of its religious element, has no right to any aid is clear injustice and unwise social policy.

you will, but discernible; particularly discernible by reason of the omission of all reference to parental rights. The public school is not a temple in which our children are to be baptized into the unity of the secular democratic faith, while those who stand without are somehow faintly heretical. Viewed realistically and with all respect for its idealisms and achievements, it is actually the symbol of our religious disunity and the sign of an experiment in dealing in a particular way—there are other ways —with the fact of that disunity. And it is the symbol of our democracy only in so far as it deals with this fact honestly and fairly, not blinking it or chipping away at it in the name of some dubious ideal of national unity. This brings me to Justice Frankfurter's second operative concept.

It is of course the concept of "pressures." Pressures by religious groups on government, "inherent pressure by the school system in the interest of religious sects" [62]—these, together with its "divisiveness," were the constitutionally damnable features of the Champaign plan. This is a pretty piece of legal unrealism. I omit the obvious fact that neither government nor any child— even James Terry McCollum—was "pressured" into doing anything it did not want to do. The unrealism is in Justice Frankfurter's implication. Take away these awful divisive sectarian pressures, and you have what he wants: "an atmosphere free from pressures in a realm in which pressures are most resisted." [63] Justice Frankfurter, although an eminent jurist, is not an expert in education; even so, this naïveté is too extreme to be credible. Thousands of educators of all religious convictions are increasingly agreed that the atmosphere of public schools is *not* free from pressures. Their supposed "neutrality" is itself a pressure. Their sheer omission of religion from the curriculum is itself a pressure against religion. In fact, the whole weight of the public school system tends to be thrown against the child's religious conscience and consciousness. Contrary to its original intention and often to the regret of its high-minded administrators and teachers, the system as such has become a formidable ally of secularism, either as a positive philosophy or as a sort of spiritual vacuum that is itself a faith *à rebours*. This, I had supposed, is

---

[62] McCollum *v.* Board of Education, 333 U.S. 203, 227 (1948).
[63] *Id.* at 216.

a well-known view, and a primary concern of very many of our leading educators.

My point is not the problem itself nor whether nor how it can be solved; I am only concerned with Justice Frankfurter's argument. Are we to suppose that "pressure by the school system in the interest of religious sects" is unconstitutional, whereas immeasurably more powerful pressure against their interests, against the idea of religion itself, is quite constitutional? To use Justice Jackson's antitheses,[64] is this "law" or "prepossessions"? One does not expect the Supreme Court to solve the problem of pressures in the public school atmosphere; likewise one does not expect it utterly to misconceive the problem. And the argument from pressures, like the wedge argument, reveals a basic misconception of the educational and sociological world we are living in. There are various kinds of pressures, and of wedges. Should the Supreme Court in the name of religious freedom throw its weight behind the secularist pressure, and in the name of separation of church and state use its hammer upon the secularist wedge?

V

Here briefly are my conclusions. First, the absolutism of the Everson and McCollum doctrine of separation of church and state is unsupported, and unsupportable, by valid evidence and reasoning—historical, political, or legal—or on any sound theory of values, religious or social. Second, in consequence of an absolutizing of separation, the very problem is misconceived; that is, the instrumental relationship of separation to the free exercise of religion is destroyed. Third, the necessary further consequence is that, when separation as an absolute principle is ruthlessly thrust into the field of education, the result is juridical damage to the freedom of religion and to the natural rights of parents. Fourth, this damage is particularly harmful in the existent religious and educational situation; in a moment of tension between contending sets of values—religious *vs.* secularist, statist

---

[64] *Id.* at 238.

vs. popular and parental values—the Court has sided with the wrong set.

If we are not to embark on "a century of error," some essential clarifications are imperative. What we need is, first, a return to the original political philosophy of the First Amendment, and second, its realistic application in a situation wherein the alignment of forces and the conflict of values is substantially different from what it was in 1791. This means development. But the essential development must take place in the concept of "freedom of religion." Woodrow Wilson in *The New Freedom* [65] showed how exclusive insistence on freedom as sheer immunity from governmental power opens the way to the tyrannies of other powers, not governmental, that gain control of governmental processes. The lesson has been heeded in the economic field; it needs to be hearkened to in the religious and educational fields. Join a rigidly negative concept of religious freedom, as sheer immunity from coercion by governmental power, to a rigidly absolute, end-in-itself concept of separation of church and state, as meaning absolutely no aid to religion by government, and you have opened the way to the subtle tyrannies of irreligion, secularist ideologies, false political and educational philosophies, and the dangerous myth of "democracy as a religion." Such a development is utterly foreign to the letter, spirit, and intent of the First Amendment, and will be consequently disastrous to American society.

Shall we have, then, a new freedom for religion, born of old American principles, made a positive empowerment by a just measure of governmental aid? Or shall we have some new tyrannies, born of the rising secularist myths, fastened on us by their alliance with the expanding power of government? That, I think, is the basic issue underlying the question presented in the Everson and McCollum cases. Is there to be cooperation between parents and public schools towards the religious education of their children, and is the right of parents to educate their children in religious schools to remain a sheer immunity or to become a genuine freedom, endowed with the full juridical status

---

[65] (1913).

that only a just measure of governmental aid can give it? These questions have a common element: How free do we want religion to be? The Court has given one answer. I think it is unreasoned and unreasonable.

Historical Note

The following notes may serve to clarify the original historical meaning of the First Amendment, as conceived by Madison and the first Congress. In the Virginia ratifying convention that met in June, 1788, when the elimination of religious tests was being discussed, Madison said: "I confess to you, sir, were *uniformity of religion* to be introduced by this system, it would, in my opinion, be ineligible; but I have no reason to conclude that *uniformity of government* will produce *that of religion*. This subject is, for the honor of America, perfectly free and unshackled. The government has *no jurisdiction* over it: the least reflection will convince us there is no danger to be feared on this ground." [66] The italicized words indicate the basic problem of the time: a national government must not mean a national religion made obligatory on all by federal law; for this would be a violation at once of the sovereignty of the states and of the individual conscience. In Madison's consistent view the danger was removed by the sheer fact that the Federal Government was one of delegated powers; and "no jurisdiction" over religion was committed to Congress. Congress has no legal power to legislate as to what the religious beliefs or practices of the American people shall be, imposing on them a national religion. Madison maintained, therefore, that no further explication on the point was necessary. However, he accepted the decision of the committee on amendments (twenty members, chairmanned by George Wythe) to submit the following amendment (its twentieth): "That religion, or the duty which we owe to our Creator, and the manner of discharging it, can be directed only by reason and conviction, not by force or violence; and therefore all men have an equal, natural and inalienable right to the free exercise of religion, according to the dictates of conscience, and

[66] III Jonathan Elliot, *The Debates in the Several State Conventions on the Adoption of the Federal Constitution* 93 (1836). [Italics supplied.]

that no particular religious sect or society ought to be favored or established, by law, in preference to others." [67] Nothing could be clearer than this statement. First, the concept of "no establishment" is subordinated to the concept of "free exercise" as means to end; second, "no establishment" means "no favor, no preference in law."

While maintaining his position that a bill of rights was not "essential" but likewise "neither improper nor altogether useless," [68] Madison assembled and presented to the first Congress the following text embodying the wishes of the states which had either explicitly (by submitting an amendment: New Hampshire, Virginia, South Carolina) or implicitly (in their ratifying resolutions: New York, North Carolina) demanded an amendment: "Fourthly. That in article Ist, section 9, between clauses 3 and 4, be inserted these clauses, to wit: The civil rights of none shall be abridged on account of religious belief or worship, nor shall any national religion be established, nor shall the full and equal rights of conscience be in any manner, or on any pretext, infringed." [68a] Again the idea is clear: political equality regardless of religion, no one national religion, equality before the law of all consciences or religions.

This draft was committed to a committee of eleven, Madison among them, by which it was reported out in this form: "No religion shall be established by law, nor shall the equal rights of conscience be infringed." [69] The brief debate turned on two points. First, was the amendment necessary? Roger Sherman of Connecticut and others thought it was not, "inasmuch as Congress had no authority whatever delegated to them by the Constitution to make religious establishments." [70] I would note that everywhere in the recorded debate "establishment of religion" was used uniformly in its proper technical sense, "to favor or prefer." The second question was, Was the amendment too radical? Peter Sylvester of New York "had some doubts about the propriety of the mode of expression used in this paragraph. He apprehended that it was liable to a construction different from what had been made by the committee. He feared it might be

---

[67] *Id.* at 659.
[68] 1 Annals of Cong 436 (1789)
[68a] *Id.* at 434.

[69] Elliot's *Debates* at 729.
[70] *Id.* at 730.

thought to have a tendency to abolish religion altogether." [71]
Benjamin Huntington of Rhode Island agreed "that the words
might be taken in such latitude as to be extremely hurtful to the
cause of religion." [72] . . . Here I pause to remark how right these
gentlemen were. . . . Elbridge Gerry of Massachusetts wanted
the intended sense made clearer: "that no religious doctrine shall
be established by law." [73]

Whereupon Madison, to calm their fears, explained the narrow and exact sense: "Mr. Madison said, he apprehended the
meaning of the words to be, that Congress should not *establish a*
religion, and *enforce* the legal observation of it by law, nor
compel men to worship God in any manner contrary to their
conscience. Whether the words are necessary or not, he did
not mean to say, but they had been required by some of the
State Conventions, who seemed to entertain an opinion that
under the clause of the Constitution, which gave power to Congress to make all laws necessary and proper to carry into execution the Constitution, and the laws made under it, enabled them
(*sic*) to make laws of such a nature as might *infringe the rights
of conscience* and establish *a national* religion; to prevent *these
effects* he presumed the amendment was intended, and he thought
it was as well expressed as the nature of the language would
admit." [74] Notice that here we have not Justice Rutledge's Madison, the fiery, implacable doctrinaire denouncing three-pence
levies, but Madison the statesman. The operative words are
italicized; the "effects" barred are (1) compulsion of conscience,
by (2) the establishment of, i.e., preference in law accorded to,
a national religion. Here Huntington expressed his wish that
"the amendment would be made in such a way as to secure the
rights of conscience, and a free exercise of the rights of religion,
but not to patronize those who professed no religion at all." [75]
. . . "O my prophetic soul!" he would exclaim today. . . .
Again Madison patiently explained the precise narrow sense of
the words: "Mr. Madison thought, if the word 'national' was
inserted before religion, it would satisfy the minds of [the]
honorable gentlemen. He believed that the people feared *one*

[71] *Id*. at 729.   [73] *Ibid*.
[72] *Id*. at 730.   [74] *Ibid*. (Italics supplied.)
[75] *Id*. at 730–731.

sect might obtain a preeminence, or two combine together, and *establish* a religion to which they would compel others to conform. He thought if the word 'national' was introduced, it would point the amendment directly to *the object* it was intended to prevent." [76]. . . . Again we are very, very far from Mr. Rutledge's Madison. . . . And again the sense of the Amendment is luminously not the sense attributed to it by Justice Black.

There is no need here to comment on the other three versions through which the text passed in the House, nor on the original Senate version: "Congress shall make no law establishing articles of faith or a mode of worship or prohibiting the free exercise of religion. . . ." [77] This was reconciled with the final House version by a conference committee, by a linguistic compromise that issued in the present version. The essential point is that from beginning to end of the debate the legislative intent was perfectly clear and unanimously agreed on: the primary thing was that there were to be no legal constraints on freedom of conscience and on the free exercise of religion; secondly, to this end there was to be no one national religion endowed with legal privilege for its beliefs. It is utterly impossible to get out of the legislative history of the Amendment that construction which Justice Black and Justice Rutledge, supposedly under appeal to history, attempted to put upon it.

As a final indication of an intimate concern of the first Congress I would add the remark of Thomas Scott of Pennsylvania made in another connection: "My design is to guard against those who are of no religion." [78] The whole problem of the relation between government and religious education in its various forms was not even remotely glimpsed by the first Congress, and the First Amendment can be brought to bear on it only by a process of interpretation and extension of meaning. If the first Congress, however, were doing the interpreting, this concern would be active, lest "those who are of no religion" should somehow use the First Amendment as a club with which to battle their way to a privileged place in American law for "no religion." As the McCollum doctrine is at variance with the

[76] *Id.* at 731. [Italics supplied.]
[77] Records of the U.S. Senate, Sept. 9, 1789 (National Archives).
[78] 1 Annals, *supra* note 68, at 767.

original sense of the First Amendment, so it is (in its tendency) in conflict with the spirit of the First Amendment.

I said in the text that Virginia's hostile reception of the First Amendment destroys Justice Black's central contention that the Amendment in design, letter, and spirit is a faithful rendition of the radical Virginian ideas, which therefore become the canon for its interpretation. The pertinent text is a statement by eight Virginia state senators recently uncovered and incorporated by appellee in his McCollum brief: "The third amendment [our First Amendment] recommended by Congress does not prohibit the rights of conscience from being violated or infringed; and although it goes to restrain Congress from passing laws establishing any national religion, they might, notwithstanding, levy taxes to any amount for the support of religion or its preachers; and any particular denomination of Christians might be so favored and supported by the general government, as to give it a decided advantage over the others, and in the process of time render it powerful and dangerous as if it was established as the national religion of the country . . . This amendment then, when considered as it relates to any of the rights it is pretended to secure, will be found totally inadequate, and betrays an unreasonable, unjustifiable, but a studied departure from the amendment proposed by Virginia . . . We conceive that this amendment is dangerous and fallacious. . . ." [79] This text makes it clear that distance has lent some manner of enchantment, but certainly no clarity or exactness, to Justice Black's and Justice Rutledge's view of the historical meaning of the First Amendment.

I add this historical note simply for the record, with no great hope that it will matter in the result. It seems quite clear from the tenor of the Everson and McCollum decisions that the original idea of the First Amendment, as revealed by the facts of its legislative history, is today in the judicial mind a matter simply of antiquarian interest—rather like the original idea behind the electoral college, for instance. If, however, I had a hope in

---

[79] Brief for Appellees, *supra* note 8, at 51–54 citing Journal of Virginia Senate, 1789, 61–64 (1828), as reprinted in *The Daily Advertiser* (New York City) for Jan. 26, 1790, and *The Virginia Independence Chronicle.*

the matter, it would merely be that in the future we might be spared "historical arguments" that are neither historical nor arguments, but simply a process of selecting pegs from the past on which to hang a philosophy consisting, as Justice Jackson well said, of one's "own ideas of what is good in public instruction." [80]

---

[80] McCollum *v.* Board of Education, 333 U.S. 203, 237 (1948).

CHAPTER ELEVEN

The Constitution and
Racial Equality

THE PROBLEM OF RACIAL DISCRIMINATION AND THE CONSTITU-tion brings into dramatic focus practically all the major issues with which the preceding essays in this volume have been concerned. In order to decide cases in this field, the Court has been forced to wade neck-deep through masses of historical material designed to reveal the "intent of the framers" of the Fourteenth Amendment; the decisions therefore raise acutely the question mentioned in the introduction to Beard's essay, viz: to what extent should historical evidence guide the path of modern doctrine? It has been obliged to ponder deeply the problem of scope raised by Thayer, and its decisions constitute in themselves an illuminating study in "the logic and rhetoric of constitutional law." The student who examines the cases can hardly help concluding that they require and perhaps rest on a redefinition of the Court's role in relation to the American socio-economic context, so that Lerner's construct, as has already been suggested, needs to be drastically recast. In short, it is hard to think of a broad question about the Supreme Court and the Constitution which is *not* brought up, either directly or inferentially, by the Court's treatment of the discrimination issue.

One way of summarizing all this would be to say that the race question has confronted the Court with the most formidable task of judicial statesmanship it has faced in many years. On the one hand is the letter of the Constitution, which declares that no state shall "deny to any person within its jurisdiction the equal protection of the laws." Combined with this constitutional mandate is the evident conviction of the justices that enforced legal separation of the races is on its face a violation of that mandate. On the other hand, there is the fact that a discriminatory pattern is deeply rooted in the mores of many American states and cannot be extirpated by a wave of the judicial hand. The weighty responsibility of the Court is to chart a course of judicial wisdom in these perilous circumstances.

Nor do the difficulties imposed by such a responsibility lessen when they are examined more closely. J. D. Hyman's essay, which follows, is largely devoted to a discussion of the logical brier patch which springs up in the world of concrete fact no matter which way the Court turns in fashioning its holdings. A wise judge is aware, as the public is sometimes not, that the decision he hands down today in response to a simple plea that race discrimination is immoral may lead constitutional law into unforeseen bypaths as we follow out the course of its logic. He must be sure then that he will want to go where it takes him not only today, but tomorrow. Moreover, if constitutional history has taught him anything, he will be wary of the practical as well as the logical consequences of his decision and will choose his ground cautiously. Yet—to carry the catalog of judicial perplexities one step farther—he must at the same time take care not to leave the impression that his decision is opportunistic. For Americans are inclined to demand, somewhat unreasonably perhaps, that the courts will both do what they want them to do and defend the right unflinchingly; we will attack the court as wilful or pertinacious if it disagrees with us or as pusillanimous if it agrees with someone else.

Before examining a little further this proposition that the judge's lot is not an altogether happy one, it is desirable to touch a few matters that may need clarification and to carry the story of discrimination and the Constitution from the point where Hyman dropped it in 1950 up to the present.

One important reason for including this particular essay in this volume is that it is not limited to an isolated discrimination issue, like segregation in the public schools, but rather deals with a wide range of constitutional questions involving race relationships. As Mr. Hyman says, many of those questions were in the minds of the framers of the Fourteenth and Fifteenth Amendments at the time of ratification, but the Supreme Court of the late 19th century chose to ignore most of them, and for a long time the issue of racial discrimination played a relatively insignificant part in our constitutional law. By the 1930's however, the pendulum began to swing back, so that in the modern era the Court has exhibited a plain intention to do its level best to mitigate racial inequality in the United States. Nevertheless, it has not (and obviously feels that it cannot) entirely taken leave of the premises inherited from the earlier period, and one of these premises is particularly constraining and particularly important to understand.

It is, of course, the premise that the Fourteenth and Fifteenth Amendments control only the action of states and do not apply to the action of private individuals. Constitutional historians have diligently argued the merits of this interpretation for many years, but the question of whether or not the framers meant so to limit the scope of their brainchildren seems almost impossible to answer conclusively, and it need not detain us here. Whatever the intentions of the congressional sponsors may have been, the fact remains that the amendments refer in terms only to state action: "Nor shall any *State* . . . deny to any person within its jurisdiction the equal protection of the laws" (Amendment XIV); "The right of citizens of the United States to vote shall not be denied or abridged . . . by any *State* on account of race, color, or previous condition of servitude" (Amendment XV). The italics are mine. The Court has taken this language to mean that the National Constitution leaves the problem of private discrimination to the disposal of the states, and the justification usually advanced is that any other interpretation would profoundly alter the federal system. If a state, or its agent, unjustly discriminates between Negroes and whites, the amendments come into action. But if a private person discriminates, the amendments have no bearing.

With that background, we can go on to outline briefly the course of doctrinal development in recent years. For purposes of discussion, the subject can be divided into several major problem areas. To begin with, there is the question raised by the "enforcement clauses" of the two amendments. Both Amendment XIV and Amendment XV grant Congress the authority to enforce the articles by "appropriate legislation," and in the reconstruction fervor after the Civil War, a number of laws were passed by Congress in pursuance of these provisions. The lawmakers' aim at the time seems to have been the broad protection of the rights of racial minorities against all who attempted to abuse them, but subsequent amendments and judicial decisions narrowed the statutes' scope considerably. (See R. H. Carr, *Federal Protection of Civil Rights* [1947]; and T. I. Emerson and David Haber, *Political and Civil Rights in the United States* [1952], Chapter I.) The difficulties encountered in very recent years have been in deciding A. What individuals, if any, *could* be reached by federal laws protecting civil rights (bearing in mind that the two amendments proscribe state, not individual action); and, B. How far Congress *meant* to reach when it passed the laws in question. The answers so far arrived at by the Supreme Court are far too tentative and complex to be presented in capsule form. However, it should be generally observed that the Court's modern tendency has been to avoid holdings that would delimit Congress' *power*, but at the same time to circumscribe rather straitly the *application* of the civil rights laws. Thus in Screws v. United States, mentioned by Mr. Hyman, a clear majority of the Court agreed that Congress could punish a local police officer who in the course of his official duties deprived a prisoner of civil rights, because the action of the officer could be regarded as the action of a state and thus within the purview of the Fourteenth Amendment's provisions. Nevertheless, the federal statute in question was construed so as to invalidate the officer's conviction. Similarly, when Hardyman v. Collins, also mentioned by Mr. Hyman, reached the Supreme Court, it was held that the facts of the case failed to present a cause of action under the statute, but Mr. Justice Jackson, speaking for the

majority, explicitly refused to say whether Congress could protect against private invasions the right to assemble and discuss
governmental questions. (See 341 U.S. 651, 662 [1951]). Congress, the Court seems to say, may enact a broader civil rights
code if it wishes to do so. But considering that the laws now
invoked were passed long ago in an extremely heated atmosphere,
and considering that their language and intent are, to say the
least, ambiguous, we will not "compete with Congress or attempt
to replace it as the Nation's law-making body" (*Ibid.*, at 663)
by judicially stretching the scope of statutory civil rights protection.

However, if it is the responsibility of Congress to decide
how the enforcement clauses shall be implemented, it is the plain
responsibility of the Supreme Court to cope with state laws that
deny racial equality. When the legal action of a state violates the
terms of the Amendments, then the Court is obliged, under the
doctrine of judicial review, to provide a judicial remedy. As has
already been said, the modern Court has taken its duty in this
regard very seriously and has assailed legalized discrimination
in many areas, only a few of which can be touched on here.

One such area is that of the electoral franchise. A number
of American states in the past tried to prevent Negro citizens
from voting, and perhaps the most successful device for accom-
plishing this was the so-called "white primary." A state law
denying Negroes the right to vote in general elections would
have been a flat violation of the Amendments. But, it was argued,
primary elections are not state affairs; they are arrangements by
which a private organization—say the Democratic Party—chooses
candidates for office. Therefore the amendments do not apply,
and the Party may, with impunity, exclude Negroes from par-
ticipating in its private prerogative of choice. By a course of
reasoning that now seems nearly incredible, the Supreme Court
in 1935 upheld this argument (Grovey *v.* Townsend, 295 U.S.
45).

Nine years later that decision was reversed in Smith *v.* Allwright (321 U.S. 649 [1944]). The Court held that a political
party is an agent of the state and that its discriminatory practices
therefore constitute state action within the meaning of the
amendments. An otherwise qualified Negro voter must be

granted a primary election ballot. Several states sought to evade the effects of this holding in various ways, the most interesting of which was the "depublicizing" of the primary election process. South Carolina, for example, repealed all laws relating to primaries and then proceeded to argue that the membership rules of the Democratic party had once more become a purely private affair. A Court of Appeals held, however, that the Amendments nevertheless applied (Rice *v.* Elmore, 165 F.2d 387), and when the Supreme Court refused to review that holding, it became apparent that the legal white primary was a lost cause. Yet later cases emphasize the fact already referred to both in Mr. Hyman's essay and in this preface—that obviously just decision may lead to thorny bypaths as we follow its logic out. A county organization in Texas colorfully named "The Jaybird Democratic Association" had been, since 1889, endorsing candidates at each Democratic primary election. Its membership policies excluded Negroes, and since the Jaybird endorsement was a practical guarantee of election to county office, Negro residents urged that their rights under the amendments were violated. The Supreme Court agreed (Terry *v.* Adams, 345 U.S. 461 [1953]), but the judges were so divided in their reasons for agreeing that the difficulties of the problem were brought into sharp focus. The Jaybird Association did not itself conduct the Democratic primary, and Negroes were still perfectly free to participate in either the primary or the general election. If the Jaybird proceedings constitute state action, where is the line between state and private action to be drawn? Would a private social club whose activities sometimes touch on political matters become thereby an agent of the state and subject to the anti-discrimination provisions of the amendments? If not, why not, especially if the club is politically potent? But if so, what becomes of the Amendments' distinction between governmental and private action? No doubt reasonable distinctions can still be devised, but the obvious difficulties these problems present may serve to emphasize the point that constitutional logic does not take care of itself. Someone has to preside over it and nurture it carefully at every stage.

Similar problems rise up in connection with another area of discriminatory action—housing. It has been plain since Buchanan *v.* Warley (245 U.S. 60 [1917]) that no state or subdivision thereof can constitutionally deny Negroes the access to housing that is permitted to whites. A standard method of bypassing this rule, however, was to make private "restrictive convenants," which amounted to agreements between buyers and sellers that they would not sell or lease to Negroes. For many years these agreements were regarded like other contracts, as enforceable through state court action, but in Shelley *v.* Kraemer, discussed by Mr. Hyman, the Supreme Court held that such enforcement violated the Fourteenth Amendment, since the state represented by its courts in effect was helping to carry out a discriminatory policy. Again the justice of the particular holding is hard to impeach, but again it raises some nice problems for courts of the future to chew on. Suppose that a prejudiced man consistently picks up only white hitchhikers at a certain corner on his way to work, and suppose that a Negro insists on clambering aboard despite the motorist's protests. Could the motorist call a policeman to his aid in ejecting the uninvited guest, or would the policeman, agent of the state, be enjoined from assisting by the Fourteenth Amendment? One might agree that the New York housing project mentioned by Mr. Hyman was semi-public because of the help the state had granted it; but most of our privileges are state-insured in one way or another, and it is not easy to say at what point the Constitution should become unconcerned about how we discriminate in exercising these privileges. Mr. Hyman makes some suggestions that merit very serious consideration, but it should be understood that the judiciary has so far made little progress in drawing the lines that the Shelley decision seems to call for.

This problem in only slightly different forms is also raised by the decisions involving public education. Mr. Hyman's essay was written before the decision in the Public School Segregation Cases was handed down (Brown *v.* Board of Education, 347 U.S. 483 [1954]), and it is therefore necessary to say a few words about this extremely important constitutional event. As Hyman says, until 1954 the Supreme Court had avoided a holding that segregation of races in public education was per se in violation of the Fourteenth Amendment, and had contented itself with insisting on strict standards of equality in the facilities available to both races. In fact, the standard of equality required by such decisions as Sweatt *v.* Painter (339 U.S. 629 [1950]) was so stringent that it seemed very nearly impossible for the state to comply with it, and one might argue that, logically speaking, segregated education had received its quietus at that point. But logic is usually debatable, and it might have been possible for the Court to maintain the "separate but equal" doctrine in nominal good health while gradually undermining it by tightening the equality requirement. Whatever could have been said for such judicial gradualism however, the Court was not persuaded, and in the Brown case it forthrightly declared that racial segregation in public schools was necessarily in contravention of the Fourteenth Amendment's equality requirements. For the time being, the judges postponed deciding how the decision should be implemented, but a year later the lower courts were ordered to fashion their desegregation decrees in the light of the principles that guide the law of equity, i.e., flexibility in the shaping of remedies and due consideration to the problem of adjusting public and private needs (Brown *v.* Board, 349 U.S. 294 [1955]). Although this order was obviously designed to permit the states some leeway, the Court was undeviating in its insistence that the states concerned must make "a prompt and reasonable start" towards desegregation, and the cases evoked in the South the most impressive wave of public criticism that has beset the Court in recent years.

This criticism, ranging from demands that Congress "curb" the Supreme Court to denunciation and threats of "interposition," makes it clear that the Court was treading slippery ground when it ventured to settle the school segregation issue. It is at least worth asking whether the judges underestimated the local resistance that might develop against their ruling. Mr. Hyman apparently expected that the Court would refrain from a flat desegregation order until there was "a convincing sociological showing that the common expectation as to the depth of resistance is ill-founded." There was no such showing before the Brown decision, and subsequent events suggest that a precise sociology would have come to the conclusion that the "common expectation" was well-founded indeed. Perhaps the discreeter course would have been to acknowledge this and continue the less dramatic but more subtle policy of insisting on rigid equality standards. Yet the fact is that the segregated school system does serve to maintain Negro inferiority in the states that practice it, and the further fact is that the Fourteenth Amendment does prescribe equality before the law. The Court exposed its prestige to a formidable test when it undertook to decide this issue as it did, and no one knows just how many such ordeals of public hostility the institution of judicial review can suffer. But neither does it seem likely that a judiciary that persistently dodged facts and evaded responsibilities could retain the respect of the nation.

Apart from this question of public reaction, it is evident that the desegregation decisions, like those in the fields of voting and housing, pose again the ticklish problem of how far the law can go in enforcing the equality requirements. One obvious technique for evading the desegregation holding is to rearrange school districts so that all or most of the students attending a given district school would be white or colored, as the case might be. A Court of Appeals held in 1956 that such "gerrymandering" of school districts did not constitute good faith compliance with the Brown mandate, and the Supreme Court refused to review the judgment (Board of Education *v.* Clemons, 76 Sup. Ct. 651 [1956]). The result seems unexceptionable, but can the Supreme Court assume the formidable task of approving or disapproving the procedures followed in mapping the thousands of school districts of the nation? Still another evasion often suggested is that the state "depublicize" its public schools, turning them over to local boards which would presumably operate like the boards of trustees of private educational institutions. (On the whole question of evasion tactics see *Southern School News*, Feb., 1956, p. 2; *United States News and World Report*, May 28, 1954, pp. 21–24; 65 Yale Law Journal 630, 637–8 [1956]; and 67 Harvard Law Review 377 [1953]). If the analogy of the voting cases applies, and there is no apparent reason why it should not, the Supreme Court can be expected to frustrate this attempt to escape the effect of its rulings. But once more the question arises of how far and up what alleys the Court is prepared to go in order to pursue the logic of its original premise that racial segregation is unconstitutional.

If we put these several problems that assail the Court in a

nutshell, they might add up to this: A. To what extent can the Court undertake to decide questions against a determined, though sectionally limited, public opinion? B. To what extent should the Court be prepared to sacrifice the value of federalism in order to stamp out the evil of racial discrimination? C. To what extent is the judiciary capable of umpiring the vast administrative problems that are presented if its anti-discrimination orders are to be given full effect? As was suggested at the outset of this foreword, these queries pose further queries about the place of the Court in a constitutional democracy; the job of the judges—and of the students who study their work—is to answer all of them.

Segregation and the Fourteenth Amendment

by J. D. Hyman*

Vanderbilt Law Review,
Volume 4, Page 555 (1951)

Slightly more than 75 years ago, Senator Boutwell said:

> The thirteenth, fourteenth and fifteenth amendments did limit the power of the States; they did extend the power of the General Government; and the question we are considering almost continually is the extent to which the power of the States has been limited by these amendments and the extent to which the power of the General Government has been carried by these several amendments.[1]

However definitively some constitutional problems may have been left behind, those created by the Civil War Amendments are still before us almost in the identical terms in which Senator Boutwell stated them. Perhaps the reason is not so much that they are insoluble as that they have only recently been receiving adequate consideration.

Their eclipse and emergence can be sketched quickly. In the

---

* (1909–   ), Professor of Law, University of Buffalo since 1946; Dean since 1953.
[1] 3 Cong. Rec. 1792 (1875).

name of federalism, the Supreme Court at the outset eviscerated
the amendments and the statutes passed to implement them.[2] In
a day which hears much talk of judicial activism, it is not inappropriate to recall how deliberately judicial power was wielded
in what was believed to be a statesmanlike blocking of political
efforts to realize in fact the Christian and humanistic ideals which
were in large part responsible for the Civil War.

But the freedom of the States from federal interference was
not long-lived. Developing in response to demands wholly different from those which primarily brought about passage of the
Fourteenth Amendment,[3] the concept of substantive due process
thrust the Federal Government deeply into the affairs of the
states, although by way of the judicial veto rather than the legislative decree. Once fully developed with reference to economic
interests, it was natural that sooner or later the doctrine should
expand to bring personal liberties also under the Supreme Court's
protecting wing. This in turn resulted in a re-examination of the
reach of the Fourteenth Amendment in protecting basic personal
rights from infringement otherwise than by the formal act of
the state. That re-examination is continuing, and with particular
urgency on the question of segregation.

In considering basic doctrines which are in flux, one cannot
avoid having some convictions or attitudes about the historical
meaning of the Civil War amendments. Fortunately our generation has the benefit of a re-examination of the historical data.
When Mr. Justice Black, to support his position that the Fourteenth Amendment incorporated the first eight Amendments,[4]
planted himself on Horace Flack's 50-year-old study of the
making of the Fourteenth Amendment,[5] that study got the benefit of a new look. Professor Fairman has given us a powerful
brief [6] challenging the incorporation thesis. By the way, he has

---

[2] See Watt & Orlikoff, The Coming Vindication of Mr. Justice Harlan, 44 Ill.
L. Rev. 13 (1949).

[3] The notion that the due process clause was smuggled into the Constitution just
to protect corporate interests has been effectively upset. Graham, The "Conspiracy
Theory" of the Fourteenth Amendment, 47 Yale L.J. 371, 48 Yale L.J. 171 (1938).

[4] Dissenting, in Adamson *v.* California, 332 U.S. 46, 68, 67 Sup. Ct. 1672, 91
L. Ed. 1903 (1947).

[5] Flack, *The Adoption of the Fourteenth Amendment* (1908).

[6] Fairman, Does the Fourteenth Amendment Incorporate the Bill of Rights? 2
Stan. L. Rev. 5 (1949).

provided us with a comprehensive survey of the views expressed about the first and fifth clauses of the Fourteenth Amendment, when the Amendment was adopted in Congress and ratified by the States. Professor Frank has re-examined with care the genesis and contemporary understanding of the equal protection clause.[7] And Mr. Graham has given a luminous account of the early antecedents of sections 1 and 5 in the activities of the abolitionists of the mid-west in the 1830's and 1840's.[8]

From these studies, two conclusions emerge quite clearly. The first is that the anticipated enlargement of federal power was the heart of the controversy over the adoption of sections 1 and 5. A typical charge was that section 1 "consolidates everything in one imperial despotism." [9] The second is that there lay behind section 1 the high idealism of men who, believing slavery and all that it implied to be incompatible with the Christian ethic as well as the assumptions of American political life, and finding that their fellow citizens could not be won to corrective action by evangelical appeal, deliberately resolved to turn to national political power to achieve their goals. Mr. Graham's analysis shows how precisely the three-part formulation of section 1 reflects the ideas painfully ground out of the doctrinal controversies of thirty years earlier.

This review of the history clearly shows that sections 1 and 5 of the Fourteenth Amendment are not properly to be regarded with suspicion, as parts of a sordid scheme to maintain political power. Rather they represent the culmination of an idealistic effort to eliminate the degrading concomitants as well as the bare fact of chattel slavery.

This result should be achieved, if possible, without impairment of the essence of federalism; this much the whole structure of the Constitution demands. But if judicial ingenuity falters, and doctrines cannot be found which give adequate power to effectuate the goals of the Amendment without sweeping enlargement of federal power, then the historical record shows that the intent was to give whatever power was needed to accomplish

[7] Frank & Munro, The Original Understanding of "Equal Protection of the Laws," 50 Col. L. Rev. 131 (1950).

[8] Graham, The Early Antislavery Backgrounds of the Fourteenth Amendment, 1950 Wis. L. Rev. 479 & 610.

[9] Quoted in Fairman, *supra* note 6, at 49.

these goals, not to deny it altogether. There remain, of course, limits of a political character on the exercise of the power; they have proved to be far from insignificant.

In Plessy *v.* Ferguson,[10] the Supreme Court in 1896 had to consider the question whether by enforcing segregation between whites and Negroes the states were denying the equal protection assured by the Fourteenth Amendment. The heart of the Court's argument is contained in two famous sentences: "We consider the underlying fallacy of the plaintiff's argument to consist in the assumption that the enforced separation of the two races stamps the colored race with a badge of inferiority. If this be so, it is not by reason of anything found in the act, but solely because the colored race chooses to put that construction upon it." [11] Of all the ex-cathedra pronouncements on nonlegal questions by the Court, this must surely be the most unrealistic as well as the most blighting in its effect on American life. As Mr. Justice Harlan plainly saw and stated then, and as every person willing to look must see now, there can be no doubt but that segregation has been enforced as a means of subordinating the Negro.[12] Yet fifty years is not a short time, even in the life of social institutions. Judicial assumptions cannot be dislodged without giving some consideration to what has been built upon them. Certainly such considerations will be widely urged and courts will have to reckon with them.

Segregation is, of course, only one facet of the problem of how far the Fourteenth Amendment goes in the direction of assuring to minority groups in the United States full standing as human beings and citizens. One related development that cannot pass without notice is the recent decision of the Court of Appeals for the Ninth Circuit that the Federal Government has the power to protect against private invasion the right of persons to assemble to consider questions of national concern.[13] This holding merely honors the promise made 75 years ago in the dictum of the Cruikshank case.[14] The dissenting opinion raises

---

[10] 163 U.S. 537, 16 Sup. Ct. 1138, 41 L. Ed. 256 (1896).

[11] *Id.* at 551.

[12] Myrdal, *An American Dilemma* 575, 581–85 (1944).

[13] Hardyman *v.* Collins, 183 F.2d 308 (9th Cir. 1950), 4 Vand. L. Rev. 166, *cert. granted,* 340 U.S. 809 (1950).

[14] United States *v.* Cruikshank, 92 U.S. 542, 23. L. Ed. 588 (1875).

questions of statutory construction rather than constitutional doubts about this degree of encroachment upon state freedom. Presumably the Supreme Court has granted review in order to settle the construction of an important and rather obscurely worded statute. It would be rather a shock to find that the Federal Government lacked the power to protect its citizens in the discharge of their duties of citizenship, when hostile local sentiment led to a failure of police protection.[15] The possibility of federal intervention in this type of situation would seem calculated to awaken rather than to deaden local incentive to protect unpopular groups in their lawful public activities.

A second recent development that has bearing on the segregation problem is the firm establishment of the doctrine that the Fourteenth Amendment applies to state officials even when their improper action is unauthorized or forbidden by state law. The explicit holding to this effect in the Screws case [16] has crystallized in a growing number of lower court decisions.[17] The application of this doctrine, like the one mentioned above, involves an intrusion by the Federal Government into an area normally regarded as belonging to the states and their citizens exclusively. The result is surely in harmony with the spirit of the Fourteenth Amendment, and the most that can be said against the result is that it is possible to read the letter of the Amendment the other way.

A third and closely related development is the holding of the voting cases [18] that the Fifteenth Amendment is invoked when what is clearly a governmental function is being performed, despite efforts to strip the acting agency of all formal vestiges of

[15] A recent episode of similar character was the disturbance at Peekskill, New York, August 27 and September 4, 1949. See *Violence in Peekskill* (1950), a report of the American Civil Liberties Union. The complaint in an action growing out of these events was sustained in Robeson *v.* Fanelli, 94 F. Supp. 62 (S.D.N.Y. 1950).

[16] Screws *v.* United States, 325 U.S. 91, 65 Sup. Ct. 1031, 89 L. Ed. 1495 (1945).

[17] See, e.g., Brandhove *v.* Tenney, 183 F.2d 121 (9th Cir. 1950), *cert. granted,* 340 U.S. 903 (1950); Campo *v.* Niemeyer, 182 F.2d 115 (7th Cir. 1950); Williams *v.* United States, 179 F.2d 644 and 656 (5th Cir. 1950); *cert. granted* 340 U.S. 850 (1950); McShane *v.* Moldovan, 172 F.2d 1016 (6th Cir. 1949); Burt *v.* New York, 156 F.2d 791 (2d Cir. 1946); Picking *v.* Pennsylvania R.R., 151 F.2d 240 (3rd Cir. 1945).

[18] Smith *v.* Allwright, 321 U.S. 649, 64 Sup. Ct. 757, 88 L. Ed. 987 (1944); Rice *v.* Elmore, 165 F.2d 387 (4th Cir. 1947), *cert. denied,* 333 U.S. 875 (1948), 1 Vand. L. Rev. 645.

state authority.[19] An unresolved issue is the application of this doctrine when the function is not strictly a governmental one, but is being performed through the joint efforts of public and private groups. A state may not, it seems clear, bar Negroes from a housing project which it has constructed, any more than it could bar Negroes by ordinance from portions of the residential land.[20] But may a privately financed residential project which would have been impossible of accomplishment without substantial state assistance bar Negroes? The New York Court of Appeals said yes, in a case in which a privately owned $90 million redevelopment project was made possible by the action of New York City in exercising the condemnation power to assemble the plot, in closing certain streets, and in granting a 25-year tax exemption on the enhanced value of the property.[21] Three of the seven judges argued powerfully that the answer should be no. The case authorities are meagre, naturally, because the undertaking is of a novel character. Yet the issues are vital. Redevelopment laws are on the books of 25 states. If our cities are to be remade on a grand scale, in a pattern which will endure for several generations, it would be a major calamity for segregation in housing to be frozen into the pattern. The argument has been that private enterprise must be encouraged if redevelopment is to become a fact. The conclusive answer is that too high a price can be paid for enlisting private enterprise, and that if private enterprise wants to exploit opportunities for which it needs extensive public aid, it must forego its prejudices and accept aid on terms that the public itself would have to meet.[22] The failure of the Supreme Court to review the case would be disturbing if it were not that the broad issue was clouded by the fact that after extended discussion at an earlier stage between New York City and the builder it had been the City's deliberate decision not to demand a nondiscrimination clause in the agreement.

In education, as in housing, the limitations on official state

---

[19] Cf. Marsh v. Alabama, 326 U.S. 501, 66 Sup. Ct. 276, 90 L. Ed. 265 (1946).

[20] Buchanan v. Warley, 245 U.S. 60, 38 Sup. Ct. 16, 62 L. Ed. 149 (1917); cf. Shelley v. Kraemer, 334 U.S. 1, 68 Sup. Ct. 836, 92 L. Ed. 1161 (1948); Birmingham v. Monk, 185 F.2d 859 (5th Cir. 1950).

[21] Dorsey v. Stuyvesant Town Corp., 299 N.Y. 512, 87 N.E.2d 541 (1949), *cert. denied*, 339 U.S. 981 (1950).

[22] Cf. Abrams, "Stuyvesant Town's Threat to Our Liberties," 8 *Commentary* 426 (Nov. 1949).

action are sharply in dispute at the present time. Professor Frank's study disclosed that when the Fourteenth Amendment was adopted there was a substantial cleavage in opinion as to whether or not the equal protection sought to be guaranteed would exclude racial segregation in education.[23] There was at least strong opinion that it should. And there can be no doubt that unsegregated education, like other experiences in living, working and playing, could contribute greatly to the breakdown of the divisive group attitudes that poison so much of American life today. Yet courts as conscious agencies of social control cannot ignore the force of entrenched patterns of behaviour, hallowed by judicial pronouncements of venerable weight. In the light of present knowledge about society it cannot be doubted that segregated education is incompatible with the kind of equal protection the Fourteenth Amendment sought to provide. But an abrupt and complete outlawing of segregated education might be thought by the Supreme Court to create too violent resistance to be a wise policy, particularly so soon after the first, belated beginnings of the enforcement of the Negro right to vote and of legal pressure on segregation in certain areas.[24]

In Sweatt *v.* Painter [25] and McLaurin *v.* Oklahoma State Regents [26] the Supreme Court was invited to repudiate forthrightly the untenable dictum of Plessy. It did not do so, but elected rather to particularize the inherent lack of equality in segregated education at the professional level.[27] Analogous rea-

---

[23] Frank & Munro, The Original Understanding of "Equal Protection of the Laws," 50 Col. L. Rev. 131 (1950).

[24] Among the more adequate law review discussions of segregation in education, see Notes, 49 Col. L. Rev. 629 (1949), 17 Geo. Wash. L. Rev. 208 (1949), 3 U. of Fla. L. Rev. 358 (1950).

[25] 339 U.S. 629, 70 Sup. Ct. 848, 94 L. Ed. 1114 (1950).

[26] 339 U.S. 637, 70 Sup. Ct. 851, 94 L. Ed. 1149 (1950). And see the earlier Supreme Court cases of Missouri ex rel. Gaines *v.* Canada, 305 U.S. 337, 59 Sup. Ct. 232, 83 L. Ed. 208 (1938); Sipuel *v.* University of Oklahoma, 332 U.S. 631, 68 Sup. Ct. 299, 92 L. Ed. 247 (1948); Fisher *v.* Hurst, 333 U.S. 147, 68 Sup. Ct. 389, 92 L. Ed. 604 (1948).

[27] Among recent lower federal cases and state cases with similar holdings, see Wilson *v.* Board of Supervisors, 92 F. Supp. 986 (E.D. La. 1950); Swanson *v.* Rector and Visitors of University of Virginia, U.S.D.C., W.D. Va., Sept. 5, 1950, noted in 36 Va. L. Rev. 797 (1950); Johnson *v.* Board of Trustees, 83 F. Supp. 707 (E.D. Ky. 1949); University of Maryland *v.* Murray, 169 Md. 478, 182 Atl. 590, 103 A.L.R. 706 (1936); cf. Epps *v.* Carmichael, 93 F. Supp. 327 (M.D.N.C. 1950); State ex rel. Hawkins *v.* Board of Control, 47 So. 2d 608 (Fla. 1950).

soning could be employed to produce the same result at each level of the educational process. And it is not easy to resist the force of the analogy. Yet the Court may feel that distinctions which can be drawn achieve validity, if not from logic, then from the differing impact on established patterns of behaviour and the probable differing degrees of resistance. Certainly if the Court is to apply the analogies all the way down to and including primary education, the path will have to be smoothed by a convincing sociological showing that the common expectation as to the depth of resistance is ill-founded.

Even if the Court is unwilling to go all the way, there is an argument, particularly difficult to answer, against segregation in vocational high schools. The relationship between such schools and employers would seem to be so close as to require the conclusion that, as with law students, segregation in education precludes equal preparation and opportunity for work. If this conclusion is correct, the status of the segregated state college becomes unclear, even assuming that equality of staff can be established.[28] A possible distinction would be whether or not the college offers primarily vocational or cultural training. If the distinction seemed too thin, all secondary and higher education might be found to be too closely tied in with working opportunities to permit segregation. That would still leave primary education untouched. And it is likely that the resistance to enforced association would be at its greatest in just that area.

However the Court finally chooses among the available paths, it is certain that economic pressure is going to be increasingly exerted against segregation. Dual school systems are expensive if neither can be neglected. And courts everywhere are making continued neglect of the Negro school systems impossible. Unequal salary scales have been found to be unjustifiably discriminatory [29] and corrective action ordered, although in a Georgia

---

[28] In Parker *v.* University of Delaware, 75 A.2d 225 (Del. Ch. 1950), the undergraduate facilities of the University of Delaware and Delaware State College were found not to be equal, and admittance to the University was ordered. In State ex rel. Tolliver *v.* Board of Education, 230 S.W.2d 724 (Mo. 1950), Negro and white state teachers' colleges were held to provide substantially equal facilities. Cf. State ex rel. Hawkins *v.* Board of Control, 47 So. 2d 608 (Fla. 1950), and companion cases.

[29] Freeman *v.* County School Board, 82 F. Supp. 167 (E.D. Va. 1948) *aff'd mem.*, 171 F.2d 702 (4th Cir. 1948); cf. Whitmyer *v.* Lincoln Parish School Board, 75 F. Supp. 686 (W.D. La. 1948).

case federal court relief was held to have been improvidently granted because of failure to exhaust state administrative remedies.[30] The Court of Appeals for the Fourth Circuit has required the correction of curricular deficiencies and facilities for extracurricular work.[31] Federal district courts in Arkansas and Texas have taken similar action.[32] It may be justifiable to allow a certain amount of time to achieve equality.[33] But there is no justification for Judge Atwell's conclusion that additional courses are not to be required for the Negro school unless there are as many as ten students for each class.[34] Two school systems are likely to be uneconomical at best; they become a real luxury where the Negro population is very small. But if curricular opportunities are to be equal, as they clearly must be, this becomes a part of the necessary cost of segregation. Could white children then complain that their facilities were unequal because of the larger classes? There would seem to be no logical answer to such a complaint, if it should be presented for judicial consideration.

Apart from the economic pressure exerted by an honest insistence on equality, the application of the "separate but equal" doctrine to schools raises a difficult theoretical problem. In his dissent in the District of Columbia case, Judge Edgerton argued forcefully that equality is impossible of achievement as long as there is segregation.[35] His premise was the unassailable one that the equality guaranteed by the Constitution is individual equality.

[30] Cook v. Davis, 178, F.2d 595 (5th Cir. 1949) *cert. denied*, 340 U.S. 811 (1950); cf. East Coast Lumber Terminal v. Babylon, 174 F.2d 106 (2d Cir. 1949).

[31] Carter v. School Board, 182 F.2d 531 (4th Cir. 1950); Corbin v. County School Board, 177 F.2d 924 (4th Cir. 1949).

[32] Butler v. Wilemon, 86 F. Supp. 397 (N.D. Tex. 1949); Pitts v. Board of Trustees, 84 F. Supp. 975 (E.D. Ark. 1949). But not all suits have been successful. See Carr v. Corning, 182 F.2d 14 (D.C. Cir. 1950).

[33] Cf. Missouri ex rel. Gaines v. Canada, 305 U.S. 337, 351–52, 59 Sup. Ct. 232, 83 L. Ed. 208 (1938); Pitts v. Board of Trustees, 84 F. Supp. 975 (E.D. Ark. 1949); Wrighten v. Board of Trustees, 72 F. Supp. 948 (E.D.S.C. 1947).

[34] Butler v. Wilemon, 86 F. Supp. 397 (N.D. Tex. 1949); see McCabe v. Atchison, T. & S.F.R.R., 235 U.S. 151, 35 Sup. Ct. 69, 59 L. Ed. 169 (1914). In Brown v. Ramsey, 185 F.2d 225 (8th Cir. 1950), the court stated that instruction offered in the white schools had to be available to qualified Negro students, however few. But the court held that none of the plaintiffs had standing to raise this point. In State ex rel. Brewton v. Board of Education, 233 S.W.2d 697 (Mo. 1950), a Negro high school student not offered a course in aeromechanics in his high school was held entitled to admission to the white high school.

[35] Carr v. Corning, 182 F.2d 14, 22, 32-33 (D.C. Cir. 1950); *cf.* Mendez v. Westminster School District, 64 F. Supp. 544 (S.D. Cal. 1946), *aff'd on other grounds*, 161 F.2d 774 (9th Cir. 1947).

This proposition underlies the holding in Shelley *v.* Kraemer.[36] The Fourth Circuit Court of Appeals has also stressed that since the protected rights are individual and personal, compliance with the constitutional requirement cannot be established by averaging facilities throughout the community.[37]

Since the Constitution requires individual equality, the question arises as to the standard for determining equality: against whom is a given child to be measured? Presumably against the actual or hypothetical child similarly situated in respects relevant to school attendance such as age, ability and previous education. If the hypothetical child, being white, would have better facilities than the child in question, it would seem that there is a denial of equal protection. If the range of Negro schools is equal to the range of white schools, then, on the facts thus far stated, the white child does not have better facilities.[38] But if the factor of residential location is added to the elements being considered, the problem changes. Then individual equality is denied so long as the white child in the same area has better school facilities. But if the Negro and white schools in the same area are substantially equal, it would seem to be immaterial that white schools elsewhere are superior. Since segregated patterns of dwelling are still the fact, this conclusion would seem to permit inferior schools for Negroes. On the other hand, if the over-all school facilities for the two groups must be equal, improvement in Negro school facilities would seem to be a more likely consequence.

These problems did not confront the Supreme Court in the Shelley and Sweatt cases when they declared that the right to equal facilities was an individual one. In the Shelley case, the asserted equality lay not in the availability of accommodations equal to those being purchased, but merely equality in legal

---

[36] 334 U.S. 1, 68 Sup. Ct. 836, 92 L. Ed. 1161 (1948), 2 Vand. L. Rev. 119.

[37] Corbin *v.* County School Board, 177 F.2d 924 (4th Cir. 1949).

[38] If all white schools in a community were identical, the test of the equality of Negro schools would be the same on an individual or an averaging basis. But it is assumed that the quality of white schools in any large urban community varies considerably. Proof that this variation was the result of a deliberate practice of favoring the more well-to-do segments of the community would presumably support a claim of denial of equal protection. But the burden of proof would seem to be insurmountable; hence the determination of the equality of the Negro schools is considered in the light of the stated assumption that white schools do vary.

opportunity similarly to exclude others. In the Sweatt case, as in the Canada case,[39] the issue involved the adequacy of facilities considered on a state-wide basis, without reference to the residential location of applicants. Considering these elements of difference, the Court may define the required equality in educational facilities in terms of the facilities available in the community as a whole.[40]

A very similar problem is involved in the question of Negro access to public recreational facilities. In Lopez v. Seccombe,[41] the federal district court in California merely enjoined discriminatory exclusion of Mexicans from the San Bernardino swimming pool. There was no suggestion of other facilities being available. In a case recently arising in Baltimore, the Court of Appeals for the Fourth Circuit affirmed the dismissal of an action against city officials grounded upon segregation of athletic activities in the city's public parks and playgrounds. The petitioners there refrained from contending that equal facilities were not offered.[42] A district court recently issued an injunction against the exclusion of Negroes from the sole municipally-operated swimming pool.[43] The court rejected as unsound the argument of the city that a proposal to build a swimming pool in the Negro section of the city at some future time was a present answer to petitioners' assertion of their constitutional rights.

Thus far the problem is relatively simple; it is like the school situation considered on a city-wide basis. Complications arise

---

[39] Missouri ex rel. Gaines v. Canada, 305 U.S. 337, 59 Sup. Ct. 232, 83 L. Ed. 208 (1938).

[40] It has been held that a plan for regional education does not meet the requirements of equal protection even though the out-of-state regional school is superior to the state school. McCready v. Byrd, 73 A.2d 8 (Md. 1950) cert. denied, 340 U.S. 827 (1950); see Notes, 1 Vand. L. Rev. 403 (1948), 13 Mo. L. Rev. 286 (1948); cf. Missouri ex rel. Gaines v. Canada, 305 U.S. 337, 59 Sup. Ct. 232, 93 L. Ed. 208 (1938).

On the right of educational institutions not publicly owned, to exclude Negroes, and the effect of state contributions, compare Kerr v. Enoch Pratt Free Library, 149 F.2d 212 (4th Cir. 1945), cert. denied, 326 U.S. 721 (1945), with Norris v. Mayor and City Council of Baltimore, 78 F. Supp. 451 (D. Md. 1948).

[41] 71 F. Supp. 769 (S.D. Cal. 1944).

[42] Boyer v. Garrett, 183 F.2d 582 (4th Cir. 1950); cf. Winkler v. Maryland, 69 A.2d 674 (Md. 1949), cert. denied, 339 U.S. 919 (1950). See Harper & Rosenthal, What the Supreme Court Did Not Do in the 1949 Term—An Appraisal of Certiorari, 99 U. of Pa. L. Rev. 293, 310 (1950).

[43] Draper v. St. Louis, 92 F. Supp. 546 (E.D. Mo. 1950); cf. Lawrence v. Hancock, 76 F. Supp. 1004 (S.D. W. Va. 1948).

when the single facility is offered exclusively for the use of
different groups at different hours of the day and on different
days of the week. This solution was suggested by a district
court in upholding the arrangements for Baltimore's municipal
golf course [44] and, as adopted by the city of Miami, was upheld
by the Florida Supreme Court.[45] The United States Supreme
Court has recently told the Florida Supreme Court to re-examine
the question in the light of McLaurin.[46] No doubt individual
equality is not achieved by temporal segregation if the time in-
tervals are substantial. As they become less substantial, the discrimination approaches the trivial, as, for example, in the case of
tennis courts available to the two races on alternate hours. It is
not trivial in the Florida case, where proportionate demand by
the two races was the ostensible test, resulting, at the time of the
suit, in Negroes being allowed to use the golf course one day
a week, whites, six days. Time is certainly a factor in considering
the availability of accommodations, and where the discrepancy
is as great as here, Negroes as a class simply do not have equal facilities for golfing. The Florida court's suggestion that the system
was self-correcting because increased demand by Negroes would
increase the number of days allotted to them seems unrealistic,
because Negroes may not be in a position to make their demands
known by putting in an appearance on the prescribed day.

The obvious next question is what happens when equal facilities are offered, but at places substantially separated in space. In
the St. Louis swimming pool case, the district judge said, referring to the proposed future swimming pool for Negroes: "Even
when completed such a pool may mitigate discrimination, but it
will not validate it as to other sections of the City." [47] Assuming
the pools to be physically equal, or substantially so, any Negro has
the same opportunity that any white has to go swimming. But if
the factor of residence location is included, and if transportation
time be regarded as a material factor in considering the availability of facilities, then Negroes near the white swimming pool are

[44] Law *v.* Baltimore, 78 F. Supp. 346 (D. Md. 1950).
[45] Rice *v.* Arnold, 45 So. 2d 195 (Fla. 1950), *cert. granted,* 340 U.S. 848 (1950).
[46] In taking certiorari, the Court remanded the case to the Florida Supreme
Court "for reconsideration in the light of subsequent decisions of this Court," in
Sweatt and McLaurin. 340 U.S. 848.
[47] Draper *v.* St. Louis, 92 F. Supp. 546, 550 (E.D. Mo. 1950).

discriminated against, as are whites near the Negro swimming pool. One answer is to say that transportation is not a material factor. That answer is hardly honest, at least for the cases in which the travel time is very great. Suppose, then, the Negro swimming pool were put near the white one. This element of difference would disappear; equality would be achieved at the expense of inconvenience for the Negroes. Here, as in the case of school facilities, if segregation continues to be allowed in theory, it might be wiser to make the determination of substantial equality without reference to the residential location of individual persons entitled to use the facilities. If the average equivalence test is used, then facilities for Negroes would apparently have to be located in somewhat the same relationship to the center of Negro population that the white facilities bear to the white center of population.

These complexities emphasize the inherent defects of the proposition that segregated facilities can be equal. But unless the Court is ready to reject the proposition directly, it is not likely to permit itself to be driven to that result by logical extension of the ruling that the protected constitutional rights are individual rights. And to press the logic of the ruling too far may only result in hindering the effort to achieve practical equality.[48]

Thus far, the problems discussed have involved some immediate action by, or attributed to, the state which establishes the discrimination. At least as significant are those cases in which the attempt to discriminate is made without compulsion of state law by a person who is not an official of the state. Private discrimination in the form of exclusion of individuals on grounds of race or color results, of course, in segregation. And such segregation does not automatically assure equal facilities for the excluded groups. The problem might be described as that of state enforcement of private discrimination. It was apparently put at rest by the declaration in the Civil Right Cases,[49] that discrimination by private individuals was beyond the reach of the Fourteenth Amendment. But Shelley *v.* Kraemer reopened

---

[48] If Myrdal is correct in believing that segregation is in large measure a device for effecting discrimination (*An American Dilemma* Chap. 28), strong pressure to force equality should have a basic corrective result.

[49] 109 U.S. 3, 3 Sup. Ct. 18, 27 L. Ed. 835 (1883).

the problem by holding that state courts may not issue an injunction to support uncompelled contractual undertakings not to allow real estate to be sold to or occupied by Negroes. The result was hard to avoid in the face of the well-settled determination that states or their subdivisions were not permitted by legislation to prevent Negroes from living in certain areas. The decision does raise, however, the broad question whether all private acts of discrimination, depending as they ultimately do, upon the sanction of the state, are not forbidden by the Fourteenth Amendment. Professor Hale in two notable articles pursued this analysis to its ultimate conclusion.[50] Perhaps his thesis may be summed up in the proposition that in civilized society any exercise of rights of property or contract is possible only to the extent that the force of society stands ready to make them effective. Professor Hale's only suggestion for a limiting factor was that the subject matter of the action should be a matter of "high public interest." [51] But if the viewpoint is taken that racial discrimination is inherently evil, contributing to a malignant growth in our society, then every act of discrimination would seem to be a matter of high public concern.

Several recent cases touch upon this issue. One was before the Court of Appeals for the Sixth Circuit—Whiteside *v.* Southern Bus Lines.[52] A Negro passenger on an interstate bus trip was asked, when the bus came into Kentucky, to move from a front seat to a rear seat. Upon her refusal to comply, the bus driver called a policeman, who put her off. She instituted a common law action for damages to her person and her property. The court of appeals reversed the district court's dismissal of the complaint. The grounds of decision are not too clear. Reliance was placed on the commerce clause, although no state or local law required the bus company to segregate its passengers. The Court observed that no state action was necessary to invalidate

---

[50] Hale, Force and the State: A Comparison of "Political" and "Economic" Compulsion, 35 Col. L. Rev. 149 (1935); Hale, Rights under the Fourteenth and Fifteenth Amendments against Injuries Inflicted by Private Individuals, 6 Law Guild Rev. 627 (1946).

[51] Hale, Rights under the Fourteenth and Fifteenth Amendments against Injuries Inflicted by Private Individuals, 6 Law Guild Rev. 627, 630 (1946), taking the phrase from Mr. Justice Cardozo in Nixon *v.* Condon, 286 U.S. 73, 88, 52 Sup. Ct. 484, 76 L. Ed. 984 (1932).

[52] 177 F.2d 949 (6th Cir. 1949).

conduct which burdened interstate commerce. But the court went on to observe that if state action were required, it was to be found in the participation of the policeman.[53] The interesting point is the suggestion that forbidden state action might be involved in the assistance furnished by the policeman. What is true of public transportation vehicles should be true of all places of public resort. If a theatre owner calls a policeman to eject a Negro who has succeeded in entering the theatre against the wishes of the proprietor, are the policeman and proprietor liable in an action of trespass? The presence of a state statute or local ordinance barring Negroes from white theatres would be forbidden state action. In the absence of such a law, the justification for the assault upon the Negro would be the privilege of the property owner to exclude from his premises those whom he chose to exclude. That privilege, of course, is state-conferred. Is it, then, prohibited state action?

The Third Circuit case of Valle *v.* Stengel[54] also comes very close to presenting the question squarely. A group of Negroes and whites had gone into Palisades Amusement Park in New Jersey. Several of them had tickets for the swimming pool. When the rest sought to get tickets, the attendant refused to sell them to the Negroes. Those Negroes who did have tickets were nevertheless denied access to the pool. An argument ensued which was terminated by the eviction of the patrons by the local chief of police, who had been summoned by the management. Suit was brought under various provisions of the Civil Rights Acts and the court of appeals held the action well-founded. Various grounds were relied on. Reference was made to the rarely invoked provisions forbidding interference with the rights of person to make and enforce contracts.[55] But these provisions would seem to have been intended to penalize third persons who prevent the making and enforcing of contracts between willing parties, rather than, as here, to penalize unwilling parties for refusing to make or perform contracts with Negroes. A similar comment may be made as to the claim that denial of admission to the

---

[53] A contrary result was reached by the Fourth Circuit Court of Appeals in Day *v.* Atlantic Greyhound Corp., 171 F.2d 59 (1948).

[54] 176 F.2d 697 (3d Cir. 1949).

[55] Rev. Stat. § 1977 (1875), 8 U.S.C.A. § 41 (1942).

swimming pool, upon presentation of a ticket already purchased, was a denial of the right to lease or hold real or personal property, also protected by the statute.[56]

An additional argument relied upon by the court of appeals was that the defendants acted under color of law to deny the privileges and immunitites conferred by the Constitution.[57] Plaintiffs were residents of New York, and thereby of the United States. By New Jersey law, all persons within the jurisdiction are entitled to equal accommodations and privileges at any place of public amusement. Since any citizen of New Jersey was entitled to use the swimming pool, the court reasoned, plaintiffs, as citizens of the United States, were also entitled to use it. Denial of that right by the police chief was therefore a denial, under color of state law, of civil rights guaranteed to the plaintiffs by the Fourteenth Amendment. The corporate defendant and its managers were retained as parties defendant, one judge dissenting, on the ground that evidence might support the allegation that they had caused the unlawful acts of the official. This ground of decision seems somewhat questionable if it be assumed, as was probably the fact, that Negro citizens of New Jersey as well as of other states were being denied access to the swimming pool.

Another basis for the decision may be suggested. If the law of the state barred Negroes, clearly there would have been a denial of equal protection. Normally, in the absence of such a law, the holding of the Civil Rights Cases would appear to preclude federal action against a private landowner who discriminates against Negroes in allowing entrance upon and the use of his property. Normally, also, official assistance may be invoked by the landowner, without transgressing the Fourteenth Amendment, to effectuate his determination thus to exclude. But in the present situation that privilege of exclusion had been curtailed: the effect of New Jersey's civil rights law was to prevent operators of places of public amusement from discriminating against Negroes. Lacking the sanction derived from the existence of the privilege of the property owner, the action of the police chief

---

[56] Rev. Stat. § 1978 (1875), 8 U.S.C.A. § 42 (1942).

[57] "The Citizens of each State shall be entitled to all Privileges and Immunities of Citizens in the several States." U.S. Const. Art. IV, 2.

becomes an arbitrary interference under color of state law with the exercise of equal rights.

The line of argument gives only limited scope for the invocation of federal assistance against discrimination motivated solely by the desires of the private owner. Generally, if there are civil rights statutes in force in the state, they will afford protection and redress if it is desired. But the broader basis for intervention is also hinted at in the eighth circuit case of Watkins v. Oaklawn Jockey Club.[58] There the operator of a race track hired the local sheriff to escort Mr. Watkins from the premises, should he venture to appear. When he did appear, after duly purchasing a ticket, he was escorted out by the sheriff. No question of color was involved. The proprietor apparently had a personal dislike of Watkins' conduct. Watkins sued the club for damages for false arrest and false imprisonment and the deprivation of federally protected rights. The complaint was dismissed after trial on the ground that there was no substantial evidence to support a finding that the sheriff and his assistants, in ejecting the plaintiff, were acting in an official capacity. Rather, it was concluded, they were shown to have been acting only as agents of the club, using reasonable means to evict a person whose license to be there had been revoked by the owner of the premises. The court of appeals affirmed on these grounds.

Currently accepted doctrine certainly casts no doubt on the correctness of the result. The interesting aspect of the case is the narrow ground of decision, with the implication that perhaps the result might have been different if the sheriff and his assistants had been acting in their official capacity when they removed Watkins at the request of the operator of the race track. Unlike the Valle situation, the present one does not involve any state law limiting the privilege of the landowner to exclude. Is it the ultimate implication of the Shelley case that a landowner in the last analysis owes to the state any effective right he may have to exclude unwanted persons from his property and, therefore, any official action which supports such exclusion is within the reach of the Fourteenth Amendment? If so, and if the policeman had been acting in an official capacity, he and the race track

---

[58] 183 F.2d 440 (8th Cir. 1950).

operator would have been subject to suit under whatever of the civil rights statutes might be construed to fit, or in a common law action in which the obvious defenses would be disallowed as unconstitutional.

This conclusion, of course, would appear to upset the long-repeated pronouncement of the Civil Rights Cases that the Fourteenth Amendment has nothing to do with private acts of discrimination.

Before re-examining the Civil Rights Cases, it may be appropriate to see if there is any earlier stopping point to the holding of the Shelley case. A possible argument is that the case merely prohibits the use of the injunction to support private discrimination; that an injunction, being such a unique and powerful form of judicial intervention, has a special character, akin to legislation. This suggestion is not very persuasive. What an injunction does is exert state judicial power in a particular way to induce a contracting party to discharge his obligations. Whether or not an action for damages for breach of contract would be an equally effective persuader would depend upon a variety of factors. Such an action could be most effective in the particular kind of situation here under consideration. A landowner contemplating the sale of real estate to Negroes in violation of a restrictive covenant might well be deterred by the threat of multiple suits by cocovenantors. There may be some legal difficulties in the way of proving damages. But that would be rather meagre comfort, particularly in a community in which judge and jury could be expected to be hostile to the seller. In the light of the practical problem involved, the distinction between state coercion in the form of an injunction and state coercion in the form of damage actions seems too trivial to hold. The Missouri Supreme Court thought it would.[59] But Judge Holtzoff, in the District of Columbia, seems to have been clearly right in rejecting the distinction. He stated the holding of the Shelley case to be "that it was contrary to the Fourteenth and Fifteenth Amendments to the Constitution and contrary to public policy to aid in the enforcement of such covenants by judicial proceedings."[60]

Judicial enforcement of contractual obligations to discrimi-

---

[59] Weiss *v.* Leaon, 225 S.W.2d 127 (Mo. 1949).
[60] Roberts *v.* Curtis, 93 F. Supp. 604 (D.D.C. 1950).

nate in ways that would be prohibited by the Fourteenth Amendment if required by legislation seems to be banned. The principle might be restated as follows: states are prohibited by the Fourteenth Amendment from compelling private individuals to discriminate, irrespective of whether the obligation to discriminate is imposed by a legislative command or is voluntarily assumed by entering into a contract. In the latter case, of course, individual contract rights are frustrated. But the rights frustrated are somewhat remote: the person most directly involved is seeking to escape a restraint on his own freedom of action.

This principle is a plausible one upon which to stand in attempting to delimit the implications of the Shelley case. But even if plausible, there is the question of whether it goes far enough to serve the purposes of the Fourteenth Amendment. But there are other plausible stopping points, short of a ban upon all private discrimination, which would give greater scope to the Amendment without excessive impairment of the principles of federalism.

Deserving of examination in this connection is the proposition that the failure by the state to bar discrimination is state action denying the equal protection of the laws. That state inaction is properly to be regarded as state action under some circumstances is not a novel idea.[61] By general acceptance the kind of federal antilynching legislation least vulnerable to constitutional attack is the assessment of penalties against local officials and communities by whose connivance or neglect lynchings occur.[62] In international law the responsibility of a state for injuries to persons or property as a result of the inaction of the state and its agencies has long been recognized. Professor Hyde has stated that in presenting claims against foreign states the United States "has correctly asserted that when any agency of a territorial sovereign either wantonly or passively fails to use the means at its disposal to prevent violence or to prosecute the perpetrators, a delinquency in an international sense is apparent and responsibility for the consequences of the action of the mob comes into being. . . ."[63] And Professor Frank has shown that the members of

---

[61] Cf. Catlette *v.* United States, 152 F.2d 902, 907 (4th Cir. 1943).

[62] See Notes, 47 Mich. L. Rev. 369 (1949), 57 Yale L.J. 855 (1948).

[63] 2 Hyde, *International Law Chiefly as Interpreted and Applied by the United States* 951 (2d ed. 1947).

Congress in 1871 believed that a state denied equal protection of the laws when it permitted widespread abuses against them because of their color.[64]

We are here concerned with something more than failure to protect against violence to person or property. But the concept of equal protection of the laws involves more. It may be thought to involve the right to be protected against arbitrary restrictions, like those based on color, wherever the power of the state reaches. This would mean that a state denied equal protection to the extent that, in the face of actual discrimination, it failed to exercise available legislative power to correct it. The Fourteenth Amendment would then be flouted by a state's failure to pass laws prohibiting discrimination in private employment, private schools, perhaps private rental housing, and all places of public accommodation.[65] The measure of the state's obligation would simply be the limits of its power under due process to prohibit discrimination. Presumably under this limitation it would still be permissible for a home-owner to exclude all of his Negro acquaintances from a garden party. But it would not be permissible to exclude Negroes as such from private rental housing, schools and employment. In these areas self-enforcement of the equal protection clause by invalidation of defenses in trespass actions would not be feasible since contractual understandings must be arrived at. An unwanted seeker of employment removed from the premises of the employer would hardly be able to overcome the property owner's defense of his privilege by pleading discriminatory denial of the chance to become an employee. If this analysis were accepted, therefore, it would seem to provide at most a basis for federal legislation.

Such a broad extension of the area to which the concept of equal protection applies is obviously open to attack. It hardly fell within the contemplation of the draftsmen that the owner of rental real estate would be prohibited, by force of the Amendment, from selecting and rejecting tenants on any basis, however arbitrary.

---

[64] Frank & Munro, The Original Understanding of "Equal Protection of the Laws," 50 Col. L. Rev. 131, 165 (1950).

[65] State civil rights laws are collected in Konvitz, *The Constitution and Civil Rights* (1947).

It is not so easy to brush aside the suggestion that the equal protection of the laws means the right to be free of restrictions upon access to places of public resort. The proprietor who selects individually those with whom he will deal is in a quite different position from the proprietor who throws open his doors to the public at large. The latter would seem to have foregone his right to pick and choose by deliberately seeking the more extensive patronage which will be attracted by wide-open doors. For a state to permit such a person to exclude solely on the basis of color would seem to be a denial of equal protection. Hotels, restaurants, inns, taverns, stores, theatres, places of recreation and public carriers fall within this class. Yet there is under state law a widely accepted differentiation within the class. Unless a franchise has been granted, the right of the owner arbitrarily to exclude individuals from a place thrown open to the public at large has been recognized.[66] Since the equal protection clause goes beyond discrimination on the basis of color and covers all arbitrary discrimination against individuals,[67] it is arguable that the state's infraction would exist only with respect to those enterprises which under state law are forbidden to exclude individuals on an arbitrary basis. Yet for constitutional purposes, the state distinction could reasonably be ignored, and the state's obligation measured by the broader class.

Whether the equal protection clause be construed to stand in the way of racial discrimination by enterprises which by state law are required to be available to all who present themselves, or by all places of public resort, the question of conflict with the Civil Rights Cases arises. The proposition of law announced in those cases was that the Fourteenth Amendment does not confer upon the Federal Government the power to prohibit discrimination by private persons. The holding of the case, while far from clear, is certainly less broad. Some language in the opinion of Mr. Justice Bradley states quite plainly that the effect of section 5 of the Fourteenth Amendment was merely to authorize federal legislation which would render null and void state laws which,

---

[66] See Madden *v.* Queens County Jockey Club, 296 N.Y. 249, 72 N.E.2d 697 (1947); cf. Powell *v.* Utz, 87 F. Supp. 811 (E.D. Wash. 1949); Nash *v.* Air Terminal Service, 85 F. Supp. 545 (E.D. Va. 1949).

[67] Burt *v.* New York, 156 F.2d 791 (2d Cir. 1946).

contrary to section 2, required establishments to discriminate on grounds of color.[68] Yet the decision appears to have been predicated upon the assumption that state laws did require equal access for all: "Innkeepers and public carriers, by the laws of all the States, so far as we are aware, are bound, to the extent of their facilities, to furnish proper accommodations to all unobjectionable persons who in good faith apply for them." [69] Bradley then continued with the observation that if the state laws themselves made any unjust discrimination, Congress had power to afford a remedy. Elsewhere, assuming that admission to a public place is the right of all classes of men, he asked, "is the Constitution violated until the denial of the right has some State sanction or authority?" [70] Again, in the famous passage declaring that the Amendment was intended only to remedy a denial of rights, "for which the States alone were or could be responsible," Bradley stated: "civil rights . . . cannot be impaired by the wrongful acts of individuals unsupported by State authority. . . . [R]ights remain in full force and may presumably be vindicated by resort to the laws of the State. . . ." [71] It appears, therefore, that he did not address himself to the question here being considered, as to the situation in the absence of state legislation. What Bradley appeared to fear most was the Federal Government's taking over the job of enforcing all rights of every character, irrespective of their recognition or enforcement by the states; an entire machinery superimposed on, and largely superseding, that of the states. The statute was stricken down because it "applies equally to cases arising in States which have the justest laws respecting the personal rights of citizens and whose authorities are ever ready to enforce such laws, and to those which arise in States that may have violated the prohibition of the Amendment." [72]

The Civil Rights Cases may continue to stand for the proposition that general federal action is not authorized to prohibit pri-

---

[68] Civil Rights Cases, 109 U.S. 3, 11, 13, 3 Sup. Ct. 18, 27 L. Ed. 835 (1883).
[69] *Id.* at 25. Bradley did not refer to the status of theatres, which were involved in one of the cases.
[70] *Id.* at 24.
[71] *Id.* at 17.
[72] *Id.* at 14.

vate persons from discriminating on the ground of color. The decision does not appear to stand in the way of federal legislation limited to those states where color is a tolerated basis of exclusion from places traditionally open to the public at large.

No attempt seems to have been made to explore the way in which such federal legislation might be appropriately limited in scope to meet the objections explicitly raised in the opinion. Granted that a need for federal action must be shown, how is it to be shown? Would a congressional finding, not wholly devoid of plausibility, suffice? Or would the Court, because of the issues of federalism at stake, insist upon the closer scrutiny usually given to legislation restricting civil rights? Assuming a need in some states, how is the application of the statute to be limited to those states? These questions should be examined further. The recent court of appeals cases discussed above reflect a new ferment of ideas stimulated by the Screws and Shelley cases. The time has come for reconsideration of the scope of federal power to cut down discrimination in places of public resort. The foregoing discussion has the very limited purpose of suggesting avenues to be explored and suggesting that the Civil Rights Cases do not present as large an obstacle as is commonly assumed.

Sociologists have rejected the old concept, enshrined in William Graham Sumner's *Folkways*, published in 1906, that law must come from the mores, and cannot go beyond them. It is now generally accepted that legal action, within limits, can influence ways of living.[73] Dramatic demonstrations of the validity of the present concepts have been furnished by the extension of Negro suffrage in the South and by the enlargement of federal protection of bodily security under the drive of Supreme Court decisions broadening the reach of the Fourteenth and Fifteenth Amendments. Equally important are the current steps to destroy the pattern of second-class education for Negroes, whether they are to be limited to rigorous insistence on equality in educational facilities or enlarged to upset the entire concept of segregation. The commerce clause has proved an effective tool for breaking down the barriers of discrimination and segregation in interstate

---

[73] See generally, Williams, *The Reduction of Intergroup Tensions* (Soc. Sci. Res. Council Bull. 57, 1947).

transportation,[74] and it appears to be adequate for this purpose in the case of employment.[75] It has been suggested here that the possibility exists for effective action in other areas. The possibility should not be foreclosed by a return to a grudging, restrictive interpretation of the Fourteenth Amendment.

---

[74] See e.g., Henderson *v.* United States, 339 U.S. 816, 70 Sup. Ct. 843, 94 L. Ed. 1302 (1950); Morgan *v.* Virginia, 328 U.S. 373, 66 Sup. Ct. 1050, 90 L. Ed. 1317 (1946). The latest important federal case—Chance *v.* Lambeth, 186 F.2d 879 (4th Cir. 1951)—is the subject of a comment, 4 Vand. L. Rev. 689 (1951), which collects and analyzes the authorities.

[75] See Hyman, Constitutional Aspects of the Covenant, 14 Law & Contemp. Prob. 451, 475–76 (1949); Hunt, The Proposed Fair Employment Practices Act; Facts and Fallacies, 32 Va. L. Rev. 1, 3–4 (1945); Cf. Steele *v.* Louisville & N.R.R., 323 U.S. 192, 65 Sup. Ct. 226, 89 L. Ed. 173 (1944); Betts *v.* Easley, 161 Kan. 459, 169 P.2d 831 (1946).

CHAPTER TWELVE

Criminal Procedures and Judicial Control

L AYMEN ARE SOMETIMES INCLINED TO THINK OF LEGAL PROCE-
dure as a farrago of technicalities cooked up by lawyers to
obscure the obvious and perpetuate the profession. But the more
one ponders the law, the more the conviction grows that procedure lies very close to the core of justice itself. As the late Mr.
Justice Jackson observed:

Only the untaught layman or the charlatan lawyer can answer that
procedures matter not. Procedural fairness and regularity are of the
indispensable essence of liberty. Severe substantive laws can be endured if they are fairly and impartially applied. Indeed, if put to
the choice, one might well prefer to live under Soviet substantive law
applied in good faith by our common-law procedures than under
our substantive law enforced by Soviet procedural practices.
(Shaughnessy v. United States, 345 U.S. 206, 224 (1953).

John Raeburn Green's essay, which follows, is concerned
with only one of this vital subject's major aspects—the constitutional requirements for procedure in state criminal trials. But his

penetrating criticism of the recent record in this field can serve
to suggest how grave and how perplexing is the Supreme Court's
problem of supervising the legal process throughout the nation.

The trouble is, of course, that procedural questions, like most
others that reach the Court, require the adjustment of closely
competing values. Manifest though the point may seem, it is
sometimes forgotten that our legal system operates within a
fairly well-defined channel of limiting assumptions, and the cases
in which those assumptions have been directly and obviously
flouted are comparatively rare. By the time a case has worked its
way through lower appellate tribunals and has been accepted for
review by the Supreme Court, the easy questions have almost
invariably been deleted. Mr. Justice Holmes once remarked that
"hard cases" make bad law (Northern Securities Co. *v.* United
States, 193 U.S. 197, 400 [1904]). If so, our constitutional law
must be in a parlous bad state, for it is hardly an exaggeration
to say that nothing but hard cases ever get to the Supreme Court.

What makes them hard is the fact that they pit one set of
crucial values against another in a near balance, and the criminal
procedure cases illustrate this nicely. As Mr. Green points out,
the modern Court has chosen to protect against state abridgment
only those procedural rights which can be ranked, in the Court's
opinion, as "fundamental principles of liberty and justice which
lie at the base of all our civil and political institutions." Concurrently, it has devised the "fair trial rule" which prescribes that a
state trial procedure is repugnant to the Federal Constitution
only if "the totality of facts" adds up to an unfair trial. Within
these somewhat enigmatic boundaries, the states may rove as
they will. What are the competing value considerations that have
brought the Court to these much-criticized and perhaps tentative
conclusions?

At first blush, it might be said that the conflict is simply
bilateral. On the one hand we have the value of protecting the
innocent; on the other, we have society's need to suppress crime
by swift and certain punishment. The more strictly subordinate
courts are supervised, the more likely it is that the innocent will
be protected, but the more likely it also is that the guilty will
escape the hand of justice. The Supreme Court's task is to strike
a balance between these ideal objectives. But unhappily the prob-

lem is more complicated than that, and the complexity is further aggravated when we are talking about the states, rather than the federal court system.

In fact, as every student of the Constitution knows, the span of the Supreme Court's effective supervisory control is extremely limited. There are, not counting "quasi-judicial" agencies, more than 100 courts in the federal court system alone. In addition, each of the 48 states has its own judicial hierarchy. It would be quite impossible for the Supreme Court of the United States to supervise even a small percentage of these courts in the minutiae of their daily operations; nor is it even practical to formulate a system of rules that will close all loopholes and anticipate every contingency. No matter how earnestly the Supreme Court tries to insure the innocent a fair deal, it must count heavily on the good intentions and good judgment of the lower courts and their officers. This is true even of the federal tribunals, which are directly subject to the Supreme Court's rule-making power; it is all the more true of the state courts, which operate under their own several codes, rules, and statutes, and whose doings come to the attention of the Supreme Court only on those infrequent occasions when appeals are carried to that tribunal.

In a very important sense then, the vitality of procedural rights in the United States depends on the far-flung state judicial systems, and the Supreme Court's problem is to insure, as well as it can, that the states use their power responsibly. Will the appropriate feeling of responsibility be best cultivated by imposing a fairly strict set of rules for the guidance of state judicial proceedings? Or is it better, considering that rules can never be fully adequate, to give the states wide leeway on the theory that responsibility breeds a sense of responsibility? Rightly or wrongly the Supreme Court has leaned towards the latter alternative; it is this choice that is represented by such judicial doctrines as the "fair trial rule." And the point is, not that the Court has preferred to weight the scales in favor of the prosecution and against the value of protecting the innocent, but rather that the Court believes the innocent will be *better* protected in the long run by a system whose officials have learned responsibility by exercising it.

Insofar as we subscribe to this belief, the objection that the fair trial rule creates uncertainty loses some of its force. For the very aim of the rule is to maintain a wide margin of uncertainty, so that the self-educating potentialities of decentralization can be realized. But even leaving this matter aside, there are further objections that might be filed against the fair trial rule, and its near-relative, the "Palko doctrine."

Perhaps the most serious objection, as Mr. Green says, arises from the arbitrary and subjective role they seem to imply for the Supreme Court. Mr. Justice Frankfurter, who must be acknowledged as the chief modern architect of these doctrines, argues of course that the standards involved are not unduly "idiosyncratic," and alternatively, that even if they *are*, it is the duty of the Court to make the most of it. Little can be added to Mr. Green's discussion of these points. If these doctrines are not subjective in their drift, it would be hard to imagine any that were. And as for the "duty" of the Court, it is, as Mr. Green says, self-imposed, and fairly recently self-imposed at that.

The real question is, not whether the standards are subjective or whether the Court is duty-bound to put up with them, but whether judicial subjectivity is, in this field, an evil or a virtue. Mr. Green, Justices Black and Douglas, and others like it not; and the reasons for their hostility seem pretty cogent when we remember the old Supreme Court and the havoc it wrought with the doctrine of "reasonableness" in the area of economic legislation. But it might be argued that procedural due process is an entirely different cup of tea, that judicial competence in the economic world is questionable indeed, while fairness in the procedures of arrest and trial is precisely a subject that judges are likely to know a lot about. Here if anywhere, we might say, the case for judicial leeway is strong, on the theory that where competence is greater, the need to obey set rules is correspondingly less. If we accept this, and if we grant (as of course we need not) that a loose rein on local courts will encourage responsibility and serve the ultimate cause of justice, then the flexibility of these doctrines may be warranted after all. Whether it is or not is a question that can be left, as usual, to the reader.

The Bill of Rights, the Fourteenth Amendment and the Supreme Court*

by John Raeburn Green * *

Michigan Law Review,
Volume 46, Page 869 (1948)

The first enforcement of any of the First Amendment freedoms against the states, through the Fourteenth Amendment, was in 1927.[1] In the twenty years since, these freedoms have, one by one, been brought within the protection of the due process clause of the Fourteenth Amendment, as integral parts of the "liberty" which is safeguarded against state denial—the process having been completed in 1947 by the *dictum* that the prohibition of the establishment of religion ran against the states.[2] The chronology of the struggle to enforce the Bill of Rights against the states, as well as other circumstances, suggests that the progress may not have been unrelated to the advance of federal power over the individual and its progressive exclusion of state power as the latter also attempted to advance. Both the advances and the rising tide of liberty were set in motion by the same fundamental cause— our transformation into an industrial society—and in particular by the development (still continuing) of transportation and communication.

A study of the judicial process as revealed in the opinions of the Supreme Court of the United States relating to the enforcement of the guaranties of the Bill of Rights against the states must

---

* This article is part of a paper prepared for the volume of essays to be published in honor of Professor Max Radin. It deals with the decisions through November, 1947.

I have drawn upon three papers entitled "Liberty Under the Fourteenth Amendment," in which the decisions through the 1943 term are considered on the merits: 27 Wash. Univ. L.Q. 497 (1942), for the period to 1942; 28 Wash. Univ. L.Q. 251 (1943), for the 1942 term; and 43 Mich. L. Rev. 437 (1944) for the 1943 term.

I am indebted to Milton I. Goldstein, Esq., of the Saint Louis Bar, for great help in the revision of this paper.

* * (1894–   ), Lawyer and author, St. Louis, Missouri.

[1] Fiske *v.* Kansas, 274 U.S. 380, 47 S. Ct. 655 (1927). This was also the first successful invocation in the Court of any of the guaranties of the First Amendment against either a state or the United States.

[2] Everson *v.* Board of Education, 330 U.S. 1, 67 S. Ct. 504 (1947).

therefore deal largely with recent decisions. This miniature mirror, which compensates for its size by its bright contemporary lighting, reflects the culmination of a struggle which commenced with the adoption of the Constitution; and the greatest intensity of the conflict is displayed in the decisions of the last eight years, which were made by a court in the main newly constituted and scarcely equalled in the past for its vigor. The climax was reached in three decisions of the last day of the 1946 term of the Court.[3]

The sections following deal with the rights of one accused or convicted of crime.

I

The Power of the Dictum: Palko v. *Connecticut*

The extent to which the decisions now enforcing liberty against the states rest upon obiter dicta is extraordinary. The expansion of "liberty" to include freedom of speech and of the press has consistently been founded on the ambiguous dictum in Gitlow v. New York.[4] The clear and present danger rule, which in applying these freedoms has so greatly enlarged them, is still being rested upon Mr. Justice Holmes' dictum in Schenck v. United States.[5] The application of clear and present danger to the free exercise of religion at this moment rests only upon a dictum.[6] The line of cases which commenced with Thornhill v. Alabama,[7] protecting picketing as free speech, rests upon Mr. Justice Brandeis' dictum in Senn v. Tile Layers Protective Union.[8] There is also observable the impressive influence of the dicta in the Slaughter-House Cases,[9] in the decisions dealing with these rights under the

---

[3] Adamson v. California, 332 U.S. 46, 67 S. Ct. 1672 (1947); Gayes v. New York, 332 U.S. 145, 67 S. Ct. 1711 (1947); and Foster and Payne v. Illinois, 332 U.S. 134, 67 S. Ct. 1716 (1947).

[4] "For present purposes we may and do assume that freedom of speech and of the press—which are protected by the First Amendment from abridgment by Congress—are among the fundamental personal rights and 'liberties' protected by the due process clause of the Fourteenth Amendment from impairment by the States." 268 U.S. 652 at 666, 45 S. Ct. 625 (1925).

[5] 249 U.S. 47 at 52, 39 S. Ct. 247 (1919).

[6] In West Virginia State Bd. of Ed. v. Barnette, 319 U.S. 624 at 639, 63 S. Ct. 1178 (1943). The statement there was obiter because the holding was not based on the free exercise of religion.

[7] Thornhill v. Alabama, 310 U.S. 88, 60 S. Ct. 736 (1940).

[8] 301 U.S. 468 at 478, 57 S. Ct. 857 (1937).

[9] 16 Wall. (83 U.S.) 36 (1873).

privileges or immunities clause. It is as if the Court, while conscious of the need for the expansion and wider application of liberty, was yet reluctant to take a new step forward without some color of precedent—either the dicta or the dissenting opinions of earlier, and bolder, Justices.

Whether Mr. Justice Cardozo had the power of the dictum in mind, when in 1937 he delivered the opinion of the Court in Palko *v.* Connecticut,[10] cannot be ascertained.[11] What is certain is that if he had been determined to turn back the rising tide of liberty in respect to the rights of the accused in criminal prosecutions, he could hardly have done it more effectively than by this opinion. The facts were simple. The appellant was tried for murder in the first degree, found guilty of murder in the second degree and sentenced to life imprisonment. Under a statute permitting the state to appeal upon any question of law, the state appealed; the judgment was reversed; and on new trial appellant was convicted of murder in the first degree and sentenced to death. He contended (1) that this was the double jeopardy prohibited by the Fifth Amendment and (2) that the right against double jeopardy embodied in the Fifth Amendment was protected against the states by the due process clause of the Fourteenth Amendment.[12] It would seem that here it was necessary for the Court to decide at least one of these two questions, and if either was answered in the affirmative, to decide the other also. But Mr. Justice Cardozo was careful to refrain from deciding either that the statute did not subject the accused to the double jeopardy prohibited by the Fifth Amendment,[13] or that a state might subject an accused to such double jeopardy.[14] Either or both disclaimers may have been inserted to obtain the concur-

---

[10] 302 U.S. 319, 58 S. Ct. 149 (1937). This was the last opinion he delivered in person.

[11] He had earlier said: "I own that it is a good deal of a mystery to me how judges, of all persons in the world, should put their faith in dicta." *The Nature of the Judicial Process* 29 (1921).

[12] He contended also that the right was protected by the privileges or immunities clause of the Fourteenth Amendment. Mr. Justice Cardozo disposed of this in a single sentence: "Maxwell *v.* Dow gives all the answer that is necessary." 302 U.S. 319 at 329, 58 S. Ct. 149 (1937).

[13] *Id.* at 322: "We do not find it profitable to mark the precise limits of the prohibition of double jeopardy in federal prosecutions."

[14] *Id.* at 328: "What the answer would have to be if the state were permitted after a trial free from error to try the accused over again or to bring another case against him, we have no occasion to consider."

rence of other Justices, for this was an eight-to-one opinion; [15] and its tenor was sharply counter to the opinion of Mr. Justice Sutherland, for a unanimous Court, in Grosjean *v.* American Press Co.,[16] only the previous year.

All that the case decided was that Palko must die, for the "kind of double jeopardy to which the statute has subjected him" was not "a hardship so acute and shocking that our polity will not endure it"; it did not violate "fundamental principles of liberty and justice." Mr. Justice Cardozo supported this by arguing that since in Kepner *v.* United States [17] four Justices (Holmes, White, McKenna and Brown) had dissented from the holding that a second trial at the government's instance was forbidden by the double jeopardy clause of the Fifth Amendment, "right-minded men could reasonably believe that in espousing that conclusion they were not favoring a practice repugnant to the conscience of mankind." While this was said of the dissent of four Justices, it would seem to apply almost equally to the dissent of one. The effect of this is perhaps to extend the philosophy developed by Mr. Justice Holmes in the liberty of contract cases (and carried on by Mr. Justice Frankfurter in the flag salute cases later) [18] that legislation must be upheld if a reasonable man could have done what the legislature did. We have "right-minded" instead of "reasonable" and we have no explicit reference to the legislature; but if the argument is carried to its logical conclusion, it must mean that whenever a single Justice dissents, the legislation must be upheld, his dissent being in itself sufficient evidence of the reasonableness of the legislative action. To extend the doctrine in this way would, of course, vitiate the Bill of Rights, for in effect it would give a veto to a single Justice in the application of the due process clause to protect any of the rights of the accused [19] against legislative invasion—and perhaps judicial invasion also.

---

[15] Mr. Justice Butler dissented without opinion.

[16] Grosjean *v.* American Press Co., 297 U.S. 233, 56 S. Ct. 444 (1936). The contrast (at 243–244) with the dicta of the Palko opinion is striking.

[17] 195 U.S. 100, 24 S. Ct. 797 (1904).

[18] See his opinion for the Court in Minersville School District *v.* Gobitis, 310 U.S. 586, 60 S. Ct. 1010 (1940), and in particular his dissenting opinion in West Virginia State Board of Education *v.* Barnette, 319 U.S. 624, 63 S. Ct. 1178 (1943).

[19] It is not clear, but apparently Mr. Justice Cardozo did not intend to apply this test to legislation invading the First Amendment freedoms.

What must, more than the decision, detain us is the vast array of dicta in which Mr. Justice Cardozo indulged. The appellant's thesis, he said, was that whatever would be a violation of the Bill of Rights if done by the federal government was now equally unlawful by force of the Fourteenth Amendment if done by a state. Mr. Justice Cardozo denied this general rule and undertook to draw a line, placing on one side those "privileges and immunities" which "have been found to be implicit in the concept of ordered liberty, and thus, through the Fourteenth Amendment, become valid as against the states." If the Fourteenth Amendment has absorbed these, he said, "the process of absorption has had its source in the belief that neither liberty nor justice would exist if they were sacrificed." On this side of the line he placed freedom of speech, freedom of the press, and free exercise of religion,[20] the right of peaceable assembly, and the right of one accused of crime to the benefit of counsel.[21] These the Fourteenth Amendment "may" make it unlawful for a state to abridge.[22] He conceded also that the thought that condemnation shall be rendered only after trial was fundamental "in the concept of due process," and that the trial must be a real one, not a sham or pretense. This, he said, was the reason why it had been held [23] that the right to the "aid of counsel" [24] was protected, that decision turning upon the fact that "in the particular situation laid before us in the evidence the benefit of counsel was essential to the substance of a hearing."

On the other side of the line, Mr. Justice Cardozo placed the right to trial by jury in criminal prosecutions, guaranteed by the Sixth Amendment, and the immunity from prosecution except after a grand jury indictment, guaranteed (in the case of "capital, or otherwise infamous crime") by the Fifth. These, he said, "may have value and importance," but they are "not of the very essence of a scheme of ordered liberty," and to abolish them would not violate a " 'principle of justice so rooted in the traditions and

---

[20] This was three years in advance of the first holding to that effect, Cantwell *v.* Connecticut, 310 U.S. 296, 60 S. Ct. 900 (1940).

[21] 302 U.S. 319 at 324–327, 58 S. Ct. 149 (1937).

[22] *Id.* at 324.

[23] The reference was to Powell *v.* Alabama, 287 U.S. 45, 53 S. Ct. 55 (1932).

[24] He apparently intended to distinguish between the right to representation by counsel, with its corollaries, and the right to appointment of counsel for an indigent accused.

conscience of our people as to be ranked as fundamental.'" What was true of them was true also of the immunity against compulsory self-incrimination, guaranteed by the Fifth Amendment—"this too might be lost, and justice still be done." Arguing that "compulsory self-incrimination is part of the established procedure in the law of Continental Europe" [25] (and that "double jeopardy, too, is not everywhere forbidden"), he observed—and not with disapproval—that "today as in the past there are students of our penal system who look upon the immunity [against self-incrimination] as a mischief rather than a benefit and who would limit its scope or destroy it altogether." "Justice," he added, "would not perish if the accused were subject to a duty to respond to orderly inquiry," although "no doubt there would remain the need to give protection against torture, physical or mental." [26] He implied that the prohibition of the Fourth Amendment against unlawful searches and seizures,[27] and "other provisions of the Sixth," were to be treated in the same way.[28]

While the opinion supported the exclusion of these rights by authority, the cases cited [29] were in 1937 no longer authoritative,

---

[25] Mr. Justice Cardozo might well have looked twice at this argument, for even in 1937 it was evident that the totalitarian states—notably Russia and Germany—were depending largely on compelled self-incrimination in their administration of what may euphemistically be called criminal justice.

[26] 302 U.S. 319 at 325–326, 58 S. Ct. 149 (1937).

[27] In the New York Court of Appeals he had held that evidence illegally obtained, without a search warrant, was admissible. People *v.* Defore, 242 N.Y. 13, 150 N.E. 585 (1926).

[28] 302 U.S. 319 at 324, 58 S. Ct. 149 (1937).

[29] Hurtado *v.* California, 110 U.S. 516, 4 S. Ct. 111, 292 (1884) and Gaines *v.* Washington, 277 U.S. 81 at 86, 48 S. Ct. 468 (1928) on grand jury indictment; Twining *v.* New Jersey, 211 U.S. 78, 29 S. Ct. 14 (1908) on self-incrimination; Maxwell *v.* Dow, 176 U.S. 581, 20 S. Ct. 448, 494 (1900), on trial by jury in criminal cases; Weeks *v.* United States, 232 U.S. 383 at 398, 34 S. Ct. 341 (1914) on the Fourth Amendment; and West *v.* Louisiana, 194 U.S. 258, 24 S. Ct. 650 (1904) on "other provisions of the Sixth." The only case later than 1925 is the Gaines case, decided less than a year after the first holding which enforced the Gitlow dictum. There the Court in a single sentence said that for a state to provide prosecution by information instead of indictment was "not a violation of the Federal Constitution" (citing the Hurtado case); but at the same time said (at 85–86): "It is contended, however, that due process of law exacted in the Fourteenth Amendment in causes tried in state courts must be construed as equivalent to the Sixth Amendment in Federal trials. The question has not arisen in any case cited to us. . . . But we need not pass on that question now." As to Hurtado *v.* California, only the year before the Palko opinion, Mr. Justice Sutherland, for a unanimous Court, had said that the Court had "held that in the light of subsequent decisions the sweeping language of the Hurtado case could not be accepted without qualification." Grosjean *v.* American Press Co., 297 U.S. 233 at 243, 56 S. Ct. 444 (1936). Mr. Justice Cardozo had concurred in this opinion.

for there had since occurred the expansion of liberty made by the Gitlow case in 1925. The contention which Mr. Justice Cardozo was considering was that double jeopardy was *now* prohibited by the due process clause, and the most recent successors of the Gitlow decision were expressly relied on by the appellant.[30] Mr. Justice Cardozo might as well have catalogued the limits of the commerce power on the basis of the decisions of 1890. And these superannuated decisions had not considered these rights with respect to their inclusion in "liberty," but solely with respect to their protection as "privileges or immunities," or as included in historical due process. For either of these grounds of protection there was indeed much to be said, as is shown by Mr. Justice Harlan's powerful and prophetic dissents, [31] which time is now vindicating; but they did not present the question before the Court in the Palko case.

No reader of the Palko opinion would suppose that the validity of these rights against the states, so categorically and so briefly denied by Mr. Justice Cardozo, had from the days of the Slaughter-House Cases [32] troubled and divided the Court, as indeed the problem is to this day troubling and dividing it, more than ever before. Nor could it be discovered from this opinion that the struggle over protection of these rights was simply the latest phase of a century-old conflict, in which, since the Gitlow decision, the prospect of success for the advocates of protection had become much greater. Mr. Charles Warren had at the time observed of that case, that if the Gitlow doctrine was "carried to its logical and inevitable conclusion, every one of the rights contained in the Bill of Rights ought to be and must be included in 'liberty,' " and thus guaranteed by the due process clause against

---

[30] Grosjean *v.* American Press Co., 297 U.S. 233 at 243, 56 S. Ct. 444 (1936); Powell *v.* Alabama, 287 U.S. 45 at 65–68, 53 S. Ct. 55 (1931); Near *v.* Minnesota, 283 U.S. 697, 51 S. Ct. 625 (1931). See summary of brief in 82 L. Ed. 288–289.

[31] See his vigorous dissenting opinions in Hurtado *v.* California, 110 U.S. 516 at 538, 4 S. Ct. 111, 292 (1884); in Twining *v.* New Jersey, 211 U.S. 78 at 114, 29 S. Ct. 14 (1908) (where he suggested that the privilege against self-incrimination was, in addition, a part of liberty); and in Maxwell *v.* Dow, 176 U.S. 581 at 605, 20 S. Ct. 448, 494 (1900). In West *v.* Louisiana, 194 U.S. 258, 24 S. Ct. 650 (1904), where the Court discussed, but did not decide, whether the right to confrontation with witnesses was a part of due process, he dissented without opinion. Mr. Justice Harlan was not a member of the Court when the other two cases relied on by Mr. Justice Cardozo were decided.

[32] 16 Wall. (83 U.S.) 36 (1873).

state denial, for their claim to inclusion at least equalled that of freedom of speech. He had pointed out that as a matter of fact, of history and of law, freedom of speech was not "in any degree as 'fundamental' as most of the other rights recited in the Bill of Rights," since, prior to the First Amendment, "while no state had in its Bill of Rights a declaration of right to freedom of speech, practically every state had a declaration of right to freedom of religion, of right to keep and bear arms, of right to be free from unreasonable search and seizure, and of right to jury trial." [33]

The propositions advanced by Mr. Justice Cardozo on the strength of these authorities were obiter pure and simple, for they were not answers to the questions (which after all concerned only double jeopardy) before the Court for decision—but not decided. The essence of this belletristic essay, which gave the scantiest consideration to profoundly important matters, was that the rights of the accused guaranteed by the Bill of Rights were nice things to have, no doubt, but luxuries, not necessities. They were all lesser rights, without the law, unless in the particular case the evidence convinced a majority of the Court that they were "essential to the substance of a hearing"—that burden Mr. Justice Cardozo placed on the accused in every case. Jove was never more omniscient.

In this deliberate fashion Mr. Justice Cardozo went out of his way to crush to earth all libertarian heresy. This opinion was the foundation for the turning of the Fair Trial Rule against the rights of the accused. How great the difference was between protecting a right guaranteed by the Bill of Rights because it was a fundamental right, and protecting it only when "in the particular situation . . . in the evidence" a majority of the Court considered it to have been fundamental to the particular defendant, was to be demonstrated in the future.

---

[33] Warren, The New "Liberty" under the Fourteenth Amendment, 39 Harv. L. Rev. 431 at 460–461 (1926). Cf. Powell, *The Supreme Court and State Police Power, 1922–30,* p. 52 (1932): "It is no longer worth while to spend time in considering whether there are liberties not within the assumed contemplation of the official progenitors of the Fourteenth Amendment." Cf. also Brown, Due Process of Law, Police Power, and the Supreme Court, 40 Harv. L. Rev. 943 at 950 (1927): "The fact is that the cases tend to establish Mr. Justice Harlan's statement in his dissent in Taylor *v.* Beckham [178 U.S. 548 1900], that the words [life, liberty or property] . . . 'should be interpreted as embracing every right that may be brought within judicial cognizance.'"

II

Truth and Justice: Betts v. *Brady*

The protection of the rights of the accused against state invasion had perhaps made more progress since 1925 than might have been inferred from the Palko opinion. Two of the rights guaranteed by the Sixth Amendment—the rights to notice of the nature and cause of the accusation, and to trial by an impartial tribunal—had from an early date been recognized to be essential parts of procedural due process.[33a] Of a third such right, that of confrontation with witnesses, Mr. Justice Cardozo, for the five-to-four majority, had said in Snyder v. Massachusetts,[34] in 1934, that "for present purposes, we assume that the privilege is re-enforced by the Fourteenth Amendment, though this has not been squarely held." But Mr. Justice Roberts (in whose dissenting opinion Justices Brandeis, Sutherland and Butler joined) had replied sharply: "It is not a matter of assumption but a certainty that the Fourteenth Amendment guarantees the observance of" this right.[35] The dissenters protested that the Court ought not "to convert the inquiry from one as to the denial of the right into one as to the prejudice suffered by the denial," that "to pivot affirmance on the question of the amount of harm done the accused is to beg the constitutional question involved." [36] Mr. Justice Cardozo's avoidance of this right in his Palko catalogue will be noted.

In 1936, in Brown v. Mississippi,[37] a unanimous Court held that the use of a confession extorted by brutality and violence was a denial of due process, remarking, however, that "the privilege against self-incrimination is not here involved." But, notwithstanding Palko, the doctrine of this case was in 1940–1942 carried much beyond "torture, physical or mental." In Chambers v. Florida [38] it was held that the use of a confession obtained by questioning over a period of five days was a denial of due process.

[33a] See Holden v. Hardy, 169 U.S. 366 at 389–390, 18 S. Ct. 383 (1898).

[34] 291 U.S. 97, 54 S. Ct. 330 (1934). His opinion here was consistent with the Palko opinion, although not so elaborate.

[35] *Id.* at 131.

[36] *Id.* at 136.

[37] 297 U.S. 278, 56 S. Ct. 461 (1936). Mr. Justice Cardozo referred to this in the Palko opinion.

[38] 309 U.S. 227, 60 S. Ct. 472 (1940).

From that it was but a short step [39] to Lisenba *v.* California,[40] where Mr. Justice Roberts said (for the Court, but as dictum) that "the concept of due process would void a trial in which, by threats or promises . . . a defendant was induced to testify against himself." This did not sound far removed, if removed at all, from the privilege against self-incrimination.

In 1932, in Powell *v.* Alabama,[41] Mr. Justice Sutherland, for the seven-to-two majority, had held that the right to have "the assistance of counsel," guaranteed by the Sixth Amendment, was protected against state denial. The convictions set aside here were of Negroes, sentenced to death for rape. The Court did not speak of the right as part of liberty, but rather as an essential part of procedural due process. It based the decision, however, in part upon the enlargement of liberty to include freedom of speech and of the press; and Mr. Justice Cardozo's statement in Palko five years later that here the right to counsel had "been found to be implicit in the concept of ordered liberty" was essentially true.

At the same time the Court had been engaged in developing the Fair Trial Rule. This had its origin in expressions in cases where a trial, although superficially conforming to due process, was simply a mask for a conviction due to mob violence, to public passion or to perjured testimony.[42] In 1941, in Smith *v.* O'Grady [43] the Court held that a conviction on a plea of guilty, made because of a promise of leniency which was not performed by an ignorant and bewildered layman without counsel and without knowledge of the charge, was lacking in due process, and later that year Mr. Justice Roberts stated the rule:

> As applied to a criminal trial, denial of due process is the failure to observe that fundamental fairness essential to the very concept of justice. In order to declare a denial of it we must find that the ab-

---

[39] The intervening cases were Canty *v.* Alabama, 309 U.S. 629, 60 S. Ct. 612 (1940); White *v.* Texas, 310 U.S. 530, 60 S. Ct. 1032 (1940); Lomax *v.* Texas, 313 U.S. 544, 61 S. Ct. 956 (1941), and Vernon *v.* Alabama, 313 U.S. 547, 61 S. Ct. 1092 (1941).

[40] 314 U.S. 219 at 237, 62 S. Ct. 280 (1941).

[41] 287 U.S. 45, 53 S. Ct. 55 (1932).

[42] See Mr. Justice Holmes' dissenting opinion in Frank *v.* Mangum, 237 U.S. 309 at 345, 35 S. Ct. 582 (1915); Moore *v.* Dempsey, 261 U.S. 86, 43 S. Ct. 265 (1923); and Mooney *v.* Holohan, 294 U.S. 103, 55 S. Ct. 340 (1935).

[43] 312 U.S. 329, 61 S. Ct. 572 (1941).

sence of that fairness fatally infected the trial; the acts complained of must be of such quality as necessarily prevents a fair trial.[44]

As originally applied, the rule took nothing away from the rights of the accused, nor did it add to them—it simply required that due process be accorded in fact, as well as in form. "Due process" must always have meant real due process, not merely its simulation. It is true that in 1941–1942 [45] the rule seemed to be developing to an extent which threatened to place upon the Court a burden it could hardly support. But even then it seemed that the Court was attempting to work out, laboriously and piecemeal, its own bill of rights for criminal prosecutions. In the confessions cases, indeed, the Court seemed not only to be arriving at the same result as the privilege against self-incrimination would produce,[46] but even to be formulating a rule which in terms resembled the privilege. While it was not clear why the Court need undertake in this fashion to discard Madison's Bill of Rights and prepare its own, the progress in the confessions cases gave ground for hope that what would finally emerge would not be much different. And there the crystallizing process seemed to be progressing rapidly.[47]

This was the situation when in 1942 Betts *v.* Brady [48] for the first time turned the Fair Trial Rule against the rights of the accused. In the Powell case ten years earlier the Court had held (1) that the hearing required by due process historically [49] and in practice had "always included the right to the aid of counsel when desired and provided by the party asserting the right"; and (2) that, assuming the defendant's inability to employ counsel

---

[44] Lisenba *v.* California, 314 U.S. 219 at 236, 62 S. Ct. 280 (1941).

[45] See Lisenba *v.* California, and Hysler *v.* Florida, 315 U.S. 411, 62 S. Ct. 688 (1942).

[46] Bram *v.* United States, 168 U.S. 532, 18 S. Ct. 183 (1897).

[47] The process is illustrated in Ward *v.* Texas, 316 U.S. 547 at 555, 62 S. Ct. 1139 (1942), where the Court said that it had set aside convictions "based upon confessions extorted from ignorant persons who have been subjected to persistent and protracted questioning, or who have been threatened with mob violence, or who have been unlawfully held incommunicado without advice of friends or counsel, or who have been taken at night to lonely and isolated places for questioning. Any one of these grounds would be sufficient cause for reversal. . . . The use of a confession obtained under such circumstances is a denial of due process. . . ."

[48] 316 U.S. 455, 62 S. Ct. 1252 (1942).

[49] See Radin, The Myth of Magna Carta, 60 Harv. L. Rev. 1060 at 1088 (1947).

"even if opportunity had been given," under the circumstances "the necessity of counsel was so vital and imperative that the failure of the trial court to make an effective appointment of counsel was likewise a denial of due process." The Court said that the United States by statute and every state in the Union required a trial judge to appoint counsel for an accused who was unable to employ counsel (although in a few states this was limited to "the more serious crimes" or to capital cases), and that a rule so unanimously adopted "reflects if it does not establish" the "inherent" and "fundamental" right to appointment of counsel, "at least in cases like the present." The court then said:

> Whether this would be so in other criminal prosecutions, or under other circumstances, we need not determine. All that it is necessary now to decide, as we do decide, is that in a capital case, where the defendant is unable to employ counsel, and is incapable adequately of making his own defense because of ignorance, feeble-mindedness, illiteracy, or the like, it is the duty of the court, whether requested or not, to assign counsel for him as a necessary requisite of due process of law. . . .[50]

It will be observed that notwithstanding the disclaimer of the first sentence, the second sentence announces a rule of general application.

Upon this whole opinion its author, Mr. Justice Sutherland, had placed a broader gloss. Four years later in the Grosjean case [51] he had said that in the Powell case, "we concluded" that certain rights guaranteed by the Bill of Rights were protected against the states by the due process clause, "and among them the fundamental right of the accused to the aid of counsel in a criminal prosecution." The Palko opinion, as has been seen, dealt with the right to counsel with some ambiguity; but twice thereafter the Court had again used broad language with respect to the right; [52] and in one of these cases, Johnson v. Zerbst,[53] in 1938, it had now held that the Sixth Amendment's guarantee of the "Assistance of Counsel" required in federal prosecutions the ap-

---

[50] 287 U.S. 45 at 71, 53 S. Ct. 55 (1932).
[51] Grosjean v. American Press Co., 297 U.S. 233 at 243–244, 56 S. Ct. 444 (1936).
[52] Johnson v. Zerbst, 304 U.S. 458 at 462, 58 S. Ct. 1019 (1938); Avery v. Alabama, 308 U.S. 444 at 447, 60 S. Ct. 321 (1940).
[53] 304 U.S. 458, 58 S. Ct. 1019 (1938).

pointment of counsel for an indigent defendant, unless there was an intelligent and competent waiver of the right.

But now Mr. Justice Roberts, for the six-to-three majority in Betts *v.* Brady, took a different view of the Powell case. The petitioner, a penniless farmhand of little education, accused of robbery, had asked the Maryland court to appoint counsel for him. The court refusing, he defended himself as best he could, was (not surprisingly) convicted, and sentenced to eight years in prison. Mr. Justice Roberts admitted that "expressions in the opinions of this court lend color to the argument" that "in every case, whatever the circumstances, one charged with crime, who is unable to obtain counsel, must be furnished counsel by the State." [54] Rejecting this, he pointed out that in each of those cases a state statute had required the appointment of counsel, while here it did not; that historically and at present there was a great diversity in the states with respect to the appointment of counsel; and that from this it was demonstrated that "the considered judgment of the people, their representatives and their courts" was "that appointment of counsel is not a fundamental right, essential to a fair trial." [55] He added, quoting from the opinion of the Maryland court of appeals, that the petitioner's contention would make no distinction between criminal charges of different magnitude and that presumably it would be argued " 'that trials in the Traffic Court would require it.' " [56] "Asserted denial" of due process, he said, "is to be tested by an appraisal of the totality of facts in a given case," for "that which may, in one setting, constitute a denial of fundamental fairness, shocking to the universal sense of justice, may, in other circumstances, and in the light of other considerations, fall short of such denial." [57] The Fourteenth Amendment, he concluded, "prohibits the conviction . . . of one whose trial is offensive to the common and fundamental ideas of fairness and right," but "we cannot say that the Amendment embodies an inexorable command that no trial of any offense, or in any court, can be fairly conducted," [58] without representation by counsel.

---

[54] 316 U.S. 455 at 462–463, 62 S. Ct. 1252 (1942). He referred to the Powell and Avery cases and to Smith *v.* O'Grady, 312 U.S. 329, 61 S. Ct. 572 (1941).
[55] 316 U.S. 455 at 471.   [57] *Id.* at 462.
[56] *Id.* at 473.   [58] *Id.* at 473

While the Court here was influenced by the "all or none" argument, it seemed to rely chiefly upon the Fair Trial Rule, as well as the fact that the state statute here did not require the appointment. The state statute could not, of course, be relevant in determining the fairness of the trial.[59] Mr. Justice Roberts here was as tenacious to condition the right to appointment of counsel on the amount of harm done the accused by its denial, as in Snyder v. Massachusetts [60] he had been to refuse to condition the right to confrontation with witnesses on the "amount of harm done the accused" by that denial. But he did not make clear how the right of confronting the witnesses, however "fundamental" it was, could be of its full value to a defendant who lacked counsel to cross-examine them.

In the Betts case Mr. Justice Black (with whom Justices Douglas and Murphy joined) dissented, saying that it would be "a little like mockery to secure to a pauper the solemn constitutional guaranties for a fair and full trial . . . , and yet say to him, when on trial, that he must employ his own counsel, who could alone render these guaranties of any real permanent value to him." [61] He observed that even under "the prevailing view of due process, . . ." reflected in Mr. Justice Roberts' opinion, which gives "this Court such vast supervisory powers that I am not prepared to accept it without grave doubts," the judgment should be reversed. And he added: "I believe that the Fourteenth Amendment made the Sixth applicable to the states. But this view, although often urged in dissents, has never been accepted by a majority of this Court and is not accepted today." [62] This passage (citing the purpose of the Fourteenth Amendment as disclosed by the debates in Congress) heralded the revival in 1947 of the struggle over the application of the privileges or immunities

---

[59] Except as a basis for comparison with other trials in the same state, which is by no means what the Fair Trial Rule had meant.

[60] 291 U.S. 97, 54 S. Ct. 330 (1934).

[61] 316 U.S. 455 at 476, 62 S. Ct. 1252 (1942), quoting Carpenter v. Dane County, 9 Wis. 274 at 276–277 (1859).

[62] 316 U.S. 455 at 475, 474, 62 S. Ct. 1252 (1942). In 1940 in Chambers v. Florida, 309 U.S. 227 at 235, note 8, 60 S. Ct. 472 (1940), he had said: "There has been a current of opinion—which this court has declined to adopt in many previous cases—that the Fourteenth Amendment was intended to make secure against State invasion all the rights, privileges and immunities protected . . . by the Bill of Rights" (citing Mr. Justice Harlan's dissents).

clause, which had divided the Court from the Slaughter-House Cases in 1873 until the death of Mr. Justice Harlan in 1911.

In the Snyder case, Mr. Justice Roberts had said that "where the conduct of a trial is involved, the guarantee of the Fourteenth Amendment is not that a just result shall have been obtained, but that the result, whatever it be, shall be reached in a fair way." [63] He did not repeat this now, where it would have had much application. The due process clause does not guarantee justice because it cannot; it is not that justice is unattainable, but that it is unascertainable. Even when exact justice is attained, we cannot know that for certain. Justice depends first upon full knowledge of the facts; but truth lies at the bottom of a well, even in a trial court. There is the fact, now well-known, that all witnesses suffer to greater or less extent from errors of observation and of memory, permitting them to testify with complete sincerity to what did not happen. There is of course perjury. There is often the reluctance of both parties to place on the stand the one witness who is in a position to know the truth. An agreed statement of facts in a civil case is frequently, if not usually, a compromise acceptable to both parties, the result of bargaining, and for that reason not containing the whole truth. In the same way a plea of guilty is the result of bargaining—though the bargaining is often not at arm's length—and even when the defendant is represented by counsel, it may be more or less than the foundation for justice. It was Bacon, not St. John, who described Pilate (a judge of some years' experience) as "jesting" when he asked, "What is truth?" [64]

In an appellate court, with a record so artificial, the well where truth lies has of course become much deeper. [65] How often have

---

[63] 291 U.S. 97 at 137, 54 S. Ct. 330 (1934).

[64] Cf. John 18:38 with Bacon's Essay on Truth. As to Pilate's experience see Radin, *The Trial of Jesus of Nazareth* 176–208 (1931).

[65] See Judge Lamm in Creamer *v.* Bivert, 214 Mo. 473 at 479–480, 113 S.W. 1118 (1908): "Truth does not always stalk boldly forth naked, but modest withal, in a printed abstract in a court of last resort. She oft hides in nooks and crannies visible only to the mind's eye of the judge who tries the case. To him appears the furtive glance, the blush of conscious shame, the hesitation, the sincere or the flippant or sneering tone, the heat, the calmness, the yawn, the sigh, the candor or lack of it, the scant or full realization of the solemnity of an oath, the carriage and mien. The brazen face of the liar, the glibness of the schooled witness in reciting a lesson or the itching over-eagerness of the swift witness, as well as

the parties and counsel read an appellate court's statement of the facts in their case with surprise, sometimes indeed astonishment! If the whole truth and nothing but the truth could be before a Court, justice would still have to contend with the fallibility of mortals, but the condition cannot be often met.

Since it is evident that the prerequisite of justice, knowledge of the truth in its full integrity, will with difficulty be available to a court, it becomes all the more necessary that courts approach it as closely as possible, by exhausting to the utmost the possibilities of the method of ascertaining truth to which we are committed. That is the adversary system, which is itself a part of due process. We depend upon what is resolved from the struggle of the parties, long experience having caused us to believe that truth is more likely to emerge from this struggle than from direct search.[66] The process cannot demand absolute equality in the skill of counsel for the contending parties, but its success depends upon the equality of both parties in the possession of counsel. In a criminal prosecution the accused, as was said in the Powell case, "lacks both the skill and knowledge adequately to prepare his defense, even though he have a perfect one;" and the judge is limited (more so in state courts than federal) in calling witnesses not called by the parties, in suggesting objections, in commenting on the credibility of witnesses, and generally in attempting to discover the truth in avenues not opened by the parties—that is, by their counsel.[67] If it is thought that an accused can present his case adequately without counsel (as Mr. Justice Roberts apparently thought that Betts could), consider what would happen in law enforcement if the state were required to prosecute and try without counsel. If the state needs counsel, the accused must need it at least as much, for the balance in a criminal prosecution is

---

honest face of the truthful one, are alone seen by him. In short, one witness may give testimony that reads in print, here, as if falling from the lips of an angel of light and yet not a soul who heard it, *nisi,* believed a word of it; and another witness may testify so that it reads brokenly and obscurely in print and yet there was that about the witness that carried conviction of truth to every soul who heard him testify."

[66] Even where the investigative system is used, in Continental Europe, it has been recognized that "truth is more easily understood if it is approached from two directions," and that the public interest requires counsel for both prosecution and defense. Calamandrei, *Eulogy of Judges,* Adams' and Phillips' trans., 54–55 (1942).

[67] See I Wigmore, *Evidence,* 3d ed., 374 (1940).

weighted in favor of the state, the presumption of innocence being called in to redress that. However it may have been earlier, in 1947 no one can doubt the truth of Mr. Justice Sutherland's observation that the accused "requires the guiding hand of counsel at every step in the proceedings against him." [68]

Betts *v.* Brady failed to take these considerations into account. While it seemed to leave the accused with a "fundamental" right to confer with his counsel (which could not be affected by whether or not the Court thought that necessary for "fairness" in the particular case), yet if he was without funds to employ counsel he might still be hurried to trial and conviction unless the lack of "fairness" was sufficiently evident to shock "the universal sense of justice," as interpreted by a majority of the Court hearing his appeal. Its greatest vice lay in the substitution of subjective judgment, varying in each case, for the objective and inflexible requirement of the Bill of Rights.

III

Natural Law and Liberty: Adamson v. *California*

While the storm did not break until 1947, the four years after Betts *v.* Brady showed that the winds were rising.[69] At the 1943 term the confessions rule was carried further in Ashcraft *v.* Tennessee,[70] where the Court, through Mr. Justice Black, held that the use of a confession obtained after thirty-six hours of continuous questioning, in relays, was in violation of the due process clause (even though a jury had found that the confession was voluntary) because the situation was "inherently coercive." [71] Mr. Justice Jackson (with whom Justices Roberts and Frankfurter joined) dissented in an opinion of great vigor. "The

---

[68] In Powell *v.* Alabama, 287 U.S. 45 at 69, 53 S. Ct. 55 (1932).

[69] The cases at the 1943, 1944 and 1945 terms are collected and analyzed in Stockham, Summary of Civil Liberties Cases in the 1943 Term of the Supreme Court, 2 Nat. B.J. 95 (1944); Summary of Civil Liberties Cases in the 1944 Term of the Supreme Court of the United States, 3 Nat. B.J. 189 (1945); and Summary of the Civil Liberties Cases in the 1945 Term of the Supreme Court of the United States, 4 Nat. B.J. 287 (1946).

[70] 322 U.S. 143, 64 S. Ct. 921 (1944).

[71] *Id.* at 154. *Id.*, note 9, Mr. Justice Black indicated the close approach of this line of cases to the privilege against self-incrimination.

Constitution," he said, "requires that a conviction rest on a fair trial," from which forced confessions are ruled out. Of course questioning for thirty-six hours was "inherently coercive," but so was questioning for one hour, so was arrest itself. The Court, Mr. Justice Jackson observed, does not quite say that the Constitution prohibits the use of all confessions made after arrest, but "it is moving far and fast in that direction." [72]

But this progress was soon checked. In Lyons *v.* Oklahoma [73] the Court, through Mr. Justice Reed, held that use of a second confession obtained twelve hours after the accused had made a confession admittedly involuntary had not deprived the accused of a fair trial, nor denied due process. [74] Mr. Justice Murphy (with whom Mr. Justice Black concurred), dissenting, said:

> The Fifth Amendment prohibits the federal government from convicting a defendant on evidence that he was compelled to give against himself. . . . Decisions of this Court in effect have held that the Fourteenth Amendment makes this prohibition applicable to the states. [75]

In Malinski *v.* New York, [76] the latest of the confessions cases, [77] the Court held, five-to-four, that a coerced confession, not introduced in evidence but referred to by witnesses and the prosecutor, was in fact "employed to obtain a conviction," which was a denial of due process. [78]

In the meantime the Fair Trial Rule had received further consideration from the Justices who had now become its chief

---

[72] *Id.* at 159, 161. He added: "The use of the due process clause to disable the States in protection of society from crime is quite as dangerous and delicate a use of federal judicial power as to use it to disable them from social or economic experimentation," *Id.* at 174.

[73] 322 U.S. 596, 64 S. Ct. 1208 (1944).

[74] Mr. Justice Douglas concurred in the result. Mr. Justice Rutledge dissented without opinion.

[75] 322 U.S. 596 at 605, 64 S. Ct. 1208 (1944). He cited Chambers *v.* Florida, Canty *v.* Alabama, Lisenba *v.* California, and the Ashcraft case.

[76] 324 U.S. 401, 65 S. Ct. 781 (1945).

[77] Except that Ashcraft *v.* Tennessee came to the Court a second time in 327 U.S. 274, 66 S. Ct. 544 (1946), the state court, on new trial, having excluded the confession but permitted witnesses to testify regarding it. The second conviction was reversed without dissent.

[78] For criticism of the "ambiguous language" and "inconsistencies in application of a stated formula" in these cases, see Morgan, The Law of Evidence, 1941–1945, 59 Harv. L. Rev. 481 at 538–541 (1946).

proponents. In 1943, in Buchalter *v.* New York,[79] Mr. Justice
Roberts stated that the due process clause required that state
action be "consistent with the fundamental principles of liberty
and justice," but did not "draw to itself the provisions of state
constitutions or state laws." This seemed at variance with the
distinction he had made in the Betts case as to state statutes requiring appointment of counsel. In two cases [80] at the 1944 term
Mr. Justice Frankfurter had discussed the difference—which indeed seemed fairly obvious—between the Court's review of federal convictions under the Bill of Rights and its review of state
convictions under the Fair Trial Rule. In a concurring opinion
in the Malinski case he now made a defense of the rule, taking
one small step toward rendering it intelligible. Instead of "the
universal sense of justice," and similar expressions, he confined
this phrase to "the notions of justice of English-speaking peoples." [81] Considering European events, one could be thankful for
this much. He added that the fact that judges might differ
among themselves whether in a particular case a trial offends
"accepted notions of justice" did not disprove "that general
rather than idiosyncratic standards were applied," "alert deference" to the state court's judgment being "an important safeguard against such merely individual judgment." [82]

But his chief defense of the Fair Trial Rule was a vigorous
attack on the concept that specific provisions of the Bill of
Rights were protected by the Fourteenth Amendment. The Bill
of Rights was approached with Mr. Justice Cardozo's spirit:
"Eighteenth-century statesmen" had formulated these safeguards,
some of which (right of trial by a jury of twelve, and the requirement of grand-jury indictment) "were built on experience
of relative and limited validity," while others expressed funda-

---

[79] 319 U.S. 427 at 429–430, 63 S. Ct. 1324 (1943).

[80] United States *v.* Mitchell, 322 U.S. 65 at 68, 64 S. Ct. 896 (1944); Feldman *v.* United States, 322 U.S. 487 at 490–491, 64 S. Ct. 1082 (1944).

[81] 324 U.S. 401 at 416–417, 65 S. Ct. 781 (1945). The phrase was still a
long way from the point where it had started, "fundamental principles of liberty
and justice which lie at the base of all our civil and political institutions," used
(in construing a state statute) in Hebert *v.* Louisiana, 272 U.S. 312 at 316, 47
S. Ct. 103 (1926). The phrase in the Hebert opinion was taken verbatim from
Hurtado *v.* California, 110 U.S. 516 at 535, 4 S. Ct. 111, 292 (1883), where it
was used in the paragraph of that opinion which the Court has since rejected (see
note 84, *infra*.). In the Hebert opinion the Court did not mention the Hurtado case.

[82] 324 U.S. 401 at 417, 65 S. Ct. 781 (1945).

mental principles of liberty and justice. But, said Mr. Justice
Frankfurter, "we can hardly select one provision of the Bill of
Rights and reject another," for this "leads inevitably to a warped
construction of specific provisions to bring within their scope
conduct clearly condemned by due process but not easily fitting
into the pigeon-holes of the specific provisions." And he revived
the argument originally made in Hurtado v. California [83] (to
which the Court had given a definitive answer in the Powell and
Grosjean cases [84]) that the due process clause of the Fifth
Amendment would be redundant and meaningless if it included
the rights specifically guaranteed elsewhere in the Bill of Rights;
that the due process clause in the Fourteenth Amendment must
have the same meaning as in the Fifth; and that therefore these
rights could not be included in it.[85]

On the other hand, Mr. Justice Black had gone out of his
way to expand the "grave doubts" regarding the rule which he
had mentioned in the Betts case. In International Shoe Co. v.
Washington [86] he said: "Superimposing the natural justice concept on the Constitution's specific prohibitions could operate as
a drastic abridgment of democratic safeguards they embody,
such as freedom of speech, press and religion, and the right to
counsel. This has already happened [in] Betts v. Brady. For
application of this natural law concept, whether under the
terms 'reasonableness,' 'justice,' or 'fair play,' makes judges the
supreme arbiters of the country's laws and practices. . . ." In a

---

[83] 110 U.S. 516 at 534–535, 4 S. Ct. 111, 292 (1883).

[84] Powell v. Alabama, 287 U.S. 45 at 65–68, 53 S. Ct. 55 (1932); Grosjean v.
American Press Co., 297 U.S. 233 at 243, 56 S. Ct. 444 (1936). Mr. Justice
Roberts also had dealt with it summarily in Snyder v. Massachusetts, 291 U.S. 97
at 133–134, 54 S. Ct. 330 (1934). These answers cited the line of cases, commencing
with Chicago, B. & Q. R.R. Co. v. Chicago, 166 U.S. 226 at 241, 17 S. Ct. 581
(1897), which had held that the Fifth Amendment's explicit guarantee that private
property shall not be taken for public use without just compensation, was included
in the due process clause of the Fourteenth. They relied also on the protection
of First Amendment rights by the due process clause. But long before these inclusions Mr. Justice Harlan, dissenting in the Hurtado case, had made an answer
equally effective in principle. See 110 U.S. 516 at 547–550, 4 S. Ct. 111, 292
(1883).

[85] Mr. Chief Justice Stone (with whom Justices Roberts, Reed and Jackson
joined), dissenting, said (324 U.S. 401 at 438, 65 S. Ct. 781): "We agree that
the controlling principles upon which this Court reviews on constitutional grounds
a state court conviction for crime, are as stated in the opinion of Mr. Justice
Frankfurter."

[86] 326 U.S. 310 at 325–326, 66 S. Ct. 154 (1945).

footnote he added that rights protected at a particular time only because the Court, as then constituted, believed them to be "a requirement of fundamental justice" might under the same rule be left unprotected by another court, "with a different belief as to fundamental justice."

The further conflict over the right to appointment of counsel had been less sharp. The first cases [87] after Betts *v.* Brady were Williams *v.* Kaiser [88] and Tomkins *v.* Missouri,[89] at the 1944 term. There a seven-to-two majority, through Mr. Justice Douglas, held that petitions for habeas corpus should not have been dismissed by the Missouri court without a hearing. The petitioners had pleaded guilty, without counsel, to robbery with a deadly weapon and to murder, respectively—both capital offenses. Williams had been sentenced to imprisonment for fifteen years and Tomkins to life imprisonment. Williams alleged that he had asked for counsel, but no appointment was made; Tomkins alleged that he did not know of his right to counsel under the state statute. The Court was careful to use the language of the Powell case and to avoid that of the Betts case, pointing out that "a layman is usually no match for the skilled prosecutor" and that this was a reason why "the right to counsel is 'fundamental.'" Mr. Justice Frankfurter (with whom Mr. Justice Roberts joined) dissented in both cases on the ground that there appeared to be an adequate state ground for dismissal of the petitions. In none of the opinions was any reference made to Betts *v.* Brady, although the briefs had by no means been silent regarding that case.

Other cases followed now in rapid sequence. House *v.* Mayo,[90] White *v.* Ragen,[91] and Hawk *v.* Olson,[92] dealt primarily with the denial of opportunity to consult with counsel; but in the first two the per curiam memoranda [93] nevertheless spoke of

---

[87] Except for Ex Parte Hawk, 321 U.S. 114, 64 S. Ct. 448 (1944), where it was held that the petitioner had not exhausted his state remedies.

[88] 323 U.S. 471, 65 S. Ct. 363 (1945).

[89] 323 U.S. 485, 65 S. Ct. 370 (1945).

[90] 324 U.S. 42, 65 S. Ct. 517 (1945).

[91] 324 U.S. 760, 65 S. Ct. 978 (1945).

[92] 326 U.S. 271, 66 S. Ct. 116 (1945).

[93] In the House case Mr. Justice Roberts dissented from the holding that there was a denial of due process. In the White case the petitions were dismissed on the theory that the State Court might have dismissed them upon the ground of

the right to appointment of counsel, saying: "Compare Betts
v. Brady with Williams *v.* Kaiser and Tomkins *v.* Missouri."
This cryptic remark was not explained. In the Hawk case
Mr. Justice Reed, holding, for a unanimous Court, that there
was a violation of the Fourteenth Amendment, cited the Williams and Tomkins cases, but not the Betts case. In Rice
v. Olson,[94] petitioner had been convicted of burglary and sentenced to from one to seven years. The offense seemed indis-
tinguishable from that in the Betts case and the punishment was
less; but Mr. Justice Black, for the six-to-three majority, stress-
ing the complexity of a question of jurisdiction arising from the
petitioner's allegation that the offense had been committed on an
Indian Reservation, held that he was entitled to appointment of
counsel unless there was an intelligent and understanding
waiver.[95] The Williams and Tomkins cases were cited but Betts
v. Brady was not. In Canizio *v.* New York,[96] Mr. Justice Black,
for the six-to-two majority, held that the petitioner had in fact
had the benefit of counsel, while Justices Murphy and Rutledge,
in separate dissenting opinions, appraised the circumstances differently. In Woods *v.* Nierstheimer [97] the petitioner claimed use
of a confession induced by threats and beatings, plus an inef-
fective appointment of counsel, but Mr. Justice Black, for a
unanimous Court, dismissed the petition on the ground that
the Illinois court's denial of habeas corpus had been because that
was not the proper remedy.

At the 1946 term, in Carter v. Illinois,[98] the Court, through
Mr. Justice Frankfurter, returned for the first time to the Fair
Trial language of the Betts case, dismissing the petition on the
ground that an intelligent waiver of counsel could be inferred.
Mr. Justice Douglas (with whom Justices Black and Rutledge
joined), dissenting, and Mr. Justice Murphy, dissenting sepa-

---

state procedure, Mr. Justice Roberts concurring in the result. In a footnote in the
White case the Court remarked that 225 petitions for certiorari had in the last
two terms been filed to review denial by the Illinois Supreme Court of leave to
file petitions for habeas corpus.

[94] 324 U.S. 786, 65 S. Ct. 989 (1945).

[95] The dissent of Justices Frankfurter, Roberts and Jackson urged only that
the Nebraska court's action should be regarded as a denial of habeas corpus on
allowable state grounds.

[96] 327 U.S. 82, 66 S. Ct. 452 (1946).

[97] 328 U.S. 211, 66 S. Ct. 996 (1946).

[98] 329 U.S. 173, 67 S. Ct. 216 (1946).

rately, urged that "at least in a capital case" it was the duty of the Court to appoint counsel whether requested or not, if the accused was incapable of making his own defense, the Williams case being the authority for this. A little later, in De Meerleer *v.* Michigan,[99] a per curiam memorandum reversed the denial of a new trial to a seventeen-year-old boy, who had on the same day been arraigned, tried, convicted of murder and sentenced to life imprisonment, without being told of his right to counsel, nor of the consequences of his plea of guilty. This deprived him of "rights essential to a fair hearing under the Federal Constitution," it was said.

With the exception of the Carter case, there had not been in any of these cases a reaffirmance of the Fair Trial doctrine, and indeed from some of them the inference seemed to be that the Betts case had been substantially limited. Many of the opinions seem to be designed with some care not to reopen the conflict in the Court. But that conflict now broke out in Louisiana *v.* Resweber,[100] which set the stage for the decisions of June 23, 1947. Here a Negro boy, convicted of murder, was sentenced to electrocution. The executioner threw the switch, but because of some mechanical difficulty death did not result. (There was evidence that the current had reached the boy.) The petitioner claimed that to proceed again with the electrocution would violate the due process clause of the Fourteenth Amendment because of the double jeopardy provision of the Fifth Amendment and the cruel and unusual punishment provision of the Eighth. There were three opinions, but no one of them commanded a majority of the Court. Mr. Justice Reed (with whom Mr. Chief Justice Vinson and Justices Black and Jackson joined) examined the circumstances "under the assumption, but without so deciding, that violation of the principles" of the Bill of Rights "as to double jeopardy and cruel and unusual punishment, would be violative of the due process clause of the Fourteenth Amendment," adding (on the authority of Re Kemmler [101]) that this clause would prohibit "execution by a state in a cruel manner." They considered that there was no double jeopardy involved; while as to cruel

---

[99] 329 U.S. 663, 67 S. Ct. 596 (1947).
[100] 329 U.S. 459, 67 S. Ct. 374 (1947).
[101] 136 U.S. 436 at 446, 10 S. Ct. 930 (1890).

and unusual punishment, it was said that the cruelty was the result of accident, and further did not lie in the electrocution sought to be prohibited but in the first attempt. There was nothing here to suggest the application of the Palko doctrine, the language being either favorable or neutral as to the inclusion of the specific rights in the due process clause. This may explain why Mr. Justice Black concurred in the opinion, but Mr. Justice Frankfurter did not.

As the Palko opinion had made clear, the concept that the due process clause restrained the states in their administration of justice only when a violation of a "fundamental principle of justice" would ensue—which has here been called (because of its origin and for convenience) the "Fair Trial Rule"—was not to be confined to the rights of the accused at his trial, but extended as well to the provisions of the Fourth, Fifth and Eighth Amendments. Mr. Justice Frankfurter, concurring separately in the Resweber case, expanded the defense of this concept which he had made in the Malinski case. He considered that some of the safeguards of the Bill of Rights "have perduring validity," but "some grew out of transient experience or formulated remedies which time might well improve." The Fourteenth Amendment, he said, "did not mean to imprison the states into the limited experience of the eighteenth century," but "did mean to withdraw" from them "the right to act in ways that are offensive to a decent respect for the dignity of man, and heedless of his freedom." These, he admitted, "are very broad terms by which to accommodate freedom and authority," and "as has been suggested from time to time, they may be too large to serve as the basis for adjudication, in that they allow much room for individual notions of policy." But that, he said, "is not our concern," for "the duty of such adjudication on a basis no less narrow has been committed to this Court." In the language of the Snyder and Palko cases, he concluded that the execution, under these circumstances, was not "repugnant to the conscience of mankind." [102]

Mr. Justice Burton (with whom Justices Murphy, Douglas and Rutledge joined), in a dissenting opinion which had the

---

[102] The privileges or immunities clause (which does not appear to have been before the Court) he dismissed on the authority of the earlier cases.

appearance of having been written in the first instance as the opinion of the Court, considered that there was cruel and unusual punishment here, and a violation of "constitutional due process."

The climax of the struggle to enforce the rights of the accused against the states was reached in three decisions on the last day of the 1946 term. Foster *v.* Illinois [103] and Gayes *v.* New York [104] both dealt with the right to counsel. In the Foster case, Mr. Justice Frankfurter, for the five-to-four majority, relying upon the Palko and Betts cases, held that due process did not require a state court to offer counsel upon a plea of guilty, the court having previously advised the defendant of his "rights of Trial." In every case in which due process had been found wanting, he said, "the prisoner sustained the burden of proving, or was prepared to prove but denied opportunity," that for lack of counsel "an ingredient of unfairness actively operated" in his conviction. Mr. Justice Black (with whom Justices Douglas, Murphy and Rutledge joined), dissenting, said that the Court now "waters down the Bill of Rights guarantee to counsel" so as "to make it compatible with the Court's standards of decency and a fair trial," as it had the same day (in the Adamson case discussed below) watered down the privilege against self-incrimination. "We cannot know," he continued, "what Bill of Rights provision will next be attenuated by the Court." The Betts case was precedent for this decision, "but it is the kind of precedent that I had hoped this Court would not perpetuate." Mr. Justice Rutledge, speaking separately for the same dissenters, considered that the Sixth Amendment's guarantee of counsel was applicable against the states, but that aside from that, even on the Court's "fair trial" basis, there was a lack of due process. In the Gayes case the Court divided in the same way as to the conviction as a second offender of a boy who at sixteen had been convicted of burglary, having waived counsel. The basis of the decision was that in his second trial he might have contested whatever infirmity there was in the first sentence. [105]

---

[103] 332 U.S. 134, 67 S. Ct. 1716 (1947).
[104] 332 U.S. 145, 67 S. Ct. 1711 (1947).
[105] Mr. Justice Burton concurred in the result. Mr. Justice Rutledge, for the four dissenters, pointed out that so far as appeared, Gayes had lacked counsel in his second trial.

In the third of these cases, Adamson *v.* California,[106] the judicial debate on the Fair Trial Rule and the Bill of Rights was extended and frank. The appellant, convicted of murder, had claimed that permitting the prosecutor to comment on his failure to testify violated the Fifth Amendment's privilege against self-incrimination which, he said, was protected against state invasion by both the privileges or immunities clause and the due process clause of the Fourteenth. Through Mr. Justice Reed, the Court said that it would assume, without deciding, that what had occurred here would violate the privilege against self-incrimination,[107] but that it was "settled law" that this privilege was not protected by the privileges or immunities clause; and that the due process clause, while it protected "the right to a fair trial," did not "draw all the rights of the federal Bill of Rights under its protection." To require the accused to testify would not necessarily deprive him of a fair trial and there was nothing "unfair" in permitting the prosecutor to comment upon his silence.

Mr. Justice Frankfurter, concurring separately, confined his opinion to the due process clause.[108] He further elaborated the views he had expressed in the Malinski and Resweber cases, relying upon the Palko case and Twining *v.* New Jersey [109] as Mr. Justice Reed had done. The suggestion that some of the first eight amendments "express the restricted views of Eighteenth-Century England" was repeated, and the right to grand-jury indictment, the right to trial by a jury of twelve in criminal cases, and the Seventh Amendment were again cited. If the due process clause was intended to incorporate the Bill of Rights, "it is a strange way of saying it." Indeed, he continued, that suggestion "is not unambiguously urged"—what is urged is a

---

[106] 332 U.S. 46, 67 S. Ct. 1672 (1947).

[107] Mr. Justice Frankfurter, concurring, conceded that this comment was barred, in a federal prosecution, by the privilege, as it was also by act of Congress. Mr. Justice Black, dissenting, said that the Court's opinion, while assuming that the privilege was a bar in federal prosecutions, "strongly implies" that it is not. He made the same assumption as the Court.

[108] He "put to one side" the privileges or immunities clause because of "the mischievous uses to which that clause would lend itself" if its scope were not confined as it had been by the decisions which had denied its application.

[109] 211 U.S. 78, 29 S. Ct. 14 (1908).

"selective incorporation"; [110] and "if the basis of selection is merely" the incorporation of those provisions "which commend themselves to individual justices as indispensable to the dignity and happiness of a free man, we are thrown back to a merely subjective test." But, he said, "the judicial judgment in applying the Due Process Clause" must move within the limits of accepted notions of justice and is not to be based upon the idiosyncrasies of a merely personal judgment." He once more resurrected the discredited Hurtado doctrine of interpretation of the due process clause,[111] and suggested again that "alert deference" to the judgment of the state court was "an important safeguard" in applying the Fair Trial Rule. The evidence adduced in Mr. Justice Black's dissent regarding the purpose of the Fourteenth Amendment he disposed of summarily.[112]

Mr. Justice Black (with whom Mr. Justice Douglas joined), dissenting, said that the decision reasserts the constitutional theory that the Court "is endowed by the Constitution with boundless power under 'natural law' periodically to expand or contract constitutional standards to conform to the Court's conception of what at a particular time constitutes 'civilized decency' and 'fundamental liberty and justice.'" This theory at once degrades the safeguards of the Bill of Rights and appropriates for the Court a broad power not authorized by the Constitution. The Twining case had been undercut by the confessions cases. The purpose of the Fifth, Sixth and Eighth Amendments had been to confine judicial exercise of power "within precise boundaries." He considered that "one of the chief objects" of the first section of the Fourteenth Amendment was to make the Bill of Rights applicable to the states, which purpose "has never received full consideration or exposition in any opin-

---

[110] "Some are in and some are out, but we are left in the dark as to which are in and which are out. Nor are we given the calculus for determining which go in and which stay out."

[111] See note 84, *supra.*

[112] "Any evidence of design or purpose not contemporaneously known could hardly have influenced those who ratified the Amendment. Remarks of a particular proponent of the Amendment, no matter how influential, are not to be deemed part of the Amendment. What was submitted for ratification was his proposal, not his speech." 332 U.S. 46 at 64, 67 S. Ct. 1672 (1947).

ion of this Court. . . ." He referred to the exclusion in Maxwell *v.* Dow [113] of the Senate debate with regard to the purpose of the Amendment, and the fact that in the Twining case the question had been held to be "no longer open," although the Court there admitted that its action resulted in giving " 'much less effect to the Fourteenth Amendment than some of the public men active in framing it' had intended . . ." [114] Mr. Justice Black now brought before the Court, in a lengthy appendix to his opinion, the committee reports and the debates in Congress, indicating that the purpose of the privileges or immunities clause was to enforce the first eight amendments against the states. He renewed, in the strongest terms, his attack on the "natural-law-due-process" formula, which "subtly conveys to the courts, at the expense of legislatures, ultimate power over public policies in fields where no specific provision of the Constitution limits legislative power." This had been rejected by a majority of the Court in the Slaughter-House Cases, but subsequently the Court, departed from the Slaughter-House philosophy of judicial tolerance of state regulation of business activities, had used the due process clause to protect "property rights under natural law concepts," and at the same time had contracted the Amendment as a protection against state infringement of the Bill of Rights. He could not consider the Bill of Rights to be "an outworn eighteenth century 'straight jacket,' " for the evils which it was designed to meet, though ancient, "have emerged from century to century wherever excessive power is sought by the few at the expense of the many."

If he had to choose, Mr. Justice Black said, "between the selective process of the Palko decision applying some of the Bill of Rights to the States," or applying none of them, he would choose the selective process. But rather than accept either of these choices, he would follow the purpose of the Amendment, "to extend to all the people of the nation the complete protection

---

[113] 176 U.S. 581, 20 S. Ct. 448, 494 (1900).

[114] Twining *v.* New Jersey, 211 U.S. 78 at 96–98, 29 S. Ct. 14 (1908). He quoted also from this opinion (at 113): "Much might be said in favor of the view that the privilege [against self-incrimination] was guaranteed against state impairment as a privilege and immunity of National Citizenship, but . . . the decisions of this court have foreclosed that view."

of the Bill of Rights." [115] The possibility that the Court was now wise enough to improve upon it by substituting natural law concepts he considered "entirely too speculative" to justify taking that course.

Mr. Justice Murphy (with whom Mr. Justice Rutledge joined) dissented separately, saying that "while in substantial agreement with the views of Mr. Justice Black, I have one reservation and one addition to make." He agreed that the Bill of Rights should be "carried over intact into the first section of the Fourteenth Amendment," but he would not limit the latter to the Bill of Rights "entirely and necessarily." There might be occasions where failure to conform to "fundamental standards of procedure" would "warrant constitutional condemnation . . . despite the absence of a specific provision in the Bill of Rights." [116]

IV

The Four Alternatives: Fair Trial, Privileges or Immunities, Due Process and Liberty

After a century and a half, the struggle to enforce the Bill of Rights against the states has in 1947 come closer to complete victory than ever before. The rights of the accused, while still largely outside the shelter of the Fourteenth Amendment, nevertheless in the Adamson case commanded four votes for inclusion *in toto*. It is even possible, notwithstanding Mr. Justice Reed's expression there, that if the question had been compelled testimony (in the literal language of the Fifth Amendment) instead of comment on failure to testify, the privilege against self-incrimination would have commanded a majority. Many of these cases presented, not clear violations of the basic rights, but violations of more or less necessary corollaries to them, corollaries only lately—or sometimes not even yet—recognized by

---

[115] 332 U.S. 46 at 69, 70, 72, 74, 75, 89, 67 S. Ct. 1672 (1947). However, elsewhere he said: "Whether this Court ever will, or whether it now should, in the light of past decisions, give full effect to what the Amendment was intended to accomplish is not necessarily essential to a decision here." *Id.* at 75.

[116] 332 U.S. 46 at 123–124, 67 S. Ct. 1672 (1947).

the Court to be included in the Bill of Rights' protection, and having a debatable right to such inclusion. Thus the right to appointment of counsel was not held to be protected by the Sixth Amendment until 1938,[117] the privilege against self-incrimination has not yet been held to bar comment on failure to testify,[118] and the Palko opinion indicated doubt whether the Court was there prepared to follow the single five-to-four decision which had held that a second trial at the instance of the government amounted to double jeopardy. The progress of the Court's thinking might have been more rapid if the cases dealing with these rights had involved unmistakable violations of the basic rights themselves. The rapid progress which for a time was made in the confessions cases at any rate suggests that conclusion.

The rule of "fairness," which we may perhaps still call the "Fair Trial Rule," seems bound to undergo further consideration in the Court. The Court has in the past considered its value to lie in permitting relief in a particular case where justice clearly required relief, while at the same time (as it supposed) not opening the door to other cases where justice might not be so demanding. At the time when Betts *v.* Brady was decided, it was observed that the Fair Trial Rule placed upon the Court a burden which it was hardly likely to be able to sustain; that it "opens the door to arbitrary and purely subjective judgment, unrestrained by any rule; it leaves all state courts uncertain of their powers; and it deprives persons accused of crime of any assurance regarding their rights." [119] The experience of the five years since seems to have fulfilled these misgivings. The purely administrative burden which the rule has placed upon the Court has now so grown that of the 1356 cases which came to the Court at the 1946 term, roughly 528, or 39 per cent, were petitions from state convicts.[120]

---

[117] Johnson *v.* Zerbst, 304 U.S. 458, 58 S. Ct. 1019 (1938).

[118] As 28 U.S.C. (1940) § 632 bars comment on the failure of an accused to testify, in federal prosecutions, the Court has not needed to consider whether this result would there be guaranteed by the Fifth Amendment, without a statute. Similarly, the Court's delay until Johnson *v.* Zerbst, in holding that the Sixth Amendment guaranteed the appointment of counsel in federal prosecutions, was doubtless due to the existence of 18 U.S.C. (1940) § 563, requiring the assignment of counsel in cases of "treason, or other capital crime."

[119] Green, Liberty Under the Fourteenth Amendment, 27 Wash. Univ. L.Q. 497 at 534 (1942).

[120] A table supplied by the kindness of the Clerk of the Court shows the

Two-fifths of the matters which come before the Court are now reviews of state criminal convictions, the ratio increasing each year. Since the Court by the terms of the Fair Trial Rule is bound to make its own "independent examination of the record" in each case, it appears that the rule, if applied whole-heartedly, has placed on the Court a burden which it can no longer sustain. Yet this burden will increase, for it requires little acquaintance with inmates of the penitentiaries to discover that almost every prisoner considers that there was something "unfair" in his prosecution, conviction or punishment. The deluge has not yet really begun, and there is nothing the Court can do to check it (so long as it adheres to the Fair Trial Rule) except to refuse the applications without too much regard to their merits, thus defeating the purpose of the rule. The great decrease in the num-

---

number of in forma pauperis cases from the 1930 term through the 1946 term, as follows:

TERM	NUMBER FILED	NUMBER GRANTED
1930	22	3
1931	24	1
1932	38	4
1933	66	10
1934	54	4
1935	59	8
1936	60	4
1937	97	15
1938	85	7
1939	117	18
1940	120	19
1941	178	16
1942	147	8
1943	214	12
1944	339	10
1945	393	15
1946	528	8

The figures include federal as well as state cases, and include also a few state cases arising under the equal protection of the laws clause of the Fourteenth Amendment; but it is estimated that the number of federal and equal protection cases is less than ten per cent, and that the state cases in which costs were paid would be sufficient to make these figures roughly accurate as a tabulation of all state cases involving review of criminal convictions under the due process clause.

As early as the 1944 term the Court had commented on the great number of petitions for certiorari filed to review denial by the Illinois Supreme Court of leave to file habeas corpus petitions. See note 93, *supra*. At the 1946 term no less than 322 of the in forma pauperis cases came from Illinois, these dealing largely with the right to counsel. The Illinois cases, even without adding to them the cases in which the costs were paid, amounted to nearly one-fourth of the 1356 matters which came before the Court at the last term.

ber of in forma pauperis cases in which the Court took jurisdiction, set out in the margin, suggests that the Court is beginning to realize this, the percentage having declined from more than 15 per cent at the 1937 term to 1½ per cent at the 1946 term. And in the cases where the Court did take jurisdiction, the attenuating process is suggested by the increasing emphasis placed upon prior exhaustion of state remedies and questions of state procedure, and the search (as in the Gayes and Foster cases) to find in the record something which might be stretched into a waiver of the right.

The rule has not only placed this insupportable burden upon the Court, but it has deprived persons accused of crime of any assurance regarding their rights, substituting instead a hope which is usually shattered; and it has left state courts and prosecutors in uncertainty regarding their powers and duties, to such an extent as already to be the subject of complaint in state courts.[121] This is true of the confessions cases, but even more so of the right to counsel cases, where the Court has most often used this rule. There the rule is by its terms in most cases impossible for a trial court to apply. As the Court has often said, the appointment, if it is to be effective, must be made at the very outset of the trial, before the accused pleads. The trial court cannot know at that time what the testimony will disclose, nor what the accused's defenses on the evidence and on the law

---

[121] See, e.g., Newman *v.* State, 148 Tex. Cr. App. 645 at 651–652, 187 S.W. 2d 559 (1945), where the Texas court said:

"As applied to a criminal trial, denial of due process is the failure to observe that fundamental fairness essential to the very concept of justice [citing the Supreme Court decisions].

". . . . There is no escape from the conclusion that the Supreme Court of the United States has potential jurisdiction in all State cases where it is claimed by the accused that the conviction was based upon his involuntary confession. . . .

"The difficult feature of our position rests in the fact that we are called upon to determine the question from a dual standpoint—first, under the laws and decisions of this State and second, under the decisions of the Supreme Court of the United States. The latter, being conclusions reached by the Court from its examination of the particular facts of each case, constitute a precedent or guide only in cases involving the same fact situations.

"If the Supreme Court would prescribe some formula by which we may be guided, our task would be much easier. . . ."

The lower federal courts and the state courts are similarly burdened by the Rule. See Hilliard *v.* Johnston, (D.C. Cal. 1947) 73 F. Supp. 956; Goodman, Use and Abuse of the Writ of Habeas Corpus, 7 F.R.D. 313 at 315 (1947). Criticism from trial courts would be even more emphatic.

may be. It often will have only the slightest knowledge of the extent of the accused's education, or of his familiarity or lack of it, with court procedure. But in Betts *v.* Brady the Court said that all of these are essential elements in the determination of whether or not the accused needs counsel in order to make his defense adequately and thus to have a fair trial.

These are substantial objections to the "fair trial" doctrine, but the greatest is, of course, that stated by Mr. Justice Black in the Adamson case. The Court's judgment under the rule is purely arbitrary and subjective. It varies from case to case, unrestrained by any measurable standard, according to the Justices' opinion of "fairness" after their examination of the record. No doubt every member of the Court in reaching his conclusion makes the utmost effort to eliminate any opinion as to guilt or innocence which the record may have forced into his mind, but can he ever be certain that this has not entered subconsciously into his determination of "fairness"?

When the Court applies the rule, it is of course converting the inquiry into one as to the prejudice suffered by the denial of the right, and is pivoting affirmance on the question of the amount of harm done the accused, to use Mr. Justice Roberts' language in Snyder *v.* Massachusetts.[122] Quite apart from the fact that in such an inquiry there may subconsciously enter considerations of guilt or innocence arising from the "independent examination of the record," it must be observed that the doctrine here applied is one which would be shocking to the framers of our Constitution. The Fair Trial Rule is natural law at its worst; it is subjective judgment unrestrained except by the most general concept of justice, producing a variable result in each case.[123] The crystallizing process, which in the confessions cases has seemed to offer hope of reducing the Rule to precise terms, went no further after Betts *v.* Brady. The result of the rule in a given case remains by hypothesis unpredictable.

"The fundamental principles of liberty and justice which lie

---

[122] 291 U.S. 97, 54 S. Ct. 330 (1934).
[123] Cf. Betts *v.* Brady, 316 U.S. 455, 62 S. Ct. 1252 (1942), with Rice *v.* Olson, 324 U.S. 786, 65 S. Ct. 989 (1945), as to the crime, the punishment and the result.

at the base of all our civil and political institutions," a phrase
used in Hebert *v.* Louisiana [124] in a different connection,[125] was
in the Fair Trial cases combined with the early cases where due
process was found to have been accorded in form but not in
fact, to produce the rule. But this language was plainly referable
to the Constitution (including the Bill of Rights) and the Declaration of Independence.[126] While in the Fair Trial opinions the
phrase has usually been quoted, it is remarkable how often
the objective elements of its last twelve words are omitted in the
more frequent paraphrases. And in particular "liberty" seems
somehow to drop out. The phrase is of course far removed from
"the universal sense of justice" or "the common and fundamental
ideas of fairness and right" which Mr. Justice Roberts applied
in the Betts case, and it is by no means the equivalent of "repugnant to the conscience of mankind," to use Mr. Justice Cardozo's
language in the Palko case. "Universal" is a broad word, even if
it is confined to this planet. So confined, we must recognize, however regretfully, that the universal sense of justice literally would
not include notice or hearing, nor exclude torture or unmention-
able mutilation. Confine it, as Mr. Justice Frankfurter is now
attempting,[127] to "the notions of justice of English-speaking peoples" (however odd these "notions" may be), and it is still so
broad as to be meaningless, for the American Revolution was
fought because of a difference of opinion as to these "notions
of justice." Confine it to the United States, and many of these
cases, as Brown *v.* Mississippi,[128] show how widely these "notions" vary. Confine it to a single state, and we find in Massachusetts some disagreement as to the fairness of the convictions of
Sacco and Vanzetti. Confine it to the Court, and we find that
what shocks the sense of justice of one judge fails to shock that
of another—hence the dissents in many of these cases.

Mr. Justice Frankfurter answered this suggestion in the

---

[124] 272 U.S. 312 at 316, 47 S. Ct. 103 (1926).

[125] It was used in denying a claim that a state court's alleged error in construction of a state statute amounted to a denial of due process. See note 81, *supra,* as
to the origin of the phrase.

[126] As to interpreting the Constitution in the spirit of the Declaration of Independence, see Gulf Colo. & Santa Fe R. Co. *v.* Ellis, 165 U.S. 150 at 160, 17 S. Ct.
255 (1897).

[127] In his concurring opinions in the Malinski and Adamson cases.

[128] 297 U.S. 278, 56 S. Ct. 461 (1936).

Malinski and Adamson cases by saying that the fact that judges might differ among themselves as to whether a particular trial offended "accepted notions of justice" did not disprove "that general rather than idiosyncratic standards were applied." [129] But no matter how justices may try to apply "general standards," and no matter how well they may think they are succeeding, the result of applying these "notions of justice" is bound to be idiosyncratic. Mr. Justice Frankfurter also says that an "alert deference" to the judgment of the state court is "an important safeguard" against "merely individual judgment"; but this, if it means anything, means that the rule is not to be applied effectively at all, for the state court's "fairness" is what, by hypothesis, is to be examined. It seems evident that what the phrase really means (excluding such "alert deference") is the particular notions of the particular Justice in the particular case, with no objective point of reference whatever. It is, in short, the purest and most absolute form of arbitrary and uncontrolled power, a retreat into the deepest jungle of natural law, from the clearing which the Bill of Rights has created.

The "vague contours" of the due process clause, of which Mr. Justice Holmes spoke,[130] were never so vague as those of the Fair Trial Rule. Mr. Justice Frankfurter's most recent answer [131] to this is that if the rule allows too much room for "individual notions of policy," that is not the Court's concern, for the duty of adjudication on this broad basis "has been committed to this Court." But this is precisely the answer that the old Court used to make in the liberty of contract cases, when it struck down state economic and social legislation. The duty has not been committed to the Court except by the Court itself. The inclusion of the Fair Trial Rule is quite as much an expansion of the due process clause as would be the inclusion of the Bill of Rights. The rule is the more shocking because this objective and precise alternative has been and is still available.

---

[129] Cf. Mr. Justice Holmes, Natural Law, 32 Harv. L. Rev. 40 at 41 (1918): "The jurists who believe in natural law seem to me to be in that naive state of mind that accepts what has been familiar and accepted by them and their neighbors as something that must be accepted by all men everywhere."

[130] In Adkins *v*. Children's Hospital, 261 U.S. 525 at 568, 43 S. Ct. 394 (1923).

[131] In Louisiana *v*. Resweber, 329 U.S. 459 at 466 *et seq.*, 67 S. Ct. 374 (1947).

"The Constitution," thundered Erskine to Lord Mansfield, "never intended to invest Judges with a discretion which cannot be tried and measured by the plain and palpable standard of law. . . . On a special verdict for murder the life of the prisoner does not depend on the religious, moral or philosophical ideas of the Judges. . . . If he is condemned . . . his conduct is brought to a precise, clear, intelligible standard, and cautiously measured by it: it is the law therefore, and not the Judge, which condemns him. . . ." [132]

This was said of another constitution, of trial judges, and—it must be confessed—in the Eighteenth Century. But one would suppose that to us, who in the Twentieth have seen the end result of arbitrary power in the concentration camps of Germany and Russia, it would have still some force. The rights of the accused must be defined specifically for precisely the same reason that the elements of the crime must be defined. As the Court (through Mr. Justice Matthews) said long ago:

When we consider the nature and theory of our institutions of government, the principles upon which they are supposed to rest, and review the history of their development, we are constrained to conclude that they do not mean to leave room for the play and action of purely personal and arbitrary power. [133]

Let us consider next the desire of Justices Murphy and Rutledge to include the Bill of Rights in the Fourteenth Amendment, but to retain the Fair Trial Rule as a supplement to, rather than a substitute for, the Bill of Rights. It is a persuasive suggestion to one who does not forget that in these cases life or liberty depends upon the decisions. But it is still arbitrary power, and moreover it is delusive. In which of the twenty-five or more cases in which the Fair Trial Rule has been applied has it voided a conviction which would not have been voided by either the Bill of Rights or procedural due process? None will be found. Indeed, in the cases where the Fair Trial Rule has voided a conviction it has often done so only by the support of the Bill of Rights bloc,[134] a majority of the Fair Trial adherents being op-

---

[132] Argument in the King's Bench in the Dean of St. Asaph's Case (1784). I *The Speeches of Thomas Erskine when at the Bar*, Ridgway ed., 331 (1813).
[133] In Yick Wo *v.* Hopkins, 118 U.S. 356 at 369, 6 S. Ct. 1064 (1886).
[134] Their compromises with the Fair Trial Rule seem, as a matter of hindsight, to have been unfortunate. More rapid progress in the long run might have been made by sticking to the Bill of Rights propositions.

posed to the result. When in Feldman *v.* United States,[135] a federal prosecution, Mr. Justice Black attempted to use the rule to supplement the privilege against self-incrimination, he met with the failure that might have been expected. Considering this, and considering also the reasons why Justices Black and Douglas, originally among the most enthusiastic in their application of the rule, have now turned against it, it would seem that the suggestion is unfortunate.

It seems unlikely that the Fair Trial Rule can contain much longer the rising tide of liberty, which, since Betts *v.* Brady, it has been used to dam and divert. The alternatives to it—there are several—therefore demand comprehensive consideration. In this consideration it should be remembered that Madison and the First Congress never intended to guarantee a fair trial in criminal prosecutions simply by "due process." That was guaranteed, they thought, chiefly by the specific rights protected in the Bill of Rights. The sum of these, plus procedural due process, were the essential elements of a fair trial. The fact that a specific right was included in the Bill of Rights ought therefore to strengthen its claim for inclusion in the Fourteenth Amendment, rather than prejudice it, as it has sometimes seemed to do.

Consideration should include also some analysis of the position of the leading proponent of the rule, Mr. Justice Frankfurter. His objection to the inclusion of the rights of the accused in the due process clause of course does not stem from any lack of appreciation of the value of these rights—on the contrary, his great devotion to them has often been demonstrated.[136] And

---

[135] 322 U.S. 487 at 494–495, 64 S. Ct. 1082 (1944).

[136] See his opinion in McNabb *v.* United States, 318 U.S. 332, 63 S. Ct. 608 (1943), excluding evidence obtained in violation of legal rights, and remarking (at 347): "The history of liberty has largely been the history of observance of procedural safeguards." See also his remark in Williams *v.* Kaiser, 323 U.S. 471 at 482, 65 S. Ct. 363 (1945): "Nothing is a more fundamental characteristic of a civilized society than those securities which safeguard a fair trial for one accused of crime"; and his opinion in Bollenbach *v.* United States, 326 U.S. 607 at 615, 66 S. Ct. 402 (1946): "In view of the place of importance that trial by jury has in our Bill of Rights, it is not to be supposed that Congress intended to substitute the belief of appellate judges in the guilt of an accused, however justifiably engendered by the dead record, for ascertainment of guilt by a jury under appropriate judicial guidance, however cumbersome that process may be."

Note in particular his dissenting opinion in Harris *v.* United States, 331 U.S. 145 at 164, 67 S. Ct. 1098 (1947), with regard to the scope and the importance of the Fourth Amendment: "To find authority for ransacking a home merely from

it will be observed that in his Malinski, Resweber and Adamson
opinions he was most careful to avoid the deprecation with
which Mr. Justice Cardozo spoke of the privilege against self-
incrimination. The consideration which has produced Mr. Justice Frankfurter's vigorous opinions in these cases seems to be
closely related to that which produced his opinions in the flag
salute cases and in the commerce clause cases as well, that is, reluctance to interfere with the power of the states any more than
strict constitutional necessity requires. It is the doctrine of Mr.
Justice Holmes again, applied to state action of a different kind.
The doctrine is understandable, but the result of its application
in this field is not. For the Fair Trial Rule seems to interfere
far more with the administration of criminal justice by
the states than would enforcement of the privilege against self-
incrimination, of the right to counsel, or of other specific and
well-defined rights. The interference is in incalculable directions,
affecting every detail of every trial, over which the Supreme
Court now has unlimited supervision; and the state courts are
left without guide or precedent as to how to proceed.[137] On the
other hand, state courts have been entirely willing to apply the
specific rights, if the Court will tell them that the Fourteenth
Amendment so requires.[138]

The alternative to the Fair Trial Rule which Mr. Justice
Black suggests is to construe all the rights secured by the Bill of
Rights to be "privileges or immunities" within the meaning of

---

authority for arrest of a person is to give a novel and ominous rendering to a
momentous chapter in the history of Anglo-American freedom."

As to the privilege against self-incrimination and the requirement of a unanimous verdict by a jury of twelve, he said long ago: "All this preoccupation with
the restrictions upon the criminal process due to the privilege against self-crimina-
tion and the requirement of a unanimous verdict by a jury of twelve is largely a
deflection of energy and attention. We are doomed to deep disappointment if we
act on the belief that ancient experience in these matters is no longer relevant, and
look for substantial diminution in crime by departing from the procedural wisdom
of the Bill of Rights." Frankfurter, *The Public and Its Government* 60–61 (1930).

[137] See Newman *v.* State, 148 Tex. Cr. App. 645, 187 S.W. 2d 559 (1945).

[138] When Williams *v.* Kaiser, 323 U.S. 471, 65 S. Ct. 363 (1945) and Tomkins
v. Missouri, 323 U.S. 485, 65 S. Ct. 370 (1945), were returned to the Supreme
Court of Missouri for hearing, the Missouri court, which had previously felt
obliged to dismiss the petitions because of Betts *v.* Brady, promptly took steps, in
conjunction with its Judicial Conference, to formulate a procedure whereby an
accused in a felony case would be provided with counsel unless an intelligent waiver
was made; and the record would show precisely what had transpired. See Special
Reports Nos. 3 and 4 of the Judicial Conference of Missouri; and 1 Mo. B.J. 73,
87 (1945); 2 Mo. B.J. 17 (1946).

that clause of the Amendment. Thus the battle so long and gallantly fought by Mr. Justice Harlan [139] is re-opened. Most history is ironic, but the vein of irony in the history of this clause runs deep. The best-beloved child of the Reconstruction Congress became the step-child of the Court; the clause into which the most detailed specifications were read by Congress, and from which the most was expected, has for eighty years been denied all except tautological meaning by the Court.[140]

Since the evidence of the purpose of this clause is fairly conclusive (not even Mr. Justice Black's long Appendix in the Adamson case exhausting it [141]), it is understandable that the battle should be reopened; but whether this is the wisest method of enforcing the Bill of Rights against the states seems debatable. While the Bill of Rights and the due process clause both protect aliens as well as citizens, if the privileges or immunities clause were given life it might be interpreted to run only to "citizens of the United States." Although these seem words of definition, not of limitation, the possibility of such an interpretation cannot be ruled out. More important, taking the Bill of Rights into the Fourteenth Amendment by virtue of this clause means (almost necessarily in view of the Congressional reports and debate on which the inclusion must be based) that the Bill of Rights must be included in its entirety. The evidence of the Congressional intention to include *in toto* is strong; and in Maxwell *v.* Dow,[142] where a small part of this was presented, the Court to exclude it had to resort to an extraordinary theory of interpretation of constitutional amendments, apparently reserved for this clause alone, and one which seems understandable only as perhaps a delayed reaction to the Court's having earlier been deceived by misquotation from the Congressional records into believing that "persons" (in the due process and equal protection clauses) was

---

[139] Justices Bradley, Swaine, Field and Clifford, at least, shared his view. See the Appendix in the Adamson case.

[140] Except that it was given a small and brief vitality in Colgate *v.* Harvey, 296 U.S. 404, 56 S. Ct. 252 (1935), overruled by Madden *v.* Kentucky, 309 U.S. 83, 60 S. Ct. 406 (1940). Other recent efforts to give it vitality commanded the support of two Justices in Hague *v.* C.I.O., 307 U.S. 496, 59 S. Ct. 954 (1939), and of four in Edwards *v.* California, 314 U.S. 160, 62 S. Ct. 164 (1941).

[141] In this connection see 2 Warren, *The Supreme Court in United States History* 539–541 (1937), for contemporary comment on the Slaughter-House Cases.

[142] 176 U.S. 581, 20 S. Ct. 448, 494 (1900).

deliberately used in order to include corporations.[143] And Twining *v.* New Jersey [144] said no more as to the privileges or immunities clause than that "the weighty arguments" for inclusion of the whole Bill of Rights could not profitably be examined, "for the question is no longer open in this court." To a Court which has rightly considered [145] that, when convinced of former error, it is not constrained to follow precedent, and that this is particularly true in constitutional questions, where correction depends upon amendment and not upon legislative action, these cases present no insurmountable difficulty.

But, while the argument for "privileges or immunities" is persuasive, the trouble lies in the thesis itself, which brings one face to face with the "all or none" argument which has so often been made. The two chief stumbling blocks in the way of such "all or none" acceptance are, as may have been gathered, the Fifth Amendment's requirement of grand jury indictment (in the case of "a capital, or otherwise infamous crime") and the Seventh Amendment's guarantee of trial by jury in civil cases where the "value in controversy" exceeds twenty dollars. Mr. Justice Frankfurter has not failed to emphasize the problems which would now arise from these two requirements.[146] His suggestion that the Bill of Rights would imprison state courts in an "Eighteenth Century strait-jacket" (the phrase comes straight from the Twining case) is not so formidable as it sounds. He is perhaps the first in forty years to imply that the administration of justice is less efficient in federal courts than in state; for it is precisely in this "strait-jacket" that federal courts function. The states could without doubt use the same methods by which those courts have found it possible to avoid the difficulties which might lie in the indictment requirement,[147] and in trial by jury in civil

---

[143] See Graham, The "Conspiracy Theory" of the Fourteenth Amendment, 47 Yale L.J. 371; 48 ibid. 171 (1938); Fairman, *Mr. Justice Miller and the Supreme Court* 186–189 (1939); Curtis, *Lions under the Throne* 274–275 (1947).

[144] 211 U.S. 78 at 98, 29 S. Ct. 14 (1908).

[145] Smith *v.* Allwright, 321 U.S. 649, 64 S. Ct. 757 (1944).

[146] He referred also in the Adamson case to "a trial by jury of twelve in a criminal case," but that presents no serious difficulty. The quotation from him in note 136, *supra*, also applies here. In any case it is the Court, not the Bill of Rights, which has added "of twelve."

[147] Rule 7 of Federal Criminal Rules permits prosecution by information if indictment is waived, and that course is now often followed. See Holtzoff, New Federal Criminal Procedure in Operation, 30 J. Am. Jud. Soc. 134 (1946). The

cases.[148] Legislation would certainly be required, but the strait-jacket would not be found too tight once it was fitted. The greatest problem would consist of the thousands of prisoners who lie in state penitentiaries as the result of convictions following information rather than indictment. Even that could perhaps be overcome,[149] but, when one adds to the practical difficulties of including these two rights, surmountable though they may be, the fact that there is very little to be said for their inclusion, it seems probable that a majority of the Court will continue to have the greatest reluctance to protect the Bill of Rights in its entirety. At any rate it seems clear that the Court would more easily—and more wisely—accept the "selective process," to which Mr. Justice Black referred in the Adamson case.

It is the due process clause which makes the selective process available. In the Twining case Mr. Justice Moody, obviously troubled, said that "it is possible that some of the personal rights safeguarded by the first eight Amendments against national action may also be safeguarded against state action, because a denial of them would be a denial of due process of law." [150] This is very far from being—as Mr. Justice Frankfurter seemed to suggest in the Adamson case—a basis for the Fair Trial Rule. It is, indeed, a denial of that concept. What might be protected by the clause were the "rights," which of course applied in every case, not merely in such cases as the Court, on a subjective basis, might select. The passage seems entirely clear as to this and so is the authority [151] on which Mr. Justice Moody relied, which was the holding that one of the rights guaranteed by the Fifth Amend-

procedure was criticized in 31 J. Am. Jud. Soc. 62 (1947) as permitting one day arraignment, trial, conviction and sentence. But it has been held not to violate the Fifth Amendment. Barkman *v.* Sanford (C.C.A. 5th, 1947) 162 F.2d 592, cert. den., Nov. 10, 1947, 16 U.S. Law Week 3148.

[148] See Federal Rules of Civil Procedure, Rule 38. This is substantially the limitation previously set up by the statutes of many states.

[149] This could be controlled if the rule was stated to apply only to the future—a solution which has been suggested in other situations. See Pekelis, The Case for a Jurisprudence of Welfare, 6 Lawyers Guild Rev. 611 at 620 (1946): "Judges should be able to set aside a precedent for the future only, while still applying the old law to the case at hand." Cf. Great Northern R. Co. *v.* Sunburst Oil & Refining Co., 287 U.S. 358 at 364, 53 S. Ct. 145 (1932); Warring *v.* Colpoys, 74 App. D.C. 303, 122 F.2d 642 (1941); and Anderson *v.* Mt. Clemens Pottery Co., (D.C. Mich. 1947) 69 F. Supp. 710 at 721.

[150] 211 U.S. 78 at 99, 29 S. Ct. 14 (1908).

[151] Chicago B. & Q. R.R. Co. *v.* Chicago, 166 U.S. 266, 17 S. Ct. 581 (1897), as to which see note 84, *supra*.

ment—the guaranty that private property should not be taken for public use without just compensation—was protected by the due process clause as a right in all cases, not simply in such cases as it might seem "fair" to a majority of the Court to afford the protection. In fact, the philosophy of the Court—until Mr. Justice Cardozo came—was always, without exception, that if the right was protected by the due process clause it was protected in every case and not simply in those cases which, on examination of the record, might for one reason or another seem to a majority of the Court to suggest an element of "unfairness" in its denial. It is on this uniform and objective basis that the First Amendment liberties and other rights have been read into the due process clause. The distinction is basic, and it was not pointed out in the Adamson case.[152]

The manner of inclusion of these liberties and rights also provides the obvious answer to the argument that if any of the rights of the accused are enforced against the states, all of them must be. The First Amendment rights, for example, were not included on an "all or none" basis, but one at a time, over a period of twenty-two years. Each stood on its own claims to inclusion, although it is true that the early inclusions paved the way for the later.

Defending the Fair Trial Rule against the attack that it was subjective, Mr. Justice Frankfurter in the Adamson case made the point that selecting certain rights as "indispensable to the dignity and happiness of a free man" also threw us back to "a merely subjective test." This is not true of the inclusion of a right in "due process" (for which objective tests are available), nor would the test for inclusion in "liberty" be quite that which Mr. Justice Frankfurter suggests. And the element of subjective judgment which is required for the latter is precisely that which was required for the expansion of "liberty" to include the First Amendment freedoms. The subjective judgment involved in

---

[152] Mr. Justice Frankfurter approached it there when he said: "If all that is meant is that due process contains within itself certain minimal standards which are 'of the very essence of a scheme of ordered liberty' [citing the Palko case], putting upon this Court the duty of applying these standards from time to time, then we have merely arrived at the insight which our predecessors long ago expressed." 332 U.S. 19 at 65, 67 S. Ct. 1658 (1947). But to arrive at the suggestion in the Twining case, "rights secured by the Bill of Rights" must be substituted for "minimal standards." These were Madison's "minimal standards."

reaching a determination as to whether a right must necessarily be included in the concept of liberty is certainly much less to be feared than the exercise of subjective judgment as to the "fairness" of the trial of each petitioner, from case to case on a variable basis.

Each right should be considered on its own merits, not each trial on its own merits. The Bill of Rights safeguards the rights of the accused, not simply to aid a particular individual in a particular trial, but in order to protect a free society against the excesses of power and to provide an efficient administration of justice. The rights ought then to be examined, one at a time, as they come to the Court, with regard to their inclusion either in "due process" or in "liberty." In the Twining case the privilege against self-incrimination was excluded from due process (over Mr. Justice Harlan's dissent) primarily on the historical basis, Mr. Justice Moody there observing that the practice of compulsory self-incrimination had existed for four hundred years after Magna Carta, not beginning to be seriously questioned until the reign of Charles I, had "gained at least some foothold among the early colonists of this country, and was not entirely omitted at trials in England until the eighteenth century." [153] As in Patterson v. Colorado [154] (decided a year earlier) we are in effect told that the Constitution is to be interpreted not even in terms of 1789, but of a considerably earlier date—due process is imprisoned in a Seventeenth Century strait-jacket. [155] On the other hand, if due process in the Fourteenth Amendment is to be

---

[153] 211 U.S. 78 at 102, 29 S. Ct. 14 (1908). He resorted also to the trial of Ann Hutchinson in 1637, as Mr. Justice Black points out in the Adamson case. He further argued (at 109) that as four of the original states when ratifying the Constitution had insisted on incorporating a guaranty against self-incrimination, separately and in addition to due process, the privilege could not then have been considered to be inherent in due process. But this argument may be to the contrary, for the other nine states may have considered that due process included the privilege.

[154] 205 U.S. 454, 27 S. Ct. 556 (1907).

[155] See Pittman, The Colonial and Constitutional History of the Privilege Against Self Incrimination in America, 21 Va. L. Rev. 763 (1935), which makes clear the historical inaccuracies of the Twining opinion. At 774: "The implication to be found in" the Twining opinion "that the privilege against self-incrimination was never regarded in England as the constitutional landmark that our own Constitution makers of 1789 regarded it, seems unjustifiable." At 781: "The privilege came to be fairly well established in the New England Colonies before 1650 and in Virginia shortly thereafter." It was well established in England by the early 1650's.

interpreted in terms of 1868, the date of the adoption of the Amendment, every state then protected the privilege against self-incrimination. If it is to be interpreted in contemporary terms, as one might perhaps suppose, every state protects it now,[156] although the confessions cases indicate that the protection is not always enforced.

The inclusion in due process of the right to the appointment of counsel would be more difficult, as the Betts case suggests. But if this and other rights for historical or other reasons cannot qualify as due process, nevertheless they may be found to be essential parts of liberty. The broad expanse of the latter has too often been overlooked in recent years. It is natural to think of these rights of trial as procedural, and hence to resort first to due process for their inclusion. But perhaps a better case may be made out for the inclusion in "liberty" of the rights which have been most insistently clamoring for admission—the right to appointment of counsel and the privilege against self-incrimination. The inclusion there may not have precisely the same effect, for "liberty" is qualified by "without due process," while "due process" of course does not qualify itself. If, therefore, the right is included in due process it is an absolute, not subject to qualification as it would be if included in liberty. But the practical effect is near enough. Is it possible, to paraphrase Mr. Justice Harlan, to conceive of liberty, as secured by the Fourteenth Amendment against hostile action by the states, which does not embrace the privilege against self-incrimination,[157] or the right of an indigent

---

[156] The protection of the privilege rests on constitutional provisions in all the states except New Jersey and Iowa, where it is accorded by statute. Iowa Code (1939) §§ 11267 *et seq.;* N.J. Rev. Stat. (1937) § 2:97–7. In the Adamson case it was said that only four states, California, New Jersey, Ohio and Vermont, lacked a prohibition against comment to the jury on the failure of the accused to testify. The Twining case, like the Adamson involved not compelled testimony, but only such comment. The Court [211 U.S. 78 at 114, 29 S. Ct. 14 (1908)] said that it assumed "only for the purpose of discussion" that such comment infringed the privilege, but that "we do not intend . . . to lend any countenance to the truth of that assumption."

[157] As the Court, through Mr. Justice Bradley, said in Boyd *v.* United States, 116 U.S. 616 at 631, 633, 6 S. Ct. 524 (1886): "And any compulsory discovery by extorting the party's oath, or compelling the production of his private books and papers, to convict him of crime, or to forfeit his property, is contrary to the principles of a free government. It is abhorrent to the instincts of an Englishman; it is abhorrent to the instincts of an American. It may suit the purposes of despotic power, but it cannot abide the pure atmosphere of political liberty and personal freedom. . . . And we have been unable to perceive that the seizure of a man's

accused to the appointment of counsel when all the machinery of the state is invoked to convict him of crime? Does not indeed liberty require that the state do as much to defend the accused who is helpless to defend himself, as it does to prosecute him? Are not these rights to a considerable number of persons more valuable essentials of liberty than any of the First Amendment rights which guarantee freedoms of no use to them, when they face death or imprisonment, alone and helpless? "Constitutional law, like other mortal contrivances, has to take some chances," [158] but the inclusion of these rights in liberty seems to be taking very few. For the chance of upsetting the balance between federal and state power, which is apparently undisturbed by the far more powerful and frequent onslaughts of the commerce clause, must certainly here be slight.

As Justices Harlan and Sutherland more than once observed, "liberty" is a word of wide meaning. Under the Fourteenth Amendment there is no reason why the standard of justice should be lower in state courts than in federal.

---

private books and papers, to be used in evidence against him, is substantially different from compelling him to be a witness against himself."

Cf. Holden *v.* Hardy, 169 U.S. 366 at 389–390, 18 S. Ct. 383 (1898): "This court has never attempted to define with precision the words 'due process of law,' nor is it necessary to do so in this case. It is sufficient to say that there are certain immutable principles of justice which inhere in the very idea of free government which no member of the Union may disregard, as that no man shall be condemned in his person or property without due notice and an opportunity of being heard in his defence."

[158] Mr. Justice Holmes in Blinn *v.* Nelson, 222 U.S. 1 at 7, 32 S. Ct. 1 (1911).

Table of Cases

Abrams v. United States, 303, 309
Adair v. United States, 152, 154
Adams v. Tanner, 152
Adamson v. California, 358, 386, 410 et seq., 418, 424, 426, 428
Adkins v. Children's Hospital, 151, 154, 419
Adm'rs of Byrne v. Adm'rs of Stewart, 68
Albizu v. United States, 306
Allgeyer v. Louisiana, 133, 134, 136
Amalgamated Ass'n of Street, Elec. Ry., & M.C. Employees v. Wisconsin Employment Relations Board, 169
American Power & Light Co. v. SEC, 174
Anderson v. Mt. Clemens Pottery Co., 425
Asakura v. Seattle, 229
Ashcraft v. Tennessee, 401, 402
Avery v. Alabama, 396

Bailey v. Drexel Furniture Co., 198
Baldwin v. Missouri, 61
Barkman v. Sanford, 425
Bayard v. Singleton, 43, 65
Belt v. Lawes, 75
Best & Co. v. Maxwell, 163
Bethlehem Steel Co. v. New York State Labor Board, 169
Betts v. Brady, 395 et seq.
Betts v. Easley, 380
Birmingham v. Mond, 362
Blinn v. Nelson, 429
Board of Education v. Barnette, 337
Board of Education v. Clemons, 356
Bob-Lo Excursion Co. v. Michigan, 160
Bollenbach v. United States, 421
Botiller v. Dominquez, 265
Bowles v. Willingham, 155

Boyd v. United States, 428
Boyer v. Garrett, 367
Bram v. United States, 395
J. L. Brandeis & Sons v. NLRB, 177
Brandhove v. Tenney, 361
Brimmer v. Rebman, 166, 167
Brown v. Board of Education, 354, 355
Brown v. Maryland, 131, 204
Brown v. Mississippi, 393, 418
Brown v. Ramsey, 365
Bryant v. United States, 306
Buchalter v. New York, 403
Buchanan v. Warley, 354, 362
Bunting v. Oregon, 98
Burt v. New York, 361, 377
Butler v. Wilemon, 365

Calder v. Bull, 56
California v. Zook, 158, 160, 168, 169
Campo v. Niemeyer, 361
Canizio v. New York, 406
Cantwell v. Connecticut, 389
Canty v. Alabama, 394, 402
Cap. & Counties Bank v. Henty, 75, 78
Carmichael v. Southern Coal and Coke Co., 207
Carolene Products Co. v. United States, 156
Carpenter v. Dane County, 398
Carr v. Corning, 365
Carter v. Carter Coal Co., 151, 152, 170, 202
Carter v. Illinois, 406
Carter v. School Board, 365
Chae Chan Ping v. United States, 231
Catlette v. United States, 375
Chambers v. Florida, 393, 398, 402
Champlin Refining Co. v. Corporation Commission, 161
Chance v. Lambeth, 380

Charles River Bridge *v.* Warren Bridge, 73

Charlton *v.* Kelly, 245, 265

Chicago & Southern Air Lines, Inc. *v.* Waterman S.S. Corp., 230

Chicago, B. & Q. R.R. Co. *v.* Chicago, 404, 425

Chicago Board of Trade *v.* Olsen, 152, 169, 174

Chicago, M. & St. P. Ry. Co. *v.* Minnesota, 60, 75, 136

Chisholm *v.* Georgia, 109

Cities Service Oil Co. *v.* Peerless Oil & Gas Co., 155, 156, 159, 160, 162, 165

Civil Rights Cases, 369, 372, 374, 377, 378

Clark *v.* Allen, 228

Colgate *v.* Harvey, 423

Collector *v.* Day, 105

Colonial Airlines, Inc. *v.* Adams, 243, 244

Commonwealth *v.* Call, 67

Commonwealth *v.* Caton, 28, 41

Commonwealth *v.* Five Cents Sav. Bank, 70

Commonwealth *v.* Isenstadt, 292

Commonwealth *v.* Smith, 66

Connecticut General Life Ins. Co. *v.* Johnson, 15, 23

Consolidated Edison Co. *v.* NLRB, 173

Cook *v.* Davis, 365

Cooley *v.* Board of Wardens, 132, 157, 201

Cooper *v.* Telfair, 68

Coppage *v.* Kansas, 152, 154

Corbin *v.* County School Board, 365, 366

Coronado Coal Co. *v.* United Mine Workers, 152, 169

Cotton *v.* The County Commissioners, 70

Creamer *v.* Bivert, 399

Cunard S.S. Co. *v.* Mellon, 231

Currin *v.* Wallace, 173

Daniel *v.* Family Security Life Ins. Co., 156

Dartmouth College Trustees *v.* Woodward, 72, 129

Davis *v.* Beeson, 289

Day *v.* The Atlantic Greyhound Corporation, 371

Dean Milk Co. *v.* Madison, 163

In re Debs, 259, 267

De Meerleer *v.* Michigan, 407

Dennis *v.* United States, 276, 278, 280, 300 *et seq.*

DiSanto *v.* Pennsylvania, 151, 159

Dorsey *v.* Stuyvesant Town Corp., 362

Draper *v.* St. Louis, 367, 368

Dred Scott *v.* Sanford, 15, 110, 117, 132

Dunne *v.* United States, 301

Eakin *v.* Raub, 72, 76

East Coast Lumber Terminal *v.* Babylon, 365

Edwards *v.* California, 163, 423

Egan *v.* United States, 177

Epps *v.* Carmichael, 363

Everson *v.* Board of Education, 310, 315, 316 *et seq.*, 385

Factor *v.* Laubenheimer, 245

Fairfax's Devisee *v.* Hunter's Lessee, 226, 228

Federal Trade Commission *v.* Morton Salt Co., 174

Feiner *v.* New York, 157

Feldman *v.* United States, 403, 421

First Iowa Hydro-Electric Co-op *v.* Federal Power Commission, 169

Fiske *v.* Kansas, 385

Fletcher *v.* Peck, 76, 129

Foster *v.* Neilson, 212, 228

Foster and Payne *v.* Illinois, 386, 409, 416

Frank *v.* Mangum, 394

Freeman *v.* County School Board, 364

Fujii *v.* State, 228

Gaines *v.* Washington, 390

Gayes *v.* New York, 386, 409, 416

Geofroy *v.* Riggs, 228, 231

In re Giacomo, 245

Gibbons *v.* Ogden, 131, 152, 157, 172, 199, 203

Gitlow *v.* New York, 275, 289, 301, 302, 303, 307, 386, 391

Glass *v.* The Sloop Betsey, 56

Great Northern R. Co. *v.* Sunburst Oil & Refining Co., 425
Grimball *v.* Ross, 68
Grosjean *v.* American Press Co., 388, 390, 391, 396, 404
Ex parte Grossman, 262
Grovey *v.* Townsend, 352
Guaranty Trust Co. *v.* United States, 234
Gulf Colo. & Sante Fe R. Co. *v.* Ellis, 418
Gwin, White & Price *v.* Henneford, 163

Hague *v.* C.I.O., 423
Hammer *v.* Dagenhart, 151, 198, 206
Hampton & Co. *v.* United States, 195
Hardyman *v.* Collins, 351, 360
Harris *v.* United States, 421
Hauenstein *v.* Lynham, 228
Ex parte Hawk, 405
Hawk *v.* Olson, 405, 406
Hayburn's Case, 28, 36, 56
Head Money Cases, 231
Hebert *v.* Louisiana, 403, 419
Heisler *v.* Thomas Colliery Co., 170
Helvering *v.* Davis, 207
Henderson *v.* United States, 380
Herndon *v.* Lowry, 278, 301
Hilliard *v.* Johnston, 416
Hoke *v.* United States, 206
Holden *v.* Hardy, 363, 429
Hood & Sons *v.* DuMond, 159, 161, 163
Hooe *v.* United States, 266
Hopkins *v.* United States, 151
House *v.* Mayo, 405
Houston E. & W. T. Ry. *v.* United States, 169, 174
Hurtado *v.* California, 390, 391, 403, 404, 411
Hylton *v.* United States, 55
Hysler *v.* Florida, 395

Illinois Natural Gas Co. *v.* Central Ill. Pub. Serv. Co., 160
Industrial Ass'n *v.* United States, 170
International Brotherhood of Electrical Workers *v.* NLRB, 177
International Salt Co. *v.* United States, 174

International Shoe Co. *v.* Washington, 404
International Union of Automobile Workers *v.* O'Brien, 169

Johnson *v.* Board of Trustees, 363
Johnson *v.* Duncan, 70
Johnson *v.* Zerbst, 396, 414
Juillard *v.* Greenman, 117

Kansas City Southern Ry. *v.* Kaw Valley, 162
In re Kemmler, 407
Kemper *v.* Hawkins, 66, 67
Kentucky *v.* Dennison, 204
Kentucky Whip & Collar Co. *v.* Illinois Cent. R.R., 174
Kepner *v.* United States, 388
Kerr *v.* Enoch Pratt Free Library, 367
Kiddy *v.* Pearson, 170
Kirschbaum Company *v.* Walling, 176
Kovacs *v.* Cooper, 157
Kunz *v.* New York, 157

Law *v.* Baltimore, 368
Lawrence *v.* Hancock, 367
Lawson *v.* Commonwealth, 289
Legal Tender Cases, 126
Leisy *v.* Hardin, 151
Lessee of Jackson *v.* Burns, 224
Lewis *v.* Graves, 333
Lewis *v.* Spaulding, 334
License Cases, 201
Lincoln Union *v.* Northwestern Iron Co., 155
Lindsay *v.* Com'rs, 66
Lisenba *v.* California, 394, 395, 402
Little *v.* Barreme, 263, 271, 272
Local 167 *v.* United States, 152, 169, 173, 174
Lochner *v.* New York, 5, 15, 24, 60, 84, 91, 98, 134, 136, 152
Lomax *v.* Texas, 394
Lopez *v.* Seccombe, 367
Louisiana *v.* Resweber, 407, 408, 410, 419
Loveman, Joseph, & Loeb *v.* NLRB, 177
Lyons *v.* Oklahoma, 402

Mabee *v.* White Plains Publishing Co., 176

McCabe *v.* Atchison, T. & S.F.R.R., 365

Ex parte M'Collum, 70

McCollum *v.* Board of Education, 311, 315, *et seq.*

McCready *v.* Byrd, 367

McCulloch *v.* Maryland, 78, 131, 171, 191, 199, 200, 203, 204, 205, 215, 267

McDermott *v.* Wisconsin, 175, 176

MacKenzie *v.* Hare, 256

McLaurin *v.* Board of Regents, 363, 368

McNabb *v.* United States, 421

McShane *v.* Moldovan, 361

Madden *v.* Kentucky, 423

Madden *v.* Queen's County Jockey Club, 377

Madsen *v.* Kinsella, 264

Malinski *v.* New York, 402, 403, 404, 408, 410, 419

Mandeville Island Farms *v.* American Crystal Sugar Co., 170, 171, 174, 176, 178

Marbury *v.* Madison, 55, 66, 258

Marsh *v.* Alabama, 362

Martin *v.* Hunter's Lessee, 200, 224, 226

Martino *v.* Michigan Window Cleaning Co., 176

Maryland *v.* Baltimore Radio Show, Inc., 301

Massachusetts *v.* Mellon, 196

Maurer *v.* Hamilton, 162

Maxwell *v.* Dow, 387, 390, 391, 412, 423

Mayo *v.* Lakeland Highlands Canning Co., 156

Mendez *v.* Westminister School District, 365

Milk Control Board *v.* Eisenberg, 159

Ex parte Milligan, 4

Milliken *v.* Stone, 231

Minersville School District *v.* Gobitis, 62, 337, 388

Minnesota *v.* Barber, 166

Missouri *ex rel.* Gaines *v.* Canada, 363, 365, 367

Missouri *v.* Holland, 229, 231, 238, 246, 247

Mitchell *v.* Harmony, 269

Mooney *v.* Holohan, 394

Moore *v.* Dempsey, 394

Morehead *v.* Tipaldo, 151, 152, 154

Morgan *v.* Virginia, 159, 160, 162, 380

Moscow Fire Ins. Co. *v.* Bank of New York, 234

Moser *v.* United States, 231

Mulford *v.* Smith, 173, 203

Muller *v.* Oregon, 137

Munn *v.* Illinois, 87, 133

Murdock *v.* Pennsylvania, 337

Myers *v.* United States, 191, 257, 259

NLRB *v.* Denver Building & Construction Trades Council, 177

NLRB *v.* Fainblatt, 175

NLRB *v.* Friedman-Harry Marks Clothing Co., 175

NLRB *v.* Fruehauf Trailer Company, 175

NLRB *v.* J. L. Hudson Co., 177

NLRB *v.* Jones & Laughlin Steel Corp., 154, 173, 175, 202

NLRB *v.* Kudile, 177

NLRB *v.* Local 74, 177

NLRB *v.* M. E. Blatt Co., 177

NLRB *v.* Suburban Lumber Company, 177

Nash *v.* Air Terminal Service, 377

In re Neagle, 259

Near *v.* Minnesota, 391

Nebbia *v.* New York, 152, 154

New State Ice Co. *v.* Liebmann, 15, 151

New York *v.* Miln, 201

Newman *v.* State, 416, 422

Nielsen *v.* Johnson, 229

Nietmotko *v.* Maryland, 157

Nixon *v.* Condon, 370

Norris *v.* Mayor and City Council of Baltimore, 367

North American Co. *v.* SEC, 172, 174, 178

Ogden *v.* Saunders, 69

O'Gorman & Young *v.* Hartford Fire Ins., 152

Oklahoma *ex rel.* Phillips *v.* Guy V. Atkinson Co., 173
Oliver Mining Co. *v.* Lord, 170
Olsen *v.* Nebraska, 155
Osborne *v.* Bank of the United States, 82

Palko *v.* Connecticut, 387 *et seq.*, 426
Panhandle Oil Co. *v.* Knox, 327
Parker *v.* Brown, 161
Parker *v.* University of Delaware, 364
Patterson *v.* Colorado, 427
People *v.* Budd, 143
People *v.* Defore, 390
People *v.* The Supervisors of Orange, 70
Perry *v.* Keene, 70, 76
Pickering Phipps *v.* Ry. Company, 76
Picking *v.* Pennsylvania R.R., 361
Pierce *v.* Society of Sisters, 335
Pitts *v.* Board of Trustees, 365
Plessy *v.* Ferguson, 6, 360
Polish National Alliance *v.* NLRB, 172, 178, 209
Pollock *v.* Farmers Loan & Trust Co., 92, 134, 136
Portsmouth Harbor Land & Hotel Co. *v.* United States, 269, 270
Powell *v.* Alabama, 389, 394, 396, 397, 400, 401, 404
Powell *v.* Utes, 377
Prigg *v.* Commonwealth of Pennsylvania, 204
Prudential Insurance Co. *v.* Benjamin, 168, 187

Railroad Commission *v.* Rowan & Nichols Oil Co., 156
Railroad Comm'n of Wisconsin *v.* Chicago B. & Q. R.R., 169
Railroad Retirement Board *v.* Alton R.R., 151
Railway Express Agency *v.* United States, 155
Reynolds *v.* United States, 289
Ribnik *v.* McBride, 151
Rice *v.* Arnold, 368
Rice *v.* Elmore, 353, 361

Rice *v.* Olson, 406, 417
Rice *v.* Sante Fe Elevator Co., 169
Riggs *v.* State, 75
Roberts *v.* Curtis, 374
Robeson *v.* Fanelli, 361

Sage Stores *v.* Kansas, 155
Saia *v.* New York, 157
San Mateo *v.* Southern Pacific Ry. Co., 133
Santa Cruz Fruit Packing Co. *v.* NLRB, 175
Santa Clara County *v.* Southern Pacific R., 136
Santiago *v.* Nagueras, 264
Schechter Corp. *v.* United States, 151
Schenck *v.* United States, 277, 386
Screws *v.* United States, 351, 361
Seery *v.* United States, 212
Senn *v.* Tile Layers Protective Union, 386
Shelley *v.* Kraemer, 354, 362, 366, 369, 373, 374
Ex parte Siebold, 267
Sinclair *v.* United States, 265
Sinking Fund Cases, 69
Sipuel *v.* University of Oklahoma, 363
Slaughter-House Cases, 133, 245, 386, 391, 399, 412
Smith *v.* Allwright, 352, 361, 424
Smith *v.* O'Grady, 394, 397
Smythe *v.* Ames, 136
Snyder *v.* Massachusetts, 398, 399, 404, 408, 417
South Carolina Highway Dep't *v.* Barnwell Bros., 162
Southern Pacific Co. *v.* Arizona, 158, 159, 160, 162, 168
Southern Pacific Co. *v.* Jensen, 95
Southern Ry. *v.* United States, 170
Stafford *v.* Wallace, 152, 169
Standard Oil Co. *v.* United States, 152
State *ex rel.* Brewton *v.* Board of Education, 365
State *ex rel.* Hawkins *v.* Board of Control, 363, 364
State *ex rel.* Tolliver *v.* Board of Education, 364
Steele *v.* Louisville & N. R.R., 380

Stettler v. Oregon, 87
Steward Machine Co. v. Davis, 206
Sunshine Anthracite Coal Co. v.
    Adkins, 155
Swanson v. Rector and Visitors of
    University of Virginia, 363
Sweatt v. Painter, 355, 363, 366, 368
Swift & Co. v. United States, 152,
    170, 172
Syndics of Brooks v. Weyman, 70

Taylor v. Beckham, 392
Taylor v. Place, 362
Terminal Railroad Ass'n v. Brother-
    hood of Railroad Trainmen, 159
Terminiello v. City of Chicago, 302
Terry v. Adams, 353
Terry v. Anderson, 76
Texas & New Orleans R.R. v. Broth-
    erhood of Railway Clerks, 152
Thomas v. Collins, 157
Thornhill v. Alabama, 386
Tomkins v. Missouri, 405, 406, 422
Toomer v. Witsell, 163
Tucker v. Alexandroff, 264
Twining v. New Jersey, 390, 391,
    410, 411, 412, 424, 426, 427, 428
Tyson v. Banton, 10, 11, 151

Union Brokerage Co. v. Jensen, 160
United Automobile Workers v. Wis-
    consin Employment Relations
    Board, 169
United Mine Workers v. Coronado
    Coal Co., 151
United States v. Ballard, 289
United States v. Belmont, 234
United States v. Butler, 8, 82, 151,
    152, 197
United States v. Capps, 212
United States v. Carolene Products
    Co., 149, 155, 203
United States v. Causby, 266
United States v. Clark, 75
United States v. Cruikshank, 360
United States v. Curtiss-Wright,
    255, 269
United States v. Darby, 155, 171,
    174, 175, 178, 202, 206
United States v. E. C. Knight Co.,
    136, 151

United States v. Frankfort Distill-
    eries, 177
United States v. Guy W. Capps,
    Inc., 247
United States v. Lee, 259
United States v. Lovett, 15
United States v. McCullagh, 229
United States v. Midwest Oil Co.,
    268
United States v. Minnesota, 231
United States v. Mitchell, 403
United States v. Moscow Fire Ins.
    Co., 234
United States v. North American
    Co., 266
United States v. Patten, 170, 174
United States v. Pewee Coal Co.,
    266, 270
United States v. Pink, 234, 242, 270
United States v. Rock Royal Co-op.,
    155
United States v. Russell, 269
United States v. Shauver, 229
United States v. South-Eastern Un-
    derwriters, 172, 178, 187
United States v. Sullivan, 175, 176
United States v. The William, 198
United States v. Williams, 245
United States v. Women's Sports-
    wear Ass'n, 174, 175
United States v. Wrightwood Dairy
    Co., 171, 174
University of Maryland v. Murray,
    363
Utah Power & Light Co. v. Pfost,
    170

Valentine v. United States, 245
Valle v. Stengel, 371
Vanhorne's Lessee v. Dorrance, 66
Veazie v. Moor, 170
Vernon v. Alabama, 394
Virginian Ry. v. System Federation
    No. 40, 154

Walton v. Southern Package Corp.,
    176
Ward v. Texas, 395
Ware v. Hylton, 54, 68, 224, 225, 226
Warren-Bradshaw Drilling Co. v.
    Hall, 176
Warring v. Colpoys, 425

Waterman Steamship Corp. *v.* Jones, 246

Watkins *v.* Oaklawn Jockey Club, 373

Wayman *v.* Southard, 268

Weeks *v.* United States, 390

Weiss *v.* Leaon, 374

Wellington *et. al.*, Petitioners, 69, 74

West *v.* Louisiana, 390, 391

West Coast Hotel *v.* Parrish, 4, 5, 9, 61, 154

West Virginia State Board of Education *v.* Barnette, 150, 386, 388

White *v.* Ragen, 405

White *v.* Texas, 394

Whiteside *v.* Southern Bus Lines, 370

Whitmyer *v.* Lincoln Parish School Board, 364

Whitney *v.* California, 278, 301, 303, 307

Whittington *v.* Polk, 66

Wickard *v.* Filburn, 170, 172, 174, 176, 178, 247

Williams *v.* Kaiser, 405, 406, 421

Williams *v.* Standard Oil Co., 151

Williams *v.* United States, 361

Wilson *v.* Board of Supervisors, 363

Winkler *v.* Maryland, 367

Wolff Packing Co. *v.* Court of Industrial Relations, 151

Woods *v.* Nierstheimer, 406

Wrighten *v.* Board of Trustees, 365

Yakus *v.* United States, 155

Yick Wo *v.* Hopkins, 420

Youngstown Sheet & Tube Co. *v.* Sawyer, 257 *et. seq.*

Zorach *v.* Clauson, 311, 315

A NOTE ON THE TYPE

This book was set on the Linotype in JANSON, *a recutting made direct from the type cast from matrices made by Anton Janson. Whether or not Janson was of Dutch ancestry is not known, but it is known that he purchased a foundry and was a practicing type-founder in Leipzig during the years 1660 to 1687. Janson's first specimen sheet was issued in 1675. His successor issued a specimen sheet showing all of the Janson types in 1689.*

His type is an excellent example of the influential and sturdy Dutch types that prevailed in England prior to the development by William Caslon of his own incomparable designs, which he evolved from these Dutch faces. The Dutch in their turn had been influenced by Garamond in France. The general tone of Janson, however, is darker than Garamond and has a sturdiness and substance quite different from its predecessors. It is a highly legible type, and its individual letters have a pleasing variety of design. Its heavy and light strokes make it sharp and clear, and the full-page effect is characterful and harmonious.

This book was composed, printed, and bound by Kingsport Press, Inc., Kingsport, Tennessee. Paper manufactured by S. D. Warren Company, Boston, Massachusetts. Typography by David Rogers.